STOCK
TRADER'S
ALMANAC
2008

Jeffrey A. Hirsch & Yale Hirsch

BICENTENNIAL
1807
WILEY
2007
BICENTENNIAL

John Wiley & Sons, Inc.

www.stocktradersalmanac.com

Editor in Chief	Jeffrey A. Hirsch
Editor at Large	Yale Hirsch
Director of Research	J. Taylor Brown
Statistics Director	Christopher Mistal
Graphic Design	Darlene Dion Design

For general information on our other products and services, or technical support, please contact our Customer Care Department within the United States at 800-762-2974, outside the United States at 317-572-3993 or fax 317-572-4002.

Wiley also publishes its books in a variety of electronic formats. Some content that appears in print may not be available in electronic books.

For more information about Wiley products, visit our Web site at www.wiley.com.

ISBN-13 978-0-470-10985-4
ISBN-10 0-470-10985-8

10 9 8 7 6 5 4 3 2 1
Printed in China

This Forty-First Edition is respectfully dedicated to:

Robert Cardwell

Savvy trader, seasoned skeptic, brilliant writer, mentor, and most importantly, friend. Thank you for imparting to us your keen eye for stocks, your lucid analysis and your salient opinions on the markets and the world.

INTRODUCTION TO THE FORTY-FIRST EDITION

We are pleased and proud to introduce the Forty-First Edition of the *Stock Trader's Almanac*. The Almanac provides you with the necessary tools to invest successfully in the twenty-first century.

J.P. Morgan's classic retort "Stocks will fluctuate" is often quoted with a wink-of-the-eye implication that the only prediction one can make about the stock market is that it will go up, down, or sideways. Many investors agree that no one ever really knows which way the market will move. Nothing could be further from the truth.

We discovered that while stocks do indeed fluctuate, they do so in well-defined, often predictable patterns. These patterns recur too frequently to be the result of chance or coincidence. How else do we explain that since 1950 practically all the gains in the market were made during November through April compared to almost nothing May through October? (See page 48.)

The *Almanac* is a practical investment tool. It alerts you to those little-known market patterns and tendencies on which shrewd professionals enhance profit potential. You will be able to forecast market trends with accuracy and confidence when you use the Almanac to help you understand:

You will be able to forecast market trends with accuracy and confidence when you use the Almanac to help you understand:

- How our Presidential Elections affect the economy and the stock market — just as the moon affects the tides. Many investors have made fortunes following the political cycle. You can be sure that money managers who control billions of dollars are also political cycle watchers. Astute people do not ignore a pattern that has been working effectively throughout most of our economic history.

- How the passage of the Twentieth Amendment to the Constitution fathered the January Barometer. This barometer has an outstanding record for predicting the general course of the stock market each year with only five major errors since 1950 for a 91.2% accuracy ratio. (See page 16.)

- Why there is a significant market bias at certain times of the day, week, month and year.

Even if you are an investor who pays scant attention to cycles, indicators and patterns, your investment survival could hinge on your interpretation of one of the recurring patterns found within these pages. One of the most intriguing and important patterns is the symbiotic relationship between Washington and Wall Street. Aside from the potential profitability in seasonal patterns, there's the pure joy of seeing the market very often do just what you expected.

The *Stock Trader's Almanac* is also an organizer. Its wealth of information is presented on a calendar basis. The Almanac puts investing in a business framework and makes investing easier because it:

- Updates investment knowledge and informs you of new techniques and tools.

- Is a monthly reminder and refresher course.

- Alerts you to both seasonal opportunities and dangers.

- Furnishes an historical viewpoint by providing pertinent statistics on past market performance.

- Supplies forms necessary for portfolio planning, record keeping and tax preparation.

 The WITCH Icon signifies THIRD FRIDAY OF THE MONTH on calendar pages and alerts you to extraordinary volatility due to expiration of equity and index options and index futures contracts. Triple-witching days appear during March, June, September and December.

The BULL Icon on calendar pages signifies favorable trading days based on the S&P 500 rising 60% or more of the time on a particular trading day during the 21-year period January 1986 to December 2006. A BEAR Icon on calendar pages signifies unfavorable trading days based on the S&P falling 60% or more of the time for the same 21-year period.

Also, to give you even greater perspective we have listed next to the date every day that the market is open the Market Probability numbers for the same 21-year period for the Dow (D), S&P 500 (S) and NASDAQ (N). You will see a "D," "S" and "N" followed by a number signifying the actual Market Probability number for that trading day based on the recent 21-year period. On pages 121-128 you will find complete Market Probability Calendars both long term and 21-year for the Dow, S&P and NASDAQ as well as for the Russell 1000 and Russell 2000 indices.

Other seasonalities near the ends, beginnings and middles of months; options expirations, around holidays and other times are noted for *Almanac* investors' convenience on the weekly planner pages. We are not able to carry FOMC Meeting dates as they are no longer available at press-time. Only the first meeting of 2008, the two-day affair on January 29-30, 2008, has been scheduled. However, the rest of the FOMC Meeting dates and all other important economic releases are provided in the Strategy Calendar every month in our newsletter, *Almanac Investor*.

Historically bullish, this election year may prove to buck the trend. More often than not, a lame duck president uses the balance of his remaining political cache to pave the way for his veep. Not only does the sitting president have the lowest poll ratings in history, but this election year is the first since 1952 in which a member of the incumbency has not run for the top office in the land.

On page 78 you will find a perspective of presidential election years. Among the research you will find that there has only been one loss in the last seven months of an election year (page 52) and how the government manipulates the economy to stay in power (page 34). Market charts for election years are available on page 30 and compare market behavior when incumbent parties have won and lost on page 36.

After a major restructuring last year, we have maintained a similar layout this go around. As a reminder to long-time *Almanac* readers, the ten years of monthly Daily Dow Point Changes have moved from their respective *Almanac* pages to the Databank section toward the rear of this book. We continue to rely on the clarity of this presentation to observe market tendencies. In response to newsletter subscriber feedback, we include our well-received Monthly Vital Stats on the *Almanac* pages.

The Year in Review is back again on page 6. It should be helpful to have the major events of the past year in the *Almanac*. Our research had been restructured to flow better with the rhythm of the year. This has also allowed us more room for added data. Again, we have included historical data on the Russell 1000 and Russell 2000 indices. The Russell 2K is an excellent proxy for small and mid caps, which we have used over the years, and the Russell 1K provides a broader view of large caps. Annual highs and lows for all five indices covered in the *Almanac* appear on pages 149-151. We've tweaked the Best & Worst section and brought back Option Trading Codes on page 190.

In order to cram in all the new material, we had to cut some of our Record Keeping section. We have converted many of these paper forms into computer spreadsheets for our own internal use. As a service to our faithful readers, we are making these forms available our Web site *www.stocktradersalmanac.com*.

We are constantly searching for new insights and nuances about the stock market and welcome any suggestions from our readers.

Have a healthy and prosperous 2008!

YEAR IN REVIEW

2006

Jun 25 – Warren Buffett gives $31 billion to the Gates Foundation
Jul 12 – Israel launches major onslaught in Lebanon after Hezbollah attack
Jul 14 – Crude oil hits closing NYMEX high of $78.71
Jul 18 – Undersea earthquake off Java, Indonesia, causes tsunami (over 800 people die)
Aug 14 – UN brokers peace between Israel and Hezbollah in Lebanon
Sep 29 – US Representative Mark Foley (R-FL) resigns after sex scandal
Oct 17 – United States population reaches 300 million
Oct 19 – Dow closes over 12,000 first time
Nov 7 – Democrats control House (233/202) and Senate (51/49) first time since 1994
Nov 8 – Secretary of Defense Donald Rumsfeld resigns
Dec 30 – Former Iraq president Saddam Hussein executed in Baghdad by hanging
Dec 30 – American death toll in Iraq reaches 3000

2007

Jan 2 – Market closed for Ford funeral
Jan 4 – Nancy Pelosi (D-CA) becomes first woman Speaker of the House
Feb 2 – UN scientific panel declares evidence of global warming unequivocal
Feb 28 – After China market drops 9%, Dow plummets 416 points (3.3%)
Mar 6 – Scandal intensifies over fired federal prosecutors
Mar 6 – Lewis "Scooter" Libby, Cheney's Chief of Staff, found guilty in CIA leak case
Apr 2 – Subprime lender New Century Financial files for Chapter 11 bankruptcy
Apr 4 – British sailors captured in Iran are freed
Apr 13 – Outstanding U.S. public debt tops $8.89 trillion just prior to federal tax deadline
Apr 16 – Virginia Tech college student guns down 32 before committing suicide
Apr 25 – Dow closes above 13,000 first time
May 8 – Pentagon notifies 35,000 soldiers to prepare for deployment to Iraq this fall
May 20 – Gasoline hits record of $3.18 a gallon, topping 1981 inflation-adjusted high

2008 OUTLOOK

Sporting only two minor losses and an average Dow gain of 18.5% in twelve decades, "eighth" years rank second only to "fifth" years. In the last fifty years, election years have ended lower twice in eleven occurrences with an average Dow gain of 9.2%. Over the same fifty years, fifteen bear markets have occurred. Four (1960, 1968, 1976, 2000) have commenced in an election year and just three (1960, 1980, 1984) have ended in election years.

A bear market was averted in midterm 2006. Global economic growth, cheap Chinese goods, and a weak dollar helped the U.S. economy navigate a soft landing between inflation and recession. A press time, from their 2006 midterm lows to their pre-election-year highs, the Dow is up 27.1%, about half its average 50% gain since 1914 and NASDAQ is up 28.1%, a third of its average since 1974.

The absence of a bear market the last four and a half years in conjunction with a slowing U.S. economy, a crumbling housing market, uncertainty on inflation, deteriorating market internal suggests further gains in 2007 will come in below historic averages. Whether or not the market gets comeuppance in 2007, a full-fledged bear market is not currently anticipated in election year 2008.

"Priming of the pump" by incumbent parties has tended to prop up market gains in election year Save a political meltdown in Washington, an international debacle or a run on The Street, any major market damage is expected to be contained to, at worst, a steep, swift 2007 pre-election-year decline with lost ground quickly reclaimed; followed by modest gains in 2008.

Prospects for the market may depend on President Bush's remaining political capital. He may not have the cache or credibility to effectively extol economic conditions for political ends, potential limiting upside in 2008. However, any severe declines or bear market are likely to be staved off until post-election 2009 or midterm 2010.

— *Jeffrey A. Hirsch, May 24, 2007*

THE 2008 STOCK TRADER'S ALMANAC

CONTENTS

DIRECTORY OF TRADING PATTERNS & DATABANK

STRATEGY PLANNING AND RECORD SECTION

2008 STRATEGY CALENDAR

(Option expiration dates circled)

	MONDAY	TUESDAY	WEDNESDAY	THURSDAY	FRIDAY	SATURDAY	SUNDAY
JANUARY	31	1 JANUARY New Year's Day	2	3	4	5	6
	7	8	9	10	11	12	13
	14	15	16	17	(18)	19	20
	21 Martin Luther King Day	22	23	24	25	26	27
	28	29	30	31	1 FEBRUARY	2	3
FEBRUARY	4	5	6 Ash Wednesday	7	8	9	10
	11	12	13	14 ♥	(15)	16	17
	18 Presidents' Day	19	20	21	22	23	24
	25	26	27	28	29	1 MARCH	2
MARCH	3	4	5	6	7	8	9 Daylight Saving Time Begins
	10	11	12	13	14	15	16
	17 ♣ St. Patrick's Day	18	19	(20)	21 Good Friday	22	23 Easter
	24	25	26	27	28	29	30
	31	1 APRIL	2	3	4	5	6
APRIL	7	8	9	10	11	12	13
	14	15 Tax Deadline	16	17	(18)	19	20 Passover
	21	22	23	24	25	26	27
	28	29	30	1 MAY	2	3	4
MAY	5	6	7	8	9	10	11 Mother's Day
	12	13	14	15	(16)	17	18
	19	20	21	22	23	24	25
	26 Memorial Day	27	28	29	30	31	1 JUNE
JUNE	2	3	4	5	6	7	8
	9	10	11	12	13	14	15 Father's Day
	16	17	18	19	(20)	21	22
	23	24	25	26	27	28	29

Market closed on shaded weekdays; closes early when half-shaded.

2008 STRATEGY CALENDAR
(Option expiration dates circled)

MONDAY	TUESDAY	WEDNESDAY	THURSDAY	FRIDAY	SATURDAY	SUNDAY	
30	1 JULY	2	3	4 Independence Day	5	6	JULY
7	8	9	10	11	12	13	
14	15	16	17	(18)	19	20	
21	22	23	24	25	26	27	
28	29	30	31	1 AUGUST	2	3	
4	5	6	7	8	9	10	AUGUST
11	12	13	14	(15)	16	17	
18	19	20	21	22	23	24	
25	26	27	28	29	30	31	
1 SEPTEMBER Labor Day	2	3	4	5	6	7	SEPTEMBER
8	9	10	11	12	13	14	
15	16	17	18	(19)	20	21	
22	23	24	25	26	27	28	
29	30 Rosh Hashanah	1 OCTOBER	2	3	4	5	OCTOBER
6	7	8	9 Yom Kippur	10	11	12	
13 Columbus Day	14	15	16	(17)	18	19	
20	21	22	23	24	25	26	
27	28	29	30	31	1 NOVEMBER	2 Daylight Saving Time Ends	NOVEMBER
3	4 Election Day	5	6	7	8	9	
10	11 Veterans' Day	12	13	14	15	16	
17	18	19	20	(21)	22	23	
24	25	26	27 Thanksgiving	28	29	30	
1 DECEMBER	2	3	4	5	6	7	DECEMBER
8	9	10	11	12	13	14	
15	16	17	18	(19)	20	21	
22 Chanukah	23	24	25 Christmas	26	27	28	
29	30	31	1 JANUARY New Year's Day	2	3	4	

JANUARY ALMANAC

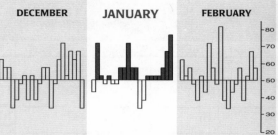

Market Probability Chart above is a graphic representation of the S&P 500 Recent Market Probability Calendar on page 124.

◆ January Barometer predicts year's course with .754 batting average (page 16) ◆ Every down January on the S&P since 1950, *without exception*, preceded a new or extended bear market, or a flat market (page 42); six election years followed suit ◆ S&P gains January's first five days preceded full-year gains 86.1% of the time; in election years, only years 1988 & 1956 have been wrong (page 14) ◆ November, December and January constitute the year's best three-month span, a 4.9% S&P gain (pages 44 & 147) ◆ January NASDAQ powerful 3.7% since 1971 (pages 56 & 148) ◆ "January Effect" now starts in mid-December and favors small-cap stocks (pages 104 & 106) ◆ Since 1972 election-year Januarys are #1 for Dow and S&P, #2 for NASDAQ

January Vital Statistics

	DJIA	S&P 500	NASDAQ	Russell 1K	Russell 2K
Rank	4	3	1	2	1
Up	39	37	26	20	18
Down	19	21	11	9	11
Avg % Change	1.3%	1.4%	3.7%	1.7%	2.7%
Election Year	0.5%	0.7%	3.4%	1.1%	3.0%
Best & Worst January					
	% Change	% Change	% Change	% Change	% Change
Best	1976 14.4	1987 13.2	1975 16.6	1987 12.7	1985 13.1
Worst	1960 −8.4	1970 −7.6	1990 −8.6	1990 −7.4	1990 −8.9
Best & Worst January Weeks					
Best	1/9/76 6.1	1/31/75 5.5	1/12/01 9.1	1/9/87 5.3	1/9/87 7.0
Worst	1/24/03 −5.3	1/28/00 −5.6	1/28/00 −8.2	1/28/00 −5.5	1/7/05 −5.9
Best & Worst January Days					
Best	1/17/91 4.6	1/3/01 5.0	1/3/01 14.2	1/3/01 5.3	1/3/01 4.7
Worst	1/8/88 −6.9	1/8/88 −6.8	1/2/01 −7.2	1/8/88 −6.1	1/2/01 −4.4
First Trading Day of Expiration Week: 1980-2007					
Record (#Up - #Down)	19-9	17-11	16-12	16-12	17-11
Current streak	U1	U1	D2	U1	D2
Avg % Change	0.11	0.15	0.16	0.13	0.22
Options Expiration Day: 1980-2007					
Record (#Up - #Down)	13-15	14-14	17-11	14-14	16-12
Current streak	D3	U1	U1	U1	U1
Avg % Change	−0.12	−0.06	−0.10	−0.08	−0.07
Options Expiration Week: 1980-2007					
Record (#Up - #Down)	15-13	13-15	17-11	13-15	16-12
Current streak	U1	D3	D3	D3	D3
Avg % Change	0.08	0.33	0.65	0.32	0.69
Week After Options Expiration: 1980-2007					
Record (#Up - #Down)	6-12	18-10	17-11	18-10	19-9
Current streak	D1	D1	D1	D1	U4
Avg % Change	0.11	0.36	0.30	0.32	0.31
First Trading Day Performance					
% of Time Up	56.9	46.6	54.1	37.9	41.4
Avg % Change	0.19	0.06	0.03	−0.04	−0.12
Last Trading Day Performance					
% of Time Up	60.3	65.5	67.6	65.5	79.3
Avg % Change	0.27	0.31	0.38	0.45	0.32

Dow & S&P 1950-April 2007, NASDAQ 1971-April 2007, Russell 1K & 2K 1979-April 2007.

20th Amendment made "Lame Ducks" disappea
Now, "As January goes, so goes the odd-numbered year

DECEMBER/JANUARY 2008

Last Day of the Year, NASDAQ Down 7 Straight After Being Up 29 in a Row!
Dow Down 7 of Last 11

MONDAY

D 38.1
S 33.3
N 66.7

31

If I had my life to live over again, I would elect to be a trader of goods rather than a student of science.
I think barter is a noble thing. — Albert Einstein (German/American physicist, 1921 Nobel Prize, 1934, 1879-1955)

New Year's Day (Market Closed)

TUESDAY

1

It's a lot of fun finding a country nobody knows about. The only thing better is finding a country everybody's bullish on
and shorting it. — Jim Rogers (Financier, *Investment Biker*, b. 1942)

First Trading Day of the Year, NASDAQ Up 8 of Last 10

WEDNESDAY

D 61.9
S 42.9
N 61.9

2

America, this brash and noble container of dreams, this muse to artists and inventors and entrepreneurs,
his beacon of optimism, this dynamo of energy, this trumpet blare of liberty. — Peter Jennings
Canadian-born anchor ABC World News Tonight, July 2003 after gaining U.S. citizenship, 1938-2005)

Second Trading Day of the Year, Dow Up 11 of Last 14

THURSDAY

D 71.4
S 71.4
N 81.0

3

---

he years teach much which the days never know.
– Ralph Waldo Emerson (American author, poet and philosopher, *Self-Reliance*, 1803-1882)

FRIDAY

D 47.6
S 52.4
N 61.9

4

---

he symbol of all relationships among such men, the moral symbol of respect for human beings, is the trader.
– Ayn Rand (Russian-born American novelist and philosopher, John Galt's Speech, *Atlas Shrugged*, 1957, 1905-1982)

SATURDAY

5

January Almanac Investor Seasonalities: See Pages 114 & 116

SUNDAY

6

JANUARY'S FIRST FIVE DAYS: AN EARLY WARNING SYSTEM

The last 36 up First Five Days were followed by full-year gains 31 times, for an 86.1% accuracy ratio and a 13.7% average gain in all 36 years. The five exceptions include flat 1994 and four related to war. Vietnam military spending delayed start of 1966 bear market. Ceasefire imminence early in 1973 raised stocks temporarily. Saddam Hussein turned 1990 into a bear. The war on terrorism, instability in the Mideast and corporate malfeasance shaped 2002 into one of the worst years on record. The 21 down First Five Days were followed by 11 up years and 10 down (less than 50% accurate).

Bullish 4-year election cycle forces have given this indicator a 12-2 record in election years. Two of four down years have been wrong. However, a bear market began in 1956 with concern over Eisenhower's heart condition, the Suez Canal Crisis, and Russia's suppression of the Hungarian Revolution. A mini-crash on the fifth day of 1988 felled the S&P 6.8%.

THE FIRST-FIVE-DAYS-IN-JANUARY INDICATOR

Chronological Data

	Previous Year's Close	January 5th Day	5-Day Change	Year Change
1950	16.76	17.09	2.0%	21.8%
1951	20.41	20.88	2.3	16.5
1952	23.77	23.91	0.6	11.8
1953	26.57	26.33	−0.9	−6.6
1954	24.81	24.93	0.5	45.0
1955	35.98	35.33	−1.8	26.4
1956	45.48	44.51	−2.1	2.6
1957	46.67	46.25	−0.9	−14.3
1958	39.99	40.99	2.5	38.1
1959	55.21	55.40	0.3	8.5
1960	59.89	59.50	−0.7	−3.0
1961	58.11	58.81	1.2	23.1
1962	71.55	69.12	−3.4	−11.8
1963	63.10	64.74	2.6	18.9
1964	75.02	76.00	1.3	13.0
1965	84.75	85.37	0.7	9.1
1966	92.43	93.14	0.8	−13.1
1967	80.33	82.81	3.1	20.1
1968	96.47	96.62	0.2	7.7
1969	103.86	100.80	−2.9	−11.4
1970	92.06	92.68	0.7	0.1
1971	92.15	92.19	0.04	10.8
1972	102.09	103.47	1.4	15.6
1973	118.05	119.85	1.5	−17.4
1974	97.55	96.12	−1.5	−29.7
1975	68.56	70.04	2.2	31.5
1976	90.19	94.58	4.9	19.1
1977	107.46	105.01	−2.3	−11.5
1978	95.10	90.64	−4.7	1.1
1979	96.11	98.80	2.8	12.3
1980	107.94	108.95	0.9	25.8
1981	135.76	133.06	−2.0	−9.7
1982	122.55	119.55	−2.4	14.8
1983	140.64	145.23	3.3	17.3
1984	164.93	168.90	2.4	1.4
1985	167.24	163.99	−1.9	26.3
1986	211.28	207.97	−1.6	14.6
1987	242.17	257.28	6.2	2.0
1988	247.08	243.40	−1.5	12.4
1989	277.72	280.98	1.2	27.3
1990	353.40	353.79	0.1	−6.6
1991	330.22	314.90	−4.6	26.3
1992	417.09	418.10	0.2	4.5
1993	435.71	429.05	−1.5	7.1
1994	466.45	469.90	0.7	−1.5
1995	459.27	460.83	0.3	34.1
1996	615.93	618.46	0.4	20.3
1997	740.74	748.41	1.0	31.0
1998	970.43	956.04	−1.5	26.7
1999	1229.23	1275.09	3.7	19.5
2000	1469.25	1441.46	−1.9	−10.1
2001	1320.28	1295.86	−1.8	−13.0
2002	1148.08	1160.71	1.1	−23.4
2003	879.82	909.93	3.4	26.4
2004	1111.92	1131.91	1.8	9.0
2005	1211.92	1186.19	−2.1	3.0
2006	1248.29	1290.15	3.4	13.6
2007	1418.30	1412.11	−0.4	??

Ranked By Performance

Rank		5-Day Change	Year Change
1	1987	6.2%	2.0
2	1976	4.9	19.1
3	1999	3.7	19.5
4	2003	3.4	26.4
5	2006	3.4	13.6
6	1983	3.3	17.3
7	1967	3.1	20.1
8	1979	2.8	12.3
9	1963	2.6	18.9
10	1958	2.5	38.1
11	1984	2.4	1.4
12	1951	2.3	16.5
13	1975	2.2	31.5
14	1950	2.0	21.8
15	2004	1.8	9.0
16	1973	1.5	−17.4
17	1972	1.4	15.6
18	1964	1.3	13.0
19	1961	1.2	23.1
20	1989	1.2	27.3
21	2002	1.1	−23.4
22	1997	1.0	31.0
23	1980	0.9	25.8
24	1966	0.8	−13.1
25	1994	0.7	−1.5
26	1965	0.7	9.1
27	1970	0.7	0.1
28	1952	0.6	11.8
29	1954	0.5	45.0
30	1996	0.4	20.3
31	1959	0.3	8.5
32	1995	0.3	34.1
33	1992	0.2	4.5
34	1968	0.2	7.7
35	1990	0.1	−6.6
36	1971	0.04	10.8
37	2007	−0.4	??
38	1960	−0.7	−3.0
39	1957	−0.9	−14.3
40	1953	−0.9	−6.6
41	1974	−1.5	−29.7
42	1998	−1.5	26.7
43	1988	−1.5	12.4
44	1993	−1.5	7.1
45	1986	−1.6	14.6
46	2001	−1.8	−13.0
47	1955	−1.8	26.4
48	2000	−1.9	−10.1
49	1985	−1.9	26.3
50	1981	−2.0	−9.7
51	1956	−2.1	2.6
52	2005	−2.1	3.0
53	1977	−2.3	−11.5
54	1982	−2.4	14.8
55	1969	−2.9	−11.4
56	1962	−3.4	−11.8
57	1991	−4.6	26.3
58	1978	−4.7	1.1

Based on S&P 500

JANUARY

owe a million dollars I am lost. But if I owe $50 billion the bankers are lost. — Celso Ming (Brazilian journalist)

nuary's First Five Days Act as an "Early Warning" (Page 14)

ense concentration hour after hour can bring out resources in people they didn't know they had.
Edwin Land (Polaroid inventor & founder, 1909-1991)

ery great advance in natural knowledge has involved the absolute rejection of authority.
Thomas H. Huxley (British scientist and humanist, defender of Darwinism, 1825-1895)

here is only one corner of the universe you can be certain of improving, and that's yourself.
- Aldous Huxley (English author, *Brave New World*, 1894-1963)

a man has no talents, he is unhappy enough; but if he has, envy pursues him in proportion to his ability.
- Leopold Mozart (to his son Wolfgang Amadeus, 1768)

THE INCREDIBLE JANUARY BAROMETER (DEVISED 1972) ONLY FIVE SIGNIFICANT ERRORS IN 57 YEARS

Devised by Yale Hirsch in 1972, our January Barometer states that as the S&P goes in January, so goes the year. The indicator has registered **only five major errors since 195** for a **91.2% accuracy ratio**. Vietnam affected 1966 and 1968; 1982 saw the start of a majo bull market in August; two January rate cuts and 9/11 affected 2001; and the anticipation o military action in Iraq held down the market in January 2003. (*Almanac Investor* newslette subscribers were warned at the time not to heed the January Barometer's negative reading a it was being influenced by Iraqi concerns.)

Including the nine flat years (less than +/- 5%) yields a 75.4% accuracy ratio. A fu comparison of all monthly barometers for the Dow, S&P and NASDAQ in our newslette archives (March 2004) at *www.stocktradersalmanac.com* details January's market forecastin prowess. Bear markets began or continued when Januarys suffered a loss (see page 42). Fu years followed January's direction in ten of the last 14 election years. The four errors occurre when January was down. See pages 18, 22 and 24 for more January Barometer items.

AS JANUARY GOES, SO GOES THE YEAR

Market Performance in January

Year	Previous Year's Close	January Close	January Change	Year Change	
1950	16.76	17.05	1.7%	21.8%	
1951	20.41	21.66	6.1	16.5	
1952	23.77	24.14	1.6	11.8	
1953	26.57	26.38	−0.7	− 6.6	
1954	24.81	26.08	5.1	45.0	
1955	35.98	36.63	1.8	26.4	
1956	45.48	43.82	−3.6	2.6	flat
1957	46.67	44.72	−4.2	−14.3	
1958	39.99	41.70	4.3	38.1	
1959	55.21	55.42	0.4	8.5	
1960	59.89	55.61	−7.1	− 3.0	flat
1961	58.11	61.78	6.3	23.1	
1962	71.55	68.84	−3.8	−11.8	
1963	63.10	66.20	4.9	18.9	
1964	75.02	77.04	2.7	13.0	
1965	84.75	87.56	3.3	9.1	
1966	92.43	92.88	0.5	−13.1	X
1967	80.33	86.61	7.8	20.1	
1968	96.47	92.24	−4.4	7.7	X
1969	103.86	103.01	−0.8	−11.4	
1970	92.06	85.02	−7.6	0.1	flat
1971	92.15	95.88	4.0	10.8	
1972	102.09	103.94	1.8	15.6	
1973	118.05	116.03	−1.7	−17.4	
1974	97.55	96.57	−1.0	−29.7	
1975	68.56	76.98	12.3	31.5	
1976	90.19	100.86	11.8	19.1	
1977	107.46	102.03	−5.1	−11.5	
1978	95.10	89.25	−6.2	1.1	flat
1979	96.11	99.93	4.0	12.3	
1980	107.94	114.16	5.8	25.8	
1981	135.76	129.55	−4.6	−9.7	
1982	122.55	120.40	−1.8	14.8	X
1983	140.64	145.30	3.3	17.3	
1984	164.93	163.41	−0.9	1.4	flat
1985	167.24	179.63	7.4	26.3	
1986	211.28	211.78	0.2	14.6	
1987	242.17	274.08	13.2	2.0	flat
1988	247.08	257.07	4.0	12.4	
1989	277.72	297.47	7.1	27.3	
1990	353.40	329.08	−6.9	−6.6	
1991	330.22	343.93	4.2	26.3	
1992	417.09	408.79	−2.0	4.5	flat
1993	435.71	438.78	0.7	7.1	
1994	466.45	481.61	3.3	−1.5	flat
1995	459.27	470.42	2.4	34.1	
1996	615.93	636.02	3.3	20.3	
1997	740.74	786.16	6.1	31.0	
1998	970.43	980.28	1.0	26.7	
1999	1229.23	1279.64	4.1	19.5	
2000	1469.25	1394.46	−5.1	−10.1	
2001	1320.28	1366.01	3.5	−13.0	X
2002	1148.08	1130.20	−1.6	−23.4	
2003	879.82	855.70	−2.7	26.4	X
2004	1111.92	1131.13	1.7	9.0	
2005	1211.92	1181.27	−2.5	3.0	flat
2006	1248.29	1280.08	2.5	13.6	
2007	1418.30	1438.24	1.4	??	

Ranked by Performance

Rank		January Change	Year Change	
1	1987	13.2%	2.0%	
2	1975	12.3	31.5	
3	1976	11.8	19.1	
4	1967	7.8	20.1	
5	1985	7.4	26.3	
6	1989	7.1	27.3	
7	1961	6.3	23.1	
8	1997	6.1	31.0	
9	1951	6.1	16.5	
10	1980	5.8	25.8	
11	1954	5.1	45.0	
12	1963	4.9	18.9	
13	1958	4.3	38.1	
14	1991	4.2	26.3	
15	1999	4.1	19.5	
16	1971	4.0	10.8	
17	1988	4.0	12.4	
18	1979	4.0	12.3	
19	2001	3.5	−13.0	X
20	1965	3.3	9.1	
21	1983	3.3	17.3	
22	1996	3.3	20.3	
23	1994	3.3	− 1.5	f
24	1964	2.7	13.0	
25	2006	2.5	13.6	
26	1995	2.4	34.1	
27	1972	1.8	15.6	
28	1955	1.8	26.4	
29	1950	1.7	21.8	
30	2004	1.7	9.0	
31	1952	1.6	11.8	
32	2007	1.4	??	
33	1998	1.0	26.7	
34	1993	0.7	7.1	
35	1966	0.5	−13.1	X
36	1959	0.4	8.5	
37	1986	0.2	14.6	
38	1953	−0.7	−6.6	
39	1969	−0.8	−11.4	
40	1984	−0.9	1.4	fl
41	1974	−1.0	−29.7	
42	2002	−1.6	−23.4	
43	1973	−1.7	−17.4	
44	1982	−1.8	14.8	X
45	1992	−2.0	4.5	fl
46	2005	−2.5	3.0	fl
47	2003	−2.7	26.4	X
48	1956	−3.6	2.6	fl
49	1962	−3.8	−11.8	
50	1957	−4.2	−14.3	
51	1968	−4.4	7.7	X
52	1981	−4.6	−9.7	
53	1977	−5.1	−11.5	
54	2000	−5.1	−10.1	
55	1978	−6.2	1.1	fl
56	1990	−6.9	−6.6	
57	1960	−7.1	—3.0	fl
58	1970	—7.6	0.1	f.

X = 5 major errors   *Based on S&P 5*

JANUARY

Trading Day of January Expiration Week, Dow Up 11 of Last 15

MONDAY
D 47.6
S 57.1
N 66.7
14

...ts are unimportant! It's what they are perceived to be that determines the course of events.
...arl Hadady (Bullish Consensus, Contrary Opinion)

TUESDAY
D 66.7
S 71.4
N 61.9
15

...d eight hours to chop down a tree, I'd spend six sharpening my axe. — Abraham Lincoln (16th U.S. president, 1809-1865)

WEDNESDAY
D 61.9
S 57.1
N 66.7
16

...have been three great inventions since the beginning of time: The fire, the wheel, and central banking.
...Rogers (American humorist and showman, 1879-1935)

THURSDAY
D 42.9
S 57.1
N 71.4
17

...n some, you lose some. And then there's that little-known third category.
...ert Gore (U.S. vice president 1993-2000, former 2000 presidential candidate, quoted at the 2004 DNC)

...uary Expiration Day, Dow Down 8 of Last 9 with Big Losses

FRIDAY
D 38.1
S 33.3
N 33.3
18

...uy when the 10-week moving average crosses the 30-week moving average and the slope of both averages is up.
...tor Sperandeo (Trader Vic — Methods of a Wall Street Master)

SATURDAY
19

SUNDAY
20

JANUARY BAROMETER IN GRAPHIC FORM SINCE 1950

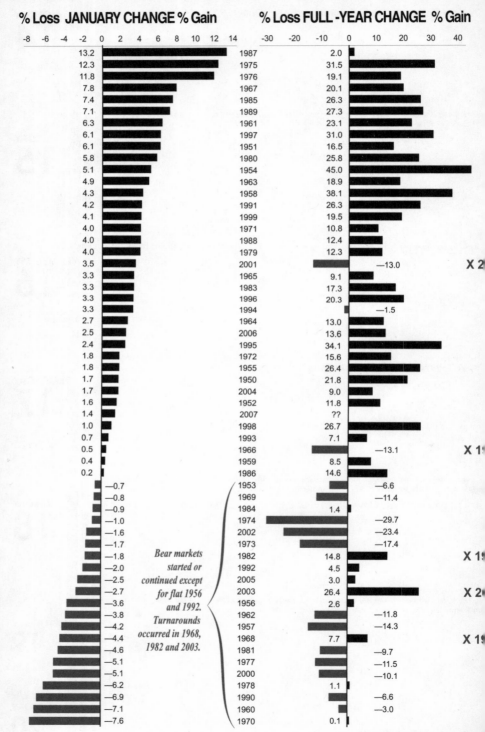

% Loss JANUARY CHANGE % Gain   % Loss FULL -YEAR CHANGE % Gain

Bear markets started or continued except for flat 1956 and 1992. Turnarounds occurred in 1968, 1982 and 2003.

X = 5 major errors   Based on S&P 500

n Luther King Jr. Day (Market Closed)

MONDAY
21

ıd, we will remember not the words of our enemies, but the silence of our friends.
ın Luther King Jr. (Civil rights leader, 1964 Nobel Peace Prize, 1929-1968)

TUESDAY
22
D 33.3
S 38.1
N 47.6

w you're right when the other side starts to shout. — I. A. O'Shaughnessy (American oilman, 1885-1973)

WEDNESDAY
23
D 52.4
S 52.4
N 52.4

re there are no rewards or punishments; there are consequences. — Horace Annesley Vachell (*The Force of Clay*)

ıary Barometer" 91.2% accurate (Page 16)
nac Investor Subscribers Emailed Official Reading Alert

THURSDAY
24
D 42.9
S 52.4
N 57.1

vill a man penetrate deeper into error than when he is continuing on a road that has led him to great success.
drich von Hayek (*Counterrevolution of Science*)

FRIDAY
25
D 71.4
S 52.4
N 42.9

asure of success is not whether you have a tough problem to deal with, but whether it's the same problem you had last year.
ı Foster Dulles (secretary of state under Eisenhower, 1888-1959)

SATURDAY
26

ıary Almanac Investor Seasonalities: See Pages 114 & 116

SUNDAY
27

FEBRUARY ALMANAC

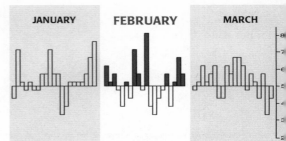
JANUARY FEBRUARY MARCH

Market Probability Chart above is a graphic representation of the S&P 500 Recent Market Probability Calendar on page 12

◆ February is the weak link in "Best Six Months" (pages 44, 58 & 147)
◆ RECENT RECORD improving: S&P 15 up, 8 down, average change 0.6% for 2 years ◆ #1 NASDAQ month in election years average 3.4%, up 6, down 3 (page 157), but #9 S&P and #11 Dow (pages 153 & 155), both up 5, down 4 ◆ Day before Presidents' Day weekend S&P down 14 of 16, 11 straight 1992-2002, day after improving lately, up 9 of 16 (see page 84 & 133) ◆ Many technicians modify market predictions based on January's market

February Vital Statistics

	DJIA	S&P 500	NASDAQ	Russell 1K	Russell 2K
Rank	8	11	8	11	5
Up	33	31	19	17	16
Down	25	27	18	12	13
Avg % Change	0.2%	−0.1%	0.5%	0.2%	1.3%
Election Year	0.1%	0.1%	3.4%	0.3%	3.4%
Best & Worst February					
	% Change	% Change	% Change	% Change	% Change
Best	1986 8.8	1986 7.1	2000 19.2	1986 7.2	2000 16.4
Worst	2000 −7.4	2001 −9.2	2001 −22.4	2001 −9.5	1999 −8.2
Best & Worst February Weeks					
Best	2/22/74 4.4	2/8/91 4.8	2/4/00 9.2	2/8/91 4.6	2/1/91 6.6
Worst	2/11/00 −4.9	2/23/01 −4.3	2/9/01 −7.1	2/23/01 −4.4	2/10/84 −4.6
Best & Worst February Days					
Best	2/24/84 2.7	2/22/99 2.7	2/11/99 4.2	2/22/99 2.6	2/29/00 3.6
Worst	2/27/07 −3.3	2/27/07 −3.5	2/16/01 −5.0	2/27/07 −3.4	2/27/07 −3.8
First Trading Day of Expiration Week: 1980-2007					
Record (#Up - #Down)	17-11	19-9	14-14	19-9	15-13
Current streak	D3	D2	D2	D2	D2
Avg % Change	0.39	0.33	0.04	0.28	0.08
Options Expiration Day: 1980-2007					
Record (#Up - #Down)	13-15	10-18	11-17	11-17	12-16
Current streak	U1	D2	D4	D2	U1
Avg % Change	−0.07	−0.16	−0.33	−0.16	−0.07
Options Expiration Week: 1980-2007					
Record (#Up - #Down)	16-12	13-15	13-15	12-16	16-12
Current streak	U2	U2	U2	U2	U2
Avg % Change	0.40	0.13	−0.05	0.13	0.19
Week After Options Expiration: 1980-2007					
Record (#Up - #Down)	12-16	13-15	17-11	13-15	17-11
Current streak	D2	D1	U3	D1	U4
Avg % Change	−0.22	−0.11	−0.03	−0.06	0.12
First Trading Day Performance					
% of Time Up	60.3	60.3	67.6	65.5	62.1
Avg % Change	0.11	0.09	0.25	0.07	0.16
Last Trading Day Performance					
% of Time Up	51.7	58.6	56.8	62.1	65.5
Avg % Change	0.08	0.08	0.05	0.11	0.33

Dow & S&P 1950-April 2007, NASDAQ 1971-April 2007, Russell 1K & 2K 1979-April 2007.

Either go short, or stay away
The day before Presidents' Day

JANUARY/FEBRUARY

<table>
<tr><td></td><td>MONDAY</td></tr>
<tr><td>D 66.7
S 52.4
N 76.2</td><td>28</td></tr>
</table>

...less you love EVERYBODY, you can't sell ANYBODY. — (From Jerry Maguire, 1996)

OMC Meeting (2 Days)

<table>
<tr><td></td><td>TUESDAY</td></tr>
<tr><td>D 52.4
S 57.1
N 66.7</td><td>29</td></tr>
</table>

Montag & Caldwell
INVESTMENT COUNSEL

JANET B. BUNCH, CFA
EXECUTIVE VICE PRESIDENT

...eum Director)

MONTAG & CALDWELL, INCORPORATED
3455 PEACHTREE ROAD, NE • SUITE 1200
ATLANTA • GEORGIA • 30326-3248
www.montag.com

404-836-7114
FAX: 404-836-7192
EMAIL: jbunch@montag.com

<table>
<tr><td></td><td>WEDNESDAY</td></tr>
<tr><td>D 61.9
S 66.7
N 57.1</td><td>30</td></tr>
</table>

18)

...not that I am so smart; it's just that I stay with problems longer.
Albert Einstein (German/American physicist, 1921 Nobel Prize, 1879-1955)

<table>
<tr><td></td><td>THURSDAY</td></tr>
<tr><td>D 71.4
S 76.2
N 71.4</td><td>31</td></tr>
</table>

...ery truth passes through three stages before it is recognized. In the first it is ridiculed; in the second it is opposed;
...the third it is regarded as self evident. — Arthur Schopenhauer (German philosopher, 1788-1860)

...rst Trading Day in February, Dow Up 7 of Last 8 and Last Five in a
...ow

<table>
<tr><td></td><td>FRIDAY</td></tr>
<tr><td>D 61.9
S 61.9
N 81.0</td><td>1</td></tr>
</table>

...e worst mistake investors make is taking their profits too soon, and their losses too long.
Michael Price (Mutual Shares Fund)

<table>
<tr><td>SATURDAY</td></tr>
<tr><td>2</td></tr>
</table>

<table>
<tr><td>SUNDAY</td></tr>
<tr><td>3</td></tr>
</table>

HOT JANUARY INDUSTRIES BEAT S&P NEXT 11 MONTHS

The S&P 500 in January tends to predict the market's direction for the year. In turn, Standard & Poor's top 10 industries in January outperform the index over the next 11 months.

Our friend Sam Stovall, chief investment strategist at S&P, has crunched the numbers over the years. He calls it the "January Barometer Portfolio," or JBP. Since 1970 a portfolio of the top 10 S&P Industries during January has beaten the S&P 500 itself — and performed even better in years when January was up.

The JBP went on to outperform the S&P 500 during the remaining 11 months of the year 73% of the time, 15.8% to 7.0%, on average. When the S&P 500 is up in January, a top-10 industries portfolio increases the average portfolio gain to 20.5% for the last 11 months of the year vs. 12.7% for the S&P.

For more check Sam's Sector Watch at *businessweek.com* or our March 2007 *Almanac Investor* newsletter in the archives at *www.stocktradersalmanac.com*. Also highlighted are Sam's selected stocks from within the top 10 sectors.

AS JANUARY GOES, SO GOES THE YEAR
FOR TOP-PERFORMING INDUSTRIES
January's Top 10 Industries vs. S&P 500 Next 11 Months

	11 Month % Change		S&P Jan	After S&P Up in January		After S&P Down in January	
	Portfolio	S&P	%	Portfolio	S&P	Portfolio	S&P
1970	− 4.7	− 0.3	− 7.6			− 4.7	− 0.3
1971	23.5	6.1	4.0	23.5	6.1		
1972	19.7	13.7	1.8	19.7	13.7		
1973	5.2	− 20.0	− 1.7			5.2	− 20.0
1974	− 29.2	− 30.2	− 1.0			− 29.2	− 30.2
1975	57.3	22.2	12.3	57.3	22.2		
1976	16.3	8.1	11.8	16.3	8.1		
1977	− 9.1	− 9.6	− 5.1			− 9.1	− 9.6
1978	7.3	6.5	− 6.2			7.3	6.5
1979	21.7	8.1	4.0	21.7	8.1		
1980	38.3	20.4	5.8	38.3	20.4		
1981	5.0	− 6.9	− 4.6			5.0	− 6.9
1982	37.2	18.8	− 1.8			37.2	18.8
1983	17.2	13.9	3.3	17.2	13.9		
1984	− 5.0	− 1.1	− 0.9			− 5.0	− 1.1
1985	28.2	20.8	7.4	28.2	20.8		
1986	18.1	19.4	0.2	18.1	19.4		
1987	− 1.5	− 8.9	13.2	− 1.5	− 8.9		
1988	18.4	10.4	4.0	18.4	10.4		
1989	16.1	22.1	7.1	16.1	22.1		
1990	− 4.4	− 3.3	− 6.9			− 4.4	− 3.3
1991	35.7	19.4	4.2	35.7	19.4		
1992	14.6	4.7	− 2.0			14.6	4.7
1993	23.7	7.2	0.7	23.7	7.2		
1994	− 7.1	− 4.6	3.3	− 7.1	− 4.6		
1995	25.6	30.9	2.4	25.6	30.9		
1996	5.4	16.5	3.3	5.4	16.5		
1997	4.7	23.4	6.1	4.7	23.4		
1998	45.2	25.4	1.0	45.2	25.4		
1999	67.9	14.8	4.1	67.9	14.8		
2000	23.6	− 5.3	− 5.1			23.6	− 5.3
2001	− 13.1	− 16.0	3.5	− 13.1	− 16.0		
2002	− 16.2	− 22.2	− 1.6			− 16.2	− 22.2
2003	69.3	29.9	− 2.7			69.3	29.9
2004	9.9	7.1	1.7	9.9	7.1		
2005	20.7	5.7	− 2.5			20.7	5.7
2006	− 0.3	10.8	2.5	− 0.3	10.8		
2007			1.4				
Averages	15.8%	7.0%		20.5%	12.7%	8.2%	− 2.4%

FEBRUARY

MONDAY
4

D 47.6
S 52.4
N 71.4

m the gods would destroy, they first put on the cover of BusinessWeek.
aul Krugman (Economist, *NY Times* 8/17/2001, referring to Enron CEO, cover 2/12, scandal 6/23, quits 8/16)

TUESDAY
5

D 42.9
S 57.1
N 57.1

et for the things we did can be tempered by time; it is regret for the things we did not do that is inconsolable.
ydney J. Harris (American journalist and author, 1917-1986)

h Wednesday

WEDNESDAY
6

D 47.6
S 47.6
N 61.9

thing always happens that you really believe in. The belief in a thing makes it happen.
rank Lloyd Wright (American architect)

THURSDAY
7

D 42.9
S 38.1
N 52.4

e money and the whole nation will conspire to call you a gentleman. — George Bernard Shaw (Irish dramatist, 1856-1950)

SDAQ Flattened in February 2001, Down 22.4%

FRIDAY
8

D 47.6
S 52.4
N 57.1

raging down in a bear market is tantamount to taking a seat on the down escalator at Macy's.
Richard Russell (*Dow Theory Letters*, 1984)

SATURDAY
9

SUNDAY
10

1933 "LAME DUCK" AMENDMENT: REASON JANUARY BAROMETER WORKS

There would be no January Barometer without the passage in 1933 of the Twentieth "Lame Duck" Amendment to the Constitution. Since then it has essentially been "As January goes so goes the year." January's direction has correctly forecasted the major trend for the market in most of the subsequent years.

Prior to 1934, newly elected senators and representatives did not take office until December of the following year, 13 months later (except when new presidents were inaugurated). Defeated congressmen stayed in Congress for all of the following session. They were known as "lame ducks."

Since 1934, Congress convenes in the first week of January and includes those members newly elected the previous November. Inauguration Day was also moved up from March 4 to January 20. As a result several events have been squeezed into January, which affects our economy and our stock market and quite possibly those of many nations of the world.

The basis for January's predictive capacity comes from the fact that so many important events occur in this month: new Congresses convene; the president gives the State of the Union message, presents the annual budget and sets national goals and priorities. Switch these events to any other month and chances are the January Barometer would become a memory.

The table shows the January Barometer in odd years. In 1935 and 1937, the Democrats already had the most lopsided congressional margins in history, so when these two Congresses convened it was anticlimactic.

The January Barometer in subsequent odd-numbered years had compiled a perfect record until two January interest rate cuts and the 9/11 attack affected 2001, the anticipation of military action in Iraq held the market down in January 2003, and we experienced a flat 2005. The disastrous Indian Ocean tsunami on December 26, 2004, may have impacted stocks in January 2005.

See the January Barometer compared to prior "New Congress Barometers" at *www.stocktradersalmanac.com*.

JANUARY BAROMETER (ODD YEARS)

January % Change	12 Month % Change	Same	Opposite
− 4.2%	41.2%		1935
3.8	− 38.6		1937
− 6.9	− 5.4	1939	
− 4.8	− 17.9	1941	
7.2	19.4	1943	
1.4	30.7	1945	
2.4	N/C	1947	
0.1	10.3	1949	
6.1	16.5	1951	
− 0.7	− 6.6	1953	
1.8	26.4	1955	
− 4.2	− 14.3	1957	
0.4	8.5	1959	
6.3	23.1	1961	
4.9	18.9	1963	
3.3	9.1	1965	
7.8	20.1	1967	
− 0.8	− 11.4	1969	
4.0	10.8	1971	
− 1.7	− 17.4	1973	
12.3	31.5	1975	
− 5.1	− 11.5	1977	
4.0	12.3	1979	
− 4.6	− 9.7	1981	
3.3	17.3	1983	
7.4	26.3	1985	
13.2	2.0	1987	
7.1	27.3	1989	
4.1	26.3	1991	
0.7	7.1	1993	
2.4	34.1	1995	
6.1	31.0	1997	
4.1	19.5	1999	
3.5	− 13.0		2001
− 2.7	26.4		2003
− 2.5	3.0		2005
1.4	??	2007?	2007?

12 month's % change includes January's % change
Based on S&P 500

FEBRUARY

*nday Before February Expiration, Dow Down 3 in a Row
er a Run of 11 Straight Winners

MONDAY
11

D 52.4
S 42.9
N 47.6

words "I am…" are potent words; be careful what you hitch them to. The thing you're claiming
a way of reaching back and claiming you. — A. L. Kitselman (Author, math teacher)

TUESDAY
12

D 61.9
S 71.4
N 61.9

e sure you have a jester because people in high places are seldom told the truth.
adio caller to President Ronald Reagan

WEDNESDAY
13

D 52.4
S 57.1
N 47.6

determined person can make a significant difference; a small group of determined people can change the course of history.
onia Johnson (Author, lecturer)

entine's Day ♥

THURSDAY
14

D 52.4
S 47.6
N 61.9

er buy at the bottom and I always sell too soon.
aron Nathan Rothchild's success formula (London Financier, 1777-1836)

oruary Expiration Day, S&P Down 10 of Last 14
/ Before Presidents' Day, S&P Down 14 of Last 16

FRIDAY
15

D 81.0
S 81.0
N 71.4

olitical problem of mankind is to combine three things: economic efficiency, social justice, and individual liberty.
hn Maynard Keynes (British economist, 1883-1946)

SATURDAY
16

SUNDAY
17

THE EIGHTH YEAR OF DECADES

An average Dow gain of 18.5% in 12 decades, with just two minor losses, ranks "eighth" year second only to "fifth" years. The 10% November drop after Truman beat Dewey left 1948 loser; following 1978's "October Massacre," the Dow ended the year slightly down while the S&P was up a bit. Bullish election year forces are expected to produce modest gains in 2008.

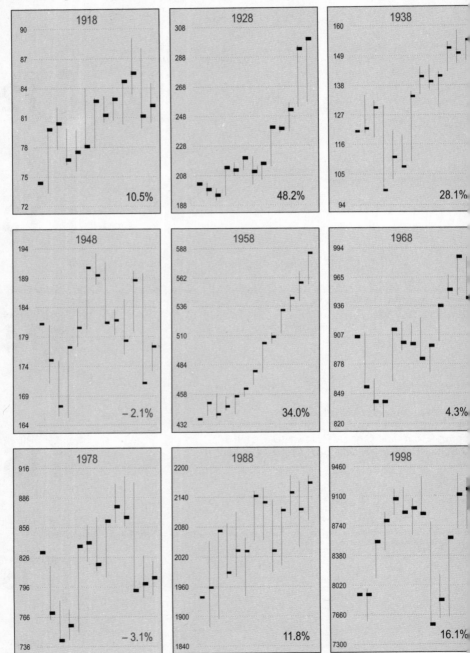

Based on Dow Jones Industrial Average monthly ranges and closing pric

FEBRUARY

esidents' Day (Market Closed)

MONDAY
18

eakened White House creates uncertainty on Wall Street.
Robert Hormats (Vice chairman, Goldman Sachs Int'l, CNN 10/28/2005)

y After Presidents' Day, a Mixed Bag, 7 of Last 8 S&P Losses Down >1%

TUESDAY
19

D 38.1
S 38.1
N 38.1

an will fight harder for his interests than his rights. — Napoleon Bonaparte (Emperor of France 1804-1815, 1769-1821)

WEDNESDAY
20

D 28.6
S 33.3
N 42.9

e history of the financial markets, arrogance has destroyed far more capital than stupidity.
ason Trennert (Managing Partner, Strategas Research Partners, March 27, 2006)

THURSDAY
21

D 52.4
S 42.9
N 42.9

me a stock clerk with a goal and I will give you a man who will make history. Give me a man without a goal,
I will give you a stock clerk. — James Cash Penney (J.C. Penney founder)

FRIDAY
22

D 57.1
S 47.6
N 42.9

omics is a very difficult subject. I've compared it to trying to learn how to repair a car when the engine is running.
en Bernanke (Fed chairman 2006, June 2004 *Region* interview as Fed governor)

SATURDAY
23

rch Almanac Investor Seasonalities: See Pages 114 & 116

SUNDAY
24

MARCH ALMANAC

MARCH							APRIL						
S	M	T	W	T	F	S	S	M	T	W	T	F	S
						1			1	2	3	4	5
2	3	4	5	6	7	8	6	7	8	9	10	11	12
9	10	11	12	13	14	15	13	14	15	16	17	18	19
16	17	18	19	20	21	22	20	21	22	23	24	25	26
23	24	25	26	27	28	29	27	28	29	30			
30	31												

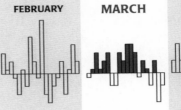

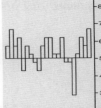

Market Probability Chart above is a graphic representation of the S&P 500 Recent Market Probability Calendar on page 12

◆ Early and mid-month strength and late-month weakness are most evident abov
◆ RECENT RECORD: S&P 16 up, 8 down, average gain 0.9%, seventh be:
◆ Rather stormy in recent years with wild fluctuations and large gains and losse
◆ March has been taking some mean end-of-quarter hits (page 134), down 146
Dow points March 9-22, 2001 ◆ Last three or four days Dow a net loser 13 out o
last 16 years ◆ NASDAQ hard hit in 2001, down 14.5% after 22.4% drop i
February ◆ Market much luckier the day before St. Patrick's Day ◆ Wor:
NASDAQ month during election years, average drop 2.5%, up 4, down 5

March Vital Statistics

	DJIA	S&P 500	NASDAQ	Russell 1K	Russell 2K
Rank	6	5	9	8	8
Up	37	38	23	19	20
Down	21	20	14	10	9
Avg % Change	0.9%	1.0%	0.3%	0.7%	0.7%
Election Year	0.5%	0.8%	−2.5%	−1.1%	−3.0%

Best & Worst March

	% Change	% Change	% Change	% Change	% Change
Best	2000 7.8	2000 9.7	1999 7.6	2000 8.9	1979 9.7
Worst	1980 −9.0	1980 −10.2	1980 −17.1	1980 −11.5	1980 −18.5

Best & Worst March Weeks

Best	3/21/03 8.4	3/21/03 7.5	3/3/00 7.1	3/21/03 7.4	3/3/00 7.4
Worst	3/16/01 −7.7	3/16/01 −6.7	3/16/01 −7.9	3/16/01 −6.8	3/7/80 −7.6

Best & Worst March Days

Best	3/16/00 4.9	3/16/00 4.8	3/13/03 4.8	3/16/00 4.9	3/28/80 4.8
Worst	3/12/01 −4.1	3/12/01 −4.3	3/12/01 −6.3	3/12/01 −4.4	3/27/80 −6.6

First Trading Day of Expiration Week: 1980-2007

Record (#Up - #Down)	18-10	19-9	14-14	19-9	16-12
Current streak	U1	U3	U3	U3	U3
Avg % Change	0.16	0.07	−0.27	0.02	−0.28

Options Expiration Day: 1980-2007

Record (#Up - #Down)	16-12	17-11	14-14	15-13	13-15
Current streak	D1	D1	D1	D1	D1
Avg % Change	0.05	0.005	−0.03	0.003	−0.04

Options Expiration Week: 1980-2007

Record (#Up - #Down)	18-10	17-11	15-13	16-12	14-14
Current streak	D1	D1	D1	D1	D1
Avg % Change	0.80	0.61	−0.19	0.54	−0.06

Week After Options Expiration: 1980-2007

Record (#Up - #Down)	12-16	9-19	13-15	9-19	13-15
Current streak	U2	U1	U2	U1	U2
Avg % Change	−0.55	−0.38	−0.20	−0.39	−0.25

First Trading Day Performance

% of Time Up	69.0	63.8	64.9	58.6	69.0
Avg % Change	0.24	0.24	0.35	0.29	0.38

Last Trading Day Performance

% of Time Up	39.7	37.9	64.9	44.8	86.2
Avg % Change	−0.14	−0.04	0.14	0.04	0.39

Dow & S&P 1950-April 2007, NASDAQ 1971-April 2007, Russell 1K & 2K 1979-April 2007.

March has Ides and St. Patrick's D
Begins bullishly, then fades awe

FEBRUARY/MARCH

MONDAY
D 52.4
S 57.1
N 57.1
25

hose who are of the opinion that money will do everything may very well be suspected to do everything for money.
— Sir George Savile (British statesman and author, 1633-1695)

TUESDAY
D 38.1
S 38.1
N 57.1
26

norance is not knowing something; stupidity is not admitting your ignorance. — Daniel Turov (Turov on Timing)

WEDNESDAY
D 47.6
S 52.4
N 52.4
27

e whole secret to our success is being able to con ourselves into believing that we're going to change the world
en though] we are unlikely to do it. — Tom Peters (American writer, In Search of Excellence, Fortune 11/13/2000)

THURSDAY
D 57.1
S 66.7
N 61.9
28

rt-term volatility is greatest at turning points and diminishes as a trend becomes established.
ieorge Soros (Financier, philanthropist, political activist, author and philosopher, b. 1930)

SDAQ Crushed in March 2001, Down 14.5%
er a 22.4% Drop in February

FRIDAY
D 47.6
S 57.1
N 52.4
29

eading of all good books is indeed like a conversation with the noblest men of past centuries, in which they reveal to us
est of their thoughts. — René Descartes (French philosopher, mathematician & scientist, 1596-1650)

SATURDAY
1

SUNDAY
2

MARKET CHARTS OF PRESIDENTIAL ELECTION YEARS

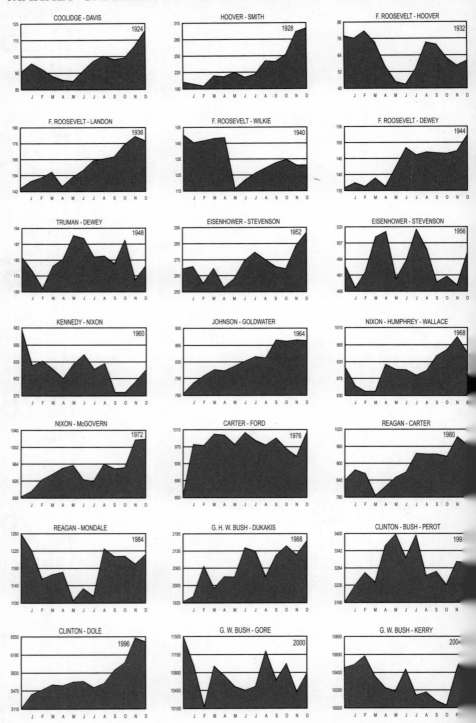

Based on Dow Jones Industrial Average monthly closing pr

MARCH

t Trading Day in March, Dow Up 9 of Last 12

MONDAY

D 57.1
S 47.6
N 66.7

3

live each day as if it was your last, someday you'll most certainly be right.
orite quote of Steve Jobs (CEO Apple & Pixar, Stanford University commencement address, 6/15/05)

TUESDAY

D 61.9
S 52.4
N 42.9

4

not believe any group of men adequate enough or wise enough to operate without scrutiny or without criticism…
ly way to avoid error is to detect it, that the only way to detect it is to be free to inquire…in secrecy error undetected
ourish and subvert. — J. Robert Oppenheimer (American physicist, father of A-bomb, 1904-1967)

ch Historically Strong Early in the Month

WEDNESDAY

D 61.9
S 61.9
N 71.4

5

twenty-two presidential elections from 1900 through 1984, Americans chose the most optimistic-sounding candidate
en times. — Martin E. Seligman, Ph.D. (Professor of Psychology, University of Pennsylvania, Learned Optimism, 1990)

THURSDAY

D 52.4
S 52.4
N 57.1

6

been said that politics is the second oldest profession. I have learned that it bears a striking resemblance to the first.
nald Reagan (40th U.S. president, 1911-2004)

Down 1469 Points March 9-22 in 2001

FRIDAY

D 57.1
S 57.1
N 61.9

7

hington people tell the truth off the record and lie on the record. In the Middle East they lie off the record and
e truth on the record. — Thomas L. Friedman (NY Times Foreign Affairs columnist, "Meet the Press" 12/17/06)

SATURDAY

8

ight Saving Time Begins

SUNDAY

9

PROFIT ON DAY BEFORE ST. PATRICK'S DAY

We first published Saint Patrick's Day bullishness in the 1977 Almanac. Dan Turov, editor of *Tur* *on Timing*, notes gains the day before Saint Patrick's Day have proved best, outperforming the da before many legal holidays for an average gain of 0.30% on the S&P. Irish luck, or coincidence?

During the past 55 years, Saint Patrick's Day itself has posted just a wee gain of 0.16% The day before Saint Pat's 2007 landed on Triple-Witching Friday and suffered a loss as t market started a new rally.

Saint Patrick's Day 2008 falls on Monday before Triple-Witching. However, Frida before March Triple-Witching have been down 5 of the last 6 election years and down ov 1% twice and more than 2% thrice. Monday of Triple-Witching Week has been mu stronger. March has been volatile in election years, so we would not press our luck, b going long the day before may prove fortunate in 2008.

Perhaps it's the anticipation of the patron saint's holiday that boosts the market and t distraction of the parade down Fifth Avenue that holds the market back — or is it the absent, a then hung-over, traders? Or maybe it's the fact that Saint Pat's usually falls in Triple-Witching Wee

ST. PATRICK'S DAY TRADING RECORD (DAYS BEFORE AND AFTER)

Year	St. Pat's Day	% Change 2 Days Prior	% Change 1 Day Prior	S&P 500 St. Pat's Day or Next *	% Change St. Pat's Day *	% Chan Day Aft
1953	Tue	0.19%	0.15%	26.33	0.42%	− 0.34
1954	Wed	− 0.45	− 0.04	26.62	0.23	0.41
1955	Thu	2.15	0.76	36.12	0.39	0.17
1956	Sat	0.97	0.31	48.59	0.93	0.58
1957	Sun	0.07	− 0.05	43.85	− 0.45	0.43
1958	Mon	0.12	− 0.31	42.04	− 0.69	− 0.36
1959	Tue	0.12	− 1.08	56.52	0.82	− 0.23
1960	Thu	0.77	0.55	54.96	− 0.15	0.09
1961	Fri	0.30	1.01	64.60	0.61	0.40
1962	Sat	0.21	− 0.17	70.85	− 0.13	− 0.27
1963	Sun	− 0.47	0.50	65.61	− 0.49	− 0.21
1964	Tue	0.08	N/C	79.32	0.23	0.08
1965	Wed	0.03	− 0.13	87.02	− 0.13	− 0.24
1966	Thu	− 0.57	0.58	88.17	0.35	0.41
1967	Fri	0.95	1.01	90.25	0.18	− 0.06
1968	Sun	− 1.90	0.88	89.59	0.55	− 0.67
1969	Mon	− 0.67	− 0.40	98.25	0.26	0.24
1970	Tue	− 0.53	− 1.08	87.29	0.44	0.29
1971	Wed	1.14	0.50	101.12	− 0.09	0.07
1972	Fri	0.13	− 0.23	107.92	0.39	− 0.31
1973	Sat	− 0.75	− 0.51	112.17	− 1.21	− 0.20
1974	Sun	− 0.09	− 0.37	98.05	− 1.24	− 0.84
1975	Mon	0.18	1.22	86.01	1.47	− 1.02
1976	Wed	− 1.05	1.12	100.86	− 0.06	− 0.41
1977	Thu	0.55	0.19	102.08	− 0.09	− 0.22
1978	Fri	− 0.26	0.44	90.20	0.77	0.69
1979	Sat	0.15	0.83	101.06	0.37	− 0.55
1980	Mon	− 1.17	− 0.18	102.26	− 3.01	1.80
1981	Tue	− 0.06	1.18	133.92	− 0.56	0.22
1982	Wed	0.77	− 0.16	109.08	− 0.18	1.12
1983	Thu	0.35	− 1.03	149.59	− 0.14	0.21
1984	Sat	0.41	1.18	157.78	− 0.94	0.68
1985	Sun	− 0.20	− 0.74	176.88	0.20	1.50
1986	Mon	0.28	1.44	234.67	− 0.79	0.47
1987	Tue	− 0.46	− 0.57	292.47	1.47	0.11
1988	Thu	− 0.09	0.95	271.22	0.96	− 0.04
1989	Fri	0.52	0.93	292.69	− 2.25	− 0.95
1990	Sat	0.36	1.14	343.53	0.47	− 0.5
1991	Sun	− 0.29	0.02	372.11	− 0.40	− 1.48
1992	Tue	0.48	0.14	409.58	0.78	− 0.16
1993	Wed	0.36	− 0.01	448.31	− 0.68	0.80
1994	Thu	− 0.08	0.52	470.90	0.32	0.04
1995	Fri	− 0.20	0.72	495.52	0.02	0.11
1996	Sun	0.36	0.09	652.65	1.75	− 0.15
1997	Mon	− 1.83	0.46	795.71	0.32	− 0.70
1998	Tue	− 0.12	1.00	1080.45	0.11	0.47
1999	Wed	0.98	− 0.07	1297.82	− 0.66	1.44
2000	Fri	2.43	4.76	1464.47	0.41	− 0.5
2001	Sat	0.59	− 1.96	1170.81	1.76	− 2.4
2002	Sun	− 0.09	1.14	1165.55	− 0.05	0.4
2003	Mon	3.45	0.16	862.79	3.54	0.4
2004	Wed	− 1.43	0.56	1123.75	1.17	− 0.1
2005	Thu	− 0.75	− 0.81	1190.21	0.18	− 0.0
2006	Fri	0.43	0.81	1307.25	0.15	− 0.1
2007	Sat	0.37	− 0.38	1402.06	1.09	0.6
Average		**0.12%**	**0.30%**		**0.16%**	**0.0**

When St. Patrick's Day falls on Saturday or Sunday, the following trading day is used. Based on S&P 500.

MARCH

MONDAY
D 52.4
S 61.9
N 47.6
10

...agination is more important than knowledge. — Albert Einstein (German/American physicist, 1921 Nobel Prize, 1879-1955)

TUESDAY
D 52.4
S 42.9
N 52.4
11

...you create an act, you create a habit. If you create a habit, you create a character. If you create a character, ...u create a destiny. — André Maurois (Novelist, biographer, essayist, 1885-1967)

WEDNESDAY
D 47.6
S 42.9
N 47.6
12

...the age of 24, I began setting clear, written goals for each area of my life. I accomplished more in the following year ...an I had in the previous 24. — Brian Tracy (Motivational speaker)

THURSDAY
D 42.9
S 61.9
N 61.9
13

...ose companies that the market expects will have the best futures, as measured by the price/earnings ratios they are accorded, ...ve consistently done worst subsequently. — David Dreman (Dreman Value Management, author, *Forbes* columnist, b. 1936)

...Market Much Luckier Day Before St. Patrick's Day (Page 32)

FRIDAY
D 61.9
S 57.1
N 52.4
14

...n't delay! A good plan, violently executed now, is better than a perfect plan next week. War is a very simple thing, ...ke stock trading] and the determining characteristics are self-confidence, speed, and audacity.
- General George S. Patton, Jr. (U.S. Army field commander WWII, 1885-1945)

SATURDAY
15

SUNDAY
16

HOW THE GOVERNMENT MANIPULATES
THE ECONOMY TO STAY IN POWER

Bull markets tend to occur in the third and fourth years of presidential terms while markets tend to decline in the first and second years. The "making of presidents" is accompanied by an unsubtle manipulation of the economy. Incumbent administrations are duty-bound to retain the reins of power. Subsequently, the "piper must be paid," producing what we have coined the "Post-Presidential Year Syndrome." Most big, bad bear markets began in such years — 1929, 1937, 1957, 1969, 1973, 1977 and 1981. Our major wars also began in years following elections — Civil War (1861), WWI (1917), WWII (1941) and Vietnam (1965). Post-election 2001 combined with 2002 for the worst back-to-back years since 1973-1974. Plus we had 9/11, the war on terror and the build-up to confrontation with Iraq.

Some cold hard facts to prove economic manipulation appeared in a book by Edward R. Tufte, *Political Control of the Economy* (Princeton University Press). Stimulative fiscal measures designed to increase per capita disposable income providing a sense of well-being to the voting public included: increases in federal budget deficits, government spending and social security benefits; interest rate reductions on government loans; and speed-ups of projected funding.

Federal Spending: During 1962-1973, the average increase was 29% higher in election years than in non-election years.

Social Security: There were nine increases during the 1952-1974 period. Half of the six election-year increases became effective in September eight weeks before Election Day. The average increase was 100% higher in presidential than in midterm election years. Annual adjustments for inflation have been the norm since then

Real Disposable Income: Accelerated in all but one election year between 1947 and 1973 (excluding the Eisenhower years). Only one of the remaining odd-numbered years (1973) showed a marked acceleration.

These moves were obviously not coincidences and explain why we tend to have a political (four-year) stock market cycle. Here are more examples of election year "generosity":

- Nixon plans to pump about $1 billion a month more than originally planned into spending programs designed to put money into the pockets of millions of currently unhappy voters...Such openhanded spending marks Nixon's conversion from unsuccessful policies of conservatism and gradualism to the activist, pump-priming Keynesian economic theory. *Time*, January 31, 1972.

- EPA Administrator Carol M. Browner today announced President Clinton's proposed fiscal year 2001 budget of $7.3 billion for the United States Environmental Protection Agency, the largest increase in the history of the Clinton/Gore Administration in spending for EPA. February 7, 2000.

- Like many of its predecessors, the Bush White House has used the machinery of government to promote the reelection of the president by awarding federal grants to strategically important states. *NY Times*, May 18, 2004.

- Even some conservatives grumble that Bush's tax cuts, expanded drug benefits for seniors and increased military spending have spurred a dramatic increase in the federal budget deficit, projected to be $477 billion in fiscal 2004, according to the Congressional Budget Office. *TheStreet.com*, July 2, 2004.

The United States does not have an exclusive on electoral spending manipulations:

- An executive increases spending to reward or cultivate loyalty to himself as the party or coalition leader. Evidence from South Korea and Taiwan between the 1970s and 2000 supports the theory. This strategy affects spending outcomes in election years. *Journal of East Asian Studies*, January 2006.

As we go to press the 2008 election campaigns have begun earlier than ever and many primaries and caucuses have been moved up earlier on the 2008 calendar as states vie for influence. The field is wide open, but should narrow quickly. President Bush and the Republicans have already primed the pump rather liberally during Bush's tenure and with approval ratings quite low, it brings into question their capacity to impact economic conditions to help sway voters.

MARCH

t. Patrick's Day ♣

Monday Before March Triple Witching, Dow Up 15 of Last 20

MONDAY
D 57.1
S 66.7
N 47.6
17

*he reasonable man adapts himself to the world; the unreasonable one persists in trying to adapt the world to himself.
herefore, all progress depends on the unreasonable man. — George Bernard Shaw (Irish dramatist, 1856-1950)*

TUESDAY
D 66.7
S 66.7
N 71.4
18

*here is only one side of the market and it is not the bull side or the bear side, but the right side.
- Jesse Livermore (Early 20th century stock trader & speculator, How to Trade in Stocks, 1877-1940)*

WEDNESDAY
D 52.4
S 61.9
N 61.9
19

*e who wants to persuade should put his trust not in the right argument, but in the right word. The power of sound
as always been greater than the power of sense. — Joseph Conrad (Polish/British novelist, 1857-1924)*

*ay Before Good Friday Worse in March — S&P Down 4 of
ast 5, Average –0.4%, March Triple Witching, Dow Down 7 of Last 12*

THURSDAY
D 61.9
S 47.6
N 61.9
20

*he only gets to the top rung on the ladder by steadily climbing up one at a time, and suddenly all sorts of powers,
l sorts of abilities, which you thought never belonged to you-suddenly become within your own possibility...
- Margaret Thatcher (British prime minister 1979-1990, b. 1925)*

good Friday (Market Closed)

FRIDAY
21

sold enough papers last year of high school to pay cash for a BMW. — Michael Dell (Founder Dell Computer, Forbes)

SATURDAY
22

aster

SUNDAY
23

INCUMBENT PARTY WINS & LOSSES

Since 1944 stocks tend to move up earlier when White House occupants are popular but do even better in November and December when unpopular administrations are ousted.

TREND OF S&P 500 INDEX IN ELECTION YEARS 1944-2004

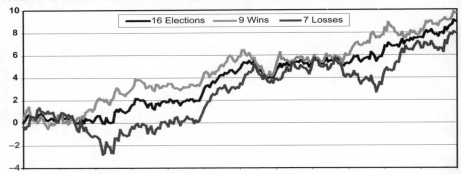

Actual percent changes reveal that March, June, October and December are best when incumbents stay in power, while July is worst. February, September and October are the worst when they are removed. Ironically, November is best when incumbents are ousted and second worst when they win.

Other interesting tidbits: there were no major losses in October (1984 off fractionally) and only one in June and December when incumbent parties retained the White House. Republican wins in November resulted in total gains of 23.6% (excluding no-decision 2000). Democratic victories produced total gains of 2.6%; however, Democrats "gained" 15.6% in December, the Republicans 7.9%.

MONTHLY % CHANGES IN S&P 500 DURING ELECTION YEARS

Incumbents Win

Year	Jan	Feb	Mar	Apr	May	Jun	Jul	Aug	Sep	Oct	Nov	Dec
1944	1.5	− 0.3	1.7	− 1.3	4.0	5.1	− 2.1	0.9	− 0.3	N/C	0.4	3.5
1948	− 4.0	− 4.7	7.7	2.7	7.8	0.3	− 5.3	0.8	− 3.0	6.8	−10.8	3.1
1956	− 3.6	3.5	6.9	− 0.2	− 6.6	3.9	5.2	− 3.8	− 4.5	0.5	− 1.1	3.5
1964	2.7	1.0	1.5	0.6	1.1	1.6	1.8	− 1.6	2.9	0.8	− 0.5	0.4
1972	1.8	2.5	0.6	0.4	1.7	− 2.2	0.2	3.4	− 0.5	0.9	4.6	1.2
1984	− 0.9	− 3.9	1.3	0.5	− 5.9	1.7	− 1.6	10.6	− 0.3	− 0.01	− 1.5	2.2
1988	4.0	4.2	− 3.3	0.9	0.3	4.3	− 0.5	− 3.9	4.0	2.6	− 1.9	1.5
1996	3.3	0.7	0.8	1.3	2.3	0.2	− 4.6	1.9	5.4	2.6	7.3	− 2.2
2004	1.7	1.2	− 1.6	− 1.7	1.2	1.8	− 3.4	0.2	0.9	1.4	3.9	3.2
Totals	**6.5**	**4.2**	**15.6**	**3.3**	**5.9**	**16.7**	**− 10.3**	**8.5**	**4.6**	**15.6**	**0.4**	**16.4**
Average	**0.7**	**0.5**	**1.7**	**0.4**	**0.7**	**1.9**	**− 1.1**	**0.9**	**0.5**	**1.7**	**0.04**	**1.8**

Incumbents Lose

Year	Jan	Feb	Mar	Apr	May	Jun	Jul	Aug	Sep	Oct	Nov	Dec
1952	1.6	− 3.6	4.8	− 4.3	2.3	4.6	1.8	− 1.5	− 2.0	− 0.1	4.6	3.5
1960	− 7.1	0.9	− 1.4	− 1.8	2.7	2.0	− 2.5	2.6	− 6.0	− 0.2	4.0	4.6
1968	− 4.4	− 3.1	0.9	8.2	1.1	0.9	− 1.8	1.1	3.9	0.7	4.8	− 4.2
1976	11.8	− 1.1	3.1	− 1.1	− 1.4	4.1	− 0.8	− 0.5	2.3	− 2.2	− 0.8	5.2
1980	5.8	− 0.4	−10.2	4.1	4.7	2.7	6.5	0.6	2.5	1.6	10.2	− 3.4
1992	− 2.0	1.0	− 2.2	2.8	0.1	− 1.7	3.9	− 2.4	0.9	0.2	3.0	1.0
2000	− 5.1	− 2.0	9.7	− 3.1	− 2.2	2.4	− 1.6	6.1	− 5.3	− 0.5	− 8.0*	0.4
Totals	**0.6**	**− 8.3**	**4.7**	**4.8**	**7.3**	**15.0**	**5.5**	**6.0**	**− 3.7**	**− 0.5**	**17.8**	**7.1**
Average	**0.1**	**− 1.2**	**0.7**	**0.7**	**1.0**	**2.1**	**0.8**	**0.9**	**− 0.5**	**− 0.1**	**2.5**	**1.0**

	Jan	Feb	Mar	Apr	May	Jun	Jul	Aug	Sep	Oct	Nov	Dec
16 Elections	**7.1**	**− 4.1**	**20.3**	**8.1**	**13.2**	**31.7**	**− 4.8**	**14.5**	**0.9**	**15.1**	**18.2**	**23.5**
Average	**0.4**	**− 0.3**	**1.3**	**0.5**	**0.8**	**2.0**	**− 0.3**	**0.9**	**0.1**	**1.0**	**1.1**	**1.5**

*Undecided election

Day After Easter, Worst Post-Holiday, S&P Down 10 of Last 14,
Up 3 of Last 4

MONDAY
D 33.3
S 57.1
N 61.9
24

10K ought to be enough for anybody.
— William H. Gates (Microsoft founder, 1981, Try running Microsoft Vista on less than a Gig)

Week After Triple Witching, Dow Down 14 of Last 20,
But Rallied 4.9% in 2000 and 3.1% in 2007

TUESDAY
D 57.1
S 52.4
N 47.6
25

Towering genius disdains a beaten path. It scorns to tread in the footsteps of any predecessor, however illustrious.
It thirsts for distinction. — Abraham Lincoln (16th U.S. president, 1809-1865)

March Historically Weak Later in the Month

WEDNESDAY
D 42.9
S 42.9
N 52.4
26

Everyone wants to make the same three things: money, a name, and a difference. What creates diversity in the human race
is how we prioritize the three. — Roy H. Williams (*The Wizard of Ads*)

THURSDAY
D 61.9
S 57.1
N 47.6
27

The only way to even begin to manage this new world is by focusing on...nation building — helping others restructure their
economies and put in place decent non-corrupt government. — Thomas L. Friedman (*NY Times* Foreign Affairs columnist)

Last Trading Day of March, Dow Down 10 of Last 13 with Major Losses

FRIDAY
D 47.6
S 33.3
N 42.9
28

In this game, the market has to keep pitching, but you don't have to swing. You can stand there with the bat on your shoulder
for six months until you get a fat pitch. — Warren Buffett (CEO Berkshire Hathaway, investor & philanthropist, b. 1930)

SATURDAY
29

April Almanac Investor Seasonalities: See Pages 114 & 116

SUNDAY
30

APRIL ALMANAC

APRIL						
S	M	T	W	T	F	S
		1	2	3	4	5
6	7	8	9	10	11	12
13	14	15	16	17	18	19
20	21	22	23	24	25	26
27	28	29	30			

MAY						
S	M	T	W	T	F	S
				1	2	3
4	5	6	7	8	9	10
11	12	13	14	15	16	17
18	19	20	21	22	23	24
25	26	27	28	29	30	31

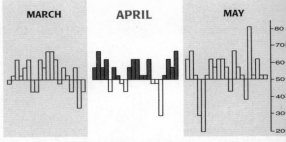

Market Probability Chart above is a graphic representation of the S&P 500 Recent Market Probability Calendar on page 124.

◆ April is still the best Dow month (average 1.8%) since 1950 (page 44) ◆ April 1999 first month ever to gain 1000 Dow points, 856 in 2001, knocked off its high horse in 2002 down 458, 2003 up 489 ◆ Prone to weakness after mid-month tax deadline ◆ Stocks anticipate great first quarter earnings by rising sharply before earnings are reported, rather than after ◆ Rarely a dangerous month except in big bear markets (like 2002), took the brunt of first-half declines in 2004 & 2005 ◆ "Best Six Months" of the year end with April (page 48) ◆ Since 1952 election-year Aprils are mediocre (#4 Dow & #8 S&P), NASDAQ net loser since 1972 ◆ End of April NASDAQ strength (pages 125 & 126)

April Vital Statistics

	DJIA		S&P 500		NASDAQ		Russell 1K		Russell 2K	
Rank	1		4		5		4		6	
Up	36		39		23		18		18	
Down	22		19		14		11		11	
Avg % Change	1.8%		1.3%		1.1%		1.3%		1.2%	
Election Year	0.8%		0.5%		−0.7%		0.6%		−0.3%	
Best & Worst April										
	% Change		% Change		% Change		% Change		% Change	
Best	1978	10.6	1978	8.5	2001	15.0	2001	8.0	2003	9.4
Worst	1970	−6.3	1970	−9.0	2000	−15.6	2002	−5.8	2000	−6.1
Best & Worst April Weeks										
Best	4/11/75	5.7	4/20/00	5.8	4/12/01	14.0	4/20/00	5.9	4/20/00	6.2
Worst	4/14/00	−7.3	4/14/00	−10.5	4/14/00	−25.3	4/14/00	−11.2	4/14/00	−16.4
Best & Worst April Days										
Best	4/5/01	4.2	4/5/01	4.4	4/5/01	8.9	4/5/01	4.6	4/18/00	5.8
Worst	4/14/00	−5.7	4/14/00	−5.8	4/14/00	−9.7	4/14/00	−6.0	4/14/00	−7.3
First Trading Day of Expiration Week: 1980-2007										
Record (#Up - #Down)	18-10		17-11		16-12		16-12		12-16	
Current streak	U1		U1		U1		U1		U1	
Avg % Change	0.29		0.22		0.26		0.21		0.11	
Options Expiration Day: 1980-2007										
Record (#Up - #Down)	19-9		18-10		16-12		18-10		17-11	
Current streak	U2		U1		U1		U1		U1	
Avg % Change	0.23		0.19		−0.09		0.17		0.13	
Options Expiration Week: 1980-2007										
Record (#Up - #Down)	23-5		21-7		19-9		19-9		21-7	
Current streak	U2		U2		U2		U2		U2	
Avg % Change	1.17		0.90		0.96		0.87		0.68	
Week After Options Expiration: 1980-2007										
Record (#Up - #Down)	18-10		18-10		19-9		18-10		18-10	
Current streak	U4		U1		U1		U1		U1	
Avg % Change	0.33		0.24		0.45		0.24		0.72	
First Trading Day Performance										
% of Time Up	56.9		60.3		40.5		55.2		41.4	
Avg % Change	0.08		0.04		−0.31		−0.03		−0.32	
Last Trading Day Performance										
% of Time Up	53.4		58.6		70.3		62.1		75.9	
Avg % Change	0.13		0.14		0.28		0.17		0.31	

Dow & S&P 1950-April 2007, NASDAQ 1971-April 2007, Russell 1K & 2K 1979-April 2007.

April "Best Month" for Dow since 1950
Day-before-Good Friday gains are nifty

MARCH/APRIL

MONDAY

D 33.3
S 42.9
N 61.9

31

*homas Alva Edison said, "Genius is 5% inspiration and 95% perspiration!" Unfortunately, many startup
genius" entrepreneurs mistakenly switch the two percentages around, and then wonder why
ey can't get their projects off the ground. — Yale Hirsch*

irst Trading Day in April, Dow Up 10 of Last 13, 6 Straight 1995-2000

TUESDAY

D 61.9
S 57.1
N 38.1

1

*ny human anywhere will blossom in a hundred unexpected talents and capacities simply by being given
e opportunity to do so. — Doris Lessing (British novelist, born in Persia 1919)*

WEDNESDAY

D 66.7
S 66.7
N 57.1

2

*ock prices tend to discount what has been unanimously reported by the mass media.
- Louis Ehrenkrantz (Ehrenkrantz, Lyons & Ross)*

*tart Looking for the Dow & S&P MACD SELL Signal (Pages 48 & 50)
lmanac Investor Subscribers Are Emailed Alert when It Triggers*

THURSDAY

D 52.4
S 57.1
N 71.4

3

ell stocks whenever the market is 30% higher over a year ago. — Eugene D. Brody (Oppenheimer Capital)

FRIDAY

D 71.4
S 61.9
N 52.4

4

*hose who cannot remember the past are condemned to repeat it.
- George Santayana (American philosopher, poet, 1863-1952)*

SATURDAY

5

SUNDAY

6

THE DECEMBER LOW INDICATOR: A USEFUL PROGNOSTICATING TOOL

When the Dow closes below its December closing low in the first quarter, it is frequently an excellent warning sign. Jeffrey Saut, managing director of investment strategy at Raymond James, brought this to our attention a few years ago. The December Low Indicator was originated by Lucien Hooper, a *Forbes* columnist and Wall Street analyst back in the 1970s. Hooper dismissed the importance of January and January's first week as reliable indicators. He noted that the trend could be random or even manipulated during a holiday-shortened week. Instead, said Hooper, "Pay much more attention to the December low. If that low is violated during the first quarter of the New Year, watch out!"

Thirteen of the 27 occurrences were followed by gains for the rest of the year — and 12 full-year gains — after the low for the year was reached. For perspective we've included the January Barometer readings for the selected years. Hooper's "Watch Out" warning was absolutely correct, though. All but two of the instances since 1952 experienced further declines, as the Dow fell an additional 10.1% on average when December's low was breached in Q1.

Only three significant drops occurred (not shown) when December's low was not breached in Q1 (1974, 1981 and 1987). Both indicators were wrong only three times and six years ended flat. If the December low is not crossed, turn to our January Barometer for guidance. It has been virtually perfect, right nearly 100% of these times (view the complete results at *www.stocktradersalmanac.com.*

YEARS DOW FELL BELOW DECEMBER LOW IN FIRST QUARTER

Year	Previous Dec Low	Date Crossed	Crossing Price	Subseq. Low	% Change Cross-Low	Rest of Year % Change	Full Year % Change	Jan Bar
1952	262.29	2/19/52	261.37	256.35	— 1.9%	11.7%	8.4%	1.6%[2]
1953	281.63	2/11/53	281.57	255.49	— 9.3	— 0.2	— 3.8	— 0.7
1956	480.72	1/9/56	479.74	462.35	— 3.6	4.1	2.3	— 3.6[2 3]
1957	480.61	1/18/57	477.46	419.79	— 12.1	— 8.7	— 12.8	— 4.2
1960	661.29	1/12/60	660.43	566.05	— 14.3	— 6.7	— 9.3	— 7.1
1962	720.10	1/5/62	714.84	535.76	— 25.1	— 8.8	— 10.8	— 3.8
1966	939.53	3/1/66	938.19	744.32	— 20.7	— 16.3	— 18.9	0.5[1]
1968	879.16	1/22/68	871.71	825.13	— 5.3	8.3	4.3	— 4.4[1 2]
1969	943.75	1/6/69	936.66	769.93	— 17.8	— 14.6	— 15.2	— 0.8
1970	769.93	1/26/70	768.88	631.16	— 17.9	9.1	4.8	— 7.6[2 3]
1973	1000.00	1/29/73	996.46	788.31	— 20.9	— 14.6	— 16.6	— 1.7
1977	946.64	2/7/77	946.31	800.85	— 15.4	— 12.2	— 17.3	— 5.1
1978	806.22	1/5/78	804.92	742.12	— 7.8	0.01	— 3.1	— 6.2[3]
1980	819.62	3/10/80	818.94	759.13	— 7.3	17.7	14.9	5.8[2]
1982	868.25	1/5/82	865.30	776.92	— 10.2	20.9	19.6	— 1.8[1 2]
1984	1236.79	1/25/84	1231.89	1086.57	— 11.8	— 1.6	— 3.7	— 0.9[3]
1990	2687.93	1/15/90	2669.37	2365.10	— 11.4	— 1.3	— 4.3	— 6.9
1991	2565.59	1/7/91	2522.77	2470.30	— 2.1	25.6	20.3	4.2[2]
1993	3255.18	1/8/93	3251.67	3241.95	— 0.3	15.5	13.7	0.7[2]
1994	3697.08	3/30/94	3626.75	3593.35	— 0.9	5.7	2.1	3.3[2 3]
1996	5059.32	1/10/96	5032.94	5032.94	NC	28.1	26.0	3.3[2]
1998	7660.13	1/9/98	7580.42	7539.07	— 0.5	21.1	16.1	1.0[2]
2000	10998.39	1/4/00	10997.93	9796.03	— 10.9	— 1.9	— 6.2	— 5.1
2001	10318.93	3/12/01	10208.25	8235.81	— 19.3	— 1.8	— 7.1	3.5[1]
2002	9763.96	1/16/02	9712.27	7286.27	— 25.0	— 14.1	— 16.8	— 1.6
2003	8303.78	1/24/03	8131.01	7524.06	— 7.5	28.6	25.3	— 2.7[1 2]
2005	10440.58	1/21/05	10392.99	10012.36	— 3.7	3.1	— 0.6	— 2.5[3]
2006	10717.50	1/20/06	10667.39	10667.39	NC	16.8	16.3	2.5[2]
2007	12194.13	3/2/07	12114.10	12050.41	— 0.5	*At Presstime – not in average*		1.4
				Average Drop	— 10.1%			

[1] January Barometer wrong [2] December Low Indicator wrong [3] Year Flat

40

APRIL

'ome men see things as they are and say "why?" I dream things that never were and say "why not?"
— George Bernard Shaw (Irish dramatist, 1856-1950)

April Is the Best Month for the Dow, Average 1.8% Since 1950

always keep these seasonal patterns in the back of my mind. My antennae start to purr at certain times of the year.
— Kenneth Ward (VP Hayden Stone, *General Technical Survey*, 1899-1976)

'ight until death over taxes? Oh, no. Women, country, God, things like that. Taxes? No.
— Daniel Patrick Moynihan (U.S. senator, New York 1977-2001, "Meet The Press" 5/23/1993, 1927-2003)

Whenever you see a successful business, someone once made a courageous decision.
— Peter Drucker (Austria-born pioneer management theorist, 1909-2005)

The ability to foretell what is going to happen tomorrow, next week, next month, and next year.
And to have the ability afterwards to explain why it didn't happen.
— Winston Churchill (British statesman, 1874-1965, when asked what qualities a politician required)

DOWN JANUARYS: A REMARKABLE RECORD

In the first third of the 20th century there was no correlation between January markets and the year as a whole (page 24). Then in 1972 we discovered that the 1933 "Lame Duck" Amendment to the Constitution changed the political calendar and the January Barometer was born — its record has been quite accurate (page 16).

Down Januarys are harbingers of trouble ahead, in the economic, political, or military arenas. Eisenhower's heart attack in 1955 cast doubt on whether he could run in 1956 — a flat year. Two other election years with down Januarys were also flat (1984 & 1982). Twelve bear markets began and five continued into second years with poor Januarys. 1968 started down as we were mired in Vietnam, but Johnson's "bombing halt" changed the climate. January 2003 closed down in the face of imminent military action in Iraq, and the market triple-bottomed in March just before U.S. led forces began their blitz to Baghdad. The fall of Baghdad combined with pre-election and recovery forces to fuel 2003 into a banner year. 2005 was flat, registering the narrowest Dow trading range on record.

Unfortunately, bull and bear markets do not start conveniently at the beginnings and ends of months or years. Though some years ended higher, **every down January since 1950 was followed by a new or continuing bear market or a flat year.** Excluding 1956, **down Januarys were followed by substantial declines averaging *minus* 13.3%,** providing excellent buying opportunities later in most years.

FROM DOWN JANUARY S&P CLOSES TO LOW NEXT 11 MONTHS

Year	January Close	% Change	11-Month Low	Date of Low	Jan Close to Low %	% Feb to Dec	Year % Change	
1953	26.38	− 0.7%	22.71	14-Sep	− 13.9%	− 6.0%	− 6.6%	bear
1956	43.82	− 3.6	44.10	28-May	0.9	6.5	2.6	FLAT
1957	44.72	− 4.2	38.98	22-Oct	− 12.8	− 10.6	− 14.3	bear
1960	55.61	− 7.1	52.30	25-Oct	− 6.0	4.5	− 3.0	bear
1962	68.84	− 3.8	52.32	26-Jun	− 24.0	− 8.3	− 11.8	bear
1968	92.24	− 4.4	87.72	5-Mar	− 4.9	12.6	7.7	Cont. bear
1969	103.01	− 0.8	89.20	17-Dec	− 13.4	− 10.6	− 11.4	bear
1970	85.02	− 7.6	69.20	26-May	− 18.6	8.4	0.1	Cont. bear
1973	116.03	− 1.7	92.16	5-Dec	− 20.6	− 15.9	− 17.4	bear
1974	96.57	− 1.0	62.28	3-Oct	− 35.5	− 29.0	− 29.7	bear
1977	102.03	− 5.1	90.71	2-Nov	− 11.1	− 6.8	− 11.5	bear
1978	89.25	− 6.2	86.90	6-Mar	− 2.6	7.7	1.1	Cont. bear
1981	129.55	− 4.6	112.77	25-Sep	− 13.0	− 5.4	− 9.7	bear
1982	120.40	− 1.8	102.42	12-Aug	− 14.9	16.8	14.8	Cont. bear
1984	163.42	− 0.9	147.82	24-Jul	− 9.5	2.3	1.4	FLAT
1990	329.07	− 6.9	295.46	11-Oct	− 10.2	0.4	− 6.6	bear
1992	408.79	− 2.0	394.50	8-Apr	− 3.5	6.6	4.5	FLAT
2000	1394.46	− 5.1	1264.74	20-Dec	− 9.3	− 5.3	− 10.1	bear
2002	1130.20	− 1.6	776.76	9-Oct	− 31.3	− 22.2	− 23.4	bear
2003	855.70	− 2.7	800.73	11-Mar	− 6.4	29.9	26.4	Cont. bear
2005	1181.27	− 2.5	1137.50	20-Apr	− 3.7	5.7	3.0	FLAT
				Totals	− 264.3%	− 18.7%	− 94.0%	
				Average	− 12.6%	− 0.9%	− 4.5%	

APRIL

MONDAY

D 71.4
S 57.1
N 57.1

14

*for an impending crash in the economy when the best seller lists are filled with books on business strategies
quick-fix management ideas.* — Peter Drucker (Austria-born pioneer management theorist, 1909-2005)

ome Tax Deadline

TUESDAY

D 71.4
S 61.9
N 47.6

15

greatest lie ever told: Build a better mousetrap and the world will beat a path to your door. — Yale Hirsch

il Prone to Weakness After Tax Deadline

WEDNESDAY

D 52.4
S 61.9
N 61.9

16

ng the first period of a man's life the greatest danger is not to take the risk.
oren Kierkegaard (Danish philosopher, 1813-1855)

THURSDAY

D 47.6
S 52.4
N 52.4

17

world hates change, but it is the only thing that has brought progress.
*harles Kettering (Inventor of electric ignition, founded Delco in 1909, 1876-1958)

il Expiration Day, Dow Up 9 of Last 11, But a Big Loser in 2001 and 2005

FRIDAY

D 52.4
S 52.4
N 47.6

18

t-rate people hire first-rate people; second-rate people hire third-rate people. — Leo Rosten (American author, 1908-1997)

SATURDAY

19

ssover

SUNDAY

20

TOP PERFORMING MONTHS PAST 57 ⅓ YEARS
STANDARD & POOR'S 500 & DOW JONES INDUSTRIALS

Monthly performance of the S&P and the Dow are ranked over the past 57 ⅓ years. NASDAQ monthly performance is shown on page 56.

January, April, November and December still hold the top four positions in both the Dow and S&P. This led to our discovery in 1986 of the market's best-kept secret. You can divide the year into two sections and have practically all the gains in one six-month section and very little in the other. September has been the worst month on both lists. (See "Best Six Months" on page 48.)

MONTHLY % CHANGES (JANUARY 1950 – APRIL 2007)

	Standard & Poor's 500					Dow Jones Industrials			
Month	Total % Change	Avg. % Change	# Up	# Down	Month	Total % Change	Avg. % Change	# Up	# Down
Jan	81.3%	1.4%	37	21	Jan	77.2%	1.3%	39	19
Feb	– 3.1	– 0.1	31	27	Feb	9.6	0.2	33	25
Mar	57.4	1.0	38	20	Mar	52.5	0.9	37	21
Apr	77.4	1.3	39	19	Apr	107.0	1.8	36	22
May	14.0	0.2	32	25	May	3.8	0.1	29	28
Jun	13.1	0.2	31	26	Jun	– 5.7	– 0.1	28	29
Jul	49.8	0.9	31	26	Jul	59.9	1.1	35	22
Aug	2.1	0.04	31	26	Aug	– 2.2	– 0.04	32	25
Sep*	– 35.1	– 0.6	24	32	Sep	– 55.1	– 1.0	21	36
Oct	52.1	0.9	34	23	Oct	33.8	0.6	33	24
Nov	100.2	1.8	39	18	Nov	96.3	1.7	39	18
Dec	96.7	1.7	43	14	Dec	99.9	1.8	41	16
% Rank					**% Rank**				
Nov	100.2%	1.8%	39	18	Apr	107.0%	1.8%	36	22
Dec	96.7	1.7	43	14	Dec	99.9	1.8	41	16
Jan	81.3	1.4	37	21	Nov	96.3	1.7	39	18
Apr	77.4	1.3	39	19	Jan	77.2	1.3	39	19
Mar	57.4	1.0	38	20	Jul	59.9	1.1	35	22
Oct	52.1	0.9	34	23	Mar	52.5	0.9	37	21
Jul	49.8	0.9	31	26	Oct	33.8	0.6	33	24
May	14.0	0.2	32	25	Feb	9.6	0.2	33	25
Jun	13.1	0.2	31	26	May	3.8	0.1	29	28
Aug	2.1	0.04	31	26	Aug	– 2.2	– 0.04	32	25
Feb	– 3.1	– 0.1	31	27	Jun	– 5.7	– 0.1	28	29
Sep*	– 35.1	– 0.6	24	32	Sep	– 55.1	– 1.0	21	36
Totals	**505.9%**	**8.7%**			**Totals**	**477.0%**	**8.4%**		
Average		**0.73%**			**Average**		**0.70%**		

*No change 1979

Anticipators, shifts in cultural behavior and faster information flow have altered seasonality in recent years. Here is how the months ranked over the past 15 ⅓ years (184 months) using total percentage gains on the S&P 500: November 36.5, October 35.4, April 24.4, December 20.5, January 16.1, May 14.6, March 9.7, June 7.3, July 0.3, September –6.3, February –6.3, August –11.1.

During the last 15 ⅓ years front-runners of our Best Six Months may have helped push October into the number-two spot. May has leapfrogged March and July into the number-six spot. January has declined in four of the last eight years. October 1987, down 21.8% (Dow –23.2%), is no longer in the most recent 15 years and we've seen some sizeable turnarounds in "bear killing" October the last nine years. Big Dow losses in the period were: August 1998 (SE Asia crisis), off 15.1%; September 2001 (9/11 attack) off 11.1%; September 2002 (Iraq war drums) off 12.4%.

APRIL

MONDAY
D 57.1
S 61.9
N 52.4
21

The punishment of wise men who refuse to take part in the affairs of government is to live under the government of unwise men.
— Plato (Greek philosopher, 427-347 BC)

TUESDAY
D 42.9
S 47.6
N 42.9
22

Get inside information from the president and you will probably lose half your money. If you get it from the chairman of the board, you will lose all your money. — Jim Rogers (Financier, b. 1942)

April 1999 First Month Ever to Gain 1000 Dow Points

WEDNESDAY
D 52.4
S 47.6
N 47.6
23

Don't fritter away your time. Create, act, take a place wherever you are and be somebody.
— Theodore Roosevelt (26th U.S. president, 1858-1919)

THURSDAY
D 33.3
S 28.6
N 42.9
24

What is conservatism? Is it not adherence to the old and tried, against the new and untried?
— Abraham Lincoln (16th U.S. president, 1809-1865)

FRIDAY
D 52.4
S 52.4
N 47.6
25

Why is it right-wing [conservatives] always stand shoulder to shoulder in solidarity, while liberals always fall out among themselves? — Yevgeny Yevtushenko (Russian poet, Babi Yar, quoted in London *Observer* December 15, 1991, b. 1933)

SATURDAY
26

May Almanac Investor Seasonalities: See Pages 114 & 116

SUNDAY
27

MAY ALMANAC

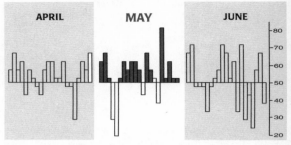

MAY								JUNE					
S	M	T	W	T	F	S		S	M	T	W	T	F	S
				1	2	3			1	2	3	4	5	6	7
4	5	6	7	8	9	10		8	9	10	11	12	13	14
11	12	13	14	15	16	17		15	16	17	18	19	20	21
18	19	20	21	22	23	24		22	23	24	25	26	27	28
25	26	27	28	29	30	31		29	30					

Market Probability Chart above is a graphic representation of the S&P 500 Recent Market Probability Calendar on page 124.

◆ "May/June disaster area" between 1965 and 1984 with S&P down 15 out of 20 Mays ◆ Between 1985 and 1997 May was the best month with 13 straight gains, gaining 3.3% per year on average, up 4, down 5 since ◆ Worst six months of the year begin with May (page 48) ◆ A $10,000 investment compounded to $578,413 for November-April in 57 years compared to a $341 gain for May-October ◆ Memorial Day week record: up 12 years in a row (1984-1995), down seven of the last eleven years ◆ Since 1952 election year Dow Mays rank last

May Vital Statistics

	DJIA		S&P 500		NASDAQ		Russell 1K		Russell 2K	
Rank	9		8		6		5		4	
Up	29		32		21		19		18	
Down	28		25		15		9		10	
Avg % Change	0.1%		0.2%		1.0%		1.3%		1.7%	
Election Year	−0.3%		0.1%		−0.6%		0.1%		0.1%	
Best & Worst May										
	% Change		% Change		% Change		% Change		% Change	
Best	1990	8.3	1990	9.2	1997	11.1	1990	8.9	1997	11.0
Worst	1962	−7.8	1962	−8.6	2000	−11.9	1984	−5.9	2000	−5.9
Best & Worst May Weeks										
Best	5/29/70	5.8	5/2/97	6.2	5/17/02	8.8	5/2/97	6.4	5/2/97	5.4
Worst	5/25/62	−6.0	5/25/62	−6.8	5/12/00	−7.5	5/2/86	−2.9	5/12/06	−5.0
Best & Worst May Days										
Best	5/27/70	5.1	5/27/70	5.0	5/30/00	7.9	5/8/02	3.7	5/30/00	4.2
Worst	5/28/62	−5.7	5/28/62	−6.7	5/23/00	−5.9	5/19/03	−2.5	5/10/00	−3.4
First Trading Day of Expiration Week: 1980-2006										
Record (#Up - #Down)	18-9		19-8		15-12		18-9		14-13	
Current streak	U2		U2		D1		U2		D1	
Avg % Change	0.29		0.30		0.19		0.26		0.04	
Options Expiration Day: 1980-2006										
Record (#Up - #Down)	12-15		14-13		13-14		14-13		13-14	
Current streak	U1		U1		U3		U1		U1	
Avg % Change	−0.17		−0.19		−0.19		−0.17		−0.06	
Options Expiration Week: 1980-2006										
Record (#Up - #Down)	15-12		14-13		15-12		13-14		16-11	
Current streak	D1		D1		D1		D1		D1	
Avg % Change	0.34		0.33		0.54		0.35		0.37	
Week After Options Expiration: 1980-2006										
Record (#Up - #Down)	16-11		17-10		19-8		17-10		19-8	
Current streak	U3		U3		U3		U3		U4	
Avg % Change	0.11		0.20		0.13		0.20		0.18	
First Trading Day Performance										
% of Time Up	56.1		56.1		58.3		50.0		64.3	
Avg % Change	0.17		0.20		0.26		0.20		0.30	
Last Trading Day Performance										
% of Time Up	64.9		63.2		72.2		57.1		71.4	
Avg % Change	0.24		0.22		0.22		0.30		0.39	

Dow & S&P 1950-April 2007, NASDAQ 1971-April 2007, Russell 1K & 2K 1979-April 2007.

Was Number One month for nine straight years
But five out of the last ten have caused May tears

APRIL/MAY

MONDAY

D 61.9
S 61.9
N 61.9

28

---

f the models are telling you to sell, sell, sell, but only buyers are out there, don't be a jerk. Buy!
— William Silber, Ph.D. (N.Y.U., *Newsweek*, 1986)

TUESDAY

D 57.1
S 57.1
N 61.9

29

Edison has done more toward abolishing poverty than all the reformers and statesmen.
— Henry Ford (Founder Ford Motors, father of moving assembly line, 1863-1947)

End of "Best Six Months" of the Year (Pages 44, 48, 50 & 147)

WEDNESDAY

D 52.4
S 66.7
N 76.2

30

A committee is a cul de sac down which ideas are lured and then quietly strangled.
— Sir Barnett Cocks (Member of Parliament, 1907-1989)

First Trading Day in May, Dow Up Solidly 7 of Last 9

THURSDAY

D 61.9
S 61.9
N 66.7

1

Every man who knows how to read has it in his power to magnify himself, to multiply the ways in which he exists, to make his life full, significant and interesting. — Aldous Huxley (English author, *Brave New World*, 1894-1963)

FRIDAY

D 66.7
S 66.7
N 76.2

2

Bill [Gates] isn't afraid of taking long-term chances. He also understands that you have to try everything because the real secret to innovation is failing fast. — Gary Starkweather (Inventor of laser printer in 1969 at Xerox, *Fortune*, July 8, 2002)

SATURDAY

3

SUNDAY

4

BEST SIX MONTHS: STILL AN EYE-POPPING STRATEGY

Our Best Six Months Switching Strategy consistently delivers. Investing in the Dow Jones Industrial Average between November 1st and April 30th each year and then switching into fixed income for the other six months has produced reliable returns with reduced risk since 1950.

The chart on page 147 shows November, December, January, March and April to be the top months since 1950. Add February, and an excellent strategy is born! These six consecutive months gained 12673.97 Dow points in 57 years, while the remaining May through October months gained 174.61 points. The S&P gained 1261.82 points in the same best six months versus 202.48 points in the worst six.

Percentage changes are shown along with a compounding $10,000 investment.

The November-April $578,413 gain overshadows May-October's $341. (S&P results were $419,782 to $9,138.) Just two November-April losses were double-digit: April 1970 (Cambodian invasion) and 1973 (OPEC oil embargo). Similarly, Iraq muted the Best 6 and inflated the Worst 6 in 2003.

When we discovered this strategy in 1986, November-April outperformed May-October by $88,145 to minus $1,520. Results improved substantially these past 21 years, $490,268 to $1,861. A simple timing indicator triples results (page 50).

SIX-MONTH SWITCHING STRATEGY

	DJIA % Change May 1-Oct 31	Investing $10,000	DJIA % Change Nov 1-Apr 30	Investing $10,000
1950	5.0%	$10,500	15.2%	$11,520
1951	1.2	10,626	− 1.8	11,313
1952	4.5	11,104	2.1	11,551
1953	0.4	11,148	15.8	13,376
1954	10.3	12,296	20.9	16,172
1955	6.9	13,144	13.5	18,355
1956	− 7.0	12,224	3.0	18,906
1957	− 10.8	10,904	3.4	19,549
1958	19.2	12,998	14.8	22,442
1959	3.7	13,479	− 6.9	20,894
1960	− 3.5	13,007	16.9	24,425
1961	3.7	13,488	− 5.5	23,082
1962	− 11.4	11,950	21.7	28,091
1963	5.2	12,571	7.4	30,170
1964	7.7	13,539	5.6	31,860
1965	4.2	14,108	− 2.8	30,968
1966	− 13.6	12,189	11.1	34,405
1967	− 1.9	11,957	3.7	35,678
1968	4.4	12,483	− 0.2	35,607
1969	− 9.9	11,247	− 14.0	30,622
1970	2.7	11,551	24.6	38,155
1971	− 10.9	10,292	13.7	43,382
1972	0.1	10,302	− 3.6	41,820
1973	3.8	10,693	− 12.5	36,593
1974	− 20.5	8,501	23.4	45,156
1975	1.8	8,654	19.2	53,826
1976	− 3.2	8,377	− 3.9	51,727
1977	− 11.7	7,397	2.3	52,917
1978	− 5.4	6,998	7.9	57,097
1979	− 4.6	6,676	0.2	57,211
1980	13.1	7,551	7.9	61,731
1981	− 14.6	6,449	− 0.5	61,422
1982	16.9	7,539	23.6	75,918
1983	− 0.1	7,531	− 4.4	72,578
1984	3.1	7,764	4.2	75,626
1985	9.2	8,478	29.8	98,163
1986	5.3	8,927	21.8	119,563
1987	− 12.8	7,784	1.9	121,835
1988	5.7	8,228	12.6	137,186
1989	9.4	9,001	0.4	137,735
1990	− 8.1	8,272	18.2	162,803
1991	6.3	8,793	9.4	178,106
1992	− 4.0	8,441	6.2	189,149
1993	7.4	9,066	0.03	189,206
1994	6.2	9,628	10.6	209,262
1995	10.0	10,591	17.1	245,046
1996	8.3	11,470	16.2	284,743
1997	6.2	12,181	21.8	346,817
1998	− 5.2	11,548	25.6	435,602
1999	− 0.5	11,490	0.04	435,776
2000	2.2	11,743	− 2.2	426,189
2001	− 15.5	9,923	9.6	467,103
2002	− 15.6	8,375	1.0	471,774
2003	15.6	9,682	4.3	492,060
2004	− 1.9	9,498	1.6	499,933
2005	2.4	9,728	8.9	544,323
2006	6.3	10,341	8.1	588,413
Average	**0.5%**		**7.9%**	
# Up	**34**		**45**	
# Down	**23**		**12**	
57-Year Gain		**$341**		**$578,413**

MONDAY

D 42.9
S 52.4
N 71.4

5

A bank is a place where they lend you an umbrella in fair weather and ask for it back again when it begins to rain.
— Robert Frost (American poet, 1874-1963)

TUESDAY

D 38.1
S 28.6
N 47.6

6

Q. What kind of grad students do you take? A. I never take a straight-A student.
A real scientist tends to be critical, and somewhere along the line, they had to rebel against their teachers.
— Lynn Margulis, (U. Mass science professor, *The Scientist*, 6/30/03)

WEDNESDAY

D 28.6
S 19.0
N 42.9

7

There's nothing wrong with cash. It gives you time to think. — Robert Prechter Jr. (*Elliott Wave Theorist*)

THURSDAY

D 61.9
S 52.4
N 66.7

8

The higher a people's intelligence and moral strength, the lower will be the prevailing rate of interest.
— Eugen von Bohm-Bawerk (Austrian economist, *Capital and Interest*, 1851-1914)

Friday Before Mother's Day, Dow Up 8 of Last 12

FRIDAY

D 66.7
S 61.9
N 47.6

9

Most people have no idea of the giant capacity we can immediately command when we focus all of our resources on mastering a single area of our lives. — Anthony Robbins (Motivator, advisor, consultant, author, entrepreneur, philanthropist, b. 1960)

SATURDAY

10

Mother's Day

SUNDAY

11

MACD-TIMING TRIPLES BEST SIX MONTHS RESULTS

Using the simple MACD (Moving Average Convergence Divergence) indicator developed by our friend Gerald Appel to better time entries and exits into and out of the Best Six Months period nearly triples the results. Sy Harding's *Riding the Bear* dubbed trading our Best Six Months Switching Strategy (page 48) with MACD triggers the "best mechanical system ever."

Our *Almanac Investor Newsletter* and *Platform* implements this system with quite a degree of success. Starting October 1 we look to catch the market's first hint of an uptrend after the summer doldrums, and beginning April 1 we prepare to exit these seasonal positions as soon as the market falters.

In up-trending markets MACD signals get you in earlier and keep you in longer. But if the market is trending down, entries are delayed until the market turns up and exit points can come a month earlier. Thus, our "Best Six Months" could be lengthened or shortened a month or so.

The results are astounding applying the simple MACD signals. Instead of $10,000 gaining $578,413 over the 57 recent years when invested only during the Best Six Months (page 48), the gain nearly tripled to $1,772,490. The $341 gain during the worst six months expanded to a loss of $6,488.

Impressive results for being invested during only 6.4 months of the year on average! For the rest of the year you could park in a money market fund, purchase index puts or bear funds, or if a long-term holder, you could write options on your positions (sell call options).

Updated signals are emailed to our monthly newsletter subscribers as soon as they are triggered. For further information on how the MACD indicator is calculated, dates when signals were given visit *www.stocktradersalmanac.com*.

SIX-MONTH SWITCHING STRATEGY+TIMING

	DJIA % Change May 1-Oct 31*	Investing $10,000	DJIA % Change Nov 1-Apr 30*	Investing $10,000
1950	7.3%	$10,730	13.3%	$11,330
1951	0.1	10,741	1.9	11,545
1952	1.4	10,891	2.1	11,787
1953	0.2	10,913	17.1	13,803
1954	13.5	12,386	16.3	16,053
1955	7.7	13,340	13.1	18,156
1956	− 6.8	12,433	2.8	18,664
1957	− 12.3	10,904	4.9	19,579
1958	17.3	12,790	16.7	22,849
1959	1.6	12,995	− 3.1	22,141
1960	− 4.9	12,358	16.9	25,883
1961	2.9	12,716	− 1.5	25,495
1962	− 15.3	10,770	22.4	31,206
1963	4.3	11,233	9.6	34,202
1964	6.7	11,986	6.2	36,323
1965	2.6	12,298	− 2.5	35,415
1966	− 16.4	10,281	14.3	40,479
1967	− 2.1	10,065	5.5	42,705
1968	3.4	10,407	0.2	42,790
1969	− 11.9	9,169	− 6.7	39,923
1970	− 1.4	9,041	20.8	48,227
1971	− 11.0	8,046	15.4	55,654
1972	− 0.6	7,998	− 1.4	54,875
1973	− 11.0	7,118	0.1	54,930
1974	− 22.4	5,524	28.2	70,420
1975	0.1	5,530	18.5	83,448
1976	− 3.4	5,342	− 3.0	80,945
1977	− 11.4	4,733	0.5	81,350
1978	− 4.5	4,520	9.3	88,916
1979	− 5.3	4,280	7.0	95,140
1980	9.3	4,678	4.7	99,612
1981	− 14.6	3,995	0.4	100,010
1982	15.5	4,614	23.5	123,512
1983	2.5	4,729	− 7.3	114,496
1984	3.3	4,885	3.9	118,961
1985	7.0	5,227	38.1	164,285
1986	− 2.8	5,081	28.2	210,613
1987	− 14.9	4,324	3.0	216,931
1988	6.1	4,588	11.8	242,529
1989	9.8	5,038	3.3	250,532
1990	− 6.7	4,700	15.8	290,116
1991	4.8	4,926	11.3	322,899
1992	− 6.2	4,621	6.6	344,210
1993	5.5	4,875	5.6	363,486
1994	3.7	5,055	13.1	411,103
1995	7.2	5,419	16.7	479,757
1996	9.2	5,918	21.9	584,824
1997	3.6	6,131	18.5	693,016
1998	− 12.4	5,371	39.9	969,529
1999	− 6.4	5,027	5.1	1,018,975
2000	− 6.0	4,725	5.4	1,074,000
2001	− 17.3	3,908	15.8	1,243,662
2002	− 25.2	2,923	6.0	1,318,314
2003	16.4	3,402	7.8	1,421,142
2004	− 0.9	3,371	1.8	1,446,723
2005	− 0.5	3,354	7.7	1,558,121
2006	4.7	3,512	14.4	1,782,490
Average	− 1.3%		10.0%	
# Up	29		50	
# Down	28		7	
57-Year Gain (Loss)		($6,488)		$1,722,490

*MACD generated entry and exit points (earlier or later) can lengthen or shorten six-month periods.

50

Monday Before May Expiration, Dow Up 17 of Last 19
Monday After Mother's Day, Dow Up 10 of Last 12

MONDAY
D 61.9
S 57.1
N 38.1
12

individualism, private property, the law of accumulation of wealth and the law of competition...
are the highest result of human experience, the soil in which, so far, has produced the best fruit.
— Andrew Carnegie (Scottish-born U.S. industrialist, philanthropist, *The Gospel of Wealth*, 1835-1919)

TUESDAY
D 61.9
S 61.9
N 57.1
13

The difference between life and the movies is that a script has to make sense, and life doesn't.
— Joseph L. Mankiewicz (Film director, writer, producer, 1909-1993)

WEDNESDAY
D 57.1
S 61.9
N 57.1
14

The task of leadership is not to put greatness into humanity, but to elicit it, for the greatness is already there.
— Sir John Buchan (Scottish author, governor general of Canada 1935-1940, 1875-1940)

THURSDAY
D 57.1
S 57.1
N 57.1
15

If you can ever buy with a P/E equivalent to growth, that's a good starting point.
— Alan Lowenstein (co-portfolio manager, John Hancock Technology Fund, *TheStreet.com* 3/12/2001)

May Day Expiration, Up 7 Down 7 Since 1993

FRIDAY
D 42.9
S 42.9
N 52.4
16

Make it idiot-proof and someone will make a better idiot. — Bumper sticker

SATURDAY
17

SUNDAY
18

ONLY ONE LOSS LAST 7 MONTHS OF ELECTION YEARS

Election years are traditionally up years. Incumbent administrations shamelessly attempt to massage the economy so voters will keep them in power. But, sometimes overpowering events occur and the market crumbles, usually resulting in a change of political control. The Republicans won in 1920 as the postwar economy contracted and President Wilson ailed. The Democrats came back during the 1932 Depression when the Dow hit its lowest level of the 20th century. A world at war and the fall of France jolted the market in 1940 but Roosevelt won an unprecedented third term. Cold War confrontations and Truman's historic upset of Dewey held markets down through the end of 1948.

Since 1948, investors have barely been bruised during election years, except for a brief span early in the year — until 2000. An undecided election plagued the country with uncertainty, hammering stock prices in November and keeping them down until December 12 when the U.S. Supreme Court prevented the Democrat's controversial bid for a manual recount of the challenged Florida vote clearing the way for George W. Bush to be elected president.

The table below presents a very positive picture for the last seven or eight months of election years.

- Since 1952 January through April losses occurred in seven of fourteen election years. Incumbent parties were ousted on five of these seven losses. Ironically, bear markets commenced following four of seven gainers in 1956, 1968, 1973 and 1976.

- Comparing month-end June with month-end April reveals gains in 1952, 1960, 1968, 1988 and 2000 for the 60-day period, when no sitting president ran for reelection.

- Of the 14 Julys since 1952, seven were losers (1960, 1968, 1976, 1984, 1988, 1996 and 2000). Five were years when, at convention time, no strong incumbent was running for reelection. Note that April through July periods had only four losers: 1972 by a small margin, 1984 as the market was turning around, 1996, and 2000 as the bubble began to work off its excesses.

- For a longer perspective, we extended the table to December. Just two losing eight-month periods in an election year are revealed and only one loss in the last seven months of all these years.

S&P 500 DURING ELECTION YEARS

Election Year	% Change First 4 Months	April	May	June	July	Dec	% Change Last 8 Months	Last 7 Months
1952*	− 1.9%	**23.32**	23.86	24.96	25.40	26.57	13.9%	11.4%
1956	6.4	**48.38**	**45.20**	46.97	49.39	46.67	− 3.5	3.3
1960*	− 9.2	**54.37**	55.83	56.92	**55.51**	58.11	6.9	4.1
1964	5.9	79.46	80.37	81.69	83.18	84.75	6.7	5.4
1968*	1.2	97.59	98.68	99.58	**97.74**	**103.86**	6.4	5.2
1972	5.5	107.67	109.53	**107.14**	107.39	118.05	9.6	7.8
1976*	12.7	**101.64**	**100.18**	104.28	**103.44**	107.46	5.7	7.3
1980*	− 1.5	106.29	111.24	114.24	121.67	**135.76**	27.7	22.0
1984	− 3.0	160.05	**150.55**	153.18	**150.66**	167.24	4.5	11.1
1988	5.8	261.33	262.16	273.50	**272.02**	277.72	6.3	5.9
1992*	− 0.5	414.95	415.35	**408.14**	424.21	435.71	5.0	4.9
1996	6.2	654.17	669.12	670.63	**639.95**	**740.74**	13.2	10.7
2000**	− 1.1	**1452.43**	**1420.60**	1454.60	**1430.83**	1320.28	− 9.1	− 7.1
2004	− 0.4	**1107.30**	1120.68	1140.84	1101.72	1211.92	9.4	8.1
Totals	**26.1%**						**102.7%**	**100.1%**
Average	**1.9%**						**7.3%**	**7.2%**

*Incumbents ousted ** Incumbent ousted & undecided election*
Down months are bold

MAY

🐻 **MONDAY**

D 57.1
S 66.7
N 66.7

19

Governments last as long as the under-taxed can defend themselves against the over-taxed.
— Bernard Berenson (American art critic, 1865-1959)

TUESDAY

D 57.1
S 57.1
N 47.6

20

If we did all the things we are capable of doing, we would literally astound ourselves.
— Thomas Alva Edison (American inventor, 1093 patents, 1847-1931)

WEDNESDAY

D 47.6
S 52.4
N 52.4

21

If each of us hires people who are smaller than we are, we shall become a company of dwarfs. But if each of us hires people who are bigger than we are, we shall become a company of giants. — David Oglivy (Advertiser, Ogilvy on Advertising, 1911-1999)

1985-1997 May Was Best S&P Month Gaining 3.3% on Average,
Up 13 Straight, Last Year Broke a 3-Year Bull Run

🐻 **THURSDAY**

D 38.1
S 38.1
N 47.6

22

The best minds are not in government. If any were, business would hire them away.
— Ronald Reagan (40th U.S. president, 1911-2004)

Friday Before Memorial Day Tends to Be Lackluster with Light Trading

🐻 **FRIDAY**

D 71.4
S 81.0
N 71.4

23

If you don't keep [your employees] happy, they're not going to keep the [customers] happy.
— David Longest (Red Lobster VP, NY Times 4/23/89)

SATURDAY

24

SUNDAY

25

JUNE ALMANAC

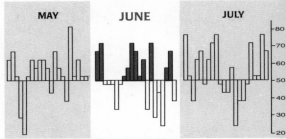

JUNE								JULY					
S	M	T	W	T	F	S		S	M	T	W	T	F	S
1	2	3	4	5	6	7				1	2	3	4	5
8	9	10	11	12	13	14		6	7	8	9	10	11	12
15	16	17	18	19	20	21		13	14	15	16	17	18	19
22	23	24	25	26	27	28		20	21	22	23	24	25	26
29	30							27	28	29	30	31		

Market Probability Chart above is a graphic representation of the S&P 500 Recent Market Probability Calendar on page 124.

◆ The "summer rally" in most years is the weakest rally of all four seasons (page 70) ◆ Week after June Triple-Witching Day Dow down 15 of last 17 (page 76) ◆ RECENT RECORD: S&P 9 up, 3 down, average gain 1.0%, ranks seventh ◆ Much stronger for NASDAQ, average gain 2.9% last 12 years ◆ Watch out for end-of-quarter "portfolio pumping" on last day of June, Dow down 13 of last 19, but NASDAQ up 14 of last 19 ◆ Since 1952 election-year Junes #2 on S&P, average 1.9% and #3 on Dow, average 1.4%, #3 on NASDAQ since 1972, average 2.9% ◆ June ends NASDAQ's best eight months ◆ NASDAQ's mid-year rally begins the third to last trading day of June (page 60)

June Vital Statistics

	DJIA		S&P 500		NASDAQ		Russell 1K		Russell 2K	
Rank	11		9		4		7		7	
Up	28		31		22		18		19	
Down	29		26		14		10		9	
Avg % Change	−0.1%		0.2%		1.2%		0.8%		1.1%	
Election Year	1.4%		1.9%		2.9%		1.8%		2.5%	
Best & Worst June										
	% Change		% Change		% Change		% Change		% Change	
Best	1955	6.2	1955	8.2	2000	16.6	1999	5.1	2000	8.6
Worst	1962	−8.5	1962	−8.2	2002	−9.4	2002	−7.5	1991	−6.0
Best & Worst June Weeks										
Best	6/7/74	6.4	6/2/00	7.2	6/2/00	19.0	6/2/00	8.0	6/2/00	12.2
Worst	6/30/50	−6.8	6/30/50	−7.6	6/15/01	−8.4	6/15/01	−4.2	6/9/06	−4.9
Best & Worst June Days										
Best	6/28/62	3.8	6/28/62	3.4	6/2/00	6.4	6/17/02	2.8	6/2/00	4.2
Worst	6/26/50	−4.7	6/26/50	−5.4	6/14/01	−3.7	6/3/02	−2.4	6/5/06	−3.2
First Trading Day of Expiration Week: 1980-2006										
Record (#Up - #Down)	15-12		16-11		12-15		15-12		10-17	
Current streak	D1		D1		D1		D1		D1	
Avg % Change	0.11		0.003		−0.23		−0.02		−0.30	
Options Expiration Day: 1980-2006										
Record (#Up - #Down)	16-11		16-11		15-12		16-11		14-13	
Current streak	D1		D1		D1		D1		D1	
Avg % Change	−0.06		0.03		−0.03		−0.02		−0.06	
Options Expiration Week: 1980-2006										
Record (#Up - #Down)	15-12		13-14		11-16		12-15		11-16	
Current streak	U4		D1		D1		D1		D1	
Avg % Change	−0.04		−0.09		−0.03		−0.16		−0.41	
Week After Options Expiration: 1980-2006										
Record (#Up - #Down)	10-17		16-11		16-11		16-11		13-14	
Current streak	D8		D4		D2		D2		D2	
Avg % Change	−0.14		0.14		0.39		0.17		0.08	
First Trading Day Performance										
% of Time Up	54.4		52.6		61.1		60.7		67.9	
Avg % Change	0.20		0.19		0.25		0.21		0.33	
Last Trading Day Performance										
% of Time Up	54.4		50.9		72.2		50.0		75.0	
Avg % Change	0.03		0.08		0.33		−0.04		0.48	

Dow & S&P 1950-April 2007, NASDAQ 1971-April 2007, Russell 1K & 2K 1979-April 2007.

Last Day of June not hot for the Dow But for stocks on NASDAQ, WOW!

MAY/JUNE

Memorial Day (Market Closed)

MONDAY

26

The time to buy is when blood is running in the streets. — Baron Nathan Rothschild (London financier, 1777-1836)

TUESDAY

D 42.9
S 52.4
N 52.4

27

The wisdom of the ages is the fruits of freedom and democracy.
— Lawrence Kudlow (Economist, 24th Annual Paulson SmallCap Conference, Waldorf Astoria NYC, 11/8/01)

WEDNESDAY

D 57.1
S 61.9
N 71.4

28

To know values is to know the meaning of the market. — Charles Dow (Co-founder Dow Jones & Co, 1851-1902)

Memorial Day Week, Dow Up Big 12 Straight 1984-1995, Down 7 of Last 11

THURSDAY

D 61.9
S 52.4
N 66.7

29

If you don't know who you are, the stock market is an expensive place to find out.
— George Goodman (*Institutional Investor, New York,* "Adam Smith," *The Money Game,* b. 1930)

FRIDAY

D 52.4
S 52.4
N 71.4

30

History is a collection of agreed upon lies. — Voltaire (French philosopher, 1694-1778)

SATURDAY

31

June Almanac Investor Seasonalities: See Pages 114 & 116

SUNDAY

1

TOP PERFORMING NASDAQ MONTHS PAST 36⅓ YEARS

NASDAQ stocks continue to run away during three consecutive months, November, December and January, with an average gain of 7.8% despite the slaughter of November 2000, down 22.9%, December 2001, up only 1.0%, January 2002, –0.8%, and December 2002, –9.7% during the three-year bear that shrank the tech-dominated index by 77.9%. Solid gains in November and December 2004 offset January 2005's 5.2% Iraq-turmoil-fueled drop.

You can see the months graphically on page 148. January by itself is impressive, up 3.7% on average. April, May and June also shine, creating our NASDAQ Best Eight Months strategy. What appears as a Death Valley abyss occurs during NASDAQ's bleakest four months: July, August, September and October. NASDAQ's Best Eight Months seasonal strategy using MACD timing is displayed on page 58.

MONTHLY % CHANGES (JANUARY 1971 — APRIL 2007)

	NASDAQ Composite*						Dow Jones Industrials			
Month	Total % Change	Avg. % Change	# Up	# Down		Month	Total % Change	Avg. % Change	# Up	# Down
Jan	135.1%	3.7%	26	11		Jan	77.2%	1.3%	39	19
Feb	18.2	0.5	19	18		Feb	9.6	0.2	33	25
Mar	12.3	0.3	23	14		Mar	52.5	0.9	37	21
Apr	40.5	1.1	23	14		Apr	107.0	1.8	36	22
May	36.1	1.0	21	15		May	3.8	0.1	29	28
Jun	43.1	1.2	22	14		Jun	– 5.7	– 0.1	28	29
Jul	– 12.5	– 0.3	17	19		Jul	59.9	1.1	35	22
Aug	10.5	0.3	19	17		Aug	– 2.2	– 0.04	32	25
Sep	– 31.3	– 0.9	19	17		Sep	– 55.1	– 1.0	21	36
Oct	23.3	0.6	19	17		Oct	33.8	0.6	33	24
Nov	78.2	2.2	25	11		Nov	96.3	1.7	39	18
Dec	69.9	1.9	21	15		Dec	99.9	1.8	41	16
% Rank						**% Rank**				
Jan	135.1%	3.7%	26	11		Apr	107.0%	1.8%	36	22
Nov	78.2	2.2	25	11		Dec	99.9	1.8	41	16
Dec	69.9	1.9	21	15		Nov	96.3	1.7	39	18
Jun	43.1	1.2	22	14		Jan	77.2	1.3	39	19
Apr	40.5	1.1	23	14		Jul	59.9	1.1	35	22
May	36.1	1.0	21	15		Mar	52.5	0.9	37	21
Oct	23.3	0.6	19	17		Oct	33.8	0.6	33	24
Feb	18.2	0.5	19	18		Feb	9.6	0.2	33	25
Mar	12.3	0.3	23	14		May	3.8	0.1	29	28
Aug	10.5	0.3	19	17		Aug	– 2.2	– 0.04	32	25
Jul	– 12.5	– 0.3	17	19		Jun	– 5.7	– 0.1	28	29
Sep	– 31.3	– 0.9	19	17		Sep	– 55.1	– 1.0	21	36
Totals	**423.4%**	**11.6%**				**Totals**	**477.0%**	**8.4%**		
Average		**0.97%**				**Average**		**0.70%**		

Based on NASDAQ composite, prior to February 5, 1971, based on National Quotation Bureau indices.

For comparison, Dow figures are shown. During this period NASDAQ averaged a 0.97% gain per month, 39 percent more than the Dow's 0.70% per month. Between January 1971 and January 1982 NASDAQ's composite index doubled in the 12 years, while the Dow stayed flat. But while NASDAQ plummeted 77.9% from its 2000 highs to the 2002 bottom, the Dow only lost 37.8%.

JUNE

First Trading Day in June, Dow Up 8 of Last 9, –2.2% in 2002

MONDAY

D 76.2
S 66.7
N 66.7

2

Tell me and I'll forget; show me and I may remember; involve me and I'll understand.
— Confucius (Chinese philosopher, 551-478 BC)

Start Looking for NASDAQ MACD Sell Signal (Page 58)
Almanac Investor Subscribers Are Emailed Alert When It Triggers

TUESDAY

D 52.4
S 71.4
N 76.2

3

A generation from now, Americans may marvel at the complacency that assumed the dollar's dominance would never end.
— Floyd Norris (Chief financial correspondent, *NY Times*, 2/2/07)

WEDNESDAY

D 52.4
S 47.6
N 52.4

4

The first human being to live to 150 years of age is alive today, but will he get Social Security for 85 years of his longer life span, more than twice the number of years he worked? — John Mauldin (Millennium Wave Advisors, 2000wave.com, 2/2/07)

THURSDAY

D 57.1
S 47.6
N 57.1

5

He who hesitates is poor. — Mel Brooks (Writer, director, comedian, b. 1926)

FRIDAY

D 52.4
S 47.6
N 47.6

6

A successful man is one who can lay a firm foundation with the bricks that others throw at him.
— Sidney Greenberg (Rabbi, author, 1918-2003)

SATURDAY

7

SUNDAY

8

GET MORE OUT OF NASDAQ'S "BEST EIGHT MONTHS" WITH MACD TIMING

NASDAQ's amazing eight-month run from November through June is hard to miss on pages 56 and 148. A $10,000 investment in these eight months since 1971 gained $354,341 versus a loss of $3,568 during the void that is the four-month period July-October.

Using the same MACD timing indicators on the NASDAQ as is done for the Dow (page 50) has enabled us to capture much of October's improved performance, pumping up NASDAQ's results considerably. Over the 36 years since NASDAQ began, the gain on the same $10,000 more than doubles to $782,291 and the loss during the four-month void increases to $7,093. Only four sizeable losses occurred during the favorable period and the bulk of NASDAQ's bear markets were avoided including the worst of the 2000-2002 bear.

Updated signals are emailed to our monthly newsletter subscribers as soon as they are triggered. For further information on how the MACD indicator is calculated visit *www.stocktradersalmanac.com.*

BEST EIGHT MONTHS STRATEGY + TIMING

MACD Signal Date	Worst 4 Months July 1-Oct 31* NASDAQ	% Change	Investing $10,000	MACD Signal Date	Best 8 Months Nov 1-June 30* NASDAQ	% Change	Investing $10,000
22-Jul-71	109.54	− 3.6	$9,640	4-Nov-71	105.56	24.1	$12,410
7-Jun-72	131.00	− 1.8	9,466	23-Oct-72	128.66	−22.7	9,593
25-Jun-73	99.43	− 7.2	8,784	7-Dec-73	92.32	−20.2	7,655
3-Jul-74	73.66	−23.2	6,746	7-Oct-74	56.57	47.8	11,314
11-Jun-75	83.60	− 9.2	6,125	7-Oct-75	75.88	20.8	13,667
22-Jul-76	91.66	− 2.4	5,978	19-Oct-76	89.45	13.2	15,471
27-Jul-77	101.25	− 4.0	5,739	4-Nov-77	97.21	26.6	19,586
7-Jun-78	123.10	− 6.5	5,366	6-Nov-78	115.08	19.1	23,327
3-Jul-79	137.03	− 1.1	5,307	30-Oct-79	135.48	15.5	26,943
20-Jun-80	156.51	26.2	6,697	9-Oct-80	197.53	11.2	29,961
4-Jun-81	219.68	−17.6	5,518	1-Oct-81	181.09	− 4.0	28,763
7-Jun-82	173.84	12.5	6,208	7-Oct-82	195.59	57.4	45,273
1-Jun-83	307.95	−10.7	5,544	3-Nov-83	274.86	−14.2	38,844
1-Jun-84	235.90	5.0	5,821	15-Oct-84	247.67	17.3	45,564
3-Jun-85	290.59	− 3.0	5,646	1-Oct-85	281.77	39.4	63,516
10-Jun-86	392.83	−10.3	5,064	1-Oct-86	352.34	20.5	76,537
30-Jun-87	424.67	−22.7	3,914	2-Nov-87	328.33	20.1	91,921
8-Jul-88	394.33	-6.6	3,656	29-Nov-88	368.15	22.4	112,511
13-Jun-89	450.73	0.7	3,682	9-Nov-89	454.07	1.9	114,649
11-Jun-90	462.79	−23.0	2,835	2-Oct-90	356.39	39.3	159,706
11-Jun-91	496.62	6.4	3,016	1-Oct-91	528.51	7.4	171,524
11-Jun-92	567.68	1.5	3,061	14-Oct-92	576.22	20.5	206,686
7-Jun-93	694.61	9.9	3,364	1-Oct-93	763.23	− 4.4	197,592
17-Jun-94	729.35	5.0	3,532	11-Oct-94	765.57	13.5	224,267
1-Jun-95	868.82	17.2	4,140	13-Oct-95	1018.38	21.6	272,709
3-Jun-96	1238.73	1.0	4,181	7-Oct-96	1250.87	10.3	300,798
4-Jun-97	1379.67	24.4	5,201	3-Oct-97	1715.87	1.8	306,212
1-Jun-98	1746.82	− 7.8	4,795	15-Oct-98	1611.01	49.7	458,399
1-Jun-99	2412.03	18.5	5,682	6-Oct-99	2857.21	35.7	622,047
29-Jun-00	3877.23	−18.2	4,648	18-Oct-00	3171.56	−32.2	421,748
1-Jun-01	2149.44	−31.1	3,202	1-Oct-01	1480.46	5.5	444,944
3-Jun-02	1562.56	−24.0	2,434	2-Oct-02	1187.30	38.5	616,247
20-Jun-03	1644.72	15.1	2,802	6-Oct-03	1893.46	4.3	642,746
21-Jun-04	1974.38	− 1.6	2,757	1-Oct-04	1942.20	6.1	681,954
8-Jun-05	2060.18	1.5	2,798	19-Oct-05	2091.76	6.1	723,553
1-Jun-06	2219.86	3.9	2,907	5-Oct-06	2306.34	9.5	792,291
30-Apr-07	2525.09						

As of April 2007, MACD Sell signal not triggered at press time

36-Year Loss ($7,093)   **36-Year Gain** $782,291

* MACD generated entry and exit points (earlier or later) can lengthen or shorten eight-month periods.

JUNE

MONDAY 9

D 42.9
S 33.3
N 38.1

I am not a member of any organized party — I am a Democrat. — Will Rogers (American humorist and showman, 1879-1935)

TUESDAY 10

D 38.1
S 47.6
N 52.4

You get stepped on, passed over, knocked down, but you have to come back.
— 90-year old Walter Watson (MD, *Fortune*, 11/13/2000)

WEDNESDAY 11

D 61.9
S 52.4
N 52.4

The difference between genius and stupidity is that genius has its limits. — Anonymous

THURSDAY 12

D 47.6
S 57.1
N 52.4

If you want to raise a crop for one year, plant corn. If you want to raise a crop for decades, plant trees.
If you want to raise a crop for centuries, raise men. If you want to plant a crop for eternities, raise democracies.
— Carl A. Schenck (German forester, 1868-1955)

FRIDAY 13

D 71.4
S 71.4
N 61.9

There are three principal means of acquiring knowledge...observation of nature, reflection, and experimentation.
Observation collects facts; reflection combines them; experimentation verifies the result of that combination.
— Denis Diderot (French philosopher, edited first modern encyclopedia in 1745, 1713-1784)

SATURDAY 14

Father's Day

SUNDAY 15

MID-YEAR RALLY: CHRISTMAS IN JULY

What's old is often new in the stock market. Nothing excites Wall Street more than the prospects for a "summer rally." Every year when the weather heats up, anticipation of an upward spike in stock prices swells. On page 70 we illustrate that the "summer rally" is the weakest of all seasonal rallies.

However, a short, tradable mid-year rally for NASDAQ has emerged in recent years. In the 1969 Almanac we quoted a *Wall Street Journal* article from June 27, 1900 (108 years ago!): "The market is more likely to advance in midsummer than at any other time. The market has in the past been essentially a railway market, controlled in summer by the outlook for crops." As the U.S. has drifted away from being an agrarian society with less than 2% farming, this "midsummer" rally has faded.

But in the mid-1980s the market began to evolve into a tech-driven market and control in summer shifted to the outlook for second quarter earnings of technology companies. NASDAQ's mid-year rally from the end of June through mid-July is strongest. The accompanying table shows NASDAQ averaging a 2.9% gain since 1987 during the 12-day period from June's third-to-last trading day through July's ninth trading day versus –0.1% for the month of July.

NASDAQ COMPOSITE 12-DAY MID-YEAR RALLY

	June Close	4th Last June Trading Day	9th July Trading Day	July Close	12-Day % Change	July Change
1985	296.20	292.30	302.39	301.29	3.5%	1.7%
1986	405.51	402.22	384.80	371.37	– 4.3	– 8.4
1987	424.67	427.20	431.14	434.93	0.9	2.4
1988	394.66	389.00	394.67	387.33	1.5	– 1.9
1989	435.29	448.55	448.90	453.84	0.1	4.3
1990	462.29	455.38	468.44	438.24	2.9	– 5.2
1991	475.92	473.30	492.71	502.04	4.1	5.5
1992	563.60	548.20	575.21	580.83	4.9	3.1
1993	703.95	694.81	712.49	704.70	2.5	0.1
1994	705.96	702.68	721.56	722.16	2.7	2.3
1995	933.45	919.56	999.33	1001.21	8.7	7.3
1996	1185.02	1172.58	1103.49	1080.59	– 5.9	– 8.8
1997	1442.07	1446.24	1523.88	1593.81	5.4	10.5
1998	1894.74	1863.25	1968.41	1872.39	5.6	– 1.2
1999	2686.12	2552.65	2818.13	2638.49	10.4	– 1.8
2000	3966.11	3858.96	4246.18	3766.99	10.0	– 5.0
2001	2160.54	2064.62	2084.79	2027.13	1.0	– 6.2
2002	1463.21	1423.99	1373.50	1328.26	– 3.5	– 9.2
2003	1622.80	1602.66	1754.82	1735.02	9.5	6.9
2004	2047.79	2025.47	1914.88	1887.36	– 5.5	– 7.8
2005	2056.96	2045.20	2152.82	2184.83	5.3	6.2
2006	2172.09	2100.25	2037.35	2091.47	– 3.0	– 3.7
				1985 Average	2.6%	– 0.4%
				1987 Average	2.9%	– 0.1%

JUNE

Monday Before June Triple Witching, Dow Down 6 of Last 10
But Back-to-Back 200+ Point Gains 2002-2003

MONDAY
D 57.1
S 66.7
N 61.9
16

What counts more than luck, is determination and perseverance. If the talent is there, it will come through. Don't be too impatient.
— Fred Astaire (The report from his first screen test stated, "Can't act. Can't sing. Balding. Can dance a little.")

TUESDAY
D 52.4
S 52.4
N 42.9
17

I want the whole of Europe to have one currency; it will make trading much easier.
— Napoleon Bonaparte (Emperor of France 1804-1815, 1769-1821)

WEDNESDAY
D 52.4
S 61.9
N 42.9
18

There is one thing stronger than all the armies in the world, and this is an idea whose time has come.
— Victor Hugo (French novelist, playwright, *Hunchback of Notre Dame* and *Les Misérables*, 1802-1885)

THURSDAY
D 33.3
S 33.3
N 42.9
19

Keep me away from the wisdom which does not cry, the philosophy which does not laugh and the greatness
which does not bow before children. — Kahlil Gibran (Lebanese-born American mystic, poet and artist, 1883-1931)

June Triple Witching, Dow Up 3 of Last 4

FRIDAY
D 57.1
S 71.4
N 57.1
20

Buy when others are despondently selling and sell when others are greedily buying.
— Mark Mobius (Fund manager Templeton Investments, on investing in foreign countries)

SATURDAY
21

SUNDAY
22

FIRST-TRADING-DAY-OF-THE-MONTH PHENOMENON
DOW GAINS MORE ONE DAY THAN ALL OTHER DAYS

Over the last 10 years the Dow Jones Industrial Average has gained more points on the first trading days of all months than all other days combined. While the Dow gained 5513.72 points between September 2, 1997 (7622.42) and May 1, 2007 (13136.14), it is incredible that 4565.51 points were gained on the first trading days of these 117 months. The remaining 2313 trading days combined gained 948.21 points during the period. This averages out to gains of 39.02 points on first days, in contrast to 0.41 points on all others.

Note: September 1997 through October 2000 racked up a total gain of 2632.39 Dow points on the first trading days of these 38 months (winners except for seven occasions). But between November 2000 and September 2002, when the last two cyclical bear markets did the bulk of their damage, frightened investors switched from pouring money into the market on that day to pulling it out, 14 months out of 23, netting a 404.80 Dow point loss.

First days of August have performed worst, falling seven times out of nine. January's first day has also been weak; down four of the last eight, as profit taking shifts to the opening of the New Year. In rising market trends first days perform much better as institutions are likely anticipating strong performance at each month's outset. S&P 500 first days track the Dow's pattern closely but NASDAQ first days are not as strong with weakness in January, April, July, August and October.

DOW POINTS GAINED ON FIRST DAY OF MONTH
FROM SEPTEMBER 1997 TO MAY 1, 2007

	1997	1998	1999	2000	2001	2002	2003	2004	2005	2006	2007	Totals
Jan		56.79	2.84	-139.61	-140.70	51.90	265.89	-44.07	-53.58	129.91	11.37	140.74
Feb		201.28	-13.13	100.52	96.27	-12.74	56.01	11.11	62.00	89.09	51.99	642.40
Mar		4.73	18.20	9.62	-45.14	262.73	-53.22	94.22	63.77	60.12	-34.29	380.74
Apr		68.51	46.35	300.01	-100.85	-41.24	77.73	15.63	-99.46	35.62	27.95	330.25
May		83.70	225.65	77.87	163.37	113.41	-25.84	88.43	59.19	-23.85	73.23	835.16
Jun		22.42	36.52	129.87	78.47	-215.46	47.55	14.20	82.39	91.97		287.93
Jul		96.65	95.62	112.78	91.32	-133.47	55.51	-101.32	28.47	77.80		323.36
Aug		-96.55	-9.19	84.97	-12.80	-229.97	-79.83	39.45	-17.76	-59.95		-381.63
Sep	257.36	288.36	108.60	23.68	47.74	-355.45	107.45	-5.46	-21.97	83.00		533.31
Oct	70.24	-210.09	-63.95	49.21	-10.73	346.86	194.14	112.38	-33.22	-8.72		446.12
Nov	232.31	114.05	-81.35	-71.67	188.76	120.61	57.34	26.92	-33.30	-49.71		503.96
Dec	189.98	16.99	120.58	-40.95	-87.60	-33.52	116.59	162.20	106.70	-27.80		523.17
Totals	749.89	646.84	486.74	636.30	268.11	-126.34	819.32	413.69	143.23	397.48	130.25	4565.51

SUMMARY FIRST DAYS VS. OTHER DAYS OF MONTH

	# of Days	Total Points Gained	Average Daily Point Gain
First days	117	4565.51	39.02
Other days	2313	948.21	0.41

JUNE

e Ends NASDAQ's "Best Eight Months" (Pages 56, 58 & 148)

🐻 **MONDAY**

D 33.3
S 28.6
N 33.3

23

nly thing that saves us from the bureaucracy is its inefficiency.
gene McCarthy (U.S. congressman & senator, Minnesota 1949-1971, 3-time presidential candidate, 1916-2005)

ek After June Triple Witching, Dow Down 8 in a Row and 15 of Last 17

TUESDAY

D 47.6
S 42.9
N 47.6

24

ology has no respect for tradition.
ter C. Lee (Merchants' Exchange CEO, quoted in Stocks, Futures & Options Magazine, May 2003)

🐻 **WEDNESDAY**

D 38.1
S 23.8
N 28.6

25

e S&P 500 companies in 1957, only 74 were still on the list in 1998 and only 12 outperformed the index itself over that period.
)20, more than 375 companies in the S&P 500 will consist of companies we don't know today.
chard Foster and Sarah Kaplan (Creative Destruction)

Day Mid-Year NASDAQ Rally Starts (Page 60)
rage 2.9% Since 1987 v. –0.1% for July

THURSDAY

D 52.4
S 57.1
N 61.9

26

ect and Emotion are partners who do not speak the same language. The intellect finds logic to justify what the emotions have decided.
THE HEARTS OF PEOPLE, THEIR MINDS WILL FOLLOW. — Roy H. Williams (*The Wizard of Ads*)

🐂 **FRIDAY**

D 57.1
S 66.7
N 66.7

27

lent firms don't believe in excellence—only in constant improvement and constant change.
m Peters (In Search of Excellence)

SATURDAY

28

Almanac Investor Seasonalities: See Pages 114 & 116

SUNDAY

29

JULY ALMANAC

JULY					
S	M	T	W	T	F	S

JULY
S M T W T F S
         1 2 3 4 5
 6 7 8 9 10 11 12
13 14 15 16 17 18 19
20 21 22 23 24 25 26
27 28 29 30 31

AUGUST
S M T W T F S
               1 2
 3 4 5 6 7 8 9
10 11 12 13 14 15 16
17 18 19 20 21 22 23
24 25 26 27 28 29 30
31

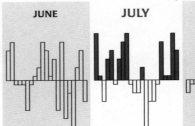

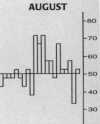

Market Probability Chart above is a graphic representation of the S&P 500 Recent Market Probability Calendar on page 124.

◆ July is the best month of the third quarter except for NASDAQ (page 74) ◆ Start of 2nd half brings an inflow of retirement funds ◆ First trading day Dow up 15 of last 18 ◆ Graph above shows strength in the beginning and end of July ◆ NASDAQ's 12-day mid-year rally gains 2.9% on average since 1987 v. -0.1% for the month of July (page 60) ◆ July closes well except if bear market in progress ◆ Huge gain in July usually provides better buying opportunity over next four months ◆ Start of NASDAQ's worst four months of the year (page 56) ◆ Election Julys average negative returns for NASDAQ (-1.8%), barely positive for Dow (0.3%) and S&P (0.2%)

July Vital Statistics

	DJIA		S&P 500		NASDAQ		Russell 1K		Russell 2K	
Rank	5		7		11		10		12	
Up	35		31		17		12		13	
Down	22		26		19		16		15	
Avg % Change	1.1%		0.9%		−0.3%		0.3%		−0.9%	
Election Year	0.3%		0.2%		−1.8%		−0.4%		−1.5%	
Best & Worst July										
	% Change		% Change		% Change		% Change		% Change	
Best	1989	9.0	1989	8.8	1997	10.5	1989	8.2	1980	11.0
Worst	1969	−6.6	2002	−7.9	2002	−9.2	2002	−7.5	2002	−15.2
Best & Worst July Weeks										
Best	7/2/99	5.6	7/2/99	5.8	7/2/99	7.4	7/2/99	5.7	7/18/80	4.2
Worst	7/19/02	−7.7	7/19/02	−8.0	7/28/00	−10.5	7/19/02	−7.4	7/19/02	−6.6
Best & Worst July Days										
Best	7/24/02	6.4	7/24/02	5.7	7/29/02	5.8	7/24/02	5.6	7/29/02	4.9
Worst	7/19/02	−4.6	7/19/02	−3.8	7/28/00	−4.7	7/19/02	−3.6	7/23/02	−4.1
First Trading Day of Expiration Week: 1980-2006										
Record (#Up - #Down)	16-11		18-9		19-8		18-9		16-11	
Current streak	U4		D1		U2		D1		D1	
Avg % Change	0.06		0.02		0.06		−0.001		−0.01	
Options Expiration Day: 1980-2006										
Record (#Up - #Down)	12-15		14-13		12-15		14-13		11-16	
Current streak	D1		D1		D1		D1		D1	
Avg % Change	−0.22		−0.25		−0.40		−0.27		−0.38	
Options Expiration Week: 1980-2006										
Record (#Up - #Down)	17-10		14-13		14-13		14-13		15-12	
Current streak	U2		U2		D1		U2		D1	
Avg % Change	0.17		−0.10		−0.26		−0.16		−0.28	
Week After Options Expiration: 1980-2006										
Record (#Up - #Down)	13-14		12-15		9-18		12-15		8-19	
Current streak	U2		U2		U2		U2		U2	
Avg % Change	−0.16		−0.41		−0.88		−0.44		−0.75	
First Trading Day Performance										
% of Time Up	63.2		68.4		55.6		67.9		57.1	
Avg % Change	0.23		0.21		−0.02		0.23		−0.16	
Last Trading Day Performance										
% of Time Up	56.1		66.7		55.6		64.3		75.0	
Avg % Change	0.13		0.18		0.07		0.15		0.12	

Dow & S&P 1950-April 2007, NASDAQ 1971-April 2007, Russell 1K & 2K 1979-April 2007.

*When Dow and S&P in July are inferior
NASDAQ days tend to be even drearier*

RESERVE YOUR *2009 ALMANAC* TODAY!

Don't miss this special discount offer! Purchase the *2009 Almanac* at 20% off the regular price. To order, just call us toll free at 800-356-5016 (in Canada call 800-567-4797) or fax us at 800-597-3299 or order online at www.stocktradersalmanac.com. Be sure to use **promo code ALMA9** when you are placing your order to receive your special discount.

RESERVE YOUR *2009 STOCK TRADER'S ALMANAC* NOW BY MAIL OR CALL 800.356.5016!

☐ **Please reserve _____ copies of the *2009 Stock Trader's Almanac*.**
Just $31.96 each (regularly $39.95) plus shipping & handling!
Deeper discounts are available for orders of 5 copies or more—call us at 800-356-5016 for details.
Shipping: US: first item $5.00, each additional $3.00; International: first item $10.50, each additional $7.00.
Bulk discounts for 5 or more copies available. Call 800-356-5016.

$_____ payment enclosed

☐ Check made payable to **John Wiley & Sons, Inc.** *(US Funds only, drawn on a US bank)*

☐ Charge Credit Card (check one):   ☐ Visa   ☐ Mastercard   ☐ AmEx

Name _____   E-mail address _____

Address _____   Account # _____

City _____   Expiration Date _____

State _____ Zip _____   Signature _____

☐ **BECOME A SUBSCRIBER! I want to stay up-to-date! Please send me future editions of the *Stock Trader's Almanac*.** You will automatically be shipped (along with the bill) future editions of the *Almanac* at the yearly pre-publication discount. It's so easy and convenient!

PROMO CODE: ALMA9   ISBN 978-0-470-22902-6

SEND ME MORE OF THE *2008 STOCK TRADER'S ALMANAC!*

☐ **Please send me _____ copies of the *2008 Stock Trader's Almanac*.**
(ISBN 978-0-470-109854)

$39.95 for single copies plus shipping
Shipping: US: first item $5.00, each additional $3.00; International: first item $10.50, each additional $7.00.
Bulk discounts for 5 or more copies available. Call 800-356-5016.

$_____ payment enclosed

☐ Check made payable to **John Wiley & Sons, Inc.** *(US Funds only, drawn on a US bank)*

☐ Charge Credit Card (check one):   ☐ Visa   ☐ Mastercard   ☐ AmEx

Name _____   E-mail address _____

Address _____   Account # _____

City _____   Expiration Date _____

State _____ Zip _____   Signature _____

RESERVE YOUR
2009 STOCK TRADER'S ALMANAC
NOW AND SAVE 20%.

Mail the postage paid card below to reserve your copy.

NO POSTAGE
NECESSARY
IF MAILED
IN THE
UNITED STATES

BUSINESS REPLY MAIL
FIRST-CLASS MAIL PERMIT NO. 2277 HOBOKEN NJ

POSTAGE WILL BE PAID BY ADDRESSEE

A SPIVAK
JOHN WILEY & SONS INC
111 RIVER ST MS 5-01
HOBOKEN NJ 07030-9442

JUNE/JULY

Last Day of Second Quarter, Dow Down 12 of Last 16 — NASDAQ Up 12 of 15

MONDAY
D 33.3
S 38.1
N 71.4
30

Technology will gradually strengthen democracies in every country and at every level. — William H. Gates (Microsoft founder)

First Trading Day in July, Dow Up 15 of Last 18 But 100+ Point Losses in 2002 & 2004

TUESDAY
D 76.2
S 76.2
N 66.7
1

Big money is made in the stock market by being on the right side of major moves. I don't believe in swimming against the tide. — Martin Zweig (Fund manager, Winning on Wall Street)

WEDNESDAY
D 57.1
S 52.4
N 47.6
2

The single best predictor of overall excellence is a company's ability to attract, motivate, and retain talented people. — Bruce Pfau (Vice chair human resources KPMG, Fortune 1998)

(Shortened Trading Day)

THURSDAY
D 38.1
S 38.1
N 38.1
3

In the realm of ideas, everything depends on enthusiasm; in the real world, all rests on perseverance. — Johann Wolfgang von Goethe (German poet and polymath, 1749-1832)

Independence Day (Market Closed)

FRIDAY
4

Nothing gives one person so much advantage over another as to remain always cool and unruffled under all circumstances. — Thomas Jefferson (3rd U.S. president, 1743-7/4/1826)

July Begins NASDAQ's "Worst Four Months" (Pages 56, 58 & 148)

SATURDAY
5

SUNDAY
6

2006 DAILY DOW POINT CHANGES (DOW JONES INDUSTRIAL AVERAGE)

Week #		Monday**	Tuesday	Wednesday	Thursday	Friday**	Weekly Dow Close	Net Point Change
1						2005 Close	10717.50	
2		Holiday	129.91	32.74	2.00	77.16	10959.31	241.81
3	J	52.59	− 0.32	31.86	− 81.08	− 2.49	10959.87	0.56
4	A	Holiday	− 63.55	− 41.46	25.85	− 213.32	10667.39	− 292.48
5	N	21.38	23.45	− 2.48	99.73	97.74	10907.21	239.82
6		− 7.29	− 35.06	89.09	− 101.97	− 58.36	10793.62	− 113.59
7	F	4.65	− 48.51	108.86	24.73	35.70	10919.05	125.43
8	E	− 26.73	136.07	30.58	61.71	− 5.36	11115.32	196.27
9	B	Holiday	− 46.26	68.11	− 67.95	− 7.37	11061.85	− 53.47
10		35.70	− 104.14	60.12	− 28.02	− 3.92	11021.59	− 40.26
11	M	− 63.00	22.10	25.05	− 33.46	104.06	11076.34	54.75
12	A	− 0.32	75.32	58.43	43.47	26.41	11279.65	203.31
13	R	− 5.12	− 39.06	81.96	− 47.14	9.68	11279.97	0.32
14		− 29.86	− 95.57	61.16	− 65.00	− 41.38	11109.32	− 170.65
15	A	35.62	58.91	35.70	− 23.05	− 96.46	11120.04	10.72
16	P	21.29	− 51.70	40.34	7.68	Holiday	11137.65	17.61
17	R	− 63.87	194.99	10.00	64.12	4.56	11347.45	209.80
18		− 11.13	− 53.07	71.24	28.02	− 15.37	11367.14	19.69
19	M	− 23.85	73.16	− 16.17	38.58	138.88	11577.74	210.60
20	A	6.80	55.23	2.88	− 141.92	− 119.74	11380.99	− 196.75
21	Y	47.78	− 8.88	− 214.28	− 77.32	15.77	11144.06	− 236.93
22		− 18.73	− 26.98	18.97	93.73	67.56	11278.61	134.55
23		Holiday	− 184.18	73.88	91.97	− 12.41	11247.87	− 30.74
24	J	− 199.15	− 46.58	− 71.24	7.92	− 46.90	10891.92	− 355.95
25	U	− 99.34	− 86.44	110.78	198.27	− 0.64	11014.55	122.63
26	N	− 72.44	32.73	104.62	− 60.35	− 30.02	10989.09	− 25.46
27		56.19	− 120.54	48.82	217.24	− 40.58	11150.22	161.13
28		77.80*	Holiday	− 76.20	73.48	− 134.63	11090.67	− 59.55
29	J	12.88	31.22	− 121.59	− 166.89	− 106.94	10739.35	− 351.32
30	U	8.01	51.87	212.19	− 83.32	− 59.72	10868.38	129.03
31	L	182.67	52.66	− 1.20	− 2.08	119.27	11219.70	351.32
32		− 34.02	− 59.95	74.20	42.66	− 2.24	11240.35	20.65
33		− 20.97	− 45.79	− 97.41	48.19	− 36.34	11088.03	− 152.32
34	A	9.84	132.39	96.86	7.84	46.51	11381.47	293.44
35	U	− 36.42	− 5.21	− 41.94	6.56	− 20.41	11284.05	− 97.42
36	G	67.96	17.93	12.97	− 1.76	83.00	11464.15	180.10
37		Holiday	5.13	− 63.08	− 74.76	60.67	11392.11	− 72.04
38	S	4.73	101.25	45.23	− 15.93	33.38	11560.77	168.66
39	E	− 5.77	− 14.09	72.28	− 79.96	− 25.13	11508.10	− 52.67
40	P	67.71	93.58	19.85	29.21	− 39.38	11679.07	170.97
41		− 8.72	56.99	123.27	16.08	− 16.48	11850.21	171.14
42	O	7.60	9.36	− 15.04	95.57	12.81	11960.51	110.30
43	C	20.09	− 30.58	42.66	19.05	− 9.36	12002.37	41.86
44	T	114.54	10.97	6.80	28.98	− 73.40	12090.26	87.89
45		− 3.76	− 5.77	− 49.71	− 12.48	− 32.50	11986.04	− 104.22
46	N	119.51	51.22	19.77	− 73.24	5.13	12108.43	122.39
47	O	23.45	86.13	33.70	54.11	36.74	12342.56	234.13
48	V	− 26.02	5.05	5.36	Holiday	− 46.78*	12280.17	− 62.39
49		− 158.46	14.74	90.28	− 4.80	− 27.80	12194.13	− 86.04
50		89.72	47.75	− 22.35	− 30.84	29.08	12307.49	113.36
51	D	20.99	− 12.90	1.92	99.26	28.76	12445.52	138.03
52	E	− 4.25	30.05	− 7.45	− 42.62	− 78.03	12343.22	− 102.30
53	C	Holiday	64.41	102.94	− 9.05	− 38.37	12463.15	119.93
TOTALS		95.74**	573.98	1283.87	193.34	− 401.28**		1745.65

Bold Color: Down Friday, Down Monday   * Shortened trading day: Jul 3, Nov 25

** Monday denotes first trading day of week, Friday denotes last trading day of week.

JULY

🐸 MONDAY
D 57.1
S 61.9
N 52.4

7

'm a great believer in luck, and I find the harder I work the more I have of it.
— Thomas Jefferson (3rd U.S. president, 1743-7/4/1826)

Watch out for Huge Market Gyrations (Both Up and Down) After July 4th

🐸 TUESDAY
D 61.9
S 66.7
N 66.7

8

Nothing will improve a person's hearing more than sincere praise. — Harvey Mackay (*Pushing the Envelope*, 1999)

WEDNESDAY
D 52.4
S 47.6
N 66.7

9

Setting a goal is not the main thing. It is deciding how you will go about achieving it and staying with that plan.
— Tom Landry (Head Coach Dallas Cowboys 1960-1988)

July Is the Best Performing Dow & S&P Month of the Third Quarter

🐸 THURSDAY
D 66.7
S 61.9
N 61.9

10

I believe in the exceptional man — the entrepreneur who is always out of money, not the bureaucrat who generates cash flow and pays dividends. — Armand Erpf (Investment banker, partner Loeb Rhoades, 1897-1971)

🐸 FRIDAY
D 61.9
S 71.4
N 76.2

11

A good manager is a man who isn't worried about his own career but rather the careers of those who work for him... Don't worry about yourself! Take care of those who work for you and you'll float to greatness on their achievements.
— H.S.M. Burns (Scottish CEO Shell Oil 1947-1960, 1900-1971)

SATURDAY

12

SUNDAY

13

DON'T SELL STOCKS ON FRIDAY

Since 1989, Monday* and Tuesday have been the most consistently bullish days of the week for the Dow, Thursday and Friday* the most bearish, as traders have become reluctant to stay long going into the weekend. Since 1989 Mondays and Tuesdays gained 9338.22 Dow points, while Thursday and Friday combined for a total loss of 1366.84 points. Also broken out are the last 6 1/3 years to illustrate Friday's deteriorating performance. During uncertain market times traders often sell before the weekend and are reluctant to jump in on Monday. See pages 66, 100 and 141-144 for more.

ANNUAL DOW POINT CHANGES FOR DAYS OF THE WEEK SINCE 1953

Year	Monday*	Tuesday	Wednesday	Thursday	Friday*	Year's DJIA Closing	Year's Point Change
1953	− 36.16	− 7.93	19.63	5.76	7.70	280.90	− 11.00
1954	15.68	3.27	24.31	33.96	46.27	404.39	123.49
1955	− 48.36	26.38	46.03	− 0.66	60.62	488.40	84.01
1956	− 27.15	− 19.36	− 15.41	8.43	64.56	499.47	11.07
1957	− 109.50	− 7.71	64.12	3.32	− 14.01	435.69	− 63.78
1958	17.50	23.59	29.10	22.67	55.10	583.65	147.96
1959	− 44.48	29.04	4.11	13.60	93.44	679.36	95.71
1960	− 111.04	− 3.75	− 5.62	6.74	50.20	615.89	− 63.47
1961	− 23.65	10.18	87.51	− 5.96	47.17	731.14	115.25
1962	− 101.60	26.19	9.97	− 7.70	− 5.90	652.10	− 79.04
1963	− 8.88	47.12	16.23	22.39	33.99	762.95	110.85
1964	− 0.29	− 17.94	39.84	5.52	84.05	874.13	111.18
1965	− 73.23	39.65	57.03	3.20	68.48	969.26	95.13
1966	− 153.24	− 27.73	56.13	− 46.19	− 12.54	785.69	− 183.57
1967	− 68.65	31.50	25.42	92.25	38.90	905.11	119.42
1968†	− 6.41	34.94	25.16	− 72.06	44.19	943.75	38.64
1969	− 164.17	− 36.70	18.33	23.79	15.36	800.36	− 143.39
1970	− 100.05	− 46.09	116.07	− 3.48	72.11	838.92	38.56
1971	− 2.99	9.56	13.66	8.04	23.01	890.20	51.28
1972	− 87.40	− 1.23	65.24	8.46	144.75	1020.02	129.82
1973	− 174.11	10.52	− 5.94	36.67	− 36.30	850.86	− 169.16
1974	− 149.37	47.51	− 20.31	− 13.70	− 98.75	616.24	− 234.62
1975	39.46	− 109.62	56.93	124.00	125.40	852.41	236.17
1976	70.72	71.76	50.88	− 33.70	− 7.42	1004.65	152.24
1977	− 65.15	− 44.89	− 79.61	− 5.62	21.79	831.17	− 173.48
1978	− 31.29	− 70.84	71.33	− 64.67	69.31	805.01	− 26.16
1979	32.52	9.52	− 18.84	75.18	0.39	838.74	33.73
1980	− 86.51	135.13	137.67	− 122.00	60.96	963.99	125.25
1981	− 45.68	− 49.51	− 13.95	− 14.67	34.82	875.00	− 88.99
1982	5.71	86.20	28.37	− 1.47	52.73	1046.54	171.54
1983	30.51	− 30.92	149.68	61.16	1.67	1258.64	212.10
1984	− 73.80	78.02	− 139.24	92.79	− 4.84	1211.57	− 47.07
1985	80.36	52.70	51.26	46.32	104.46	1546.67	335.10
1986	− 39.94	97.63	178.65	29.31	83.63	1895.95	349.28
1987	− 559.15	235.83	392.03	139.73	− 165.56	1938.83	42.88
1988	268.12	166.44	− 60.48	− 230.84	86.50	2168.57	229.74
1989	− 53.31	143.33	233.25	90.25	171.11	2753.20	584.63
SubTotal	*− 1937.20*	*941.79*	*1708.54*	*330.82*	*1417.35*		*2461.30*
1990	219.90	− 25.22	47.96	− 352.55	− 9.63	2633.66	− 119.54
1991	191.13	47.97	174.53	254.79	− 133.25	3168.83	535.17
1992	237.80	− 49.67	3.12	108.74	− 167.71	3301.11	132.28
1993	322.82	− 37.03	243.87	4.97	− 81.65	3754.09	452.98
1994	206.41	− 95.33	29.98	− 168.87	108.16	3834.44	80.35
1995	262.97	210.06	357.02	140.07	312.56	5117.12	1282.68
1996	626.41	155.55	− 34.24	268.52	314.91	6448.27	1331.15
1997	1136.04	1989.17	− 590.17	− 949.80	− 125.26	7908.25	1459.98
1998	649.10	679.95	591.63	− 1579.43	931.93	9181.43	1273.18
1999	980.49	− 1587.22	826.68	735.94	1359.81	11497.12	2315.69
2000	2265.45	306.47	− 1978.34	238.21	− 1542.06	10786.85	− 710.27
SubTotal	*7098.52*	*1594.69*	*− 327.96*	*− 1299.41*	*967.81*		*8033.65*
2001	− 389.33	336.86	− 396.53	976.41	− 1292.76	10021.50	− 765.35
2002	− 1404.94	− 823.76	1443.69	− 428.12	− 466.74	8341.63	− 1679.87
2003	978.87	482.11	− 425.46	566.22	510.55	10453.92	2112.29
2004	201.12	523.28	358.76	− 409.72	− 344.35	10783.01	329.09
2005	316.23	− 305.62	27.67	− 128.75	24.96	10717.50	− 65.51
2006 ‡	95.74	573.98	1283.87	193.34	− 401.28	12463.15	1745.65
2007 ‡	89.61	− 29.14	576.00	184.56	19.56	13264.62	801.47
Subtotal	*− 112.70*	*757.71*	*2868.00*	*953.94*	*− 1989.18*		*2477.77*
Totals	**5048.62**	**3294.19**	**4248.58**	**− 14.65**	**395.98**		**12972.72**

* Monday denotes first trading day of week, Friday denotes last trading day of week.
† Most Wednesdays closed last 7 months of 1968 ‡ Partial year through May 4, 2007.

JULY

Monday Before July Expiration, Dow Up 4 in a Row After a 3-Year Bear Run
2-Day Mid-Year NASDAQ Rally Ends July 14th (Page 60)

MONDAY
14

D 66.7
S 76.2
N 76.2

...l free governments are managed by the combined wisdom and folly of the people.
— James A. Garfield (20th U.S. president, 1831-1881)

TUESDAY
15

D 52.4
S 47.6
N 61.9

...e only things that evolve by themselves in an organization are disorder, friction and malperformance.
— Peter Drucker (Austria-born pioneer management theorist, 1909-2005)

WEDNESDAY
16

D 47.6
S 42.9
N 47.6

...he average man desires to be told specifically which particular stock to buy or sell. He wants to get something for nothing.
...e does not wish to work. — William LeFevre (Senior analyst Ehrenkrantz King Nussbaum, 1928-1997)

THURSDAY
17

D 42.9
S 42.9
N 42.9

...he word "crisis" in Chinese is composed of two characters: the first, the symbol of danger; the second, opportunity.
...uly Expiration Day, Dow Down 5 of Last 7 — Off 390 Dow Points in 2002

FRIDAY
18

D 52.4
S 57.1
N 52.4

...al knowledge is to know the extent of one's ignorance. — Confucius (Chinese philosopher, 551-478 B.C.)

SATURDAY
19

SUNDAY
20

A RALLY FOR ALL SEASONS

Most years, especially when the market sells off during the first half, prospects for the perennial summer rally become the buzz on the street. Parameters for this "rally" were defined by the late Ralph Rotnem as the lowest close in the Dow Jones Industrials in May or June to the highest close in July, August, or September. Such a big deal is made of the "summer rally" that one might get the impression the market puts on its best performance in the summertime. Nothing could be further from the truth! Not only does the market "rally" in every season of the year, but it does so with more gusto in the winter, spring, and fall than in the summer.

Winters in 44 years averaged a 13.1% gain as measured from the low in November or December to the first quarter closing high. Spring rose 11.0% followed by fall with 10.9%. Last and least was the average 9.2% "summer rally." Even 2003's impressive 14.3% "summer rally" was outmatched by spring and fall. Nevertheless, no matter how thick the gloom or grim the outlook, don't despair! There's always a rally for all seasons, statistically. NASDAQ's 12-day mid-year rally on page 60 is tradable.

SEASONAL GAINS IN DOW JONES INDUSTRIALS

	WINTER RALLY Nov/Dec Low to Q1 High	SPRING RALLY Feb/Mar Low to Q2 High	SUMMER RALLY May/Jun Low to Q3 High	FALL RALLY Aug/Sep Low to Q4 High
1964	15.3%	6.2%	9.4%	8.3%
1965	5.7	6.6	11.6	10.3
1966	5.9	4.8	3.5	7.0
1967	11.6	8.7	11.2	4.4
1968	7.0	11.5	5.2	13.3
1969	0.9	7.7	1.9	6.7
1970	5.4	6.2	22.5	19.0
1971	21.6	9.4	5.5	7.4
1972	19.1	7.7	5.2	11.4
1973	8.6	4.8	9.7	15.9
1974	13.1	8.2	1.4	11.0
1975	36.2	24.2	8.2	8.7
1976	23.3	6.4	5.9	4.6
1977	8.2	3.1	2.8	2.1
1978	2.1	16.8	11.8	5.2
1979	11.0	8.9	8.9	6.1
1980	13.5	16.8	21.0	8.5
1981	11.8	9.9	0.4	8.3
1982	4.6	9.3	18.5	37.8
1983	15.7	17.8	6.3	10.7
1984	5.9	4.6	14.1	9.7
1985	11.7	7.1	9.5	19.7
1986	31.1	18.8	9.2	11.4
1987	30.6	13.6	22.9	5.9
1988	18.1	13.5	11.2	9.8
1989	15.1	12.9	16.1	5.7
1990	8.8	14.5	12.4	8.6
1991	21.8	11.2	6.6	9.3
1992	14.9	6.4	3.7	3.3
1993	8.9	7.7	6.3	7.3
1994	9.7	5.2	9.1	5.0
1995	13.6	19.3	11.3	13.9
1996	19.2	7.5	8.7	17.3
1997	17.7	18.4	18.4	7.3
1998	20.3	13.6	8.2	24.3
1999	15.1	21.6	8.2	12.6
2000	10.8	15.2	9.8	3.5
2001	6.4	20.8	1.7	23.1
2002	14.8	7.9	2.8	17.6
2003	6.5	23.9	14.3	15.7
2004	11.6	5.2	4.4	10.6
2005	9.0	2.1	5.6	5.3
2006	8.8	8.3	9.5	13.0
2007	6.7			
Totals	**577.7%**	**474.3%**	**394.9%**	**466.6%**
Average	**13.1%**	**11.0%**	**9.2%**	**10.9%**

MONDAY
D 33.3
S 23.8
N 28.6 **21**

If you destroy a free market you create a black market. If you have ten thousand regulations you destroy all respect for the law.
— Winston Churchill (British statesman, 1874-1965)

2006 Week After July Options Expiration, Dow Up Huge 3.2%

TUESDAY
D 47.6
S 38.1
N 38.1 **22**

A gold mine is a hole in the ground with a liar on top.
— Mark Twain (1835-1910, pen name of Samuel Longhorne Clemens, American novelist and satirist)

WEDNESDAY
D 38.1
S 38.1
N 33.3 **23**

Have not great merchants, great manufacturers, great inventors done more for the world than preachers and philanthropists. Can there be any doubt that cheapening the cost of necessities and conveniences of life is the most powerful agent of civilization and progress? — Charles Elliott Perkins (Railroad magnate, 1840-1907)

July Closes Well but Can End Poorly if a Bear Market in Progress

THURSDAY
D 52.4
S 47.6
N 47.6 **24**

Anyone who has achieved excellence knows that it comes as a result of ceaseless concentration.
— Louise Brooks (Actress, 1906-1985)

FRIDAY
D 66.7
S 71.4
N 66.7 **25**

To me, the "tape" is the final arbiter of any investment decision. I have a cardinal rule: Never fight the tape!
— Martin Zweig (Fund manager, *Winning on Wall Street*)

SATURDAY

26

August Almanac Investor Seasonalities: See Pages 114 & 116

SUNDAY

27

AUGUST ALMANAC

AUGUST							SEPTEMBER						
S	M	T	W	T	F	S	S	M	T	W	T	F	S
					1	2		1	2	3	4	5	6
3	4	5	6	7	8	9	7	8	9	10	11	12	13
10	11	12	13	14	15	16	14	15	16	17	18	19	20
17	18	19	20	21	22	23	21	22	23	24	25	26	27
24	25	26	27	28	29	30	28	29	30				
31													

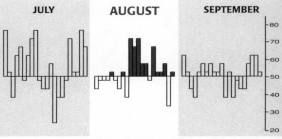

Market Probability Chart above is a graphic representation of the S&P 500 Recent Market Probability Calendar on page 124.

◆ Harvesting made August the best stock market month 1901-1951 ◆ Now that less than 2% farm, August has become the worst S&P month since 1987, second worst Dow and third worst NASDAQ month (NAS up 11.7% in 2000 but down 10.9 in 2001 ◆ Shortest bear in history (45 days) caused by turmoil in Russia, currency crisis and hedge fund debacle ended here in 1998, with a record 1344.22 point drop in the Dow, off 15.1% ◆ Saddam Hussein triggered a 10.0% slide in 1990 ◆ Best Dow gains: 1982 (11.5%) and 1984 (9.8%) as bear markets ended ◆ Last five days of August much better, up four years in a row

August Vital Statistics

	DJIA	S&P 500	NASDAQ	Russell 1K	Russell 2K
Rank	10	10	10	9	9
Up	32	31	19	18	16
Down	25	26	17	10	12
Avg % Change	−0.04%	0.04%	0.3%	0.6%	0.6%
Election Year	0.8%	0.9%	2.8%	2.3%	3.5%
Best & Worst August					
	% Change	% Change	% Change	% Change	% Change
Best	1982 11.5	1982 11.6	2000 11.7	1982 11.3	1984 11.5
Worst	1998 −15.1	1998 −14.6	1998 −19.9	1998 −15.1	1998 −19.5
Best & Worst August Weeks					
Best	8/20/82 10.3	8/20/82 8.8	8/3/84 7.4	8/20/82 8.5	8/3/84 7.0
Worst	8/23/74 −6.1	8/16/74 −6.4	8/28/98 −8.8	8/28/98 −5.4	8/28/98 −9.4
Best & Worst August Days					
Best	8/17/82 4.9	8/17/82 4.8	8/14/02 5.1	8/17/82 4.4	8/6/02 3.7
Worst	8/31/98 −6.4	8/31/98 −6.8	8/31/98 −8.6	8/31/98 −6.7	8/31/98 −5.7
First Trading Day of Expiration Week: 1980-2006					
Record (#Up - #Down)	19-8	21-6	20-7	20-7	17-10
Current streak	U4	U4	U9	U4	U7
Avg % Change	0.35	0.34	0.35	0.30	0.21
Options Expiration Day: 1980-2006					
Record (#Up - #Down)	14-13	15-12	15-12	15-12	18-9
Current streak	U4	U4	U1	U4	U5
Avg % Change	−0.13	−0.10	−0.19	−0.10	0.03
Options Expiration Week: 1980-2006					
Record (#Up - #Down)	15-12	17-10	15-12	17-10	17-10
Current streak	U1	U1	U1	U1	U1
Avg % Change	0.47	0.64	0.83	0.67	0.79
Week After Options Expiration: 1980-2006					
Record (#Up - #Down)	17-10	18-9	17-10	18-9	17-10
Current streak	D2	D2	D2	D2	D2
Avg % Change	0.13	0.14	0.29	0.12	−0.18
First Trading Day Performance					
% of Time Up	47.4	50.9	52.8	46.4	46.4
Avg % Change	−0.03	−0.01	−0.16	0.001	−0.07
Last Trading Day Performance					
% of Time Up	61.4	64.9	72.2	60.7	78.6
Avg % Change	0.16	0.15	0.11	−0.03	0.14

Dow & S&P 1950-April 2007, NASDAQ 1971-April 2007, Russell 1K & 2K 1979-April 2007.

August's a good month to go on vacation
Trading stocks will likely lead to frustration

JULY/AUGUST

ompanies which do well generally tend to report (their quarterly earnings) earlier than those which do poorly.
— Alan Abelson (Financial journalist and editor, *Barron's*)

TUESDAY
D 47.6
S 52.4
N 52.4
29

"you can buy all you want of a new issue, you do not want any; if you cannot obtain any, you want all you can buy.
— Rod Fadem (Stifel Nicolaus & Co., *Barron's* 1989)

WEDNESDAY
D 66.7
S 76.2
N 66.7
30

)nly those who will risk going too far can possibly find out how far one can go.
— T.S. Eliot (English poet, essayist and critic, *The Wasteland*, 1888-1965)

THURSDAY
D 57.1
S 66.7
N 61.9
31

f you bet on a horse, that's gambling. If you bet you can make three spades, that's entertainment.
f you bet cotton will go up three points, that's business. See the difference? — Blackie Sherrod (Sportswriter, b. 1919)

First Trading Day in August Atrocious, Dow Down 8 of Last 10

FRIDAY
D 33.3
S 42.9
N 47.6
1

The trend is your friend...until it ends. — Anonymous

SATURDAY
2

SUNDAY
3

FIRST MONTH OF QUARTERS IS THE MOST BULLISH

We have observed over the years that the investment calendar reflects the annual, semi-annual, and quarterly operations of institutions during January, April and July. The opening month of the first three quarters produces the greatest gains in the Dow Jones Industrials and the S&P 500. NASDAQ's record differs slightly.

The fourth quarter had behaved quite differently since it is affected by year-end portfolio adjustments and presidential and congressional elections in even-numbered years. But in recent years, with October 1987 not factored in, October has transformed into a bear-killing-turnaround month, posting some mighty gains in seven of the last nine years. (See pages 152-160.)

After experiencing the most powerful bull market of all time during the 1990s, followed by the ferocious bear market early in the millennium, we divided the monthly average percent changes into two groups: before 1991 and after. Comparing the month-by-month quarterly behavior of the three major U.S. averages in the table, you'll see that first months of the first three quarters perform best overall. Nasty sell-offs in April 2000, 2002, 2004 and 2005 and July 2000-2002 and 2004, hit the NASDAQ hardest. (See pages 152-160.)

Between 1950 and 1990, the S&P 500 gained 1.3% (Dow, 1.4%) on average in first months of the first three quarters. Second months barely eked out any gain, while third months, thanks to March, moved up 0.23% (Dow, 0.07%) on average. NASDAQ's first month of the first three quarters averages 1.67% from 1971-1990 with July being a negative drag.

Since 1991 major turnarounds have helped October join the ranks of bullish first months of quarters. The once-feared month has been the bulls' latter-day savior.

DOW JONES INDUSTRIALS, S&P 500 & NASDAQ
AVERAGE MONTHLY % CHANGES BY QUARTER

	DJIA 1950-1990			S&P 500 1950-1990			NASDAQ 1971-1990		
	1st Mo	2nd Mo	3rd Mo	1st Mo	2nd Mo	3rd Mo	1st Mo	2nd Mo	3rd Mo
1Q	1.5%	−0.01%	1.0%	1.5%	−0.1%	1.1%	3.8%	1.2%	0.9%
2Q	1.6	−0.4	0.1	1.3	−0.1	0.3	1.7	0.8	1.1
3Q	1.1	0.3	−0.9	1.1	0.3	−0.7	−0.5	0.1	−1.6
Tot	4.2%	−0.1%	0.2%	3.9%	0.1%	0.7%	5.0%	2.1%	0.4%
Avg	1.40%	−0.04%	0.07%	1.30%	0.03%	0.23%	1.67%	0.70%	0.13%
4Q	−0.1%	1.4%	1.7%	0.4%	1.7%	1.6%	−1.4%	1.6%	1.4%
	DJIA 1991-April 2007			S&P 500 1991-April 2007			NASDAQ 1991-April 2007		
1Q	1.0%	0.6%	0.6%	1.2%	0.02%	0.7%	3.5%	−0.4%	−0.3%
2Q	2.3	1.3	−0.5	1.4	1.2	0.2	0.4	1.2	1.4
3Q	0.9	−0.9	−1.3	0.3	−0.6	−0.5	−0.1	0.5	0.01
Tot	4.2%	1.0%	−1.2%	2.9%	0.6%	0.4%	3.8%	1.3%	1.1%
Avg	1.40%	0.33%	−0.40%	0.96%	0.21%	0.13%	1.27%	0.44%	0.37%
4Q	2.4%	2.4%	2.0%	2.3%	2.0%	2.0%	3.1%	2.9%	2.6%
	DJIA 1950-April 2007			S&P 500 1950-April 2007			NASDAQ 1971-April 2007		
1Q	1.3%	0.2%	0.9%	1.4%	−0.1%	1.0%	3.7%	0.5%	0.3%
2Q	1.8	0.1	−0.1	1.3	0.2	0.2	1.1	1.0	1.2
3Q	1.1	−0.04	−1.0	0.9	0.04	−0.6	−0.3	0.3	−0.9
Tot	4.2%	0.3%	−0.2%	3.6%	0.2%	0.6%	4.5%	1.8%	0.6%
Avg	1.40%	0.09%	−0.07%	1.20%	0.06%	0.20%	1.50%	0.60%	0.20%
4Q	0.6%	1.7%	1.8%	0.9%	1.8%	1.7%	0.6%	2.2%	1.9%

AUGUST

gust Is the Worst S&P since 1987
rvesting Made August the Best Dow Month 1901-1951

MONDAY
D 57.1
S 47.6
N 38.1
4

fect the quality of the day, that is the highest of the arts.
enry David Thoreau (American writer, naturalist and philosopher, 1817-1862)

TUESDAY
D 47.6
S 47.6
N 42.9
5

e are no secrets to success. Don't waste your time looking for them. Success is the result of perfection,
work, learning from failure, loyalty to those for whom you work, and persistence.
eneral Colin Powell (Chairman, Joint Chiefs of Staff 1989-1993, secretary of state 2001-2005)

WEDNESDAY
D 47.6
S 47.6
N 57.1
6

t spirits have always encountered violent opposition from mediocre minds.
lbert Einstein (German/American physicist, 1921 Nobel Prize, 1879-1955)

st Nine Trading Days of August Are Historically Weak

THURSDAY
D 47.6
S 52.4
N 52.4
7

does not consist mainly of facts and happenings. It consists mainly of the storm of thoughts that are forever
ing through one's mind. — Mark Twain (1835-1910, pen name of Samuel Longhorne Clemens, American novelist and satirist)

mmer Olympics Start in Beijing

FRIDAY
D 42.9
S 47.6
N 42.9
8

n Paris sneezes, Europe catches cold. — Prince Klemens Metternich (Austrian statesman, 1773-1859)

SATURDAY
9

SUNDAY
10

AURA OF THE TRIPLE WITCH – 4TH QUARTER MOST BULLISH
DOWN WEEKS TRIGGER MORE WEAKNESS WEEK AFTER

Options expire the third Friday of every month but in March, June, September and December a powerful coven gathers. Since the S&P index futures began trading on April 21, 1982, stock options, index options as well as index futures all expire at the same time four times each year — known as Triple Witching. Traders have long sought to understand and master the magic of this quarterly phenomenon.

The market is still small for fledgling single-stock futures (450 at this writing) so we do not believe the term "quadruple witching" is applicable just yet.

We have analyzed what the market does prior, during and following Triple Witching expirations in search of consistent trading patterns. This is never easy. For as soon as a pattern becomes obvious, the market almost always starts to anticipate it, and the pattern tends to shift. These are some of our findings of how the Dow Jones Industrials perform around Triple-Witching Week (TWW).

* TWWs became more bullish since 1990, except in the second quarter.
* Following weeks became more bearish. Since Q1 2000, only 9 of 28 were up, and 5 occurred in December.
* TWWs have tended to be down in flat periods and dramatically so during the 2000-2002 bear market.
* DOWN WEEKS TEND TO FOLLOW DOWN TWWs is a most interesting pattern. Since 1991, of 22 down TWWs, 17 following weeks were also down. This is surprising inasmuch as the previous decade had an exactly opposite pattern: There were 13 down TWWs then, but 12 up weeks followed them.
* TWWs in the second and third quarter (Worst Six Months May through October) are much weaker and the weeks following, horrendous. But in the first and fourth quarter (Best Six Months period November through April) only the week after Q1 expiration is negative.

Throughout the *Almanac* you will also see notations on the performance of Mondays and Fridays of TWW as we place considerable significance on the beginnings and ends of weeks (pages 66, 68, 100, 141-144). See more in our March 2004 *Almanac Investor Newsletter at stocktradersalmanac.com*.

TRIPLE WITCHING WEEK & WEEK AFTER DOW POINT CHANGES

	Expiration Week Q1	Week After	Expiration Week Q2	Week After	Expiration Week Q3	Week After	Expiration Week Q4	Week After
1991	– 6.93	– 89.36	– 34.98	– 58.81	33.54	– 13.19	20.12	167.04
1992	40.48	– 44.95	– 69.01	– 2.94	21.35	– 76.73	9.19	12.97
1993	43.76	– 31.60	– 10.24	– 3.88	– 8.38	– 70.14	10.90	6.15
1994	32.95	–120.92	3.33	–139.84	58.54	–101.60	116.08	26.24
1995	38.04	65.02	86.80	75.05	96.85	– 33.42	19.87	– 78.76
1996	114.52	51.67	55.78	– 50.60	49.94	– 15.54	179.53	76.51
1997	–130.67	– 64.20	14.47	–108.79	174.30	4.91	– 82.01	– 76.98
1998	303.91	–110.35	–122.07	231.67	100.16	133.11	81.87	314.36
1999	27.20	– 81.31	365.05	–303.00	– 224.80	–524.30	32.73	148.33
2000	666.41	517.49	–164.76	– 44.55	– 293.65	– 79.63	–277.95	200.60
2001	–821.21	–318.63	–353.36	– 19.05	–1369.70	611.75	224.19	101.65
2002	34.74	–179.56	–220.42	– 10.53	– 326.67	–284.57	77.61	–207.54
2003	662.26	–376.20	83.63	–211.70	173.27	–331.74	236.06	46.45
2004	– 53.48	26.37	6.31	– 44.57	– 28.61	–237.22	106.70	177.20
2005	–144.69	–186.80	110.44	–325.23	– 36.62	–222.35	97.01	7.68
2006	203.31	0.32	122.63	– 25.46	168.66	– 52.67	138.03	–102.30
2007	–165.91	370.60						
Up	11	6	9	2	9	3	14	12
Down	6	11	7	14	7	13	2	4

AUGUST

Monday Before August Expiration, Dow Up 10 of Last 12

MONDAY

D 47.6
S 42.9
N 42.9

11

I've never been poor, only broke. Being poor is a frame of mind. Being broke is only a temporary situation.
— Mike Todd (Movie producer, 1903-1958)

TUESDAY

D 57.1
S 52.4
N 52.4

12

The worst trades are generally when people freeze and start to pray and hope rather than take some action.
— Robert Mnuchin (Partner, Goldman Sachs)

Mid-August Stronger than Beginning and End

WEDNESDAY

D 38.1
S 38.1
N 52.4

13

I was in search of a one-armed economist so that the guy could never make a statement and then say: "on the other hand."
— Harry S. Truman (33rd U.S. president, 1884-1972)

THURSDAY

D 66.7
S 71.4
N 76.2

14

Knowledge born from actual experience is the answer to why one profits; lack of it is the reason one loses.
— Gerald M. Loeb (EF Hutton, *The Battle for Investment Survival*, predicted '29 Crash, 1900-1974)

August Expiration Day, Dow Up 4 in a Row
Down 10 of 13 Prior to Recent Bullishness

FRIDAY

D 57.1
S 66.7
N 71.4

15

The worse a situation becomes the less it takes to turn it around, the bigger the upside.
— George Soros (Financier, philanthropist, political activist, author and philosopher, b. 1930)

SATURDAY

16

SUNDAY

17

2008 PRESIDENTIAL ELECTION YEAR PERPECTIVES

ONLY ONE LOSS IN LAST SEVEN MONTHS OF ELECTION YEARS

Regardless which party is victorious, the last seven months have seen gains on the S&P in 13 of the 14 presidential election years since 1950. The one loss was in 2000 when the election's outcome was delayed for 36 tumultuous days, though the Dow did end higher. *Page 52.*

FIRST FIVE MONTHS BETTER WHEN PARTY RETAINS WHITE HOUSE

Since 1901 there have been 26 presidential elections. When the party in power retained the White House 16 times, the Dow was up 1.5% on average for the first five months, compared to a 4.5% loss the 10 times the Party was ousted. Since 1950, retaining the White House 7 times brought an average gain of 1.9%, compared to 0.5% the other 7 times.

PUBLIC USUALLY TIRES OF POLITICAL PARTIES AFTER TWO TERMS

Since the Roosevelt/Truman era the American public tends to "throw the rascals out" after two terms. Jimmy Carter lasted just one term after the Iranians took American hostages at our embassy in Tehran holding 52 for 444 days and inflation hit a post-WWII record on his watch. The Republicans held on for three terms in 1988 despite the Iran/Contra scandal and market crash in October 1987. A lackluster Democratic candidate in 1988 enabled the Reps to last for 12 years. Also, the election of a sitting vice-president was the first in 162 years.

WAR CAN BE A MAJOR FACTOR IN PRESIDENTIAL RACES

Democrats used to lose the White House on foreign shores (1920 WW1, 1952 Korea, 1968 Vietnam, 1980 Iran Crisis). Republicans, by contrast, lost it here at home (1912 party split, 1932 Depression, 1960 economy, 1976 Watergate). Homeland issues dominated elections the last three decades with the Republican loss in 1992 (economy) and the Democratic loss in 2000 (scandal). As we've learned over the years, it all depends on who the candidates are in 2008.

MARKET BOTTOMS TWO YEARS AFTER A PRESIDENTIAL ELECTION

A takeover of the White House by the opposing party in the past 50 years (1960, 1968, 1976, 1980, 1992, 2000) has resulted in a bottom two years later, with one flat market in 1994. When incumbent parties retained power (1964, 1972, 1984, 1988, 1996, 2004) stocks often bottomed two years later as well, except 1984 (three years, 1987) and 2004 (one year, flat 2005). Whatever the outcome in 2008, we could see a bottom in 2010.

REPUBLICANS WON 7 OF 8 INCUMBENT-LESS RACES SINCE 1900

Few people are aware that when there were no incumbents running in the presidential elections since 1900, Republicans won them all (1908, 1920, 1928, 1952, 1968, 1988, and 2000) with the exception of 1960, when John Kennedy beat Richard Nixon by a 118,574 margin out of a little more than 68 million votes cast.

MARKET CHARTS OF PRESIDENTIAL ELECTION YEARS

Market behavior last 21 elections including candidates and winners. *Page 30.*

HOW THE GOVERNMENT MANIPULATES THE ECONOMY TO STAY IN POWER

Money faucets get turned on, if possible, in years divisible by "4." *Page 34.*

INCUMBENT PARTY WINS & LOSSES

Markets tend to be stronger when party in power wins. *Page 36.*

AUGUST

MONDAY
18

D 66.7
S 71.4
N 61.9

The incestuous relationship between government and big business thrives in the dark.
— Jack Anderson (Washington journalist and author, *Peace, War and Politics*, 1922-2005)

TUESDAY
19

D 52.4
S 57.1
N 61.9

If you have an important point to make, don't try to be subtle or clever. Use a pile driver. Hit the point once. Then come back and hit it again. Then hit it a third time — a tremendous whack. — Winston Churchill (British statesman, 1874-1965)

Beware the "Summer Rally" Hype
Historically the Weakest Rally of All Seasons (Page 70)

WEDNESDAY
20

D 57.1
S 57.1
N 47.6

The way a young man spends his evenings is a part of that thin area between success and failure.
— Robert R. Young (U.S. financier and railroad tycoon, 1897-1958)

THURSDAY
21

D 42.9
S 47.6
N 57.1

Show me a good phone receptionist and I'll show you a good company. — Harvey Mackay (*Pushing the Envelope*, 1999)

FRIDAY
22

D 57.1
S 66.7
N 52.4

Major bottoms are usually made when analysts cut their earnings estimates and companies report earnings which are below expectations. — Edward Babbitt, Jr. (Avatar Associates)

SATURDAY
23

SUNDAY
24

A CORRECTION FOR ALL SEASONS

While there's a rally for every season (page 70), almost always there's a decline or correction, too. Fortunately, corrections tend to be smaller than rallies, and that's what gives the stock market its long-term upward bias. In each season the average bounce outdoes the average setback. On average the net gain between the rally and the correction is smallest in summer and fall.

The summer setback tends to be slightly outdone by the average correction in the fall. Tax selling and portfolio cleaning are the usual explanations — individuals sell to register a tax loss and institutions like to get rid of their losers before preparing year-end statements. The October jinx also plays a major part. Since 1964, there have been 16 fall declines of over 10%, and in nine of them (1966, 1974, 1978, 1979, 1987, 1990, 1997, 2000 and 2002) much damage was done in October, where so many bear markets end. Recent October lows were also seen in 1998, 1999, 2004 and 2005. Most often, it has paid to buy after fourth quarter or late third quarter "waterfall declines" for a rally that may continue into January or even beyond. War in Iraq affected the pattern in 2003. Anticipation of our invasion put the market down in the first quarter. Quick success inspired the bulls, which resumed their upward move through the summer.

SEASONAL CORRECTIONS IN DOW JONES INDUSTRIALS

	WINTER SLUMP Nov/Dec High to Q1 Low	SPRING SLUMP Feb/Mar High to Q2 Low	SUMMER SLUMP May/Jun High to Q3 Low	FALL SLUMP Aug/Sep High to Q4 Low
1964	− 0.1%	− 2.4%	− 1.0%	− 2.1%
1965	− 2.5	− 7.3	− 8.3	− 0.9
1966	− 6.0	− 13.2	− 17.7	− 12.7
1967	− 4.2	− 3.9	− 5.5	− 9.9
1968	− 8.8	− 0.3	− 5.5	+ 0.4
1969	− 8.7	− 8.7	− 17.2	− 8.1
1970	− 13.8	− 20.2	− 8.8	− 2.5
1971	− 1.4	− 4.8	− 10.7	− 13.4
1972	− 0.5	− 2.6	− 6.3	− 5.3
1973	− 11.0	− 12.8	− 10.9	− 17.3
1974	− 15.3	− 10.8	− 29.8	− 27.6
1975	− 6.3	− 5.5	− 9.9	− 6.7
1976	− 0.2	− 5.1	− 4.7	− 8.9
1977	− 8.5	− 7.2	− 11.5	− 10.2
1978	− 12.3	− 4.0	− 7.0	− 13.5
1979	− 2.5	− 5.8	− 3.7	− 10.9
1980	− 10.0	− 16.0	− 1.7	− 6.8
1981	− 6.9	− 5.1	− 18.6	− 12.9
1982	− 10.9	− 7.5	− 10.6	− 3.3
1983	− 4.1	− 2.8	− 6.8	− 3.6
1984	− 11.9	− 10.5	− 8.4	− 6.2
1985	− 4.8	− 4.4	− 2.8	− 2.3
1986	− 3.3	− 4.7	− 7.3	− 7.6
1987	− 1.4	− 6.6	− 1.7	− 36.1
1988	− 6.7	− 7.0	− 7.6	− 4.5
1989	− 1.7	− 2.4	− 3.1	− 6.6
1990	− 7.9	− 4.0	− 17.3	− 18.4
1991	− 6.3	− 3.6	− 4.5	− 6.3
1992	+ 0.1	− 3.3	− 5.4	− 7.6
1993	− 2.7	− 3.1	− 3.0	− 2.0
1994	− 4.4	− 9.6	− 4.4	− 7.1
1995	− 0.8	− 0.1	− 0.2	− 2.0
1996	− 3.5	− 4.6	− 7.5	+ 0.2
1997	− 1.8	− 9.8	− 2.2	− 13.3
1998	− 7.0	− 3.1	− 18.2	− 13.1
1999	− 2.7	− 1.7	− 8.0	− 11.5
2000	− 14.8	− 7.4	− 4.1	− 11.8
2001	− 14.5	− 13.6	− 27.4	− 16.2
2002	− 5.1	− 14.2	− 26.7	− 19.5
2003	− 15.8	− 5.3	− 3.1	− 2.1
2004	− 3.9	− 7.7	− 6.3	− 5.7
2005	− 4.5	− 8.5	− 3.3	− 4.5
2006	− 2.4	− 5.4	− 7.8	− 0.4
2007	− 3.7			
Totals	−265.5%	−286.6%	−376.5%	−380.7 %
Average	− 6.0%	− 6.7%	− 8.8%	− 8.9 %

AUGUST

Democratic National Convention Begins in Denver

MONDAY

D 52.4
S 52.4
N 57.1

25

A realist believes that what is done or left undone in the short run determines the long run.
— Sydney J. Harris (American journalist and author, 1917-1986)

Last 5 Days of August Much Better, Up 4 Years in a Row

TUESDAY

D 47.6
S 52.4
N 57.1

26

The whole problem with the world is that fools and fanatics are always so certain of themselves, but wiser people so full of doubts. — Bertrand Russell (British mathematician and philosopher, 1872-1970)

WEDNESDAY

D 57.1
S 57.1
N 61.9

27

In order to be a great writer (or "investor") a person must have a built-in, shockproof crap detector.
— Ernest Hemingway (American writer, 1954 Nobel Prize, 1899-1961)

August's Next to Last Day S&P, Up Only Once Last 11 Years

THURSDAY

D 28.6
S 33.3
N 57.1

28

Companies that announce mass layoffs or a series of firings underperform the stock market over a three-year period.
— Bain & Company (*Smart Money Magazine*, August 2001)

FRIDAY

D 47.6
S 52.4
N 66.7

29

I'm always turned off by an overly optimistic letter from the president in the annual report. If his letter is mildly pessimistic to me, that's a good sign. — Philip Carret (Centenarian, founded Pioneer Fund in 1928, 1896-1998)

September Almanac Investor Seasonalities: See Pages 114 & 116

SATURDAY

30

Shortest Bear Market in History (45 Days) Ended 8/31/98
S&P Lost 19.3%

SUNDAY

31

SEPTEMBER ALMANAC

SEPTEMBER
S M T W T F S
1 2 3 4 5 6
7 8 9 10 11 12 13
14 15 16 17 18 19 20
21 22 23 24 25 26 27
28 29 30

OCTOBER
S M T W T F S
1 2 3 4
5 6 7 8 9 10 11
12 13 14 15 16 17 18
19 20 21 22 23 24 25
26 27 28 29 30 31

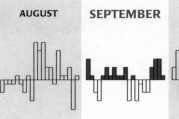

AUGUST   SEPTEMBER   OCTOBER

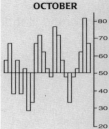

Market Probability Chart above is a graphic representation of the S&P 500 Recent Market Probability Calendar on page 124.

◆ Start of business year, end of vacations, and back to school made September a leading barometer month in first 60 years of 20th century, now portfolio managers back after Labor Day tend to clean house ◆ Biggest % loser on the S&P, Dow and NASDAQ (pages 44 & 56) ◆ Streak of four great Dow Septembers averaging 4.2% gains ended in 1999 with six losers in a row averaging –5.9% (see page 152), up two straight since ◆ Day after Labor Day Dow up 11 of last 13 ◆ Opened strong 9 of last 12 years but tends to close weak due to end-of-quarter mutual fund portfolio restructuring ◆ September Triple-Witching Week is dangerous, week after pitiful (see page 76)

September Vital Statistics

	DJIA		S&P 500		NASDAQ		Russell 1K		Russell 2K	
Rank	12		12		12		12		11	
Up	21		24		19		13		15	
Down	36		32		17		15		13	
Avg % Change	–1.0%		–0.6%		–0.9%		–0.9%		–0.7%	
Election Year	–0.2%		0.3%		0.8%		1.3%		1.7%	
Best & Worst September										
	% Change		% Change		% Change		% Change		% Change	
Best	1954	7.3	1954	8.3	1998	13.0	1998	6.5	1998	7.6
Worst	2002	–12.4	1974	–11.9	2001	–17.0	2002	–10.9	2001	–13.6
Best & Worst September Weeks										
Best	9/28/01	7.4	9/28/01	7.8	9/20/74	5.7	9/28/01	7.6	9/28/01	6.9
Worst	9/21/01	–14.3	9/21/01	–11.6	9/21/01	–16.1	9/21/01	–11.7	9/21/01	–14.0
Best & Worst September Days										
Best	9/8/98	5.0	9/8/98	5.1	9/8/98	6.0	9/8/98	5.0	9/8/98	4.3
Worst	9/17/01	–7.1	9/26/55	–6.6	9/17/01	–6.8	9/17/01	–5.0	9/17/01	–5.2
First Trading Day of Expiration Week: 1980-2006										
Record (#Up - #Down)	18-9		15-12		10-17		15-12		10-17	
Current streak	U3		U1		U3		U1		D1	
Avg % Change	–0.01		–0.06		–0.36		–0.09		–0.23	
Options Expiration Day: 1980-2006										
Record (#Up - #Down)	12-15		14-13		17-10		14-13		17-10	
Current streak	U3		U3		U3		U3		U2	
Avg % Change	–0.12		0.01		0.02		–0.01		0.04	
Options Expiration Week: 1980-2006										
Record (#Up - #Down)	13-14		14-13		13-14		14-13		12-15	
Current streak	U1		U1		U1		U1		U1	
Avg % Change	–0.76		–0.49		–0.56		–0.50		–0.61	
Week After Options Expiration: 1980-2006										
Record (#Up - #Down)	10-17		8-19		12-15		8-19		10-17	
Current streak	D5		D5		D5		D5		D5	
Avg % Change	–0.58		–0.51		–0.74		–0.51		–1.00	
First Trading Day Performance										
% of Time Up	63.2		64.9		55.6		53.6		50.0	
Avg % Change	0.05		0.02		–0.02		–0.03		0.02	
Last Trading Day Performance										
% of Time Up	40.4		43.9		52.8		53.6		71.4	
Avg % Change	–0.18		–0.12		–0.10		–0.05		0.41	

Dow & S&P 1950-April 2007, NASDAQ 1971-April 2007, Russell 1K & 2K 1979-April 2007.

September is when leaves and stocks tend to fall
On Wall Street it's the worst month of all

SEPTEMBER

Labor Day (Market Closed)
Republican National Convention Begins in St. Paul

MONDAY

1

The key to long-term profits on Wall Street is not making big killings, it's not getting killed. — Daniel Turov (*Turov on Timing*)

First Trading Day September, Dow Down 3 of Last 5 After a 7-Year Bull Run
Day After Labor Day, Dow Up 11 of Last 13 — Crushed in 2002, off 4.1%

TUESDAY

D 52.4
S 61.9
N 57.1

2

[Look for companies] where the executives have a good ownership position — not only options, but outright ownership — so that they will ride up and down with the shareholder. — George Roche (Chairman, T. Rowe Price, *Barron's* 12/18/06)

WEDNESDAY

D 61.9
S 52.4
N 66.7

3

Among the simplest truths is that market risk tends to be unusually rewarding when market valuations are low and interest rates are falling. — John P. Hussman, Ph.D. (Hussman Funds, 5/22/06)

THURSDAY

D 47.6
S 42.9
N 47.6

4

When everyone starts downgrading a stock, it's usually time to buy.
— Meryl Witmer (General partner, Eagle Capital Partners, *Barron's* 1/29/07)

FRIDAY

D 33.3
S 38.1
N 57.1

5

Liberties voluntarily forfeited are not easily retrieved. All the more so for those that are removed surreptitiously.
— Ted Koppel (Newsman, managing editor Discovery Channel, *NY Times* Op-Ed 11/6/06, b. 1940)

SATURDAY

6

SUNDAY

7

MARKET BEHAVIOR THREE DAYS BEFORE AND THREE DAYS AFTER HOLIDAYS

The *Stock Trader's Almanac* has tracked holiday seasonality annually since the first edition in 1968. Stocks used to rise on the day before holidays and sell off the day after, but nowadays each holiday moves to its own rhythm. Eight holidays are separated into seven groups. Average percent changes for the Dow, S&P 500, NASDAQ and Russell 2000 are shown.

The Dow and S&P consist of blue chips and the largest cap stocks, whereas NASDAQ and the Russell 2000 would be more representative of smaller cap stocks. This is evident on the last day of the year with NASDAQ and the Russell 2000 having a field day, while their larger brethren in the Dow and S&P are showing losses on average.

Thanks to the Santa Claus Rally the three days before and after New Year's Day and Christmas are best. NASDAQ and the Russell 2000 average gains of 1.4% to 1.9% over the six-day spans. However, trading around the first day of the year has been mixed. Traders have been selling more the first trading day of the year recently, pushing gains and losses into the New Year.

Bullishness before Labor Day and after Memorial Day is affected by strength the first day of September and June. The worst day after a holiday is the day after Easter. Surprisingly, the following day is one of the best second days after a holiday, right up there with the second day after New Year's Day.

Presidents' Day is the least bullish of all the holidays, bearish the day before and three days after. The S&P and NASDAQ have dropped 14 of the last 16 days before Presidents' Day (Dow, 12 of 16; Russell 2000, 10 of 16).

HOLIDAYS: 3 DAYS BEFORE, 3 DAYS AFTER (Average % Change 1980 – April 2007)

	– 3	– 2	– 1	Mixed	+1	+2	+3
S&P 500	0.14	0.22	– 0.14	**New Year's**	0.02	0.44	0.09
DJIA	0.09	0.16	– 0.21	**Day**	0.21	0.46	0.24
NASDAQ	0.28	0.27	0.24	*1/1/08*	– 0.02	0.84	0.29
Russell 2K	0.36	0.37	0.52		– 0.15	0.42	0.16
S&P 500	0.36	– 0.03	– 0.26	**Negative Before & After**	– 0.13	– 0.05	– 0.10
DJIA	0.37	0.001	– 0.18	**Presidents'**	– 0.06	– 0.10	– 0.14
NASDAQ	0.56	0.24	– 0.44	**Day**	– 0.52	– 0.01	– 0.04
Russell 2K	0.40	0.09	– 0.14	*2/18/08*	– 0.37	– 0.08	– 0.03
S&P 500	0.15	– 0.02	0.21	**Positive Before &**	– 0.32	0.45	0.12
DJIA	0.14	– 0.05	0.14	**Negative After**	– 0.21	0.45	0.11
NASDAQ	0.46	0.30	0.35	**Good Friday**	– 0.53	0.44	0.27
Russell 2K	0.22	0.13	0.28	*3/21/08*	– 0.50	0.37	0.11
S&P 500	0.14	0.02	0.06	**Positive Day After**	0.27	0.22	0.22
DJIA	0.12	– 0.03	– 0.003	**Memorial**	0.35	0.24	0.15
NASDAQ	0.21	0.24	0.04	**Day**	0.07	– 0.003	0.47
Russell 2K	– 0.03	0.26	0.17	*5/26/08*	0.06	0.16	0.40
S&P 500	0.08	0.80	0.10	**Negative After**	– 0.18	– 0.04	0.08
DJIA	0.06	0.06	0.07	**Independence**	– 0.12	– 0.01	0.04
NASDAQ	0.22	0.11	0.08	**Day**	– 0.22	– 0.20	0.27
Russell 2K	0.23	– 0.05	0.05	*7/4/08*	– 0.18	– 0.20	0.06
S&P 500	– 0.03	– 0.32	0.21	**Positive Day Before**	0.06	0.001	– 0.10
DJIA	– 0.03	– 0.38	0.22	**Labor**	0.15	0.09	– 0.20
NASDAQ	0.22	– 0.05	0.22	**Day**	– 0.08	– 0.19	0.09
Russell 2K	0.37	0.02	0.18	*9/1/08*	0.02	– 0.04	0.10
S&P 500	– 0.04	0.04	0.25	**Positive Before & After**	0.21	– 0.22	0.15
DJIA	0.04	0.06	0.29	**Thanksgiving**	0.16	– 0.18	0.20
NASDAQ	– 0.18	– 0.22	0.37	*11/27/08*	0.57	– 0.24	– 0.05
Russell 2K	– 0.09	– 0.13	0.29		0.44	– 0.22	0.05
S&P 500	0.19	0.17	0.19	**Christmas**	0.15	0.11	0.29
DJIA	0.26	0.25	0.25	*12/25/08*	0.20	0.10	0.25
NASDAQ	– 0.14	0.44	0.45		0.10	0.23	0.36
Russell 2K	0.17	0.35	0.38		0.17	0.36	0.48

SEPTEMBER

MONDAY

D 47.6
S 52.4
N 61.9

8

Regardless of current economic conditions, it's always best to remember that the stock market is a barometer and not a thermometer. — Yale Hirsch

TUESDAY

D 47.6
S 57.1
N 57.1

9

Things may come to those who wait, but only the things left by those who hustle.
— Abraham Lincoln (16th U.S. president, 1809-1865)

WEDNESDAY

D 61.9
S 52.4
N 57.1

10

Small business has been the first rung on the ladder upward for every minority group in the nation's history.
— S. I. Hayakawa (1947, U.S. senator, California 1977-1983, 1906-1992)

2001 4-Day Market Closing, Longest Since
9-Day Banking Moratorium in March 1933

THURSDAY

D 61.9
S 57.1
N 61.9

11

The soul is dyed the color of its thoughts. Think only on those things that are in line with your principles and can bear the light of day. The content of your character is your choice. Day by day, what you do is who you become.
— Heraclitus (Greek philosopher, 535-475 BC)

"In Memory"

FRIDAY

D 47.6
S 52.4
N 57.1

12

The universal line of distinction between the strong and the weak is that one persists, while the other hesitates, falters, trifles and at last collapses or caves in. — Edwin Percy Whipple (American essayist, 1819-1886)

SATURDAY

13

SUNDAY

14

MARKET GAINS MORE ON SUPER-8 DAYS EACH MONTH THAN ON ALL 13 REMAINING DAYS COMBINED

For many years the last day plus the first four days were the best days of the month. The market currently exhibits greater bullish bias from the last three trading days of the previous month through the first two days of the current month, and now shows significant bullishness during the middle three trading days, 9 to 11, due to 401(k) cash inflows (see pages 145 and 146). This pattern was not as pronounced during the boom years of the 1990s, with market strength all month long. It returned from 2001 to 2002 with monthly bullishness at the ends, beginnings and middles of months versus weakness during the rest of the month. Was 1999's "rest of month" heavy bullishness a bearish omen and 2002's "rest of month" large losses a bullish sign? Could early 2007's "rest of month" strength be indicating a reversal?

SUPER-8 DAYS* DOW % CHANGES VS. REST OF MONTH

	Super 8 Days	Rest of Month		Super 8 Days	Rest of Month		Super 8 Days	Rest of Month
	1999			**2000**			**2001**	
Jan	0.98%	0.08%		− 4.09%	0.47%		2.13%	− 2.36%
Feb	0.76	1.62		0.43	− 9.10		1.41	− 3.36
Mar	− 0.68	3.74		2.76	5.62		− 1.50	− 3.30
Apr	2.84	7.09		− 2.79	4.77		− 2.61	9.56
May	− 0.83	− 1.92		0.71	− 7.86		2.02	1.53
Jun	0.20	0.01		5.99	− 4.10		− 2.46	− 2.45
Jul	5.87	− 1.74		− 0.65	0.83		2.16	− 2.29
Aug	− 0.35	2.41		3.08	3.75		0.24	− 2.48
Sep	− 5.83	− 2.32		− 3.27	− 2.34		− 3.62	− 12.05
Oct	− 2.86	2.97		− 0.85	− 1.47		4.51	5.36
Nov	4.25	2.45		5.81	− 4.06		1.01	2.48
Dec	0.29	3.92		− 2.96	4.44		0.19	1.99
Totals	**4.64%**	**18.31%**		**4.17%**	**− 9.05%**		**3.48%**	**− 7.37%**
Average	**0.39%**	**1.53%**		**0.35%**	**− 0.75%**		**0.29%**	**− 0.61%**
	2002			**2003**			**2004**	
Jan	− 1.92%	− 0.24%		1.00%	− 4.86%		3.79%	− 1.02%
Feb	− 1.41	4.27		2.71	− 4.82		− 1.20	0.83
Mar	4.11	− 2.64		5.22	− 0.90		− 1.64	− 1.69
Apr	− 2.46	0.08		2.87	− 1.91		3.20	− 0.60
May	3.62	− 4.07		3.17	2.46		− 2.92	− 0.51
Jun	− 2.22	− 6.51		3.09	− 0.38		1.15	1.36
Jul	− 5.04	− 4.75		1.18	1.64		− 1.91	− 0.88
Aug	2.08	4.59		− 0.74	1.55		0.51	0.40
Sep	− 6.58	− 5.00		3.58	− 3.47		0.47	− 2.26
Oct	8.48	− 1.50		2.87	1.41		0.85	− 1.82
Nov	4.74	0.99		− 0.47	0.48		3.08	3.20
Dec	− 0.76	− 4.02		2.10	3.70		2.03	1.13
Totals	**2.64%**	**− 18.80%**		**26.58%**	**− 5.10%**		**7.41%**	**− 1.86%**
Average	**0.22%**	**− 1.57%**		**2.22%**	**− 0.43%**		**0.62%**	**− 0.16%**
	2005			**2006**			**2007**	
Jan	− 1.96%	− 1.35%		− 0.03%	0.34%		0.68%	− 0.04%
Feb	1.76	− 0.07		1.67	0.71		3.02	− 1.72
Mar	0.31	− 2.05		0.81	− 0.03		− 5.51	3.64
Apr	− 4.62	1.46		1.69	− 0.53		2.66	2.82
May	0.57	2.43		− 0.66	0.08			
Jun	1.43	− 3.00		2.39	− 4.87			
Jul	0.96	1.83		1.65	0.07			
Aug	1.36	− 3.07		1.83	0.41			
Sep	0.90	− 0.31		1.13	1.64			
Oct	1.14	− 2.18		1.58	2.59			
Nov	1.67	3.89		− 0.01	− 0.31			
Dec	0.57	− 1.96		2.40	− 0.05			
Totals	**4.09%**	**− 4.37%**		**14.45%**	**0.04%**		**0.85%**	**4.71%**
Average	**0.34%**	**− 0.36%**		**1.20%**	**0.003%**		**0.21%**	**1.18%**

	Super-8 Days*		Rest of Month (13 Days)	
100	Net % Changes	68.31%	Net % Changes	− 23.49%
Month	Average Period	0.68%	Average Period	− 0.23%
Totals	Average Day	0.09%	Average Day	− 0.02%

* Super 8 Days = Last 3 + First 2 + Middle 3

SEPTEMBER

Monday Before September Triple Witching, Dow Up 4 of Last 5

MONDAY

D 52.4
S 52.4
N 23.8

15

Genius is the ability to put into effect what is in your mind. — F. Scott Fitzgerald (author, 1896-1940)

TUESDAY

D 47.6
S 57.1
N 47.6

16

Anytime there is change there is opportunity. So it is paramount that an organization get energized rather than paralyzed.
— Jack Welch (GE CEO, *Fortune*)

Expiration Week 2001, Dow Off 1369.70 Points
Worst Weekly Dow Point Loss Ever

WEDNESDAY

D 23.8
S 38.1
N 52.4

17

Securities pricing is, in every sense a psychological phenomenon that arises from the interaction of human beings with fear.
Why not greed and fear as the equation is usually stated? Because greed is simply fear of not having enough.
— John Bollinger (Bollinger Capital Management, *Capital Growth Letter, Bollinger on Bollinger Bands*)

THURSDAY

D 47.6
S 52.4
N 66.7

18

Wall Street has a uniquely hysterical way of thinking the world will end tomorrow but be fully recovered in the long run,
then a few years later believing the immediate future is rosy but that the long term stinks. — Kenneth L. Fisher (*Wall Street Waltz*)

September Triple Witching, Dow Up 3 Straight
Back-to-back 100+ Point Losses 2000-2001

FRIDAY

D 33.3
S 38.1
N 42.9

19

The price of a stock varies inversely with the thickness of its research file.
— Martin Sosnoff (Atalanta/Sosnoff Capital, *Silent Investor, Silent Loser*)

SATURDAY

20

SUNDAY

21

SELL ROSH HASHANAH, BUY YOM KIPPUR, SELL PASSOVER

Our headline above may surprise some investors who vaguely remember the old saying on the Street, "Buy Rosh Hashanah, Sell Yom Kippur." Though it had a good record at one time, it stopped working in the middle of the last century. Still, it gets tossed around every autumn when the "high holidays" are on the minds of traders as many of their Jewish colleagues take off to observe the Jewish New Year and Day of Atonement. It's not unlike the "summer rally," which gets mentioned every year despite the fact (page 70) that it's the worst season for stock prices.

The basis for the new pattern is that with many traders and investors busy with religious observance and family, positions are closed out and volume fades creating a buying vacuum. Holiday seasonality around official market holidays is something we pay close attention to (page 84). Actual stats on the most observed Hebrew holidays have been compiled in the table here.

	ROSH HASHANAH TO YOM KIPPUR					YOM KIPPUR TO PASSOVER		
	Rosh Hashanah	Dow Close*	Yom Kippur	Dow Close*	% Change	Next Year Passover	Dow Close*	% Change
1971	Sep 20	905.15	Sep 29	883.83	– 2.4%	Mar 30	940.70	6.4%
1972	**Sep 9**	961.24	Sep 18	945.36	– 1.7%	Apr 17	953.42	0.9%
1973	Sep 27	953.27	Oct 6	971.25	1.9%	**Apr 7**	847.54	– 12.7%
1974	Sep 17	648.78	Sep 26	637.98	– 1.7%	Mar 27	770.26	20.7%
1975	**Sep 6**	835.97	Sep 15	803.19	– 3.9%	Apr 15	980.48	22.1%
1976	**Sep 25**	1009.31	Oct 4	977.98	– 3.1%	**Apr 3**	927.36	– 5.2%
1977	Sep 13	854.56	Sep 22	839.41	– 1.8%	**Apr 22**	812.80	– 3.2%
1978	Oct 2	871.36	Oct 11	901.42	3.4%	Apr 12	870.50	– 3.4%
1979	**Sep 22**	893.94	Oct 1	872.95	– 2.3%	Apr 1	784.47	– 10.1%
1980	Sep 11	941.30	**Sep 20**	963.74	2.4%	**Apr 19**	1005.58	4.3%
1981	Sep 29	847.89	Oct 8	878.14	3.6%	**Apr 8**	842.94	– 4.0%
1982	**Sep 18**	916.94	Sep 27	920.90	0.4%	Mar 29	1131.19	22.8%
1983	Sep 8	1246.14	**Sep 17**	1225.71	– 1.6%	Apr 17	1164.57	– 5.0%
1984	Sep 27	1216.76	**Oct 6**	1182.53	– 2.8%	**Apr 6**	1259.05	6.5%
1985	Sep 16	1309.14	Sep 25	1312.05	0.2%	Apr 24	1831.72	39.6%
1986	**Oct 4**	1774.18	Oct 13	1798.37	1.4%	Apr 14	2252.98	25.3%
1987	Sep 24	2566.42	**Oct 3**	2640.99	2.9%	**Apr 2**	1988.06	– 24.7%
1988	Sep 12	2072.37	Sep 21	2090.50	0.9%	Apr 20	2377.38	13.7%
1989	**Sep 30**	2692.82	Oct 9	2791.41	3.7%	Apr 11	2729.73	– 2.2%
1990	Sep 20	2518.32	**Sep 29**	2452.48	– 2.6%	**Mar 31**	2913.86	18.8%
1991	Sep 9	3007.16	Sep 18	3017.89	0.4%	**Apr 18**	3366.50	11.6%
1992	Sep 28	3276.26	Oct 7	3152.25	– 3.8%	Apr 6	3377.57	7.1%
1993	Sep 16	3630.85	**Sep 25**	3543.11	– 2.4%	**Mar 27**	3774.73	6.5%
1994	Sep 6	3898.70	Sep 15	3953.88	1.4%	**Apr 15**	4208.18	6.4%
1995	Sep 25	4769.93	Oct 4	4740.67	– 0.6%	Apr 4	5682.88	19.9%
1996	**Sep 14**	5838.52	Sep 23	5894.74	1.0%	Apr 22	6833.59	15.9%
1997	Oct 2	8027.53	**Oct 11**	8045.21	0.2%	**Apr 11**	8994.86	11.8%
1998	Sep 21	7933.25	Sep 30	7842.62	– 1.1%	Apr 1	9832.51	25.4%
1999	**Sep 11**	11028.43	Sep 20	10823.90	– 1.9%	Apr 20	10844.05	0.2%
2000	**Sep 30**	10650.92	Oct 9	10568.43	– 0.8%	**Apr 8**	9791.09	– 7.4%
2001	Sep 18	8903.40	Sep 27	8681.42	– 2.5%	Mar 28	10403.94	19.8%
2002	**Sep 7**	8427.20	Sep 16	8380.18	– 0.6%	Apr 17	8337.65	– 0.5%
2003	**Sep 27**	9313.08	Oct 6	9594.98	3.0%	Apr 6	10570.81	10.2%
2004	Sep 16	10244.49	**Sep 25**	10047.24	– 1.9%	**Apr 24**	10157.71	1.1%
2005	Oct 4	10441.11	Oct 13	10216.59	– 2.2%	Apr 13	11137.65	9.0%
2006	**Sep 23**	11508.10	Oct 2	11670.35	1.4%	Apr 3	12510.30	7.2%
Bold=Saturday or Sunday				**Average**	**– 0.4%**			**7.1%**
If on Saturday or Sunday prior close is used				**# Up**	**16**			**25**
				# Down	**20**			**11**

We present the data back to 1971 and when the holiday falls on a weekend the prior market close is used. It's no coincidence that Rosh Hashanah and Yom Kippur fall in September and/or October, two dangerous and opportune months. We then took it a step further and calculated the return from Yom Kippur to Passover, which conveniently occurs in March or April, right near the end of our "Best Six Months" strategy.

Perhaps it's Talmudic wisdom, but selling stocks before the eight-day span of the high holidays has avoided many declines, especially during uncertain times. While being long Yom Kippur to Passover has produced more than twice as many advances, averaging gains of 7.1%. It often pays to be a contrarian when old bromides are tossed around, *buying* instead of *selling* Yom Kippur.

SEPTEMBER

MONDAY

D 38.1
S 47.6
N 52.4

22

There is always plenty of capital for those who can create practical plans for using it.
— Napoleon Hill (Author, *Think and Grow Rich*, 1883-1970)

Week After September Triple Witching Awful — Dow Down 14 of Last 17

TUESDAY

D 38.1
S 42.9
N 47.6

23

Our philosophy here is identifying change, anticipating change. Change is what drives earnings growth, and if you identify the underlying change, you recognize the growth before the market, and the deceleration of that growth.
— Peter Vermilye (Baring America asset management, 1987)

WEDNESDAY

D 47.6
S 42.9
N 42.9

24

Your emotions are often a reverse indicator of what you ought to be doing. — John F. Hindelong (Dillon, Reed)

Historically September Has Closed Poorly

THURSDAY

D 57.1
S 57.1
N 52.4

25

Keep away from people who try to belittle your ambitions. Small people always do that, but the really great make you feel that you, too, can become great.
— Mark Twain (1835-1910, pen name of Samuel Longhorne Clemens, American novelist and satirist)

FRIDAY

D 57.1
S 61.9
N 42.9

26

*A day will come when all nations on our continent will form a European brotherhood...
A day will come when we shall see...the United States of Europe...reaching out for each other across the seas.*
— Victor Hugo (French novelist, playwright, *Hunchback of Notre Dame* and *Les Misérables*, 1802-1885)

SATURDAY

27

October Almanac Investor Seasonalities: See Pages 114 & 116

SUNDAY

28

OCTOBER ALMANAC

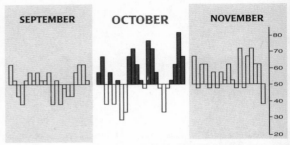

OCTOBER	NOVEMBER
S M T W T F S	S M T W T F S
1 2 3 4	1
5 6 7 8 9 10 11	2 3 4 5 6 7 8
12 13 14 15 16 17 18	9 10 11 12 13 14 15
19 20 21 22 23 24 25	16 17 18 19 20 21 22
26 27 28 29 30 31	23 24 25 26 27 28 29
	30

Market Probability Chart above is a graphic representation of the S&P 500 Recent Market Probability Calendar on page 124.

◆ Known as the jinx month because of crashes in 1929, 1987, the 554-point drop on October 27, 1997, back-to-back massacres in 1978 and 1979 and Friday the 13th in 1989 ◆ Yet October is a "bear killer" and turned the tide in 11 post-WWII bear markets: 1946, 1957, 1960, 1962, 1966, 1974, 1987, 1990, 1998, 2001 and 2002 ◆ Worst six months of the year ends with October (page 48) ◆ No longer worst month (pages 44 & 56) ◆ Best Dow & S&P month last 10 years ◆ October is a great time to buy ◆ Big October gains five years 1999-2003 after atrocious Septembers ◆ Can get into Best Six Months earlier using MACD (page 50)

October Vital Statistics

	DJIA		S&P 500		NASDAQ		Russell 1K		Russell 2K	
Rank	7		6		7		6		10	
Up	33		34		19		18		15	
Down	24		23		17		10		13	
Avg % Change	0.6%		0.9%		0.6%		1.1%		−0.4%	
Election Year	0.3%		0.6%		−0.1%		1.0%		−0.1%	
Best & Worst October										
	% Change		% Change		% Change		% Change		% Change	
Best	1982	10.7	1974	16.3	1974	17.2	1982	11.3	1982	14.1
Worst	1987	−23.2	1987	−21.8	1987	−27.2	1987	−21.9	1987	−30.8
Best & Worst October Weeks										
Best	10/11/74	12.6	10/11/74	14.1	10/11/74	9.5	10/16/98	7.6	10/16/98	7.7
Worst	10/23/87	−13.2	10/23/87	−12.2	10/23/87	−19.2	10/23/87	−12.9	10/23/87	−20.4
Best & Worst October Days										
Best	10/21/87	10.2	10/21/87	9.1	10/13/00	7.9	10/21/87	8.9	10/21/87	7.6
Worst	10/19/87	−22.6	10/19/87	−20.5	10/19/87	−11.4	10/19/87	−19.0	10/19/87	−12.5
First Trading Day of Expiration Week: 1980-2006										
Record (#Up - #Down)	23-4		21-6		20-7		22-5		23-4	
Current streak	U7		U5		U5		U5		U17	
Avg % Change	0.67		0.60		0.41		0.57		0.35	
Options Expiration Day: 1980-2006										
Record (#Up - #Down)	3-14		14-13		15-12		14-13		13-14	
Current streak	D2		U3		U3		U3		D1	
Avg % Change	−0.13		−0.25		−0.13		−0.24		−0.05	
Options Expiration Week: 1980-2006										
Record (#Up - #Down)	18-9		18-9		15-12		18-9		16-11	
Current streak	U1		U1		D1		U1		D3	
Avg % Change	0.63		0.63		0.72		0.62		0.46	
Week After Options Expiration: 1980-2006										
Record (#Up - #Down)	11-16		10-17		13-14		10-17		11-16	
Current streak	U2		U2		U3		U2		U2	
Avg % Change	−0.61		−0.59		−0.62		−0.60		−0.73	
First Trading Day Performance										
% of Time Up	49.1		49.1		50.0		53.6		50.0	
Avg % Change	0.13		0.13		−0.01		0.45		−0.07	
Last Trading Day Performance										
% of Time Up	54.4		56.1		69.4		64.3		75.0	
Avg % Change	0.11		0.21		0.65		0.52		0.72	

Dow & S&P 1950-June 2006, NASDAQ 1971-June 2006, Russell 1K & 2K 1979-June 2006.

October has killed many a bear
Buy tech stocks and soon wear a grin ear to ear

SEPTEMBER/OCTOBER

Q3 End Brings Institutional Portfolio Window Dressing & Heavy Selling

MONDAY

D 57.1
S 61.9
N 52.4

29

Bankruptcy was designed to forgive stupidity, not reward criminality.
— William P. Barr (Verizon General Counsel, calling for government liquidation of MCI-WorldCom in Chap. 7, 4/14/2003)

Rosh Hashanah

TUESDAY

D 47.6
S 52.4
N 57.1

30

Marketing is our No. 1 priority... A marketing campaign isn't worth doing unless it serves three purposes.
It must grow the business, create news, and enhance our image. — James Robinson III (American Express)

First Trading Day in October, Dow Down 2 in a Row
After Being Up 4.6% 2002, 2.1% 2003, 1.1% 2004

WEDNESDAY

D 61.9
S 57.1
N 52.4

1

When you get to the end of your rope, tie a knot and hang on. — Franklin D. Roosevelt (32nd U.S. president, 1882-1945)

October Ends Dow & S&P "Worst Six Months" (Pages 44, 48, 50 & 147)
& NASDAQ "Worst Four Months" (Pages 56, 58 & 148)

THURSDAY

D 52.4
S 66.7
N 61.9

2

Good luck is what happens when preparation meets opportunity, bad luck is what happens when
lack of preparation meets a challenge. — Paul Krugman (Economist, *NY Times* Op-Ed March 3, 2006)

FRIDAY

D 38.1
S 38.1
N 52.4

3

All you need to succeed is a yellow pad and a pencil. — Andre Meyer (Top deal maker at Lazard Freres)

SATURDAY

4

SUNDAY

5

Evidence-Based Technical Analysis: Applying the Scientific Method and Statistical Inference to Trading Signals
By David Aronson

THE BEST INVESTMENT BOOK OF THE YEAR
Reviewed by Yale Hirsch

An endorsement by Victor Niederhoffer says, "Without qualification this book should be in every serious market practitioner's collection." As technical analysis (TA) is the study of recurring stock market patterns with the intent of forecasting future price movements, Aronson asserts that many traders are using TA methods that are based on undisciplined research and can improve their results by applying the scientific method.

The book is organized in two sections. Part One establishes the methodological, philosophical, psychological, and statistical foundations of Evidence-Based Technical Analysis (EBTA). Part Two demonstrates EBTA with a case study that tests 6,402 binary buy/sell rules on the S&P 500 for 25 years of historical data.

Mr. Aronson recently impressed me when he analyzed the Best Six Months pattern I discovered in 1986 from data starting in 1950. Aronson and his colleague, Dr. Timothy Masters, put our Best Six Months Switching Strategy (page 48) through its paces and back-tested it using their scientific method to 1987, the year after I published the strategy.

They found that from 1987 through April 2006 the S&P 500 generated an annualized return of 16.3% during our Best Six Months compared to 3.9% for the Worst Six Months. Their analysis also found our Six-Month Switching Strategy to be sound, valuable and to have predictive power. The returns were considered to be statistically significant, unlike any of the 6,402 rules tested for the book.

Aronson's testing methods are in stark contrast to other "backward" tests that go back to 1925, or even 1896 and say, "Ah ha! The 80-year back-tested period (or 109-year) proves the pattern doesn't work" Exogenous factors as well as cultural shifts must also be considered. Farming made August the best month from 1900-1951. Since 1987 it is the worst S&P month. The onset of war with Iraq in early 2003 gave the Worst Six Months a better return.

Evidence-Based Technical Analysis does not derail technical analysis; it actually strengthens it with a rigorous and empirical system for verifying trading systems. This book provides traders and technical analysts with a more effective back-testing methodology for developing sound trading systems.

SAVE 20% at the *Stock Trader's Almanac* bookstore at
www.stocktradersalmanac.com by using Promo Code 8-4024.

OCTOBER

ober Is the Best Month Since 1998

MONDAY

D 61.9
S 57.1
N 61.9

6

acks near the 30-week moving average are often good times to take action. — Michael Burke (*Investors Intelligence*)

rt Looking for MACD Buy Signal (Pages 50 & 58)
anac Investor Subscribers Are Emailed Alert When It Triggers

TUESDAY

D 42.9
S 38.1
N 42.9

7

dology is the last refuge of a sterile mind. — Marianne L. Simmel (Psychologist)

WEDNESDAY

D 52.4
S 52.4
N 57.1

8

nothing grander, better exercise...more positive proof of the past, the triumphant result of faith in humankind,
well-contested national election. — Walt Whitman (American poet, 1819-1892)

Kippur

THURSDAY

D 33.3
S 28.6
N 42.9

9

ss is going from failure to failure without loss of enthusiasm. — Winston Churchill (British statesman, 1874-1965)

FRIDAY

D 28.6
S 33.3
N 47.6

10

ry generation there has to be some fool who will speak the truth as he sees it.
ris Pasternak (Russian writer and poet, 1958 Nobel Laureate in Literature, *Doctor Zhivago*, 1890-1960)

SATURDAY

11

SUNDAY

12

YEAR'S TOP INVESTMENT BOOKS

Evidence-Based Technical Analysis: Applying the Scientific Method and Statistical Inference to Trading Signals, David Aronson, Wiley, $95. <u>Best Investment Book of the Year</u>. *Page 92.*

Trend Following: How Great Traders Make Millions in Up or Down Markets, Michael W. Covel, FT Press, Soft, $17.99. Notes the traits, tactics and wisdom of a score of successful traders, including many well-known names.

The Three Skills of Top Trading: Behavioral Systems Building, Pattern Recognition, and Mental State Management, Hank Pruden, Wiley, $75. Very worthwhile read for any full-time trader. A third of the book is devoted to the techniques of Richard D. Wyckoff founder of the *Magazine of Wall Street.*

Anatomy of the Bear: Lessons from Wall Street's Four Great Bottoms, Russell Napier, CLSA Books, Soft, $34.95. Great information for those who like to see the major swings between undervaluation and overvaluation. The four bottoms are 1921, 1932, 1949, and 1982. Was the last major bottom in 2002, or is it yet to come?

The Only Three Questions That Count: Investing by Knowing What Others Don't, Ken Fisher, Wiley, $27.95. *Forbes* columnist and manager of $35 billion, Fisher has outperformed the S&P over the past 10 years, so we should pay attention to his ideas.

Where Have All the Leaders Gone? Lee Iacocca, Scribner, $25. It is hard to resist the latest book by one of America's greatest business leaders. Iacocca discusses his Nine Cs of Leadership: Curiosity, Creativity, Communication, Character, Courage, Conviction, Charisma, Competence, and Common Sense.

Candlestick and Pivot Point Trading Triggers + CD-ROM: Setups for Stock, Forex, and Futures Markets, John L. Person, Wiley, $80. Teaches you how to keep things simple to become a better trader. We rated his previous book highly in 2005.

Taking Your IRA to the Next Level: Securing Above Average Returns in Tax Sheltered Accounts, Humphrey Lloyd, Traders Press E-Book, $49.95. Dr. Lloyd did just that while Chief Pathologist at Beverly MA Hospital. Has an enormous command of strategies and indicators. Friends with a wide circle of top professional moneymakers.

Capital Ideas Evolving, Peter L. Bernstein, Wiley, $29.95. The markets are obviously changing. An analysis of the major financial theorists and how they influence managers of trillions of dollars worldwide. Investors and traders, "meet your tough competition!" Bernstein is one of the Street's sharpest minds.

The Black Swan: The Impact of the Highly Improbable, Nassim Nicholas Taleb, Random House, $26.95. In the *NY Times* book review Gregg Easterbrook says, "Taleb proclaims that the unexpected is the key to understanding not just financial markets but history itself." We rated his previous book highly in 2003.

(continued on page 96)

OCTOBER

Columbus Day (Bond Market Closed)
Monday Before October Expiration, Dow Up 23 of 27 and 7 Straight

MONDAY
D 66.7
S 66.7
N 76.2
13

...hold, my son, with what little wisdom the world is ruled.
— Count Axel Gustafsson Oxenstierna (1648 letter to his son at conclusion of Thirty Years War, 1583-1654)

TUESDAY
D 71.4
S 71.4
N 66.7
14

...om very early on, I understood that you can touch a piece of paper once...if you touch it twice, you're dead.
...erefore, paper only touches my hand once. After that, it's either thrown away, acted on or given to somebody else.
— Manuel Fernandez (Businessman, *Investor's Business Daily*)

WEDNESDAY
D 66.7
S 61.9
N 57.1
15

...ery man with a new idea is a crank until the idea succeeds.
— Mark Twain (American novelist and satirist, pen name of Samuel Longhorne Clemens, 1835-1910)

THURSDAY
D 47.6
S 52.4
N 42.9
16

...ttle minds are tamed and subdued by misfortune; but great minds rise above them.
— Washington Irving (American writer, *The Legend of Sleepy Hollow*, U.S. ambassador Spain 1842-46, 1783-1859)

October Expiration Day, Dow Up 4 of Last 7 — Down 267 Points in 1999

FRIDAY
D 52.4
S 47.6
N 38.1
17

...u must automate, emigrate, or evaporate. — James A. Baker (General Electric)

SATURDAY
18

...rash of October 19, 1987, Dow Down 22.6% in One Day

SUNDAY
19

YEAR'S TOP INVESTMENT BOOKS

(continued from page 94)

Point & Figure Charting: The Essential Application for Forecasting and Tracking Market Prices, Thomas J. Dorsey, Wiley, $65.The world's foremost expert on Point and Figure charting shows how it is done with stocks, ETFs, and market indicators.

The Last Tycoons: The Secret History of Lazard Frères & Co., William D. Cohan, Doubleday, $29.95. Compelling history of the storied investment bank from its beginnings as a New Orleans dry goods retailer in 1848 to Wall Street powerhouse packed with intrigue and insights into the world of high finance. Should make a sizzling summer read.

The Halo Effect: ... and the Eight Other Business Delusions That Deceive Managers, Phil Rosenzweig, Free Press, $25. Not the usual pablum. Sharp critique of existing management dogma that professes success still comes from old fashioned savvy, execution and a bit of luck.

The Options Doctor: Option Strategies for Every Kind of Market, Jeanette Schwarz Young, Wiley, $55. How to use options to create and protect portfolio profits in every market environment.

India: An Investor's Guide to the Next Economic Superpower, Aaron Chaze, Wiley, $35. The magic of capitalism at work. India could turn out to be one of the major success stories of the 21st century. What are the opportunities? What are the threats? See globalization at work. Enormous potential for investors who think outside the box.

Rocking Wall Street: Four Powerful Strategies that Will Shake Up the Way You Invest, Gary Marks, Wiley, $24.95. Unusual approaches to protect you from the hype masters and media "experts," and making hedging techniques the rule, not the exception.

A Demon of Our Own Design: Markets, Hedge Funds, and the Perils of Financial Innovation, Richard Bookstaber, Wiley, $27.95. This designer of some complex options and derivatives argues that many financial innovations and regulations that are supposed to level the playing field instead make the markets more dangerous for all the players.

The CRB Encyclopedia of Commodity and Financial Prices, Commodity Research Bureau, Wiley, $200. A treasure-trove of charts and data on all commodities traded. The encyclopedia is endorsed by Jim Rogers, one of the most fabulously successful commodity traders of all time. We don't see how anyone can trade commodities without having this volume, or the equivalent.

A Random Walk Down Wall Street: The Time-Tested Strategy for Successful Investing, Ninth Edition, Burton G. Malkiel, Norton, $29.95. A new revised edition of the famous classic. Very well done, but if everyone bought index funds and all brokers, fundamentalists and technicians were dismissed, what a boring world it would be. The 4-year presidential cycle, "Best Six Months," and other recurring patterns show that the market is far from always being random.

Don't Make Another Move Without the Almanac Investor Advantage!

SIGN-UP TODAY FOR THE ALMANAC INVESTOR PLATFORM

THE ALMANAC INVESTOR PLATFORM INCLUDES...

■ **The Almanac Investor Newsletter**—This monthly newsletter is designed to update and expand the proven strategies outlined in the Almanac. Each issue provides market timing, seasonal strategies, small-cap growth stocks and undervalued seasonal equities, and investment strategies focusing on ETFs.

■ **Interactive Online Research Tools and Reports**—View daily, weekly, monthly, and annual reports based on historical performance and obtain historical data downloads from each report. These handy research tools allow Almanac Investors to do their own historical research, update Almanac market indicators and strategies, as well as create their own.

■ **E-mail Alerts**—You will receive e-mail alerts such as the January Barometer, MACD Seasonal Buy and Sell Signals, stock and strategy updates, the Free-Lunch Menu, and so much more!

Receive your FREE copy of *Stock Trader's Almanac* when you subscribe to the Almanac Investor Platform TODAY for an annual rate of $179.95! That's a 40% savings off the regular $299 annual fee.

EXCLUSIVE ALMANAC INVESTOR PLATFORM TOOLS

Can you afford to ignore over 40 years of financial expertise? Few can and that's why we urge you to become a subscriber to Almanac Investor Platform. As a subscriber you'll have access to proprietary tools such as:

- **The Barometer Tool** devised by Yale Hirsch in 1972 allows you to test the January Barometer. The January Barometer indicator has a 90.9% accuracy ratio.
- **The MACD Calculator** (**M**oving **A**verage **C**onvergence/**D**ivergence) allows you to measure market sentiment for clues of trend reversals or continuation. You can track and confirm entry and exit points for the Best Months Switching Strategy.
- **The Year in Review Tool** allows you to observe daily, weekly and monthly trends.
- **Market & Stocks Tool** allows you to track your own portfolio and get updated information on nearly any stock, ETF, mutual fund.
- **Almanac Investor (AI) Watch List** allows you to create your own watch list.

These great tools and so much more are available to you at **stocktradersalmanac.c**
Take advantage of these proprietary tools by subscribing *today!*

IT'S EASY TO SUBSCRIBE...

- **Online at stocktradersalmanac.com using promo code STA8**
- **Call us toll-free at 800-356-5016**
- **Fax us at 800-597-3299**
- **Mail the self-addressed card on the reverse side to our attention**

OCTOBER

🐃 **MONDAY**
D 71.4
S 76.2
N 71.4
20

Sometimes the best investments are the ones you don't make.
— Donald Trump (Real estate mogul and entrepreneur, *Trump: How to Get Rich*, 2004)

🐃 **TUESDAY**
D 61.9
S 71.4
N 57.1
21

What technology does is make people more productive. It doesn't replace them.
— Michael Bloomberg (Founder Bloomberg, philanthropist, New York Mayor)

Late October Is Time to Buy Depressed Stocks, Especially Techs and Small Caps

WEDNESDAY
D 47.6
S 57.1
N 57.1
22

The two most abundant elements in the universe are Hydrogen and Stupidity. — Harlan Ellison (Science fiction writer, b. 1934)

THURSDAY
D 42.9
S 47.6
N 42.9
23

Drawing on my fine command of language, I said nothing.
— Robert Benchley (American writer, actor and humorist, 1889-1945)

🐻 **FRIDAY**
D 47.6
S 33.3
N 33.3
24

Early in March (1960), Dr. Arthur F. Burns called on me...Burns' conclusion was that unless some decisive action was taken, and taken soon, we were heading for another economic dip which would hit its low point in October, just before the elections.
— Richard M. Nixon (37th U.S. president, *Six Crises*, 1913-1994)

SATURDAY
25

SUNDAY
26

NOVEMBER ALMANAC

NOVEMBER							DECEMBER						
S	M	T	W	T	F	S	S	M	T	W	T	F	S
						1		1	2	3	4	5	6
2	3	4	5	6	7	8	7	8	9	10	11	12	13
9	10	11	12	13	14	15	14	15	16	17	18	19	20
16	17	18	19	20	21	22	21	22	23	24	25	26	27
23	24	25	26	27	28	29	28	29	30	31			
30													

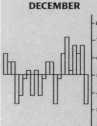

OCTOBER　　NOVEMBER　　DECEMBER

Market Probability Chart above is a graphic representation of the S&P 500 Recent Market Probability Calendar on page 12

◆ #1 S&P month and #3 on Dow since 1950, #2 on NASDAQ since 1971 (pages 44 & 56) ◆ Start of the Best Six Months of the year (page 48), NASDAQ's Eight Months and Best Three (pages 147 & 148) ◆ Simple timing indicator almost triples Best Six Months strategy (page 50), doubles NASDAQ's Best Eight (page 56) ◆ Election Novembers #1 for Dow and S&P, but #7 on NASDAQ thanks to Y2K's tech wreck ◆ Day before and after Thanksgiving Day combined, only 10 losses in 55 years (page 102) ◆ 2000 worst election year since Truman upsets Dewey in 1948 following first undecided presidential election since 1888 ◆ Last 8 other Republican victories averaged 3.0% on S&P, 7 Democrats 0.4% (page 36) ◆ 2003 broke 10-year Dow winning streak week before Thanksgiving, up last 2

November Vital Statistics

	DJIA	S&P 500	NASDAQ	Russell 1K	Russell 2K
Rank	3	1	2	1	2
Up	39	39	25	21	19
Down	18	18	11	7	9
Avg % Change	1.7%	1.8%	2.2%	2.2%	2.6%
Election Year	2.1%	2.0%	0.4%	1.7%	1.5%

Best & Worst November

	% Change		% Change		% Change		% Change		% Change	
Best	1962	10.1	1980	10.2	2001	14.2	1980	10.1	2002	8.8
Worst	1973	−14.0	1973	−11.4	2000	−22.9	2000	−9.3	2000	−10.4

Best & Worst November Weeks

		% Change		% Change		% Change		% Change		% Change
Best	11/2/62	6.3	11/5/82	6.3	11/5/82	6.8	11/5/82	6.4	11/5/82	6.6
Worst	1/2/73	−5.3	11/23/73	−4.3	11/10/00	−12.2	11/10/00	−4.9	11/10/00	−5.3

Best & Worst November Days

		% Change		% Change		% Change		% Change		% Change
Best	11/26/63	4.5	11/26/63	4.0	11/14/00	5.8	11/3/82	3.7	11/24/00	3.1
Worst	11/30/87	−4.0	11/30/87	−4.2	11/8/00	−5.4	11/30/87	−4.1	11/30/87	−3.4

First Trading Day of Expiration Week: 1980-2006

	DJIA	S&P 500	NASDAQ	Russell 1K	Russell 2K
Record (#Up - #Down)	14-13	12-15	11-16	13-14	12-15
Current streak	U3	U1	U1	U1	U1
Avg % Change	0.02	0.01	−0.06	−0.01	−0.11

Options Expiration Day: 1980-2006

	DJIA	S&P 500	NASDAQ	Russell 1K	Russell 2K
Record (#Up - #Down)	16-11	15-12	13-14	15-12	12-15
Current streak	U2	U2	D1	U2	D1
Avg % Change	−0.01	−0.07	−0.19	−0.08	−0.11

Options Expiration Week: 1980-2006

	DJIA	S&P 500	NASDAQ	Russell 1K	Russell 2K
Record (#Up - #Down)	18-9	17-10	15-12	16-11	15-12
Current streak	U2	U2	U2	U2	U2
Avg % Change	0.58	0.43	0.42	0.42	0.17

Week After Options Expiration: 1980-2006

	DJIA	S&P 500	NASDAQ	Russell 1K	Russell 2K
Record (#Up - #Down)	17-10	17-10	18-9	18-9	16-11
Current streak	D1	D1	U6	U6	U6
Avg % Change	0.66	0.53	0.64	0.51	0.55

First Trading Day Performance

	DJIA	S&P 500	NASDAQ	Russell 1K	Russell 2K
% of Time Up	64.9	64.9	66.7	75.0	71.4
Avg % Change	0.36	0.39	0.43	0.61	0.51

Last Trading Day Performance

	DJIA	S&P 500	NASDAQ	Russell 1K	Russell 2K
% of Time Up	52.6	52.6	66.7	42.9	71.4
Avg % Change	0.02	0.06	−0.19	−0.17	0.02

Dow & S&P 1950-April 2007, NASDAQ 1971-April 2007, Russell 1K & 2K 1979-April 2007.

*Astute investors always smile and remember
When stocks seasonally start soaring, and salute November*

MONDAY

D 42.9
S 47.6
N 33.3

27

The mind is not a vessel to be filled but a fire to be kindled.
— Plutarch (Greek biographer and philosopher, Parallel Lives, 46-120 AD)

1929 Crash October 28 & 29, Dow Down 23.0% in Two Days

TUESDAY

D 42.9
S 52.4
N 38.1

28

Develop interest in life as you see it; in people, things, literature, music — the world is so rich, simply throbbing with rich treasures, beautiful souls and interesting people. Forget yourself. — Henry Miller (American writer, Tropic of Cancer, Tropic of Capricorn, 1891-1980)

WEDNESDAY

D 66.7
S 61.9
N 47.6

29

Choose a job you love, and you will never have to work a day in your life. — Confucius (Chinese philosopher, 551-478 B.C.)

THURSDAY

D 76.2
S 81.0
N 71.4

30

An entrepreneur tends to lie some of the time. An entrepreneur in trouble tends to lie most of the time. — Anonymous

Halloween

FRIDAY

D 47.6
S 66.7
N 71.4

31

I invest in people, not ideas; I want to see fire in the belly and intellect. — Arthur Rock (First venture capitalist)

November Almanac Investor Seasonalities: See Pages 114 & 116

SATURDAY

1

Daylight Saving Time Ends

SUNDAY

2

TAKE ADVANTAGE OF DOWN FRIDAY/ DOWN MONDAY WARNING

For market professionals and serious traders, Fridays and Mondays are the most important days of the week. Friday is the day for squaring positions — trimming longs or covering shorts before taking off for the weekend. Pros want to limit their exposure (particularly to stocks that are not acting well) since there could be unfavorable developments before trading resumes two or more days later.

Monday is important because the market then has the chance to reflect any weekend news, plus what traders think after digesting the previous week's action and the many Monday morning research and strategy comments.

We've been watching Friday-Monday market behavior for over 30 years. In this time we have observed that a down Friday followed by down Monday is often an important market inflection point that exhibits a clearly negative bias and frequently coincides with market tops and on a few climactic occasions, such as in October 2002, near major market bottoms.

One simple way to get a quick reading on which way the market may be heading is to keep track of the performance of the Dow Jones Industrial Average on Fridays and the following Mondays. Since 1995 there have been 126 occurrences of Down Friday/Down Monday (DF/DM) with 31 falling in the bear market years of 2001 and 2002 producing an average decline of 12.7%.

DOWN FRIDAY/DOWN MONDAYS

Year	Total Number Down Friday/ Down Monday	Subsequent Average % Dow Loss*	Average Number of Days it took
1995	8	– 1.2%	18
1996	9	– 3.0%	28
1997	6	– 5.1%	45
1998	9	– 6.4%	47
1999	9	– 6.4%	39
2000	11	– 6.6%	32
2001	13	– 13.5%	53
2002	18	– 11.9%	54
2003	9	– 3.0%	17
2004	9	– 3.7%	51
2005	10	– 3.0%	37
2006	11	– 2.0%	14
2007**	4	– 4.2%	16
Average	**10**	**– 5.4%**	**35**

* Over next 3 months, ** Ending May 4, 2007

To illustrate how Down Friday/Down Monday can telegraph market infection points we created the chart below of the Dow Jones Industrials from November 2005 to April 2007 with arrows pointing to occurrences of DF/DM. Use DF/DM as a warning to examine market conditions carefully.

DOW JONES INDUSTRIALS (November 2005 – April 2007)

Arrows Indicate Down Friday/Down Monday

NOVEMBER

First Trading Day November, Dow Down 2 in a Row After 4-Year Bull Run
Up 13 in a Row 1978-1990

MONDAY

D 66.7
S 66.7
N 71.4

3

prosperity is a great teacher; adversity a greater. — William Hazlitt (English essayist, 1778-1830)

Election Day

TUESDAY

D 42.9
S 47.6
N 47.6

4

Those who cast the votes decide nothing. Those who count the votes decide everything.
— Joseph Stalin (Ruler USSR 1929-1953, 1879-1953)

WEDNESDAY

D 61.9
S 61.9
N 81.0

5

A fanatic is one who can't change his mind and won't change the subject. — Winston Churchill (British statesman, 1874-1965)

THURSDAY

D 61.9
S 61.9
N 57.1

6

Life is what happens, while you're busy making other plans. — John Lennon (Beatle, 1940-1980)

November Begins Dow & S&P Best Six Months (Pages 44, 48, 50 & 147)
& NASDAQ Best Eight Months (Pages 56, 58 & 148)

FRIDAY

D 47.6
S 47.6
N 57.1

7

When you get into a tight place and everything goes against you, till it seems as though you could not hang on a minute longer, never give up then, for that is just the place and time that the tide will turn. — Harriet Beecher Stowe (American writer and abolitionist)

SATURDAY

8

SUNDAY

9

TRADING THE THANKSGIVING MARKET

For 35 years the combination of the Wednesday before Thanksgiving and the Friday after ha
a great track record, except for two occasions. Attributing this phenomenon to the warm "ho
iday spirit" was a no-brainer. But publishing it in the 1987 Almanac was the "kiss of death
Wednesday, Friday and Monday were all crushed, down 6.6% over the three days in 1987. Sinc
1988 Wednesday-Friday lost 7 of 19 times with a total Dow point-gain of 460.99 versus
Wednesday-Monday total Dow point-gain of 472.67 with only five losses. The best strateg
appears to be coming into the week long and exiting into strength Friday or Monday.

DOW JONES INDUSTRIALS BEFORE AND AFTER THANKSGIVING

	Tuesday Before	Wednesday Before		Friday After	Total Gain Dow Points	Dow Close	Next Monday
1952	− 0.18	1.54		1.22	2.76	283.66	0.04
1953	1.71	0.65		2.45	3.10	280.23	1.14
1954	3.27	1.89		3.16	5.05	387.79	0.72
1955	4.61	0.71		0.26	0.97	482.88	− 1.92
1956	− 4.49	− 2.16		4.65	2.49	472.56	− 2.27
1957	− 9.04	10.69		3.84	14.53	449.87	− 2.96
1958	− 4.37	8.63		8.31	16.94	557.46	2.61
1959	2.94	1.41		1.42	2.83	652.52	6.66
1960	− 3.44	1.37		4.00	5.37	606.47	− 1.04
1961	− 0.77	1.10		2.18	3.28	732.60	− 0.61
1962	6.73	4.31	**T**	7.62	11.93	644.87	− 2.81
1963	32.03	− 2.52		9.52	7.00	750.52	1.39
1964	− 1.68	− 5.21	**H**	− 0.28	− 5.49	882.12	6.69
1965	2.56	N/C		− 0.78	− 0.78	948.16	− 1.23
1966	− 3.18	1.84	**A**	6.52	8.36	803.34	− 2.18
1967	13.17	3.07		3.58	6.65	877.60	4.51
1968	8.14	− 3.17	**N**	8.76	5.59	985.08	− 1.74
1969	− 5.61	3.23		1.78	5.01	812.30	− 7.26
1970	5.21	1.98	**K**	6.64	8.62	781.35	12.74
1971	− 5.18	0.66		17.96	18.62	816.59	13.14
1972	8.21	7.29	**S**	4.67	11.96	1025.21	− 7.45
1973	− 17.76	10.08		− 0.98	9.10	854.00	− 29.05
1974	5.32	2.03	**G**	− 0.63	1.40	618.66	− 15.64
1975	9.76	3.15		2.12	5.27	860.67	− 4.33
1976	− 6.57	1.66	**I**	5.66	7.32	956.62	− 6.57
1977	6.41	0.78		1.12	1.90	844.42	− 4.85
1978	− 1.56	2.95	**V**	3.12	6.07	810.12	3.72
1979	− 6.05	− 1.80		4.35	2.55	811.77	16.98
1980	3.93	7.00	**I**	3.66	10.66	993.34	− 23.89
1981	18.45	7.90		7.80	15.70	885.94	3.04
1982	− 9.01	9.01	**N**	7.36	16.37	1007.36	− 4.51
1983	7.01	− 0.20		1.83	1.63	1277.44	− 7.62
1984	9.83	6.40	**G**	18.78	25.18	1220.30	− 7.95
1985	0.12	18.92		− 3.56	15.36	1472.13	− 14.22
1986	6.05	4.64		− 2.53	2.11	1914.23	− 1.55
1987	40.45	− 16.58		− 36.47	− 53.05	1910.48	− 76.93
1988	11.73	14.58		− 17.60	− 3.02	2074.68	6.76
1989	7.25	17.49		18.77	36.26	2675.55	19.42
1990	− 35.15	9.16		− 12.13	− 2.97	2527.23	5.94
1991	14.08	− 16.10	**D**	− 5.36	− 21.46	2894.68	40.70
1992	25.66	17.56		15.94	33.50	3282.20	22.96
1993	3.92	13.41	**A**	− 3.63	9.78	3683.95	− 6.15
1994	− 91.52	− 3.36		33.64	30.28	3708.27	31.29
1995	40.46	18.06	**Y**	7.23*	25.29	5048.84	22.04
1996	− 19.38	− 29.07		22.36*	− 6.71	6521.70	N/C
1997	41.03	− 14.17		28.35*	14.18	7823.13	189.98
1998	− 73.12	13.13		18.80*	31.93	9333.08	− 216.53
1999	− 93.89	12.54		− 19.26*	− 6.72	10988.91	− 40.99
2000	31.85	− 95.18		70.91*	− 24.27	10470.23	75.84
2001	− 75.08	− 66.70		125.03*	58.33	9959.71	23.04
2002	− 172.98	255.26		− 35.59*	219.67	8896.09	− 33.52
2003	16.15	15.63		2.89*	18.52	9782.46	116.59
2004	3.18	27.71		1.92*	29.63	10522.23	− 46.33
2005	51.15	44.66		15.53*	60.19	10931.62	− 40.90
2006	5.05	5.36		− 46.78*	− 41.42	12280.17	− 158.46

*Shortened trading day

102

NOVEMBER

MONDAY

D 61.9
S 57.1
N 57.1

10

A good new chairman of the Federal Reserve Bank is worth a $10 billion tax cut.
— Paul H. Douglas (U.S. senator, Illinois 1949-1967, 1892-1976)

Veterans' Day

TUESDAY

D 38.1
S 47.6
N 57.1

11

Never overpay for a stock. More money is lost than in any other way by projecting above-average growth and paying an extra multiple for it. — Charles Neuhauser (Bear Stearns)

WEDNESDAY

D 57.1
S 57.1
N 61.9

12

The worst bankrupt in the world is the person who has lost his enthusiasm. — H.W. Arnold

THURSDAY

D 57.1
S 52.4
N 57.1

13

Investors operate with limited funds and limited intelligence, they don't need to know everything. As long as they understand something better than others, they have an edge.
— George Soros (Financier, philanthropist, political activist, author and philosopher, b. 1930)

FRIDAY

D 66.7
S 61.9
N 61.9

14

There has never been a commercial technology like this (Internet) in the history of the world, whereby the minute you adopt it, it forces you to think and act globally. — Robert Hormats (Vice chairman, Goldman Sachs Int'l)

SATURDAY

15

SUNDAY

16

MOST OF THE SO-CALLED "JANUARY EFFECT" TAKES PLACE IN THE LAST HALF OF DECEMBER

Over the years we reported annually on the fascinating January Effect, showing that small-cap stocks handily outperformed large-cap stocks during January 40 out of 43 years between 1953 and 1995. Readers saw that "Cats and Dogs" on average quadrupled the returns of blue chips in this period. Then, the January Effect disappeared over the next four years.

Looking at the graph on page 106, comparing the Russell 1000 index of large capitalization stocks to the Russell 2000 smaller capitalization stocks, shows small cap stocks beginning to outperform the blue chips in mid-December. Narrowing the comparison down to half-month segments was an inspiration and proved to be quite revealing, as you can see in the table below.

20-YEAR AVERAGE RATES OF RETURN (DEC 1987 – FEB 2007)

From mid-Dec*	Russell 1000 Change	Annualized	Russell 2000 Change	Annualized
12/15-12/31	1.7%	47.1%	3.2%	105.8%
12/15-01/15	2.2	28.3	4.0	56.7
12/15-01/31	3.0	27.2	4.9	47.5
12/15-02/15	3.9	25.8	6.5	45.9
12/15-02/28	3.2	16.8	6.6	37.1
end-Dec*				
12/31-01/15	0.5	11.0	0.8	18.2
12/31-01/31	1.2	15.4	1.6	21.0
12/31-02/15	2.1	17.8	3.1	27.2
12/31-02/28	1.5	9.8	3.2	22.0

28-YEAR AVERAGE RATES OF RETURN (DEC 1979 – FEB 2007)

From mid-Dec*	Russell 1000 Change	Annualized	Russell 2000 Change	Annualized
12/15-12/31	1.5%	40.6%	2.8%	88.3%
12/15-01/15	2.5	32.7	4.5	65.6
12/15-01/31	3.2	28.2	5.3	50.2
12/15-02/15	3.9	25.1	6.8	47.0
12/15-02/28	3.5	18.5	7.0	39.7
end-Dec*				
12/31-01/15	0.9	20.7	1.6	39.6
12/31-01/31	1.6	21.0	2.4	32.9
12/31-02/15	2.4	20.5	3.9	35.2
12/31-02/28	2.0	12.9	4.0	27.3

* Mid-month dates are the 11th trading day of the month, month end dates are monthly closes.

Small-cap strength in the last half of December became even more magnified after the 1987 market crash. Note the dramatic shift in gains in the last half of December during the 20-year period starting in 1987, versus the 28 years from 1979 to 2007. With all the beaten down small stocks being dumped for tax loss purposes, it generally pays to get a head start on the January Effect in mid-December. You don't have to wait until December either; the small-cap sector often begins to turn around toward the end of October.

NOVEMBER

Monday Before November Expiration, Dow Up 3 in a Row After 5-Year Bear Run

MONDAY

D 57.1
S 52.4
N 38.1

17

The big guys are the status quo, not the innovators. — Kenneth L. Fisher (*Forbes* columnist)

TUESDAY

D 38.1
S 47.6
N 33.3

18

Knowing others is intelligence; knowing yourself is true wisdom. Mastering others is strength; mastering yourself is true power. — Lau Tzu (Shaolin monk, founder of Taoism, circa 6th-4th century B.C.)

Week Before Thanksgiving, Dow Up 12 of Last 14, 2003 –1.4% & 2004 –0.8%

WEDNESDAY

D 71.4
S 71.4
N 57.1

19

A cynic is a man who knows the price of everything and the value of nothing. — Oscar Wilde (Irish-born writer and wit, 1845-1900)

THURSDAY

D 47.6
S 47.6
N 57.1

20

Those heroes of finance are like beads on a string, when one slips off, the rest follow. — Henrik Ibsen (Norwegian playwright, 1828-1906)

November Expiration Day, Dow Up 4 of Last 5

FRIDAY

D 71.4
S 66.7
N 61.9

21

Eighty percent of success is showing up. — Woody Allen (Filmaker)

SATURDAY

22

SUNDAY

23

JANUARY EFFECT NOW STARTS IN MID-DECEMBER

Small-cap stocks tend to outperform big caps in January. Known as the "January Effect," the tendency is clearly revealed by the graph below. The 29 years of daily data for the Russell 2000 index of smaller companies are divided by the Russell 1000 index of largest companies. Then the 29 years are compressed into a single year to show an idealized yearly pattern. When the graph is descending, big blue chips are outperforming smaller companies; when the graph is rising, smaller companies are moving up faster than their larger brethren.

In a typical year the smaller fry stay on the sidelines while the big boys are on the field. Then, around late October, small stocks begin to wake up and in mid-December, they take off. So many year-end dividends, payouts and bonuses could be a factor. Other major moves are quite evident just before Labor Day — possibly because individual investors are back from vacations — and off the low points in late October and November. After a pause in mid-January, small caps take the lead through the beginning of March.

RUSSELL 2000/RUSSELL 1000 ONE-YEAR SEASONAL PATTERN

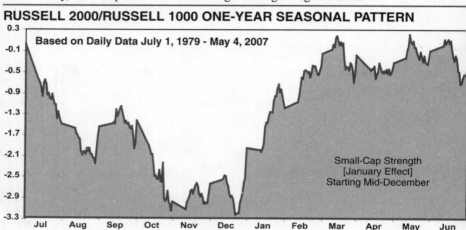

The bottom graph shows the actual ratio of the Russell 2000 divided by the Russell 1000 from 1979. Smaller companies had the upper hand for five years into 1983 as the last major bear trend wound to a close and the nascent bull market logged its first year. After falling behind for about eight years, they came back after the Persian Gulf War bottom in 1990, moving up until 1994 when big caps ruled the latter stages of the millennial bull. For six years the picture was bleak for small fry as the blue chips and tech stocks moved to stratospheric PE ratios. Small caps spiked in late 1999 and early 2000 and have been rising since the bubble burst. Note how the small cap advantage has waned at the outset of major bull moves and intensified during weak market times. As the current ratio has pulled back from near 1.1 broad market weakness may be indicated. Look for a clear move lower when the next major bull takes hold.

RUSSELL 2000/RUSSELL 1000 (1979 - APRIL 2007)

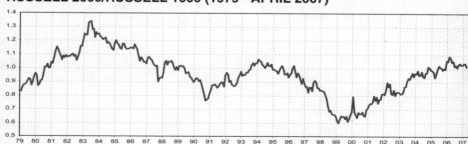

NOVEMBER

Trading Thanksgiving Market: Long into Weakness Prior,
Exit into Strength After (Page 102)

MONDAY
D 71.4
S 71.4
N 57.1
24

ge is a question of mind over matter. If you don't mind, it doesn't matter.
— Leroy Robert "Satchel" Paige (Negro League and Hall of Fame pitcher, 1906-1982)

TUESDAY
D 57.1
S 61.9
N 61.9
25

small debt produces a debtor; a large one, an enemy.
— Publilius Syrus (Syrian-born Roman mime and former slave, 83-43 B.C.)

WEDNESDAY
D 47.6
S 61.9
N 71.4
26

o profession requires more hard work, intelligence, patience, and mental discipline than successful speculation.
— Robert Rhea (The Dow Theory)

Thanksgiving (Market Closed)

THURSDAY
27

is not how right or how wrong you are that matters, but how much money you make when right and how much you do not lose
hen wrong. — George Soros (Financier, philanthropist, political activist, author and philosopher, b. 1930)

Shortened Trading Day)

FRIDAY
D 47.6
S 38.1
N 57.1
28

he knowledge of past times… is both an ornament and nutriment to the human mind.
— Leonardo da Vinci (Italian Renaissance polymath, 1452-1519)

SATURDAY
29

December Almanac Investor Seasonalities: See Pages 114 & 116

SUNDAY
30

DECEMBER ALMANAC

DECEMBER						
S	M	T	W	T	F	S
	1	2	3	4	5	6
7	8	9	10	11	12	13
14	15	16	17	18	19	20
21	22	23	24	25	26	27
28	29	30	31			

JANUARY
S	M	T	W	T	F	S
				1	2	3
4	5	6	7	8	9	10
11	12	13	14	15	16	17
18	19	20	21	22	23	24
25	26	27	28	29	30	31

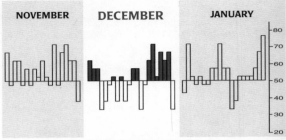

Market Probability Chart above is a graphic representation of the S&P 500 Recent Market Probability Calendar on page 124.

◆ #2 S&P and Dow month average gain 1.7% & 1.8% respectively since 1950 (page 44), #3 NASDAQ 1.9% since 1971 ◆ 2002 worst December since 1931, down over 6% Dow and S&P, –9.7% on NASDAQ (pages 152, 155 & 157) ◆ "Free lunch" served on Wall Street before Christmas (page 110) ◆ Small caps start to outperform larger caps near middle of month (pages 104 & 106) ◆ "Santa Claus Rally" visible in graph above and on page 112 ◆ In 1998 was part of best fourth quarter since 1928 (page 167) ◆ Election-year December's fare well; since 1950 Dow average 1.5%, S&P 1.2%; NASDAQ 1.4% since 1972

December Vital Statistics

	DJIA	S&P 500	NASDAQ	Russell 1K	Russell 2K
Rank	2	2	3	3	3
Up	41	43	21	22	22
Down	16	14	14	6	6
Avg % Change	1.8%	1.7%	1.9%	1.7%	2.6%
Election Year	1.5%	1.2%	1.4%	0.6%	2.6%
Best & Worst December					
	% Change	% Change	% Change	% Change	% Change
Best	1991 9.5	1991 11.2	1999 22.0	1991 11.2	1999 11.2
Worst	2002 –6.2	2002 –6.0	2002 –9.7	2002 –5.8	2002 –5.7
Best & Worst December Weeks					
Best	12/18/87 5.8	12/18/87 5.9	12/8/00 10.3	12/18/87 6.0	12/18/87 7.7
Worst	12/4/87 –7.5	12/6/74 –7.1	12/15/00 –9.1	12/4/87 –7.0	12/12/80 –6.5
Best & Worst December Days					
Best	12/14/87 3.5	12/5/00 3.9	12/5/00 10.5	12/5/00 4.4	12/5/00 4.6
Worst	12/3/87 –3.9	12/3/87 –3.5	12/20/00 –7.1	12/20/00 –3.4	12/8/80 –3.6
First Trading Day of Expiration Week: 1980-2006					
Record (#Up - #Down)	16-11	17-10	12-15	18-9	13-14
Current streak	U1	U3	U3	U3	U3
Avg % Change	0.29	0.26	0.08	0.22	–0.03
Options Expiration Day: 1980-2006					
Record (#Up - #Down)	19-8	19-8	18-9	19-8	16-11
Current streak	U1	U1	U1	U1	D3
Avg % Change	0.39	0.40	0.27	0.37	0.30
Options Expiration Week: 1980-2006					
Record (#Up - #Down)	22-5	20-7	14-13	19-8	12-15
Current streak	U6	U6	U1	U6	U1
Avg % Change	0.89	0.80	0.09	0.73	0.28
Week After Options Expiration: 1980-2006					
Record (#Up - #Down)	19-8	16-11	17-10	16-11	19-8
Current streak	D1	D1	D2	D1	D1
Avg % Change	0.76	0.43	0.70	0.46	0.84
First Trading Day Performance					
% of Time Up	49.1	52.6	63.9	57.1	57.1
Avg % Change	0.03	0.08	0.36	0.19	0.26
Last Trading Day Performance					
% of Time Up	54.4	64.9	80.6	57.1	78.6
Avg % Change	0.09	0.12	0.40	–0.09	0.52

Dow & S&P 1950-April 2007, NASDAQ 1971-April 2007, Russell 1K & 2K 1979-April 2007.

*If Santa Claus should fail to call
Bears may come to Broad and Wall*

DECEMBER

First Trading Day December, Dow 100+ Point Gains 2003-2005,
Down in 2006

MONDAY

D 57.1
S 61.9
N 76.2

1

No other wisdom is better than the financial markets themselves. They incorporate the total wisdom of everyone that has money that is willing to vote their wisdom every second of every day. — Don R. Hays (Hays Advisory, 3/14/07)

TUESDAY

D 57.1
S 57.1
N 66.7

2

Capitalism works because it encourages and rewards those who successfully take risks, adapt to change, and develop profitable opportunities. — Henry Blodget (former stock analyst, *NY Times* Op-Ed 12/20/06, *The Wall Street Self-Defense Manual*)

WEDNESDAY

D 52.4
S 57.1
N 66.7

3

Market risk tends to be poorly rewarded when market valuations are rich and interest rates are rising. — John P. Hussman, Ph.D. (Hussman Funds, 5/22/06)

THURSDAY

D 47.6
S 33.3
N 52.4

4

The investor who concentrated on the 50 stocks in the S&P 500 that are followed by the fewest Wall Street analysts wound up with a rousing 24.6% gain in [2006 versus] 13.6% [for] the S&P 500. — Rich Bernstein (Chief Investment Strategist, Merrill Lynch, *Barron's* 1/8/07)

FRIDAY

D 33.3
S 38.1
N 33.3

5

What people in the Middle East tell you in private is irrelevant. All that matters is what they will defend in public in their language. — Thomas L. Friedman (*NY Times* Foreign Affairs columnist, "Meet the Press" 12/17/06)

SATURDAY

6

SUNDAY

7

WALL STREET'S ONLY "FREE LUNCH" SERVED BEFORE CHRISTMAS

Investors tend to get rid of their losers near year-end for tax purposes, often hammering these stocks down to bargain levels. Over the years the *Almanac* has shown that NYSE stocks selling at their lows on December 15 will usually outperform the market by February 15 in the following year. Preferred stocks, closed-end funds, splits and new issues are eliminated. When there are a huge number of new lows, stocks down the most are selected, even though there are usually good reasons why some stocks have been battered.

BARGAIN STOCKS VS. THE MARKET*

Short Span* Late Dec - Jan/Feb	New Lows Late Dec	% Change Jan/Feb	% Change NYSE Composite	Bargain Stocks Advantage
1974-75	112	48.9%	22.1%	26.8%
1975-76	21	34.9	14.9	20.0
1976-77	2	1.3	− 3.3	4.6
1977-78	15	2.8	− 4.5	7.3
1978-79	43	11.8	3.9	7.9
1979-80	5	9.3	6.1	3.2
1980-81	14	7.1	− 2.0	9.1
1981-82	21	− 2.6	− 7.4	4.8
1982-83	4	33.0	9.7	23.3
1983-84	13	− 3.2	− 3.8	0.6
1984-85	32	19.0	12.1	6.9
1985-86	4	− 22.5	3.9	− 26.4
1986-87	22	9.3	12.5	− 3.2
1987-88	23	13.2	6.8	6.4
1988-89	14	30.0	6.4	23.6
1989-90	25	− 3.1	− 4.8	1.7
1990-91	18	18.8	12.6	6.2
1991-92	23	51.1	7.7	43.4
1992-93	9	8.7	0.6	8.1
1993-94	10	− 1.4	2.0	− 3.4
1994-95	25	14.6	5.7	8.9
1995-96	5	− 11.3	4.5	−15.8
1996-97	16	13.9	11.2	2.7
1997-98	29	9.9	5.7	4.2
1998-99	40	− 2.8	4.3	− 7.1
1999-00	26	8.9	− 5.4	14.3
2000-01	51	44.4	0.1	44.3
2001-02	12	31.4	− 2.3	33.7
2002-03	33	28.7	3.9	24.8
2003-04	15	16.7	2.3	14.4
2004-05	36	6.8	− 2.8	9.6
2005-06	71	12.0	2.6	9.4
2006-07	43	5.1	− 0.5	5.6
33-Year Totals		**444.7%**	**124.8%**	**319.9%**
Average		**13.5%**	**3.8%**	**9.7%**

* Dec 15 - Feb 15 (1974-1999), Dec 1999-2007 based on actual newsletter advice

In response to changing market conditions we tweaked the strategy the last eight years making our selections from stocks making new lows on the fourth-to-last trading day of the year some years, adding selections from NASDAQ, AMEX and the OTC Bulletin Board, and selling in mid-January some years. We email the lists of stocks and trading advice to our *Almanac Investor* newsletter subscribers.

Upon further review we have come to the conclusion that the most prudent course of action is to compile our list from the stocks making new lows on the Friday before Christmas, capitalizing on the Santa Claus Rally (page 112). This gives us the weekend to evaluate the issues in greater depth and weed out any glaringly problematic stocks. Subscribers will receive the list of stocks selected from the new lows made on December 21, 2007, via email.

This "Free Lunch" strategy is only an extremely short-term strategy reserved for the nimblest traders. It has performed better after market corrections and when there are more new lows to choose from. The object is to buy bargain stocks near their 52-week lows and sell any quick, generous gains, as these issues can often be real dogs.

Examination of December trades by NYSE members through the years shows they tend to buy on balance during this month, contrary to other months. See more in our *Almanac Investor Newsletters* at *stocktradersalmanac.com*.

DECEMBER

MONDAY
D 52.4
S 47.6
N 42.9
8

Don't put all your eggs in one basket. — (Market maxim)

TUESDAY
D 57.1
S 52.4
N 42.9
9

Put your eggs in one basket and watch the basket. — (An alternate strategy)

Small Cap Strength Starts in Mid-December (Pages 104 & 106)

WEDNESDAY
D 47.6
S 38.1
N 33.3
10

You try to be greedy when others are fearful, and fearful when others are greedy.
— Warren Buffett (CEO Berkshire Hathaway, investor & philanthropist, b. 1930)

THURSDAY
D 52.4
S 52.4
N 61.9
11

Life is like riding a bicycle. You don't fall off unless you stop peddling.
— Claude D. Pepper (U.S. senator, Florida 1936-1951, 1900-1989)

FRIDAY
D 42.9
S 38.1
N 33.3
12

Capitalism without bankruptcy is like Christianity without hell. — Frank Borman (CEO Eastern Airlines, April 1986)

SATURDAY
13

SUNDAY
14

IF SANTA CLAUS SHOULD FAIL TO CALL
BEARS MAY COME TO BROAD & WALL

Santa Claus tends to come to Wall Street nearly every year, bringing a short, sweet, respectable rally within the last five days of the year and the first two in January. This has been good for an average 1.5% gain since 1969 (1.5% since 1950). Santa's failure to show tends to precede bear markets, or times stocks could be purchased later in the year at much lower prices. We discovered this phenomenon in 1972.

DAILY % CHANGE IN S&P 500 AT YEAR END

| | Trading Days Before Year End | | | | | | First Days in January | | | Rally % |
	6	5	4	3	2	1	1	2	3	Change
1969	- 0.4	1.1	0.8	- 0.7	0.4	0.5	1.0	0.5	- 0.7	3.6
1970	0.1	0.6	0.5	1.1	0.2	- 0.1	- 1.1	0.7	0.6	1.9
1971	- 0.4	0.2	1.0	0.3	- 0.4	0.3	- 0.4	0.4	1.0	1.3
1972	- 0.3	- 0.7	0.6	0.4	0.5	1.0	0.9	0.4	- 0.1	3.1
1973	- 1.1	- 0.7	3.1	2.1	- 0.2	0.01	0.1	2.2	- 0.9	6.7
1974	- 1.4	1.4	0.8	- 0.4	0.03	2.1	2.4	0.7	0.5	7.2
1975	0.7	0.8	0.9	- 0.1	- 0.4	0.5	0.8	1.8	1.0	4.3
1976	0.1	1.2	0.7	- 0.4	0.5	0.5	- 0.4	- 1.2	- 0.9	0.8
1977	0.8	0.9	N/C	0.1	0.2	0.2	- 1.3	- 0.3	- 0.8	- 0.3
1978	0.03	1.7	1.3	- 0.9	- 0.4	- 0.2	0.6	1.1	0.8	3.3
1979	- 0.6	0.1	0.1	0.2	- 0.1	0.1	- 2.0	- 0.5	1.2	- 2.2
1980	- 0.4	0.4	0.5	- 1.1	0.2	0.3	0.4	1.2	0.1	2.0
1981	- 0.5	0.2	- 0.2	- 0.5	0.5	0.2	0.2	- 2.2	- 0.7	- 1.8
1982	0.6	1.8	- 1.0	0.3	- 0.7	0.2	- 1.6	2.2	0.4	1.2
1983	- 0.2	- 0.03	0.9	0.3	- 0.2	0.05	- 0.5	1.7	1.2	2.1
1984	- 0.5	0.8	- 0.2	- 0.4	0.3	0.6	- 1.1	- 0.5	- 0.5	- 0.6
1985	- 1.1	- 0.7	0.2	0.9	0.5	0.3	- 0.8	0.6	- 0.1	1.1
1986	- 1.0	0.2	0.1	- 0.9	- 0.5	- 0.5	1.8	2.3	0.2	2.4
1987	1.3	- 0.5	- 2.6	- 0.4	1.3	- 0.3	3.6	1.1	0.1	2.2
1988	- 0.2	0.3	- 0.4	0.1	0.8	- 0.6	- 0.9	1.5	0.2	0.9
1989	0.6	0.8	- 0.2	0.6	0.5	0.8	1.8	- 0.3	- 0.9	4.1
1990	0.5	- 0.6	0.3	- 0.8	0.1	0.5	- 1.1	- 1.4	- 0.3	- 3.0
1991	2.5	0.6	1.4	0.4	2.1	0.5	0.04	0.5	- 0.3	5.7
1992	- 0.3	0.2	- 0.1	- 0.3	0.2	- 0.7	- 0.1	- 0.2	0.04	- 1.1
1993	0.01	0.7	0.1	- 0.1	- 0.4	- 0.5	- 0.2	0.3	0.1	- 0.1
1994	0.01	0.2	0.4	- 0.3	0.1	- 0.4	- 0.03	0.3	- 0.1	0.2
1995	0.8	0.2	0.4	0.04	- 0.1	0.3	0.8	0.1	- 0.6	1.8
1996	- 0.3	0.5	0.6	0.1	- 0.4	- 1.7	- 0.5	1.5	- 0.1	0.1
1997	- 1.5	- 0.7	0.4	1.8	1.8	- 0.04	0.5	0.2	- 1.1	4.0
1998	2.1	- 0.2	- 0.1	1.3	- 0.8	- 0.2	- 0.1	1.4	2.2	1.3
1999	1.6	- 0.1	0.04	0.4	0.1	0.3	- 1.0	- 3.8	0.2	- 4.0
2000	0.8	2.4	0.7	1.0	0.4	- 1.0	- 2.8	5.0	- 1.1	5.7
2001	0.4	- 0.02	0.4	0.7	0.3	- 1.1	0.6	0.9	0.6	1.8
2002	0.2	- 0.5	- 0.3	- 1.6	0.5	0.05	3.3	- 0.05	2.2	1.2
2003	0.3	- 0.2	0.2	1.2	0.01	0.2	- 0.3	1.2	0.1	2.4
2004	0.1	- 0.4	0.7	- 0.01	0.01	- 0.1	- 0.8	- 1.2	- 0.4	-1.8
2005	0.4	0.04	- 1.0	0.1	- 0.3	- 0.5	1.6	0.4	0.002	0.4
2006	- 0.4	- 0.5	0.4	0.7	- 0.1	- 0.5	- 0.1	0.1	- 0.6	0.003
Avg	0.09	0.30	0.30	0.14	0.17	0.03	0.09	0.50	0.08	1.5

The couplet above was certainly on the mark in 1999, as the period suffered a horrendous 4.0% loss. On January 14, 2000, the Dow started its 33-month 37.8% slide to the October 2002 midterm election year bottom. NASDAQ cracked eight weeks later, falling 37.3% in 10 weeks, eventually dropping 77.9% by October 2002. This is reminiscent of the Dow during the Depression, when the Dow initially fell 47.9% in just over two months from 381.17 September 3, 1929, only to end down 89.2% at its 20th century low of 41.22 on July 8, 1932. Perhaps October 9, 2002, will prove to be the low for the 21st century. Saddam Hussein cancelled Christmas by invading Kuwait in 1990. Energy prices and Middle East terror woes may have grounded Santa in 2004. After an April low, 2005 registered one of the flattest years on record. Less bullishness on last day is due to last-minute portfolio restructuring. Pushing gains and losses into the next tax year often affects year's first trading day.

DECEMBER

Monday Before December Triple Witching, Dow Up 5 of Last 7

MONDAY

D 52.4
S 47.6
N 52.4

15

Resentment is like taking poison and waiting for the other person to die. — Malachy McCourt *(A Monk Swimming: A Memoir)*

TUESDAY

D 61.9
S 57.1
N 47.6

16

We are handicapped by policies based on old myths rather than current realities.
— James William Fulbright (U.S. senator, Arkansas 1944-1974, 1905-1995)

Triple-Witching Week, Dow Up 21 of Last 23 and 6 Straight

WEDNESDAY

D 52.4
S 57.1
N 47.6

17

Financial genius is a rising stock market. — John Kenneth Galbraith (Canadian/American economist and diplomat, 1908-2006)

THURSDAY

D 42.9
S 33.3
N 47.6

18

When everybody starts looking really smart, and not realizing that a lot of it was luck, I get scared. — Raphael Yavneh *(Forbes)*

December Triple Witching, Dow Up 17 of 25

FRIDAY

D 52.4
S 47.6
N 52.4

19

Bull markets are born on pessimism, grow on skepticism, mature on optimism, and die on euphoria.
— Sir John Templeton (Founder Templeton Funds, philanthropist, 1994)

SATURDAY

20

SUNDAY

21

SECTOR SEASONALITY: SELECTED PERCENTAGE PLAYS

Sector seasonality was featured in the first 1968 *Almanac*. A Merrill Lynch study showed that buying seven sectors around September or October and selling in the first few months of 1954-1964 tripled the gains of holding them for 10 years. Over the past few years we have honed this strategy significantly and now devote a large portion of our time and resources to investing during seasonably favorable periods for different sectors with Exchange Traded Funds (ETFs).

Updated seasonalities appear in the table below. We specify whether the seasonality starts or finishes in the beginning third (B), middle third (M) or last third (E) of the month. These Selected Percentage Plays are geared to take advantage of the bulk of seasonal sector bullishness.

By design entry points are in advance of the major seasonal moves, providing traders ample opportunity to accumulate positions at favorable prices. Conversely, exit points have been selected to capture the majority of the advance, getting out ahead of any seasonal weakness.

From the sampling of the major seasonalities in the table below we created the Sector Index Seasonality Strategy Calendar on page 116. Note the concentration of bullish sector seasonalities during the Best Six Months, November-April.

As the ETF universe expands at breakneck speed, more seasonal investment options become available to Almanac Investors. Check our archives at *stocktradersalmanac.com* for updates and revisions to the strategy. We provide entry and exit points to *Almanac Investor* newsletter subscribers. Top 300 ETFs appear on pages 188-189.

SECTOR INDEX SEASONALITY TABLE

Ticker	Sector Index	Start		Seasonality Finish		Average % Return † 10-Year	5-Year
XNG	Natural Gas	February	E	June	B	18.6	10.4
RXH	Healthcare Prov	March	E	June	M	13.9	8.4
XCI	Computer Tech	April	M	July	M	14.8	3.0
RXP	Healthcare Prod	April	M	July	B	9.7	2.3
MSH	High-Tech	April	M	July	M	15.5	4.0
IIX	Internet	April	M	July	B	15.1	7.5
BTK	Biotech	July	E	March	B	38.3	15.6
XAU	Gold & Silver	July	E	September	E	20.0	20.8
UTY	Utilities	July	E	January	B	12.1	13.4
CMR	Consumer	September	E	June	B	15.1	11.2
RXP	Healthcare Prod	September	E	February	M	12.3	9.6
RXH	Healthcare Prov	September	E	January	B	10.6	6.0
DRG	Pharmaceutical	September	B	February	M	9.7	3.9
XTC	Telecom	September	E	January	M	21.3	22.7
BKX	Banking	October	B	June	B	21.1	17.2
XBD	Broker/Dealer	October	B	April	M	45.7	21.6
XCI	Computer Tech	October	B	January	B	22.0	17.8
CYC	Cyclical	October	B	May	M	22.0	21.8
MSH	High-Tech	October	B	January	M	28.6	20.1
IIX	Internet	October	B	January	B	40.6	27.6
S5MATR *	Materials	October	M	May	M	18.8	17.5
RMZ	Real Estate	October	E	July	B	18.9	23.0
SOX	Semiconductor	October	E	December	B	22.0	18.7
DJT	Transports	October	B	May	B	22.5	21.1
XOI	Oil	December	M	June	B	16.0	16.4

† Average % Return based on full seasonality completion through April 2007.
* S5MATR Available @ bloomberg.com.

DECEMBER

hanukah
REE LUNCH Menu Emailed to Almanac Investor Subscribers (Page 110)

MONDAY
D 61.9
S 61.9
N 52.4
22

---

a man can see both sides of a problem, you know that none of his money is tied up in it. — Verda Ross

Watch for the Santa Claus Rally (Page 112)

TUESDAY
D 66.7
S 71.4
N 81.0
23

---

ortune favors the brave. — Virgil (Roman Poet, Aeneid, 70-19 B.C.)

Shortened Trading Day)
Last Trading Day Before Christmas, Weak Dow Down 4 of Last 5

WEDNESDAY
D 52.4
S 52.4
N 61.9
24

---

he first rule is not to lose. The second rule is not to forget the first rule.
— Warren Buffett (CEO Berkshire Hathaway, investor & philanthropist, b. 1930)

Christmas Day (Market Closed)

THURSDAY
25

---

lmost any insider purchase is worth investigating for a possible lead to a superior speculation.
But very few insider sales justify concern. — William Chidester

Shortened Trading Day)
First Trading Day After Christmas, Dow Up 9 in a Row 1990-1998,
50:50 Since

FRIDAY
D 76.2
S 66.7
N 66.7
26

---

here are very few instances in history when any government has ever paid off debt.
— Walter Wriston (Retired CEO of Citicorp and Citibank)

SATURDAY
27

January Almanac Investor Seasonalities: See Pages 114 & 116

SUNDAY
28

Sector Index Seasonality Strategy Calendar*

* Graphic representation of the Sector Index Seasonality Table on page 114.

DECEMBER/JANUARY 2009

MONDAY
29

D 61.9
S 61.9
N 61.9

Follow the course opposite to custom and you will almost always do well.
— Jean-Jacques Rousseau (Swiss philosopher, 1712-1778)

Week After December Triple Witching, Dow Up 12 of last 16

TUESDAY
30

D 47.6
S 66.7
N 61.9

Love your enemies, for they tell you your faults. — Benjamin Franklin (U.S. founding father, diplomat, inventor, 1706-1790)

Last Day of the Year, NASDAQ Down 7 Straight After Being Up 29 in a Row!
Dow Down 7 of Last 11

WEDNESDAY
31

D 38.1
S 33.3
N 66.7

The real difference between men is energy. A strong will, a settled purpose, an invincible determination,
can accomplish almost anything; and in this lies the distinction between great men and little men.
— Buckminster Fuller (American architect, author, 1895-1983)

New Year's Day (Market Closed)

THURSDAY
1

Patriotism is when love of your own people comes first. Nationalism is when hate for people other that your own comes first.
— Charles De Gaulle (French president and WWII general, 1890-1970, May 1969)

First Trading Day of the Year, NASDAQ Up 8 of Last 10

FRIDAY
2

D 61.9
S 42.9
N 61.9

Il a parent can give a child is roots and wings. — Chinese proverb

SATURDAY
3

SUNDAY
4

2009 STRATEGY CALENDAR
(Option expiration dates circled)

	MONDAY	TUESDAY	WEDNESDAY	THURSDAY	FRIDAY	SATURDAY	SUNDAY
JANUARY	29	30	31	1 JANUARY New Year's Day	2	3	4
	5	6	7	8	9	10	11
	12	13	14	15	(16)	17	18
	19 Martin Luther King Day	20	21	22	23	24	25
	26	27	28	29	30	31	1 FEBRUARY
FEBRUARY	2	3	4	5	6	7	8
	9	10	11	12	13	14 ♥	15
	16 Presidents' Day	17	18	19	(20)	21	22
	23	24	25 Ash Wednesday	26	27	28	1 MARCH
MARCH	2	3	4	5	6	7	8 Daylight Saving Time Begins
	9	10	11	12	13	14	15
	16	17 ♣ St. Patrick's Day	18	19	(20)	21	22
	23	24	25	26	27	28	29
	30	31	1 APRIL	2	3	4	5
APRIL	6	7	8	9 Passover	10 Good Friday	11	12 Easter
	13	14	15 Tax Deadline	16	(17)	18	19
	20	21	22	23	24	25	26
	27	28	29	30	1 MAY	2	3
MAY	4	5	6	7	8	9	10 Mother's Day
	11	12	13	14	(15)	16	17
	18	19	20	21	22	23	24
	25 Memorial Day	26	27	28	29	30	31
JUNE	1 JUNE	2	3	4	5	6	7
	8	9	10	11	12	13	14
	15	16	17	18	(19)	20	21 Father's Day
	22	23	24	25	26	27	28

Market closed on shaded weekdays; closes early when half-shaded.

118

2009 STRATEGY CALENDAR

(Option expiration dates circled)

MONDAY	TUESDAY	WEDNESDAY	THURSDAY	FRIDAY	SATURDAY	SUNDAY	
29	30	1 JULY	2	3	4 Independence Day	5	JULY
6	7	8	9	10	11	12	JULY
13	14	15	16	(17)	18	19	JULY
20	21	22	23	24	25	26	JULY
27	28	29	30	31	1 AUGUST	2	
3	4	5	6	7	8	9	AUGUST
10	11	12	13	14	15	16	AUGUST
17	18	19	20	(21)	22	23	AUGUST
24	25	26	27	28	29	30	AUGUST
31	1 SEPTEMBER	2	3	4	5	6	
7 Labor Day	8	9	10	11	12	13	SEPTEMBER
14	15	16	17	(18)	19 Rosh Hashanah	20	SEPTEMBER
21	22	23	24	25	26	27	SEPTEMBER
28 Yom Kippur	29	30	1 OCTOBER	2	3	4	
5	6	7	8	9	10	11	OCTOBER
12 Columbus Day	13	14	15	(16)	17	18	OCTOBER
19	20	21	22	23	24	25	OCTOBER
26	27	28	29	30	31	1 NOVEMBER Daylight Saving Time Ends	
2	3 Election Day	4	5	6	7	8	NOVEMBER
9	10	11 Veterans' Day	12	13	14	15	NOVEMBER
16	17	18	19	(20)	21	22	NOVEMBER
23	24	25	26 Thanksgiving	27	28	29	NOVEMBER
30	1 DECEMBER	2	3	4	5	6	
7	8	9	10	11	12 Chanukah	13	DECEMBER
14	15	16	17	(18)	19	20	DECEMBER
21	22	23	24	25 Christmas	26	27	DECEMBER
28	29	30	31	1 JANUARY New Year's Day	2	3	DECEMBER

DIRECTORY OF TRADING PATTERNS & DATABANK

CONTENTS

DOW JONES INDUSTRIALS MARKET PROBABILITY CALENDAR 2008

THE % CHANCE OF THE MARKET RISING ON ANY TRADING DAY OF THE YEAR*

(Based on the number of times the DJIA rose on a particular trading day during January 1954-December 2006)

Date	Jan	Feb	Mar	Apr	May	Jun	Jul	Aug	Sep	Oct	Nov	Dec
1	H	56.6	S	56.6	54.7	S	62.3	43.4	H	47.2	S	47.2
2	54.7	S	S	58.5	64.2	58.5	62.3	S	60.4	62.3	S	54.7
3	73.6	S	67.9	54.7	S	52.8	58.5	S	58.5	50.9	62.3	62.3
4	49.1	54.7	66.0	60.4	S	54.7	H	47.2	58.5	S	49.1	58.5
5	S	37.7	60.4	S	52.8	58.5	S	49.1	43.4	S	67.9	43.4
6	S	54.7	49.1	S	49.1	52.8	S	50.9	S	60.4	58.5	S
7	56.6	43.4	45.3	52.8	45.3	S	56.6	54.7	S	47.2	45.3	S
8	49.1	43.4	S	58.5	49.1	S	62.3	43.4	45.3	50.9	S	43.4
9	47.2	S	S	62.3	50.9	41.5	56.6	S	41.5	41.5	S	56.6
10	47.2	S	54.7	64.2	S	35.8	50.9	S	54.7	37.7	62.3	56.6
11	47.2	45.3	56.6	54.7	S	60.4	37.7	49.1	58.5	S	52.8	43.4
12	S	64.2	52.8	S	50.9	56.6	S	50.9	45.3	S	60.4	52.8
13	S	41.5	52.8	S	47.2	56.6	S	45.3	S	54.7	47.2	S
14	56.6	50.9	50.9	69.8	52.8	S	64.2	66.0	S	58.5	52.8	S
15	56.6	56.6	S	64.2	54.7	S	49.1	60.4	52.8	54.7	S	47.2
16	60.4	S	S	54.7	45.3	50.9	43.4	S	49.1	49.1	S	56.6
17	41.5	S	58.5	54.7	S	49.1	47.2	S	37.7	43.4	56.6	52.8
18	35.8	H	62.3	50.9	S	49.1	47.2	52.8	47.2	S	47.2	52.8
19	S	35.8	56.6	S	54.7	41.5	S	45.3	45.3	S	54.7	56.6
20	S	45.3	50.9	S	45.3	49.1	S	54.7	S	62.3	50.9	S
21	H	50.9	H	54.7	45.3	S	43.4	47.2	S	54.7	60.4	S
22	41.5	56.6	S	49.1	34.0	S	49.1	50.9	43.4	47.2	S	56.6
23	58.5	S	S	50.9	54.7	41.5	43.4	S	39.6	37.7	S	49.1
24	47.2	S	35.8	49.1	S	41.5	49.1	S	52.8	49.1	64.2	58.5
25	58.5	35.8	47.2	56.6	S	45.3	58.5	50.9	54.7	S	56.6	H
26	S	45.3	47.2	S	H	45.3	S	45.3	49.1	S	50.9	71.7
27	S	60.4	56.6	S	41.5	56.6	S	54.7	S	28.3	H	S
28	58.5	49.1	41.5	52.8	45.3	S	52.8	41.5	S	50.9	49.1	S
29	47.2	52.8	S	45.3	52.8	S	47.2	62.3	50.9	54.7	S	52.8
30	62.3		S	54.7	62.3	52.8	62.3	S	41.5	60.4	S	54.7
31	60.4		39.6		S		54.7	S		54.7		54.7

* See new trends developing on pages 68, 86, 145, and 146.

121

RECENT DOW JONES INDUSTRIALS MARKET PROBABILITY CALENDAR 2008

THE % CHANCE OF THE MARKET RISING ON ANY TRADING DAY OF THE YEAR*

(Based on the number of times the DJIA rose on a particular trading day during January 1986-December 2006**)

Date	Jan	Feb	Mar	Apr	May	Jun	Jul	Aug	Sep	Oct	Nov	Dec
1	H	61.9	S	61.9	61.9	S	76.2	33.3	H	61.9	S	57.1
2	61.9	S	S	66.7	66.7	76.2	57.1	S	52.4	52.4	S	57.1
3	71.4	S	57.1	52.4	S	52.4	38.1	S	61.9	38.1	66.7	52.4
4	47.6	47.6	61.9	71.4	S	52.4	H	57.1	47.6	S	42.9	47.6
5	S	42.9	61.9	S	42.9	57.1	S	47.6	33.3	S	61.9	33.3
6	S	47.6	52.4	S	38.1	52.4	S	47.6	S	61.9	61.9	S
7	57.1	42.9	57.1	38.1	28.6	S	57.1	47.6	S	42.9	47.6	S
8	42.9	47.6	S	52.4	61.9	S	61.9	42.9	47.6	52.4	S	52.4
9	47.6	S	S	52.4	66.7	42.9	52.4	S	47.6	33.3	S	57.1
10	47.6	S	52.4	61.9	S	38.1	66.7	S	61.9	28.6	61.9	47.6
11	57.1	52.4	52.4	52.4	S	61.9	61.9	47.6	61.9	S	38.1	52.4
12	S	61.9	47.6	S	61.9	47.6	S	57.1	47.6	S	57.1	42.9
13	S	52.4	42.9	S	61.9	71.4	S	38.1	S	66.7	57.1	S
14	47.6	52.4	61.9	71.4	57.1	S	66.7	66.7	S	71.4	66.7	S
15	66.7	81.0	S	71.4	57.1	S	52.4	57.1	52.4	66.7	S	52.4
16	61.9	S	S	52.4	42.9	57.1	47.6	S	47.6	47.6	S	61.9
17	42.9	S	57.1	47.6	S	52.4	42.9	S	23.8	52.4	57.1	52.4
18	38.1	H	66.7	52.4	S	52.4	52.4	66.7	47.6	S	38.1	42.9
19	S	38.1	52.4	S	57.1	33.3	S	52.4	33.3	S	71.4	52.4
20	S	28.6	61.9	S	57.1	57.1	S	57.1	S	71.4	47.6	S
21	H	52.4	H	57.1	47.6	S	33.3	42.9	S	61.9	71.4	S
22	33.3	57.1	S	42.9	38.1	S	47.6	57.1	38.1	47.6	S	61.9
23	52.4	S	S	52.4	71.4	33.3	38.1	S	38.1	42.9	S	66.7
24	42.9	S	33.3	33.3	S	47.6	52.4	S	47.6	47.6	71.4	52.4
25	71.4	52.4	57.1	52.4	S	38.1	66.7	52.4	57.1	S	57.1	H
26	S	38.1	42.9	S	H	52.4	S	47.6	57.1	S	47.6	76.2
27	S	47.6	61.9	S	42.9	57.1	S	57.1	S	42.9	H	S
28	66.7	57.1	47.6	61.9	57.1	S	47.6	28.6	S	42.9	47.6	S
29	52.4	47.6	S	57.1	61.9	S	47.6	47.6	57.1	66.7	S	61.9
30	61.9		S	52.4	52.4	33.3	66.7	S	47.6	76.2	S	47.6
31	71.4		33.3		S		57.1	S		47.6		38.1

* See new trends developing on pages 68, 86, 145, and 146. ** Based on most recent 21-year period.

S&P 500 MARKET PROBABILITY CALENDAR 2008

THE % CHANCE OF THE MARKET RISING ON ANY TRADING DAY OF THE YEAR*

(Based on the number of times the S&P 500 rose on a particular trading day during January 1954-December 2006)

Date	Jan	Feb	Mar	Apr	May	Jun	Jul	Aug	Sep	Oct	Nov	Dec
1	H	58.5	S	62.3	54.7	S	67.9	47.2	H	47.2	S	49.1
2	47.2	S	S	58.5	69.8	56.6	58.5	S	64.2	69.8	S	52.8
3	73.6	S	62.3	54.7	S	62.3	50.9	S	56.6	52.8	62.3	60.4
4	52.8	56.6	60.4	54.7	S	54.7	H	45.3	58.5	S	54.7	56.6
5	S	49.1	62.3	S	58.5	56.6	S	49.1	43.4	S	69.8	39.6
6	S	49.1	47.2	S	43.4	49.1	S	50.9	S	62.3	54.7	S
7	50.9	47.2	47.2	54.7	41.5	S	60.4	56.6	S	49.1	45.3	S
8	45.3	43.4	S	60.4	49.1	S	62.3	43.4	49.1	49.1	S	49.1
9	49.1	S	S	64.2	50.9	41.5	56.6	S	50.9	37.7	S	56.6
10	50.9	S	58.5	52.8	S	41.5	50.9	S	52.8	43.4	60.4	47.2
11	52.8	39.6	56.6	49.1	S	60.4	47.2	54.7	62.3	S	62.3	49.1
12	S	64.2	49.1	S	52.8	60.4	S	47.2	49.1	S	58.5	45.3
13	S	47.2	60.4	S	45.3	56.6	S	47.2	S	52.8	47.2	S
14	60.4	45.3	47.2	60.4	50.9	S	71.7	67.9	S	52.8	52.8	S
15	64.2	54.7	S	62.3	56.6	S	54.7	64.2	52.8	52.8	S	47.2
16	54.7	S	S	58.5	49.1	56.6	41.5	S	52.8	52.8	S	54.7
17	52.8	S	62.3	52.8	S	47.2	43.4	S	45.3	39.6	49.1	47.2
18	45.3	H	62.3	52.8	S	54.7	47.2	54.7	52.8	S	49.1	43.4
19	S	35.8	56.6	S	56.6	37.7	S	52.8	50.9	S	56.6	49.1
20	S	49.1	49.1	S	41.5	54.7	S	52.8	S	67.9	54.7	S
21	H	43.4	H	54.7	52.8	S	41.5	45.3	S	54.7	60.4	S
22	45.3	49.1	S	52.8	43.4	S	41.5	50.9	50.9	49.1	S	52.8
23	58.5	S	S	43.4	56.6	41.5	43.4	S	37.7	37.7	S	47.2
24	60.4	S	52.8	45.3	S	39.6	45.3	S	50.9	41.5	67.9	58.5
25	52.8	41.5	39.6	56.6	S	35.8	56.6	49.1	52.8	S	58.5	H
26	S	37.7	49.1	S	H	50.9	S	45.3	56.6	S	56.6	71.7
27	S	58.5	56.6	S	45.3	60.4	S	54.7	S	34.0	H	S
28	52.8	52.8	35.8	49.1	47.2	S	54.7	45.3	S	58.5	49.1	S
29	45.3	60.4	S	43.4	52.8	S	50.9	66.0	50.9	58.5	S	56.6
30	66.0		S	62.3	60.4	50.9	64.2	S	45.3	60.4	S	64.2
31	66.0		39.6		S		66.0	S		56.6		66.0

* See new trends developing on pages 68, 86, 145, and 146. 123

RECENT S&P 500 MARKET PROBABILITY CALENDAR 2008

THE % CHANCE OF THE MARKET RISING ON ANY TRADING DAY OF THE YEAR*

(Based on the number of times the S&P 500 rose on a particular trading day during **January 1986-December 2006****)

Date	Jan	Feb	Mar	Apr	May	Jun	Jul	Aug	Sep	Oct	Nov	Dec
1	H	61.9	S	57.1	61.9	S	76.2	42.9	H	57.1	S	61.9
2	42.9	S	S	66.7	66.7	66.7	52.4	S	61.9	66.7	S	57.1
3	71.4	S	47.6	57.1	S	71.4	38.1	S	52.4	38.1	66.7	57.1
4	52.4	52.4	52.4	61.9	S	47.6	H	47.6	42.9	S	47.6	33.3
5	S	57.1	61.9	S	52.4	47.6	S	47.6	38.1	S	61.9	38.1
6	S	47.6	52.4	S	28.6	47.6	S	47.6	S	57.1	61.9	S
7	47.6	38.1	57.1	42.9	19.0	S	61.9	52.4	S	38.1	47.6	S
8	52.4	52.4	S	57.1	52.4	S	66.7	47.6	52.4	52.4	S	47.6
9	47.6	S	S	52.4	61.9	33.3	47.6	S	57.1	28.6	S	52.4
10	47.6	S	61.9	47.6	S	47.6	61.9	S	52.4	33.3	57.1	38.1
11	57.1	42.9	42.9	42.9	S	52.4	71.4	42.9	57.1	S	47.6	52.4
12	S	71.4	42.9	S	57.1	57.1	S	52.4	52.4	S	57.1	38.1
13	S	57.1	61.9	S	61.9	71.4	S	38.1	S	66.7	52.4	S
14	57.1	47.6	57.1	57.1	61.9	S	76.2	71.4	S	71.4	61.9	S
15	71.4	81.0	S	61.9	57.1	S	47.6	66.7	52.4	61.9	S	47.6
16	57.1	S	S	61.9	42.9	66.7	42.9	S	57.1	52.4	S	57.1
17	57.1	S	66.7	52.4	S	52.4	42.9	S	38.1	47.6	52.4	57.1
18	33.3	H	66.7	52.4	S	61.9	57.1	71.4	52.4	S	47.6	33.3
19	S	38.1	61.9	S	66.7	33.3	S	57.1	38.1	S	71.4	47.6
20	S	33.3	47.6	S	57.1	71.4	S	57.1	S	76.2	47.6	S
21	H	42.9	H	61.9	52.4	S	23.8	47.6	S	71.4	66.7	S
22	38.1	47.6	S	47.6	38.1	S	38.1	66.7	47.6	57.1	S	61.9
23	52.4	S	S	47.6	81.0	28.6	38.1	S	42.9	47.6	S	71.4
24	52.4	S	57.1	28.6	S	42.9	47.6	S	42.9	33.3	71.4	52.4
25	52.4	57.1	52.4	52.4	S	23.8	71.4	52.4	57.1	S	61.9	H
26	S	38.1	42.9	S	H	57.1	S	52.4	61.9	S	61.9	66.7
27	S	52.4	57.1	S	52.4	66.7	S	57.1	S	47.6	H	S
28	52.4	66.7	33.3	61.9	61.9	S	52.4	33.3	S	52.4	38.1	S
29	57.1	57.1	S	57.1	52.4	S	52.4	52.4	61.9	61.9	S	61.9
30	66.7		S	66.7	52.4	38.1	76.2	S	52.4	81.0	S	66.7
31	76.2		42.9		S		66.7	S		66.7		33.3

* See new trends developing on pages 68, 86, 145, and 146.   ** Based on most recent 21-year period.

NASDAQ COMPOSITE MARKET PROBABILITY CALENDAR 2008

THE % CHANCE OF THE MARKET RISING ON ANY TRADING DAY OF THE YEAR*

(Based on the number of times the NASDAQ rose on a particular trading day during January 1972-December 2006)

Date	Jan	Feb	Mar	Apr	May	Jun	Jul	Aug	Sep	Oct	Nov	Dec
1	H	65.7	S	37.1	60.0	S	54.3	51.4	H	48.6	S	62.9
2	51.4	S	S	62.9	74.3	60.0	48.6	S	54.3	62.9	S	62.9
3	77.1	S	65.7	62.9	S	74.3	40.0	S	65.7	54.3	68.6	62.9
4	60.0	68.6	54.3	51.4	S	57.1	H	42.9	57.1	S	51.4	60.0
5	S	57.1	68.6	S	65.7	60.0	S	48.6	57.1	S	74.3	40.0
6	S	65.7	54.3	S	54.3	54.3	S	60.0	S	62.9	57.1	S
7	65.7	51.4	54.3	51.4	57.1	S	51.4	57.1	S	60.0	48.6	S
8	51.4	51.4	S	60.0	60.0	S	60.0	37.1	54.3	60.0	S	51.4
9	60.0	S	S	62.9	54.3	45.7	65.7	S	48.6	48.6	S	45.7
10	54.3	S	54.3	60.0	S	45.7	57.1	S	48.6	45.7	54.3	40.0
11	57.1	48.6	54.3	51.4	S	57.1	71.4	54.3	60.0	S	62.9	48.6
12	S	68.6	51.4	S	40.0	60.0	S	51.4	57.1	S	65.7	40.0
13	S	51.4	68.6	S	54.3	65.7	S	54.3	S	77.1	54.3	S
14	68.6	60.0	51.4	60.0	57.1	S	74.3	62.9	S	65.7	57.1	S
15	68.6	62.9	S	51.4	60.0	S	68.6	60.0	34.3	54.3	S	45.7
16	68.6	S	S	62.9	57.1	57.1	45.7	S	45.7	48.6	S	51.4
17	65.7	S	54.3	60.0	S	45.7	51.4	S	51.4	37.1	42.9	48.6
18	42.9	H	62.9	51.4	S	51.4	54.3	51.4	65.7	S	42.9	48.6
19	S	48.6	57.1	S	54.3	45.7	S	60.0	51.4	S	57.1	48.6
20	S	54.3	60.0	S	42.9	51.4	S	51.4	S	74.3	57.1	S
21	H	37.1	H	54.3	51.4	S	42.9	54.3	S	51.4	60.0	S
22	48.6	37.1	S	54.3	48.6	S	42.9	48.6	57.1	62.9	S	57.1
23	51.4	S	S	51.4	62.9	48.6	45.7	S	48.6	42.9	S	68.6
24	54.3	S	60.0	45.7	S	48.6	54.3	S	51.4	40.0	57.1	65.7
25	42.9	48.6	42.9	45.7	S	40.0	57.1	54.3	45.7	S	65.7	H
26	S	54.3	48.6	S	H	60.0	S	54.3	45.7	S	65.7	71.4
27	S	60.0	54.3	S	51.4	68.6	S	57.1	S	34.3	H	S
28	65.7	57.1	51.4	68.6	60.0	S	51.4	60.0	S	42.9	65.7	S
29	60.0	54.3	S	57.1	51.4	S	48.6	74.3	51.4	54.3	S	54.3
30	60.0		S	74.3	71.4	71.4	54.3	S	51.4	60.0	S	68.6
31	65.7		62.9		S		57.1	S		68.6		80.0

*See new trends developing on pages 68, 86, 145, and 146.
Based on NASDAQ composite, prior to February 5, 1971, based on National Quotation Bureau indices. 125

<u>RECENT</u> NASDAQ COMPOSITE MARKET PROBABILITY CALENDAR 2008

THE % CHANCE OF THE MARKET RISING ON ANY TRADING DAY OF THE YEAR

(Based on the number of times the NASDAQ rose on a particular trading day during January 1986–December 2006**)

Date	Jan	Feb	Mar	Apr	May	Jun	Jul	Aug	Sep	Oct	Nov	Dec
1	H	81.0	S	38.1	66.7	S	66.7	47.6	H	52.4	S	76.2
2	61.9	S	S	57.1	76.2	66.7	47.6	S	57.1	61.9	S	66.7
3	81.0	S	66.7	71.4	S	76.2	38.1	S	66.7	52.4	71.4	66.7
4	61.9	71.4	42.9	52.4	S	52.4	H	38.1	47.6	S	47.6	52.4
5	S	57.1	71.4	S	71.4	57.1	S	42.9	57.1	S	81.0	33.3
6	S	61.9	57.1	S	47.6	47.6	S	57.1	S	61.9	57.1	S
7	61.9	52.4	61.9	42.9	42.9	S	52.4	52.4	S	42.9	57.1	S
8	52.4	57.1	S	57.1	66.7	S	66.7	42.9	61.9	57.1	S	42.9
9	57.1	S	S	52.4	47.6	38.1	66.7	S	57.1	42.9	S	42.9
10	52.4	S	47.6	57.1	S	52.4	61.9	S	57.1	47.6	57.1	33.3
11	57.1	47.6	52.4	47.6	S	52.4	76.2	42.9	61.9	S	57.1	61.9
12	S	61.9	47.6	S	38.1	52.4	S	52.4	57.1	S	61.9	33.3
13	S	47.6	61.9	S	57.1	61.9	S	52.4	S	76.2	57.1	S
14	66.7	61.9	52.4	57.1	57.1	S	76.2	76.2	S	66.7	61.9	S
15	61.9	71.4	S	47.6	57.1	S	61.9	71.4	23.8	57.1	S	52.4
16	66.7	S	S	61.9	52.4	61.9	47.6	S	47.6	42.9	S	47.6
17	71.4	S	47.6	52.4	S	42.9	42.9	S	52.4	38.1	38.1	47.6
18	33.3	H	71.4	47.6	S	42.9	52.4	61.9	66.7	S	33.3	47.6
19	S	38.1	61.9	S	66.7	42.9	S	61.9	42.9	S	57.1	52.4
20	S	42.9	61.9	S	47.6	57.1	S	47.6	S	71.4	57.1	S
21	H	42.9	H	52.4	52.4	S	28.6	57.1	S	57.1	61.9	S
22	47.6	42.9	S	42.9	47.6	S	38.1	52.4	52.4	57.1	S	52.4
23	52.4	S	S	47.6	71.4	33.3	33.3	S	47.6	42.9	S	81.0
24	57.1	S	61.9	42.9	S	47.6	47.6	S	42.9	33.3	57.1	61.9
25	42.9	57.1	47.6	47.6	S	28.6	66.7	57.1	52.4	S	61.9	H
26	S	57.1	52.4	S	H	61.9	S	57.1	42.9	S	71.4	66.7
27	S	52.4	47.6	S	52.4	66.7	S	61.9	S	33.3	H	S
28	76.2	61.9	42.9	61.9	71.4	S	57.1	57.1	S	38.1	57.1	S
29	66.7	52.4	S	61.9	66.7	S	52.4	66.7	52.4	47.6	S	61.9
30	57.1		S	76.2	71.4	71.4	66.7	S	57.1	71.4	S	61.9
31	71.4		61.9		S		61.9	S		71.4		66.7

* See new trends developing on page 68, 86, 145, and 146.   ** Based on most recent 21-year period.

126

RUSSELL 1000 INDEX MARKET PROBABILITY CALENDAR 2008

THE % CHANCE OF THE MARKET RISING ON ANY TRADING DAY OF THE YEAR*
(Based on the number of times the Russell 1000 rose on a particular trading day during January 1980-December 2006)

Date	Jan	Feb	Mar	Apr	May	Jun	Jul	Aug	Sep	Oct	Nov	Dec
1	H	63.0	S	55.6	51.9	S	70.4	44.4	H	55.6	S	59.3
2	37.0	S	S	59.3	66.7	59.3	44.4	S	55.6	59.3	S	51.9
3	66.7	S	59.3	48.1	S	63.0	37.0	S	55.6	48.1	74.1	59.3
4	59.3	59.3	48.1	55.6	S	51.9	H	40.7	48.1	S	51.9	37.0
5	S	63.0	59.3	S	59.3	55.6	S	48.1	33.3	S	63.0	37.0
6	S	48.1	40.7	S	37.0	37.0	S	48.1	S	59.3	59.3	S
7	51.9	55.6	40.7	48.1	37.0	S	59.3	55.6	S	44.4	44.4	S
8	48.1	48.1	S	66.7	51.9	S	59.3	51.9	48.1	55.6	S	44.4
9	59.3	S	S	55.6	63.0	37.0	51.9	S	55.6	33.3	S	55.6
10	51.9	S	55.6	48.1	S	40.7	63.0	S	51.9	37.0	55.6	37.0
11	51.9	37.0	48.1	44.4	S	55.6	66.7	48.1	63.0	S	51.9	48.1
12	S	70.4	44.4	S	51.9	55.6	S	48.1	55.6	S	59.3	40.7
13	S	55.6	55.6	S	55.6	59.3	S	37.0	S	70.4	59.3	S
14	59.3	44.4	44.4	55.6	55.6	S	85.2	66.7	S	70.4	59.3	S
15	74.1	66.7	S	66.7	59.3	S	48.1	63.0	51.9	63.0	S	55.6
16	70.4	S	S	55.6	55.6	59.3	51.9	S	44.4	48.1	S	55.6
17	44.4	S	63.0	48.1	S	51.9	44.4	S	40.7	37.0	48.1	55.6
18	29.6	H	59.3	48.1	S	63.0	55.6	63.0	48.1	S	44.4	37.0
19	S	33.3	55.6	S	59.3	29.6	S	63.0	40.7	S	70.4	48.1
20	S	37.0	48.1	S	51.9	59.3	S	63.0	S	77.8	51.9	S
21	H	40.7	H	51.9	51.9	S	33.3	48.1	S	63.0	63.0	S
22	44.4	44.4	S	48.1	40.7	S	37.0	55.6	51.9	55.6	S	66.7
23	51.9	S	S	51.9	70.4	40.7	40.7	S	37.0	40.7	S	59.3
24	48.1	S	48.1	40.7	S	40.7	37.0	S	44.4	33.3	70.4	55.6
25	48.1	48.1	48.1	51.9	S	29.6	74.1	44.4	51.9	S	70.4	H
26	S	44.4	37.0	S	H	51.9	S	55.6	63.0	S	63.0	66.7
27	S	63.0	51.9	S	55.6	63.0	S	48.1	S	37.0	H	S
28	66.7	63.0	40.7	59.3	59.3	S	59.3	48.1	S	51.9	44.4	S
29	59.3	59.3	S	51.9	48.1	S	48.1	59.3	59.3	55.6	S	66.7
30	66.7		S	66.7	55.6	48.1	66.7	S	55.6	66.7	S	66.7
31	66.7		48.1		S		63.0	S		66.7		55.6

* See new trends developing on pages 68, 86, 145, and 146.

127

RUSSELL 2000 INDEX MARKET PROBABILITY CALENDAR 2008

THE % CHANCE OF THE MARKET RISING ON ANY TRADING DAY OF THE YEAR*

(Based on the number of times the Russell 2000 rose on a particular trading day during January 1980-December 2006)

Date	Jan	Feb	Mar	Apr	May	Jun	Jul	Aug	Sep	Oct	Nov	Dec
1	H	63.0	S	40.7	63.0	S	59.3	44.4	H	51.9	S	59.3
2	40.7	S	S	55.6	66.7	66.7	51.9	S	51.9	48.1	S	59.3
3	74.1	S	70.4	44.4	S	74.1	40.7	S	66.7	48.1	70.4	66.7
4	63.0	63.0	63.0	51.9	S	51.9	H	48.1	51.9	S	66.7	59.3
5	S	59.3	63.0	S	70.4	55.6	S	44.4	63.0	S	74.1	37.0
6	S	70.4	59.3	S	59.3	59.3	S	48.1	S	70.4	59.3	S
7	63.0	63.0	63.0	48.1	55.6	S	51.9	48.1	S	44.4	59.3	S
8	59.3	63.0	S	59.3	51.9	S	51.9	40.7	51.9	48.1	S	59.3
9	63.0	S	S	63.0	59.3	33.3	66.7	S	59.3	48.1	S	44.4
10	51.9	S	48.1	63.0	S	48.1	51.9	S	55.6	55.6	48.1	48.1
11	66.7	44.4	48.1	48.1	S	59.3	59.3	59.3	63.0	S	55.6	40.7
12	S	70.4	40.7	S	48.1	55.6	S	51.9	51.9	S	74.1	44.4
13	S	51.9	55.6	S	59.3	63.0	S	44.4	S	74.1	51.9	S
14	70.4	66.7	55.6	51.9	55.6	S	66.7	81.5	S	63.0	59.3	S
15	70.4	59.3	S	63.0	48.1	S	59.3	66.7	29.6	70.4	S	37.0
16	74.1	S	S	59.3	59.3	55.6	48.1	S	44.4	37.0	S	51.9
17	81.5	S	51.9	51.9	S	51.9	48.1	S	40.7	44.4	44.4	59.3
18	29.6	H	59.3	51.9	S	37.0	48.1	63.0	40.7	S	22.2	55.6
19	S	44.4	66.7	S	59.3	33.3	S	59.3	48.1	S	66.7	55.6
20	S	37.0	55.6	S	55.6	48.1	S	48.1	S	70.4	48.1	S
21	H	33.3	H	48.1	51.9	S	37.0	48.1	S	66.7	59.3	S
22	51.9	33.3	S	59.3	51.9	S	40.7	59.3	59.3	55.6	S	59.3
23	55.6	S	S	51.9	66.7	48.1	37.0	S	40.7	48.1	S	70.4
24	55.6	S	48.1	51.9	S	48.1	48.1	S	48.1	40.7	63.0	74.1
25	40.7	48.1	51.9	59.3	S	40.7	59.3	55.6	33.3	S	63.0	H
26	S	63.0	48.1	S	H	55.6	S	59.3	51.9	S	74.1	70.4
27	S	63.0	55.6	S	48.1	77.8	S	59.3	S	40.7	H	S
28	66.7	70.4	48.1	59.3	70.4	S	70.4	66.7	S	37.0	70.4	S
29	55.6	66.7	S	59.3	63.0	S	48.1	77.8	59.3	51.9	S	63.0
30	63.0		S	81.5	74.1	74.1	55.6	S	74.1	63.0	S	66.7
31	81.5		85.2		S		74.1	S		77.8		77.8

* See new trends developing on pages 68, 86, 145, and 14

DECENNIAL CYCLE: A MARKET PHENOMENON

By arranging each year's market gain or loss so the first and succeeding years of each decade fall into the same column, certain interesting patterns emerge — strong fifth and eighth years; weak first, seventh and zero years.

This fascinating phenomenon was first presented by Edgar Lawrence Smith in *Common Stocks and Business Cycles* (William-Frederick Press, 1959). Anthony Gaubis co-pioneered the decennial pattern with Smith.

When Smith first cut graphs of market prices into 10-year segments and placed them above one another, he observed that each decade tended to have three bull market cycles and that the longest and strongest bull markets seem to favor the middle years of a decade.

Don't place too much emphasis on the decennial cycle nowadays, other than the extraordinary fifth and zero years, as the stock market is more influenced by the quadrennial presidential election cycle, shown on page 130. Also, the last half-century, which has been the most prosperous in U.S. history, has distributed the returns among most years of the decade. Interestingly, NASDAQ suffered its worst bear market ever in a zero year, giving us the rare experience of witnessing a bubble burst.

Eighth years have the second best record next to fifth years. 2008 is also an election year, which often gets a boost as incumbent administrations try to pump up the economy to keep voters happy. It may be difficult for the market to match the historical average as the current administration may have already spent much of its political capital (see pages 26, 30, 34, 36, 78 and 130).

THE 10-YEAR STOCK MARKET CYCLE
Annual % Change in Dow Jones Industrial Average
Year of Decade

DECADES	1st	2nd	3rd	4th	5th	6th	7th	8th	9th	10th
1881-1890	3.0%	− 2.9%	− 8.5%	−18.8%	20.1%	12.4%	− 8.4%	4.8%	5.5%	−14.1%
1891-1900	17.6	− 6.6	−24.6	− 0.6	2.3	− 1.7	21.3	22.5	9.2	7.0
1901-1910	− 8.7	− 0.4	−23.6	41.7	38.2	− 1.9	−37.7	46.6	15.0	−17.9
1911-1920	0.4	7.6	−10.3	− 5.4	81.7	− 4.2	−21.7	10.5	30.5	−32.9
1921-1930	12.7	21.7	− 3.3	26.2	30.0	0.3	28.8	48.2	−17.2	−33.8
1931-1940	−52.7	−23.1	66.7	4.1	38.5	24.8	−32.8	28.1	− 2.9	−12.7
1941-1950	−15.4	7.6	13.8	12.1	26.6	− 8.1	2.2	− 2.1	12.9	17.6
1951-1960	14.4	8.4	− 3.8	44.0	20.8	2.3	−12.8	34.0	16.4	− 9.3
1961-1970	18.7	−10.8	17.0	14.6	10.9	−18.9	15.2	4.3	−15.2	4.8
1971-1980	6.1	14.6	−16.6	−27.6	38.3	17.9	−17.3	− 3.1	4.2	14.9
1981-1990	− 9.2	19.6	20.3	− 3.7	27.7	22.6	2.3	11.8	27.0	− 4.3
1991-2000	20.3	4.2	13.7	2.1	33.5	26.0	22.6	16.1	25.2	− 6.2
2001-2010	− 7.1	−16.8	25.3	3.1	− 0.6	16.3				
Total % Change	**0.1%**	**23.1%**	**66.1%**	**91.8%**	**368.0%**	**87.3%**	**−38.3%**	**221.7%**	**110.6%**	**−86.9%**
Avg % Change	**0.01%**	**1.8%**	**5.1%**	**7.1%**	**28.3%**	**6.8%**	**− 3.2%**	**18.5%**	**9.2%**	**−7.2%**
Up Years	8	7	6	8	12	8	6	10	9	4
Down Years	5	6	7	5	1	5	6	2	3	8

Based on annual close; Cowles indices 1881-1885; 12 Mixed Stocks, 10 Rails, 2 Inds 1886-1889;

20 Mixed Stocks, 18 Rails, 2 Inds 1890-1896; Railroad average 1897 (First industrial average published May 26, 1896).

PRESIDENTIAL ELECTION/STOCK MARKET CYCLE: THE 174-YEAR SAGA CONTINUES

It is no mere coincidence that the last two years (pre-election year and election year) of the 44 administrations since 1833 produced a total net market gain of 745.9%, dwarfing the 243.3% gain of the first two years of these administrations.

Presidential elections every four years have a profound impact on the economy and the stock market. Wars, recessions and bear markets tend to start or occur in the first half of the term; prosperous times and bull markets, in the latter half. After nine straight annual Dow gains during the millennial bull, the four-year election cycle appears to be back on track. 2001-2007 have been textbook examples.

STOCK MARKET ACTION SINCE 1833
Annual % Change In Dow Jones Industrial Average[1]

4-Year Cycle Beginning	Elected President	Post-Election Year	Mid-Term Year	Pre-Election Year	Election Year
1833	Jackson (D)	− 0.9	13.0	3.1	− 11.7
1837	Van Buren (D)	− 11.5	1.6	− 12.3	5.5
1841*	W.H. Harrison (W)**	− 13.3	− 18.1	45.0	15.5
1845*	Polk (D)	8.1	− 14.5	1.2	− 3.6
1849*	Taylor (W)	N/C	18.7	− 3.2	19.6
1853*	Pierce (D)	− 12.7	− 30.2	1.5	4.4
1857	Buchanan (D)	− 31.0	14.3	− 10.7	14.0
1861*	Lincoln (R)	− 1.8	55.4	38.0	6.4
1865	Lincoln (R)**	− 8.5	3.6	1.6	10.8
1869	Grant (R)	1.7	5.6	7.3	6.8
1873	Grant (R)	− 12.7	2.8	− 4.1	− 17.9
1877	Hayes (R)	− 9.4	6.1	43.0	18.7
1881	Garfield (R)**	3.0	− 2.9	− 8.5	− 18.8
1885*	Cleveland (D)	20.1	12.4	− 8.4	4.8
1889*	B. Harrison (R)	5.5	− 14.1	17.6	− 6.6
1893*	Cleveland (D)	− 24.6	− 0.6	2.3	− 1.7
1897*	McKinley (R)	21.3	22.5	9.2	7.0
1901	McKinley (R)**	− 8.7	− 0.4	− 23.6	41.7
1905	T. Roosevelt (R)	38.2	− 1.9	− 37.7	46.6
1909	Taft (R)	15.0	− 17.9	0.4	7.6
1913*	Wilson (D)	− 10.3	− 5.4	81.7	− 4.2
1917	Wilson (D)	− 21.7	10.5	30.5	− 32.9
1921*	Harding (R)**	12.7	21.7	− 3.3	26.2
1925	Coolidge (R)	30.0	0.3	28.8	48.2
1929	Hoover (R)	− 17.2	− 33.8	− 52.7	− 23.1
1933*	F. Roosevelt (D)	66.7	4.1	38.5	24.8
1937	F. Roosevelt (D)	− 32.8	28.1	− 2.9	− 12.7
1941	F. Roosevelt (D)	− 15.4	7.6	13.8	12.1
1945	F. Roosevelt (D)**	26.6	− 8.1	2.2	− 2.1
1949	Truman (D)	12.9	17.6	14.4	8.4
1953*	Eisenhower (R)	− 3.8	44.0	20.8	2.3
1957	Eisenhower (R)	− 12.8	34.0	16.4	− 9.3
1961*	Kennedy (D)**	18.7	− 10.8	17.0	14.6
1965	Johnson (D)	10.9	− 18.9	15.2	4.3
1969*	Nixon (R)	− 15.2	4.8	6.1	14.6
1973	Nixon (R)***	− 16.6	− 27.6	38.3	17.9
1977*	Carter (D)	− 17.3	− 3.1	4.2	14.9
1981*	Reagan (R)	− 9.2	19.6	20.3	− 3.7
1985	Reagan (R)	27.7	22.6	2.3	11.8
1989	G. H. W. Bush (R)	27.0	− 4.3	20.3	4.2
1993*	Clinton (D)	13.7	2.1	33.5	26.0
1997	Clinton (D)	22.6	16.1	25.2	− 6.2
2001*	G. W. Bush (R)	− 7.1	− 16.8	25.3	3.1
2005	G. W. Bush (R)	− 0.6	16.3		
Total % Gain		**67.3 %**	**176.0%**	**457.6%**	**288.3%**
Average % Gain		**1.6 %**	**4.0%**	**10.6%**	**6.7%**
# Up		19	26	32	29
# Down		24	18	11	14

*Party in power ousted **Death in office ***Resigned D—Democrat, W—Whig, R—Republican
[1] Based on annual close; Prior to 1886 based on Cowles and other indices; 12 Mixed Stocks, 10 Rails, 2 Inds 1886-1889; 20 Mixed Stocks, 18 Rails, 2 Inds 1890-1896; Railroad average 1897 (First industrial average published May 26, 1896).

DOW JONES INDUSTRIALS BULL & BEAR MARKETS SINCE 1900

Bear markets begin at the end of one bull market and end at the start of the next bull market (7/17/90 to 10/11/90 as an example). The high at Dow 3978.36 on 1/31/94, was followed by a 9.7 percent correction. A 10.3 percent correction occurred between the 5/22/96, closing high of 5778 and the intraday low on 7/16/96. The longest bull market on record ended on 7/17/98, and the shortest bear market on record ended on 8/31/98, when the new bull market began. The greatest bull super cycle in history that began 8/12/82 ended in 2000 after the Dow gained 1409% and NASDAQ climbed 3072%. The Dow gained only 497% in the eight-year super bull from 1921 to the top in 1929. NASDAQ suffered its worst loss ever, down 77.9% nearly as much as the 89.2% drop in the Dow from 1929 to the bottom in 1932. The Dow has rallied 79.3% since the 10/9/02 bear market low; S&P 500, 90.8% and NASDAQ 126.6%! At press time we have not experienced a 10% correction since March 2003. This is the third longest Dow bull since 1900. (See page 132 for S&P 500 and NASDAQ bulls and bears.)

DOW JONES INDUSTRIALS BULL AND BEAR MARKETS SINCE 1900

— Beginning —		— Ending —		Bull		Bear	
Date	DJIA	Date	DJIA	% Gain	Days	% Change	Days
9/24/00	38.80	6/17/01	57.33	47.8%	266	− 46.1%	875
11/9/03	30.88	1/19/06	75.45	144.3	802	− 48.5	665
11/15/07	38.83	11/19/09	73.64	89.6	735	− 27.4	675
9/25/11	53.43	9/30/12	68.97	29.1	371	− 24.1	668
7/30/14	52.32	11/21/16	110.15	110.5	845	− 40.1	393
12/19/17	65.95	11/3/19	119.62	81.4	684	− 46.6	660
8/24/21	63.90	3/20/23	105.38	64.9	573	− 18.6	221
10/27/23	85.76	9/3/29	381.17	344.5	2138	− 47.9	71
11/13/29	198.69	4/17/30	294.07	48.0	155	− 86.0	813
7/8/32	41.22	9/7/32	79.93	93.9	61	− 37.2	173
2/27/33	50.16	2/5/34	110.74	120.8	343	− 22.8	171
7/26/34	85.51	3/10/37	194.40	127.3	958	− 49.1	386
3/31/38	98.95	11/12/38	158.41	60.1	226	− 23.3	147
4/8/39	121.44	9/12/39	155.92	28.4	157	− 40.4	959
4/28/42	92.92	5/29/46	212.50	128.7	1492	− 23.2	353
5/17/47	163.21	6/15/48	193.16	18.4	395	− 16.3	363
6/13/49	161.60	1/5/53	293.79	81.8	1302	− 13.0	252
9/14/53	255.49	4/6/56	521.05	103.9	935	− 19.4	564
10/22/57	419.79	1/5/60	685.47	63.3	805	− 17.4	294
10/25/60	566.05	12/13/61	734.91	29.8	414	− 27.1	195
6/26/62	535.76	2/9/66	995.15	85.7	1324	− 25.2	240
10/7/66	744.32	12/3/68	985.21	32.4	788	− 35.9	539
5/26/70	631.16	4/28/71	950.82	50.6	337	− 16.1	209
11/23/71	797.97	1/11/73	1051.70	31.8	415	− 45.1	694
12/6/74	577.60	9/21/76	1014.79	75.7	655	− 26.9	525
2/28/78	742.12	9/8/78	907.74	22.3	192	− 16.4	591
4/21/80	759.13	4/27/81	1024.05	34.9	371	− 24.1	472
8/12/82	776.92	11/29/83	1287.20	65.7	474	− 15.6	238
7/24/84	1086.57	8/25/87	2722.42	150.6	1127	− 36.1	55
10/19/87	1738.74	7/17/90	2999.75	72.5	1002	− 21.2	86
10/11/90	2365.10	7/17/98	9337.97	294.8	2836	− 19.3	45
8/31/98	7539.07	1/14/00	11722.98	55.5	501	− 29.7	616
9/21/01	8235.81	3/19/02	10635.25	29.1	179	− 31.5	204
10/9/02	7286.27	4/30/07	13062.91	79.3*	1664*	*At Press Time	
			Average	85.2%	751	− 30.8%	406

Based on Dow Jones industrial average.
The NYSE was closed from 7/31/1914 to 12/11/1914 due to World War I.
DJIA figures were then adjusted back to reflect the composition change from 12 to 20 stocks in September 1916.

1900-2000 Data: Ned Davis Research

STANDARD & POOR'S 500 BULL & BEAR MARKETS SINCE 1929 NASDAQ COMPOSITE SINCE 1971

A constant debate of the definition and timing of bull and bear markets permeates Wall Street like the bell that signals the open and close of every trading day. We have relied on the Ned Davis Research parameters for years to track bulls and bears on the Dow (see page 131). Standard & Poor's 500 index has been a stalwart indicator for decades and at times marched to a different beat than the Dow. With the increasing prominence of NASDAQ as a benchmark we felt the time had come to add bull and bear data on the other two main stock averages to the Almanac. We conferred with Sam Stovall, Chief Investment Strategist at Standard & Poor's, and correlated the moves of the S&P 500 and NASDAQ to the bull & bear dates on page 131 to compile the data below on bull and bear markets for the S&P 500 and NASDAQ. Many dates line up for the three indices but you will notice quite a lag or lead on several occasions, including NASDAQ's independent cadence from 1975 to 1980.

STANDARD & POOR'S 500 BULL AND BEAR MARKETS

— Beginning —		— Ending —		Bull		Bear	
Date	S&P 500	Date	S&P 500	% Gain	Days	% Change	Days
11/13/29	17.66	4/10/30	25.92	46.8%	148	– 83.0%	783
6/1/32	4.40	9/7/32	9.31	111.6	98	– 40.6	173
2/27/33	5.53	2/6/34	11.82	113.7	344	– 31.8	401
3/14/35	8.06	3/6/37	16.68	106.9	723	– 49.0	390
3/31/38	8.50	11/9/38	13.79	62.2	223	– 26.2	150
4/8/39	10.18	10/25/39	13.21	29.8	200	– 43.5	916
4/28/42	7.47	5/29/46	19.25	157.7	1492	– 28.8	353
5/17/47	13.71	6/15/48	17.06	24.4	395	– 20.6	363
6/13/49	13.55	1/5/53	26.66	96.8	1302	– 14.8	252
9/14/53	22.71	8/2/56	49.74	119.0	1053	– 21.6	446
10/22/57	38.98	8/3/59	60.71	55.7	650	– 13.9	449
10/25/60	52.30	12/12/61	72.64	38.9	413	– 28.0	196
6/26/62	52.32	2/9/66	94.06	79.8	1324	– 22.2	240
10/7/66	73.20	11/29/68	108.37	48.0	784	– 36.1	543
5/26/70	69.29	4/28/71	104.77	51.2	337	– 13.9	209
11/23/71	90.16	1/11/73	120.24	33.4	415	– 48.2	630
10/3/74	62.28	9/21/76	107.83	73.1	719	– 19.4	531
3/6/78	86.90	9/12/78	106.99	23.1	190	– 8.2	562
3/27/80	98.22	11/28/80	140.52	43.1	246	– 27.1	622
8/12/82	102.42	10/10/83	172.65	68.6	424	– 14.4	288
7/24/84	147.82	8/25/87	336.77	127.8	1127	– 33.5	101
12/4/87	223.92	7/16/90	368.95	64.8	955	– 19.9	87
10/11/90	295.46	7/17/98	1186.75	301.7	2836	– 19.3	45
8/31/98	957.28	3/24/00	1527.46	59.6	571	– 36.8	546
9/21/01	965.80	1/4/02	1172.51	21.4	105	– 33.8	278
10/9/02	776.76	4/30/07	1482.37	90.8*	1664*	*At Press Time	
			Average	**78.8%**	**721**	**– 29.4%**	**382**

NASDAQ COMPOSITE BULL AND BEAR MARKETS

— Beginning —		— Ending —		Bull		Bear	
Date	NASDAQ	Date	NASDAQ	% Gain	Days	% Change	Days
11/23/71	100.31	1/11/73	136.84	36.4%	415	– 59.9%	630
10/3/74	54.87	7/15/75	88.00	60.4	285	– 16.2	63
9/16/75	73.78	9/13/78	139.25	88.7	1093	– 20.4	62
11/14/78	110.88	2/8/80	165.25	49.0	451	– 24.9	48
3/27/80	124.09	5/29/81	223.47	80.1	428	– 28.8	441
8/13/82	159.14	6/24/83	328.91	106.7	315	– 31.5	397
7/25/84	225.30	8/26/87	455.26	102.1	1127	– 35.9	63
10/28/87	291.88	10/9/89	485.73	66.4	712	– 33.0	372
10/16/90	325.44	7/20/98	2014.25	518.9	2834	– 29.5	80
10/8/98	1419.12	3/10/00	5048.62	255.8	519	– 71.8	560
9/21/01	1423.19	1/4/02	2059.38	44.7	105	– 45.9	278
10/9/02	1114.11	4/30/07	2525.09	126.6*	1664*	*At Press Time	
			Average	**128.0%**	**829**	**– 36.2%**	**272**

JANUARY DAILY POINT CHANGES DOW JONES INDUSTRIALS

Previous Month Close	1998	1999	2000	2001	2002	2003	2004	2005	2006	2007
Close	7908.25	9181.43	11497.12	10786.85	10021.50	8341.63	10453.92	10783.01	10717.50	12463.15
1	H	H	S	H	H	H	H	S	S	H
2	56.79	S	S	-140.70	51.90	265.89	-44.07	S	S	H*
3	S	S	-139.61	299.60	98.74	-5.83		-53.58	129.91	11.37
4	S	2.84	-359.58	-33.34	87.60	S	S	-98.65	32.74	6.17
5	13.95	126.92	124.72	-250.40	S	S	134.22	-32.95	2.00	-82.68
6	-72.74	233.78	130.61	S	S	171.88	-5.41	25.05	77.16	S
7	-3.98	-7.21	269.30	S	-62.69	-32.98	-9.63	-18.92	S	S
8	-99.65	105.56	S	-40.66	-46.50	-145.28	63.41	S	S	25.48
9	-222.20	S	S	-48.80	-56.46	180.87	-133.55	S	52.59	-6.89
10	S	S	49.64	31.72	-26.23	8.71	S	17.07	-0.32	25.56
11	S	-23.43	-61.12	5.28	-80.33	S	S	-64.81	31.86	72.82
12	66.76	-145.21	40.02	-84.17	S	S	26.29	61.56	-81.08	41.10
13	84.95	-125.12	31.33	S	S	1.09	-58.00	-111.95	-2.49	S
14	52.56	-228.63	140.55	S	-96.11	56.64	111.19	52.17	S	S
15	-92.92	219.62	S	S	32.73	-119.44	15.48	S	S	H
16	61.78	S	S	127.28	-211.88	-25.31	46.66	S	S	26.51
17	S	S	H	-68.32	137.77	-111.13	S	H	-63.55	-5.44
18	S	H	-162.26	93.94	-78.19	S	S	70.79	-41.46	-9.22
19	H	14.67	-71.36	-90.69	S	S	H	-88.82	25.85	-2.40
20	119.57	-19.31	-138.06	S	S	H	-71.85	-68.50	-213.32	S
21	-78.72	-71.83	-99.59	S	H	-143.84	94.96	-78.48	S	S
22	-63.52	-143.41	S	-9.35	-58.05	-124.17	-0.44	S	S	-88.37
23	-30.14	S	S	71.57	17.16	50.74	-54.89	S	21.38	56.64
24	S	S	-243.54	-2.84	65.11	-238.46	S	-24.38	23.45	87.97
25	S	82.65	21.72	82.55	44.01	S	S	92.95	-2.48	-119.21
26	12.20	121.26	3.10	-69.54	S	S	134.22	37.03	99.73	-15.54
27	102.14	-124.35	-4.97	S	S	-141.45	-92.59	-31.19	97.74	S
28	100.39	81.10	-289.15	S	25.67	99.28	-141.55	-40.20	S	S
29	57.55	77.50	S	42.21	-247.51	21.87	41.92	S	S	3.76
30	-66.52	S	S	179.01	144.62	-165.58	-22.22	S	-7.29	32.53
31	S	S	201.66	6.16	157.14	108.68	S	62.74	-35.06	98.38
Close	7906.50	9358.83	10940.53	10887.36	9920.00	8053.81	10488.07	10489.94	10864.86	12621.69
Change	-1.75	177.40	-556.59	100.51	-101.50	-287.82	34.15	-293.07	147.36	158.54

Ford funeral

FEBRUARY DAILY POINT CHANGES DOW JONES INDUSTRIALS

Previous Month Close	1998	1999	2000	2001	2002	2003	2004	2005	2006	2007
Close	7906.50	9358.83	10940.53	10887.36	9920.00	8053.81	10488.07	10489.94	10864.86	12621.69
1	S	-13.13	100.52	96.27	-12.74	S	S	62.00	89.09	51.99
2	201.28	-71.58	-37.85	-119.53	S	S	11.11	44.85	-101.97	-20.19
3	52.57	92.69	10.24	S	S	56.01	6.00	-3.69	-58.36	S
4	-30.64	-62.31	-49.64	S	-220.17	-96.53	-34.44	123.03	S	S
5	-12.46	-0.26	S	101.75	-1.66	-28.11	24.81	S	S	8.25
6	72.24	S	S	-8.43	-32.04	-55.88	97.48	S	4.65	4.57
7	S	S	-58.01	-10.70	-27.95	-65.07	S	-0.37	-48.51	0.56
8	S	-13.13	51.81	-66.17	118.80	S	S	8.87	108.86	-29.24
9	-8.97	-158.08	-258.44	-99.10	S	S	-14.00	-60.52	24.73	-56.80
10	115.09	44.28	-55.53	S	S	55.88	34.82	85.50	35.70	S
11	18.94	186.15	-218.42	S	140.54	-77.00	123.85	46.40	S	S
12	55.05	-88.57	S	165.32	-21.04	-84.94	-43.63	S	S	-28.28
13	0.50	S	S	-43.45	125.93	-8.30	-66.22	S	-26.73	102.30
14	S	S	94.63	-107.91	12.32	158.93	S	-4.88	136.07	87.01
15	S	H	198.25	95.61	-98.95	S	S	46.19	30.58	23.15
16	H	22.14	-156.68	-91.20	S	S	H	-2.44	61.71	2.56
17	28.40	-101.56	-46.84	S	S	H	87.03	-80.62	-5.36	S
18	52.56	103.16	-295.05	S	H	132.35	-42.89	30.96	S	S
19	-75.48	41.32	S	H	-157.90	-40.55	-7.26	S	S	H
20	38.36	S	S	-68.94	196.03	-85.64	-45.70	S	H	19.07
21	S	S	H	-204.30	-106.49	103.15	S	H	-46.26	-48.23
22	S	212.73	85.32	0.23	133.47	S	S	-174.02	68.11	-52.39
23	-3.74	-8.26	-79.11	-84.91	S	S	-9.41	62.59	-67.95	-38.54
24	-40.10	-144.75	-133.10	S	S	-159.87	-43.25	75.00	-7.37	S
25	87.68	-33.33	-230.51	S	177.56	51.26	35.25	92.81	S	S
26	32.89	-59.76	S	200.63	-30.45	-102.52	-21.48	S	S	-15.22
27	55.05	S	S	-5.65	12.32	78.01	3.78	S	35.70	-416.02
28	S	S	176.53	-141.60	-21.45	6.09	S	-75.37	-104.14	52.39
29	—	—	89.66				S			
Close	8545.72	9306.58	10128.31	10495.28	10106.13	7891.08	10583.92	10766.23	10993.41	12268.63
Change	639.22	-52.25	-812.22	-392.08	186.13	-162.73	95.85	276.29	128.55	-353.06

	1998	1999	2000	2001	2002	2003	2004	2005	2006	2007
Previous Month Close	8545.72	9306.58	10128.31	10495.28	10106.13	7891.08	10583.92	10766.23	10993.41	12268.63
1	S	18.20	9.62	-45.14	262.73	S	94.22	63.77	60.12	-34.29
2	4.73	-27.17	26.99	16.17	S	S	-86.66	-18.03	-28.02	-120.24
3	34.38	-21.73	202.28	S	S	-53.22	1.63	21.06	-3.92	S
4	-45.59	191.52	S	S	217.96	-132.99	-5.11	107.52	S	S
5	-94.91	268.68	S	95.99	-153.41	70.73	7.55	S	S	-63.69
6	125.06	S	-196.70	28.92	140.88	-101.61	S	S	-63.00	157.18
7	S	S	-374.47	138.38	-48.92	66.04	S	-3.69	22.10	-15.14
8	S	-8.47	60.50	128.65	47.12	S	-66.07	-24.24	25.05	68.25
9	-2.25	-33.85	154.20	-213.63	S	S	-72.52	-107.00	-33.46	15.62
10	75.98	79.08	-81.91	S	S	-171.85	-160.07	45.89	104.06	S
11	32.63	124.60	S	S	38.75	-44.12	-168.51	-77.15	S	S
12	-16.19	-21.09	S	-436.37	21.11	28.01	111.70	S	S	42.30
13	-57.04	S	18.31	82.55	-130.50	269.68	S	S	-0.32	-242.66
14	S	S	-135.89	-317.34	15.29	37.96	S	30.15	75.32	57.44
15	S	82.42	320.17	57.82	90.09	S	-137.19	-59.41	58.43	26.28
16	116.33	-28.30	499.19	-207.87	S	S	81.78	-112.03	43.47	-49.27
17	31.14	-51.06	-35.37	S	S	282.21	115.63	-6.72	26.41	S
18	25.41	118.21	S	S	-29.48	52.31	-4.52	3.32	S	S
19	27.65	-94.07	S	135.70	57.50	71.22	-109.18	S	S	115.76
20	103.38	S	85.01	-238.35	-133.68	21.15	S	S	-5.12	61.93
21	S	S	227.10	-233.76	-21.73	235.37	S	-64.28	-39.06	159.42
22	S	-13.04	-40.64	-97.52	-52.17	S	-121.85	-94.88	81.96	13.62
23	-90.18	-218.68	253.16	115.30	S	S	-1.11	-14.49	-47.14	19.87
24	88.19	-4.99	-7.14	S	S	-307.29	-15.41	-13.15	9.68	S
25	-31.64	169.55	S	S	-146.00	65.55	170.59	H	S	S
26	-25.91	-14.15	S	182.75	71.69	-50.35	-5.85	S	S	-11.94
27	-50.81	S	-86.87	260.01	73.55	-28.43	S	S	-29.86	-71.78
28	S	S	-89.74	-162.19	-22.97	-55.68	S	42.78	-95.57	-96.93
29	S	184.54	82.61	13.71	H	S	116.66	-79.95	61.16	48.39
30	-13.96	-93.52	-38.47	79.72	S	S	52.07	135.23	-65.00	5.60
31	17.69	-127.10	-58.33	S	S	-153.64	-24.00	-37.17	-41.38	S
Close	8799.81	9786.16	10921.92	9878.78	10403.94	7992.13	10357.70	10503.76	11109.32	12354.35
Change	254.09	479.58	793.61	-616.50	297.81	101.05	-226.22	-262.47	115.91	85.72

	1998	1999	2000	2001	2002	2003	2004	2005	2006	2007
Previous Month Close	8799.81	9786.16	10921.92	9878.78	10403.94	7992.13	10357.70	10503.76	11109.32	12354.35
1	68.51	46.35	S	S	-41.24	77.73	15.63	-99.46	S	S
2	118.32	H	S	-100.85	-48.99	215.20	97.26	S	S	27.95
3	-3.23	S	300.01	-292.22	-115.42	-44.68	S	S	35.62	128.00
4	S	S	-57.09	29.71	36.88	36.77	S	16.84	58.91	19.75
5	S	174.82	-130.92	402.63	36.47	S	87.78	37.32	35.70	30.15
6	49.82	-43.84	80.35	-126.96	S	S	12.44	27.56	-23.05	H
7	-76.73	121.82	-2.79	S	S	23.26	-90.66	60.30	-96.46	S
8	-65.02	112.39	S	S	-22.56	-1.49	-38.12	-84.98	S	S
9	103.38	-23.86	S	54.06	-40.41	-100.98	H	S	S	8.94
10	H	S	75.08	257.59	173.06	23.39	S	S	21.29	4.71
11	S	S	100.52	-89.27	-205.65	-17.92	S	-12.78	-51.70	-89.23
12	S	165.67	-161.95	113.47	14.74	S	73.53	59.41	40.34	68.34
13	17.44	55.50	-201.58	H	S	S	-134.28	-104.04	7.68	59.17
14	97.90	16.65	-617.78	S	S	147.69	-3.33	-125.18	H	S
15	52.07	51.06	S	S	-97.15	51.26	19.51	-191.24	S	S
16	-85.70	31.17	S	31.62	207.65	-144.75	54.51	S	S	108.33
17	90.93	S	276.74	58.17	-80.54	80.04	S	S	-63.87	52.58
18	S	S	184.91	399.10	-15.50	H	S	-16.26	194.99	30.80
19	S	-53.36	-92.46	77.88	51.83	S	-14.12	56.16	10.00	4.79
20	-25.66	8.02	169.09	-113.86	S	S	-123.35	-115.05	64.12	153.35
21	43.10	132.87	H	S	S	-8.75	2.77	206.24	4.56	S
22	-8.22	145.76	S	S	-120.68	156.09	143.93	-60.89	S	S
23	-33.39	-37.51	S	-47.62	-47.19	30.67	11.64	S	S	-42.58
24	-78.71	S	62.05	-77.89	-58.81	-75.62	S	S	-11.13	34.54
25	S	S	218.72	170.86	4.63	-133.69	S	84.76	-53.07	135.95
26	S	28.92	-179.32	67.15	-124.34	S	-28.11	-91.34	71.24	15.61
27	-146.98	113.12	-57.40	117.70	S	S	33.43	47.67	28.02	15.44
28	-18.68	13.74	-154.19	S	S	165.26	-135.56	-128.43	-15.37	S
29	52.56	32.93	S	S	-90.85	31.38	-70.33	122.14	S	S
30	111.85	-89.34	S	-75.08	126.35	-22.90	-46.70	S	S	-58.03
Close	9063.37	10789.04	10733.91	10734.97	9946.22	8480.09	10225.57	10192.51	11367.14	13062.91
Change	263.56	1002.88	-188.01	856.19	-457.72	487.96	-132.13	-311.25	257.82	708.56

MAY DAILY POINT CHANGES DOW JONES INDUSTRIALS

Previous Month Close	1997	1998	1999	2000	2001	2002	2003	2004	2005	2006
	7008.99	9063.37	10789.04	10733.91	10734.97	9946.22	8480.09	10225.57	10192.51	11367.14
1	-32.51	83.70	S	77.87	163.37	113.41	-25.84	S	S	-23.85
2	94.72	S	S	-80.66	-21.66	32.24	128.43	S	59.19	73.16
3	S	S	225.65	-250.99	-80.03	-85.24	S	88.43	5.25	-16.17
4	S	45.59	-128.58	-67.64	154.59	S	S	3.20	127.69	38.58
5	143.29	-45.09	69.30	165.37	S	S	-51.11	-6.25	-44.26	138.88
6	10.83	-92.92	-8.59	S	S	-198.59	56.79	-69.69	5.02	S
7	-139.67	-77.97	84.77	S	-16.07	28.51	-27.73	-123.92	S	S
8	50.97	78.47	S	25.77	-51.66	305.28	-69.41	S	S	6.80
9	32.91	S	S	-66.88	-16.53	-104.41	113.38	S	38.94	55.23
10	S	S	-24.34	-168.97	43.46	-97.50	S	-127.32	-103.23	2.88
11	S	36.37	18.90	178.19	-89.13	S	S	29.45	19.14	-141.92
12	123.22	70.25	-25.78	63.40	S	S	122.13	25.69	-110.77	-119.74
13	-18.54	50.07	106.82	S	S	169.74	-47.48	-34.42	-49.36	S
14	11.95	-39.61	-193.87	S	56.02	188.48	-31.43	2.13	S	S
15	47.39	-76.23	S	198.41	-4.36	-54.46	65.32	S	S	47.78
16	-138.88	S	S	126.79	342.95	45.53	-34.17	S	112.17	-8.88
17	S	S	-59.85	-164.83	32.66	63.87	S	-105.96	79.59	-214.28
18	S	-45.09	-16.52	7.54	53.16	S	S	61.60	132.57	-77.32
19	34.21	3.74	50.44	-150.43	S	S	-185.58	-30.80	28.74	15.77
20	74.58	116.83	-20.65	S	S	-123.58	-2.03	-0.07	-21.28	S
21	-12.77	-39.11	-37.46	S	36.18	-123.79	25.07	29.10	S	S
22	-32.56	-17.93	S	-84.30	-80.68	52.17	77.59	S	S	-18.73
23	87.78	S	S	-120.28	-151.73	58.20	7.36	S	51.65	-26.98
24	S	S	-174.61	113.08	16.91	-111.82	S	-8.31	-19.88	18.97
25	S	H	-123.58	-211.43	-117.05	S	S	159.19	-45.88	93.73
26	H	-150.71	171.07	-24.68	S	S	H	-7.73	79.80	67.56
27	37.50	-27.16	-235.23	S	S	H	179.97	95.31	4.95	S
28	-26.18	33.63	92.81	S	H	-122.68	11.77	-16.75	S	S
29	-27.05	-70.25	S	S	33.77	-58.54	-81.94	S	S	H
30	0.86	S	S	227.89	-166.50	-11.35	139.08	S	H	-184.18
31	S	S	H	-4.80	39.30	13.56	S	H	-75.07	73.88
Close	7331.04	8899.95	10559.74	10522.33	10911.94	9925.25	8850.26	10188.45	10467.48	11168.31
Change	322.05	-163.42	-229.30	-211.58	176.97	-20.97	370.17	-37.12	274.97	-198.83

JUNE DAILY POINT CHANGES DOW JONES INDUSTRIALS

Previous Month Close	1997	1998	1999	2000	2001	2002	2003	2004	2005	2006
	7331.04	8899.95	10559.74	10522.33	10911.94	9925.25	8850.26	10188.45	10467.48	11168.31
1	S	22.42	36.52	129.87	78.47	S	S	14.20	82.39	91.97
2	-41.64	-31.13	-18.37	142.56	S	S	47.55	60.32	3.62	-12.41
3	22.75	-87.44	85.80	S	S	-215.46	25.14	-67.06	-92.52	S
4	-42.49	66.76	136.15	S	71.11	-21.95	116.03	46.91	S	S
5	35.63	167.15	S	20.54	114.32	108.96	2.32	S	S	-199.15
6	130.49	S	S	-79.73	-105.60	-172.16	21.49	S	6.06	-46.58
7	S	S	109.54	77.29	20.50	-34.97	S	148.26	16.04	-71.24
8	S	31.89	-143.74	-144.14	-113.74	S	S	41.44	-6.21	7.92
9	42.72	-19.68	-75.35	-54.66	S	S	-82.79	-64.08	26.16	-46.90
10	60.77	-78.22	-69.02	S	S	55.73	74.89	41.66	9.61	S
11	36.56	-159.93	-130.76	S	-54.91	-128.14	128.33	H*	S	S
12	135.64	23.17	S	-49.85	26.29	100.45	13.33	S	S	-99.34
13	70.57	S	S	57.63	-76.76	-114.91	-79.43	S	9.93	-86.44
14	S	S	72.82	66.11	-181.49	-28.59	S	-75.37	25.01	110.78
15	S	-207.01	31.66	26.87	-66.49	S	S	45.70	18.80	198.27
16	-9.95	37.36	189.96	-265.52	S	S	201.84	-0.85	12.28	-0.64
17	-11.31	164.17	56.68	S	S	213.21	4.06	-2.06	44.42	S
18	-42.07	-16.45	13.93	S	21.74	18.70	-29.22	38.89	S	S
19	58.35	-100.14	S	108.54	-48.71	-144.55	-114.27	S	S	-72.44
20	19.45	S	S	-122.68	50.66	-129.80	21.22	S	-13.96	32.73
21	S	S	-39.58	62.58	68.10	-177.98	S	-44.94	-9.44	104.62
22	S	-1.74	-94.35	-121.62	-110.84	S	S	23.60	-11.74	-60.35
23	-192.25	117.33	-54.77	28.63	S	S	-127.80	84.50	-166.49	-30.02
24	153.80	95.41	-132.03	S	S	28.03	36.90	-35.76	-123.60	S
25	-68.08	11.71	17.73	S	-100.37	-155.00	-98.32	-71.97	S	S
26	-35.73	8.96	S	138.24	-31.74	-6.71	67.51	S	S	56.19
27	33.47	S	S	-38.53	-37.64	149.81	-89.99	S	-7.06	-120.54
28	S	S	102.59	23.33	131.37	-26.66	S	-14.75	114.85	48.82
29	S	52.82	160.20	-129.75	-63.81	S	S	56.34	-31.15	217.24
30	-14.93	-45.34	155.45	49.85	S	S	-3.61	22.05	-99.51	-40.58
Close	7672.79	8952.02	10970.80	10447.89	10502.40	9243.26	8985.44	10435.48	10274.97	11150.22
Change	341.75	52.07	411.06	-74.44	-409.54	-681.99	135.18	247.03	-192.51	-18.09

* Reagan funeral

JULY DAILY POINT CHANGES DOW JONES INDUSTRIALS

	1997	1998	1999	2000	2001	2002	2003	2004	2005	2006
Previous Month Close	7672.79	8952.02	10970.80	10447.89	10502.40	9243.26	8985.44	10435.48	10274.97	11150.22
1	49.54	96.65	95.62	S	S	-133.47	55.51	-101.32	28.47	S
2	73.05	-23.41	72.82	S	91.32	-102.04	101.89	-51.33	S	S
3	100.43	H	S	112.78*	-22.61*	47.22	-72.63*	S	S	77.8*
4	H	S	S	H	H	H	H	H	H	H
5	S	S	H	-77.07	-91.25	324.53*	S	H	68.36	-76.20
6	S	66.51	-4.12	-2.13	-227.18	S	S	-63.49	-101.12	73.48
7	-37.32	-6.73	52.24	154.51	S	S	146.58	20.95	31.61	-134.63
8	103.82	89.93	-60.47	S	S	-104.60	6.30	-68.73	146.85	S
9	-119.88	-85.19	66.81	S	46.72	-178.81	-66.88	41.66	S	S
10	44.33	15.96	S	10.60	-123.76	-282.59	-120.17	S	S	12.88
11	35.06	S	S	80.61	65.38	-11.97	83.55	S	70.58	31.22
12	S	S	7.28	56.22	237.97	-117.00	S	25.00	-5.83	-121.59
13	S	-9.53	-25.96	5.30	60.07	S	S	9.37	43.50	-166.89
14	1.16	149.33	-26.92	24.04	S	S	57.56	-38.79	71.50	-106.94
15	52.73	-11.07	38.31	S	S	-45.34	-48.18	-45.64	11.94	S
16	63.17	93.72	23.43	S	-66.94	-166.08	-34.38	-23.38	S	S
17	-18.11	9.78	S	-8.48	134.27	69.37	-43.77	S	S	8.01
18	-130.31	S	S	-64.35	-36.56	-132.99	137.33	S	-65.84	51.87
19	S	S	-22.16	-43.84	40.17	-390.23	S	-45.72	71.57	212.19
20	S	-42.22	-191.55	147.79	-33.35	S	S	55.01	42.59	-83.32
21	16.26	-105.56	6.65	-110.31	S	S	-91.46	-102.94	-61.38	-59.72
22	154.93	-61.28	-33.56	S	S	-234.68	61.76	4.20	23.41	S
23	26.71	-195.93	-58.26	S	-152.23	-82.24	35.79	-88.11	S	S
24	28.57	4.38	S	-48.44	-183.30	488.95	-81.73	S	S	182.67
25	-3.49	S	S	14.85	164.55	-4.98	172.06	S	-54.70	52.66
26	S	S	-47.80	-183.49	49.96	78.08	S	-0.30	-16.71	-1.20
27	S	90.88	115.88	69.65	-38.96	S	S	123.22	57.32	-2.08
28	7.67	-93.46	-6.97	-74.96	S	S	-18.06	31.93	68.46	119.27
29	53.42	-19.82	-180.78	S	S	447.49	-62.05	12.17	-64.64	S
30	80.36	111.99	-136.14	S	-14.95	-31.85	-4.41	10.47	S	S
31	-32.28	-143.66	S	10.81	121.09	56.56	33.75	S	S	-34.02
Close	8222.61	8883.29	10655.15	10521.98	10522.81	8736.59	9233.80	10139.71	10640.91	11185.68
Change	549.82	-68.73	-315.65	74.09	20.41	-506.67	248.36	-295.77	365.94	35.46

* Shortened trading day

AUGUST DAILY POINT CHANGES DOW JONES INDUSTRIALS

	1997	1998	1999	2000	2001	2002	2003	2004	2005	2006
Previous Month Close	8222.61	8883.29	10655.15	10521.98	10522.81	8736.59	9233.80	10139.71	10640.91	11185.68
1	-28.57	S	S	84.97	-12.80	-229.97	-79.83	S	-17.76	-59.95
2	S	S	-9.19	80.58	41.17	-193.49	S	39.45	60.59	74.20
3	S	-96.55	31.35	19.05	-38.40	S	S	-58.92	13.85	42.66
4	4.41	-299.43	-2.54	61.17	S	S	32.07	6.27	-87.49	-2.24
5	-10.91	59.47	119.05	S	S	-269.50	-149.72	-163.48	-52.07	S
6	71.77	30.90	-79.79	S	-111.47	230.46	25.42	-147.70	S	S
7	-71.31	20.34	S	99.26	57.43	182.06	64.71	S	S	-20.97
8	-156.78	S	S	109.88	-165.24	255.87	64.64	S	-21.10	-45.79
9	S	S	-6.33	-71.06	5.06	33.43	S	-0.67	78.74	-97.41
10	S	-23.17	-52.55	2.93	117.69	S	S	130.01	-21.26	48.19
11	30.89	-112.00	132.65	119.04	S	S	26.26	-6.35	91.48	-36.34
12	-101.27	90.11	1.59	S	S	-56.56	92.71	-123.73	-85.58	S
13	-32.52	-93.46	184.26	S	-0.34	-206.50	-38.30	10.76	S	S
14	13.71	-34.50	S	148.34	-3.74	260.92	38.80	S	S	9.84
15	-247.37	S	S	-109.14	-66.22	74.83	11.13	S	34.07	132.39
16	S	S	73.14	-58.61	46.57	-40.08	S	129.20	-120.93	96.86
17	S	149.85	70.29	47.25	-151.74	S	S	18.28	37.26	7.84
18	108.70	139.80	-125.70	-9.16	S	S	90.76	110.32	4.22	46.51
19	114.74	-21.37	-27.54	S	S	212.73	16.45	-42.33	4.30	S
20	103.13	-81.87	136.77	S	79.29	-118.72	-31.39	69.32	S	S
21	-127.28	-77.76	S	33.33	-145.93	85.16	26.17	S	S	-36.42
22	-6.04	S	S	59.34	102.76	96.41	-74.81	S	10.66	-5.21
23	S	S	199.15	5.50	-47.75	-180.68	S	25.58	-50.31	-41.94
24	S	32.96	-16.46	38.09	194.02	S	S	83.11	-84.71	6.56
25	-28.34	36.04	42.74	9.89	S	S	-31.23	-8.33	15.76	-20.41
26	-77.35	-79.30	-127.59	S	S	46.05	22.81	21.60	-53.34	S
27	5.11	-357.36	-108.28	S	-40.82	-94.60	-6.66	-37.09	S	S
28	-92.90	-114.31	S	60.21	-160.32	-130.32	40.42	S	S	67.96
29	-72.01	S	S	-37.74	-131.13	-23.10	41.61	S	65.76	17.93
30	S	S	-176.04	-112.09	-171.32	-7.49	S	-72.49	-50.23	12.97
31	S	-512.61	-84.85	112.09	30.17	S	S	51.40	68.78	-1.76
Close	7622.42	7539.07	10829.28	11215.10	9949.75	8663.50	9415.82	10173.92	10481.60	11381.15
Change	-600.19	-1344.22	174.13	693.12	-573.06	-73.09	182.02	34.21	-159.31	195.47

SEPTEMBER DAILY POINT CHANGES DOW JONES INDUSTRIALS

Previous Month	1997	1998	1999	2000	2001	2002	2003	2004	2005	2006
Close	7622.42	7539.07	10829.28	11215.10	9949.75	8663.50	9415.82	10173.92	10481.60	11381.15
1	H	288.36	108.60	23.68	S	S	H	−5.46	−21.97	83.00
2	257.36	−45.06	−94.67	S	S	H	107.45	121.82	−12.26	S
3	14.86	−100.15	235.24	S	H	−355.45	45.19	−30.08	S	S
4	−27.40	−41.97	S	H	47.74	117.07	19.44	S	S	H
5	−44.83	S	S	21.83	35.78	−141.42	−84.56	S	H	5.13
6	S	S	H	50.03	−192.43	143.50	S	H	141.87	−63.08
7	S	H	−44.32	2.21	−234.99	S	S	82.95	44.26	−74.76
8	12.77	380.53	2.21	−39.22	S	S	82.95	−29.43	−37.57	60.67
9	16.73	−155.76	43.06	S	S	92.18	−79.09	−24.26	82.63	S
10	−132.63	−249.48	−50.97	S	−0.34	83.23	−86.74	23.97	S	S
11	−58.30	179.96	S	−25.16	Closed*	−21.44	39.30	S	S	4.73
12	81.99	S	S	37.74	Closed*	−201.76	11.79	S	4.38	101.25
13	S	S	1.90	−51.05	Closed*	−66.72	S	1.69	−85.50	45.23
14	S	149.85	−120.00	−94.71	Closed*	S	S	−86.80	13.85	33.38
15	−21.83	79.04	−108.91	−160.47	S	S	−22.74	118.53	13.13	83.19
16	174.78	65.39	−63.96	S	S	67.49	118.53	13.13	83.19	S
17	−9.48	−216.01	66.17	S	−684.81	−172.63	−21.69	39.97	S	S
18	36.28	21.89	S	−118.48	−17.30	−35.10	113.48	S	S	−5.77
19	−5.45	S	S	20.27	−19.23	−144.27	−230.06	S	−84.31	−14.09
20	S	S	−225.43	−101.37	−382.92	43.63	S	−79.57	−76.11	72.28
21	S	37.59	−74.40	77.60	−140.40	S	S	40.04	−103.49	−79.96
22	79.56	−36.05	−74.40	81.85	S	S	−109.41	−135.75	44.02	−25.13
23	−26.77	257.21	−205.48	S	S	−113.87	40.63	−70.28	−2.46	S
24	−63.35	−152.42	−39.26	S	368.05	−189.02	−150.53	8.34	S	S
25	−58.70	26.78	S	−39.22	56.11	158.69	−81.55	S	S	67.71
26	74.17	S	S	−176.83	−92.58	155.30	−30.88	S	24.04	93.58
27	S	S	24.06	−2.96	114.03	−295.67	S	−58.70	12.58	19.85
28	S	80.07	−27.86	195.70	166.14	S	S	88.86	16.88	29.21
29	69.25	−28.32	−62.05	−173.14	S	S	67.16	58.84	79.69	−39.38
30	−46.17	−237.90	123.47	S	S	−109.52	−105.18	−55.97	15.92	S
Close	7945.26	7842.62	10336.95	10650.92	8847.56	7591.93	9275.06	10080.27	10568.70	11679.07
Change	322.84	303.55	−492.33	−564.18	−1102.19	−1071.57	−140.76	−93.65	87.10	297.92

* Market closed for four days following 9/11 terrorist attacks

OCTOBER DAILY POINT CHANGES DOW JONES INDUSTRIALS

Previous Month	1997	1998	1999	2000	2001	2002	2003	2004	2005	2006
Close	7945.26	7842.62	10336.95	10650.92	8847.56	7591.93	9275.06	10080.27	10568.70	11679.07
1	70.24	−210.09	−63.95	S	−10.73	346.86	194.14	112.38	S	S
2	12.03	152.16	S	49.21	113.76	−183.18	18.60	S	S	−8.72
3	11.05	S	S	19.61	173.19	−38.42	84.51	S	−33.22	56.99
4	S	S	128.23	64.74	−62.90	−188.79	S	23.89	−94.37	123.27
5	S	−58.45	−0.64	−59.56	58.89	S	S	−38.86	−123.75	16.08
6	61.64	16.74	187.75	−128.38	S	S	22.67	62.24	−30.26	−16.48
7	78.09	−1.29	−51.29	S	S	−105.56	59.63	−114.52	5.21	S
8	−83.25	−9.78	112.71	S	−51.83	78.65	−23.71	−70.20	S	S
9	−33.64	167.61	S	−28.11	−15.50	−215.22	49.11	S	S	7.60
10	−16.21	S	S	−44.03	188.42	247.68	−5.33	S	−53.55	9.36
11	S	S	−1.58	−110.61	169.59	316.34	S	26.77	14.41	−15.04
12	S	101.95	−231.12	−379.21	−66.29	S	S	−4.79	−36.26	95.57
13	27.01	−63.33	−184.90	157.60	S	S	89.70	−74.85	−0.32	12.81
14	24.07	30.64	54.45	S	S	27.11	48.60	−107.88	70.75	S
15	−38.31	330.58	−266.90	S	3.46	378.28	−9.93	38.93	S	S
16	−119.10	117.40	S	46.62	36.61	−219.65	−11.33	S	S	20.09
17	−91.85	S	S	−149.09	−151.26	239.01	−69.93	S	60.76	−30.58
18	S	S	96.57	−114.69	−69.75	47.36	S	22.94	−62.84	42.66
19	S	49.69	88.65	167.96	40.89	S	S	−58.70	128.87	19.05
20	74.41	39.40	187.43	83.61	S	S	56.15	−10.69	−133.03	−9.36
21	139.00	13.38	−94.67	S	S	215.84	−30.30	−21.17	−65.88	S
22	−25.79	13.91	172.56	S	172.92	−88.08	−149.40	−107.95	S	S
23	−186.88	−80.85	S	45.13	−36.95	44.11	14.89	S	S	114.54
24	−132.36	S	S	121.35	5.54	−176.93	−30.67	S	169.78	10.97
25	S	S	−120.32	−66.59	117.28	126.65	S	−7.82	−7.13	6.80
26	S	−20.08	−47.80	53.64	82.27	S	S	138.49	−32.89	28.98
27	−554.26	−66.17	92.76	210.50	S	S	25.70	113.55	−115.03	−73.40
28	337.17	5.93	227.64	S	S	−75.95	140.15	2.51	172.82	S
29	8.35	123.06	107.33	S	−275.67	0.90	26.22	22.93	S	S
30	−125.00	97.07	S	245.15	−147.52	58.47	12.08	S	S	−5.77
31	60.41	S	S	135.37	−46.84	−30.38	14.51	S	37.30	−3.76
Close	7442.08	8592.10	10729.86	10971.14	9075.14	8397.03	9801.12	10027.47	10440.07	12080.73
Change	−503.18	749.48	392.91	320.22	227.58	805.10	526.06	−52.80	−128.63	401.66

NOVEMBER DAILY POINT CHANGES DOW JONES INDUSTRIALS

Previous Month Close	1997	1998	1999	2000	2001	2002	2003	2004	2005	2006
	7442.08	8592.10	10729.86	10971.14	9075.14	8397.03	9801.12	10027.47	10440.07	12080.73
1	S	S	-81.35	-71.67	188.76	120.61	S	26.92	-33.30	-49.71
2	S	114.05	-66.67	-18.96	59.64	S	S	-18.66	65.96	-12.48
3	232.31	0.00	27.22	-62.56	S	S	57.34	101.32	49.86	-32.50
4	14.74	76.99	30.58	S	S	53.96	-19.63	177.71	8.17	S
5	3.44	132.33	64.84	S	117.49	106.67	-18.00	72.78	S	S
6	-9.33	59.99	S	159.26	150.09	92.74	36.14	S	S	119.51
7	-101.92	S	S	-25.03	-36.75	-184.77	-47.18	S	55.47	51.22
8	S	S	14.37	-45.12	33.15	-49.11	S	3.77	-46.51	19.77
9	S	-77.50	-101.53	-72.81	20.48	S	S	-4.94	6.49	-73.24
10	-28.73	-33.98	-19.58	-231.30	S	S	-53.26	-0.89	93.89	5.13
11	6.14	-40.16	-2.44	S	S	-178.18	-18.74	84.36	45.94	S
12	-157.41	5.92	174.02	S	-53.63	27.05	111.04	69.17	S	S
13	86.44	89.85	S	-85.70	196.58	12.49	-10.89	S	S	23.45
14	84.72	S	S	163.81	72.66	143.64	-69.26	S	11.13	86.13
15	S	S	-8.57	26.54	48.78	36.96	S	11.23	-10.73	33.70
16	S	91.66	171.58	-51.57	-5.40	S	S	-62.59	-11.68	54.11
17	125.74	-24.97	-49.24	-26.16	S	S	-57.85	61.92	45.46	36.74
18	-47.40	54.83	152.61	S	S	-92.52	-86.67	22.98	46.11	S
19	73.92	14.94	-31.81	S	109.47	-11.79	66.30	-115.64	S	S
20	101.87	103.50	S	-167.22	-75.08	148.23	-71.04	S	S	-26.02
21	54.46	S	S	31.85	-66.70	222.14	9.11	S	53.95	5.05
22	S	S	85.63	-95.18	H	-40.31	S	32.51	51.15	5.36
23	S	214.72	-93.89	H	125.03*	S	S	3.18	44.66	H
24	-113.15	-73.12	12.54	70.91*	S	S	119.26	27.71	H	-46.78*
25	41.03	13.13	H	S	S	44.56	16.15	H	15.53*	S
26	-14.17	H	-19.26*	S	23.04	-172.98	15.63	1.92*	S	S
27	H	18.80*	S	75.84	-110.15	255.26	H	S	S	-158.46
28	28.35*	S	S	-38.49	-160.74	H	2.89*	S	-40.90	14.74
29	S	S	-40.99	121.53	117.56	-35.59*	S	-46.33	-2.56	90.28
30	S	-216.53	-70.11	-214.62	22.14	S	S	-47.88	-82.29	-4.80
Close	7823.13	9116.55	10877.81	10414.49	9851.56	8896.09	9782.46	10428.02	10805.87	12221.93
Change	381.05	524.45	147.95	-556.65	776.42	499.06	-18.66	400.55	365.80	141.20

* Shortened trading day

DECEMBER DAILY POINT CHANGES DOW JONES INDUSTRIALS

Previous Month Close	1997	1998	1999	2000	2001	2002	2003	2004	2005	2006
	7823.13	9116.55	10877.81	10414.49	9851.56	8896.09	9782.46	10428.02	10805.87	12221.93
1	189.98	16.99	120.58	-40.95	S	S	116.59	162.20	106.70	-27.80
2	5.72	-69.00	40.67	S	S	-33.52	-45.41	-5.10	-35.06	S
3	13.18	-184.86	247.12	S	-87.60	-119.64	19.78	7.09	S	S
4	18.15	136.46	S	186.56	129.88	-5.08	57.40	S	S	89.72
5	98.97	S	S	338.62	220.45	-114.57	-68.14	S	-42.50	47.75
6	S	S	-61.17	-234.34	-15.15	22.49	S	-45.15	21.85	-22.35
7	S	54.33	-118.36	-47.02	-49.68	S	S	-106.48	-45.95	-30.84
8	-38.29	-42.49	-38.53	95.55	S	S	102.59	53.65	-55.79	29.08
9	-61.18	-18.79	66.67	S	S	-172.36	-41.85	58.59	23.46	S
10	-70.87	-167.61	89.91	S	-128.01	100.85	-1.56	-9.60	S	S
11	-129.80	-19.82	S	12.89	-33.08	14.88	86.30	S	S	20.99
12	-10.69	S	S	42.47	6.44	-50.74	34.00	S	-10.81	-12.90
13	S	-126.16	-32.11	26.17	-128.36	-104.69	S	95.10	55.95	1.92
14	S	127.70	-32.42	-119.45	44.70	S	S	38.13	59.79	99.26
15	84.29	127.70	65.15	-240.03	S	S	-19.34	15.00	-1.84	28.76
16	53.72	-32.70	19.57	S	S	193.69	106.74	14.19	-6.08	S
17	-18.90	85.22	12.54	S	80.82	-92.01	15.70	-55.72	S	S
18	-110.91	27.81	S	210.46	106.42	-88.04	102.82	S	S	-4.25
19	-90.21	S	S	-61.05	72.10	-82.55	30.14	S	-39.06	30.05
20	S	S	-113.16	-265.44	-85.31	146.52	S	11.68	-30.98	-7.45
21	S	85.22	56.27	168.36	50.16	S	S	97.83	28.18	-42.62
22	63.02	55.61	3.06	148.27	S	S	59.78	56.46	55.71	-78.03
23	-127.54	157.57	202.16	S	S	-18.03	3.26	11.23	-6.17	S
24	-31.64*	15.96*	H	S	N/C*	-45.18*	-36.07*	H	S	S
25	H	H	S	H	H	H	H	H	S	S
26	19.18*	S	S	56.88	52.80	-15.50	19.48*	S	H	64.41
27	S	S	-14.68	110.72	43.17	-128.83	S	-50.99	-105.50	102.94
28	S	8.76	85.63	65.60	5.68	S	S	78.41	18.49	-9.05
29	113.10	94.23	7.95	-81.91	S	S	125.33	-25.35	-11.44	-38.37
30	123.56	-46.34	-31.80	S	-115.49	29.07	-24.96	-28.89	-67.32	S
31	-7.72	-93.21	44.26	S	S	8.78	28.88	-17.29	S	S
Close	7908.25	9181.43	11497.12	10786.85	10021.50	8341.63	10453.92	10783.01	10717.50	12463.15
Change	85.12	64.88	619.31	372.36	169.94	-554.46	671.46	354.99	-88.37	241.22

* Shortened trading day

A TYPICAL DAY IN THE MARKET

Half-hourly data became available for the Dow Jones Industrial Average starting in January 1987. The NYSE switched 10:00am openings to 9:30am in October 1985. Below is the comparison between half-hourly performance 1987-April 27, 2007, and hourly November 1963-June 1985. Stronger openings and closings in a more bullish climate are evident. Morning and afternoon weaknesses appear an hour earlier.

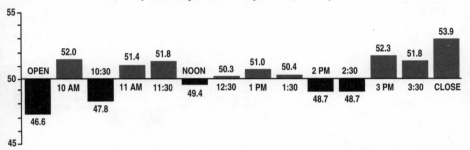

MARKET % PERFORMANCE EACH HALF-HOUR OF THE DAY
(January 1987 – April 27, 2007)

Based on the number of times the Dow Jones Industrial Average increased over previous half-hour.

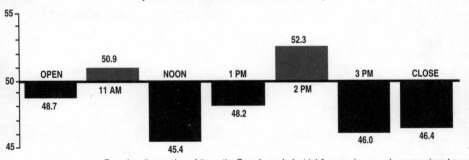

MARKET % PERFORMANCE EACH HOUR OF THE DAY
(November 1963 – June 1985)

Based on the number of times the Dow Jones Industrial Average increased over previous hour.

On the next page, half-hourly movements since January 1987 are separated by day of the week. From 1953 to 1989 Monday was the worst day of the week, especially during long bear markets, but times changed. Monday reversed positions and became the best day of the week and on the plus side 11 years in a row from 1990 to 2000.

During the last seven years (2001-April 2007) Monday and Friday are net losers, Friday the worst and the middle three days are net gainers, Wednesday the best. On all days stocks do tend to firm up near the close with weakness early morning and from 2 to 2:30 frequently.

THROUGH THE WEEK ON A HALF-HOURLY BASIS

From the chart showing the percentage of times the Dow Jones Industrial Average rose over the preceding half-hour (January 1987–April 27, 2007*) the typical week unfolds.

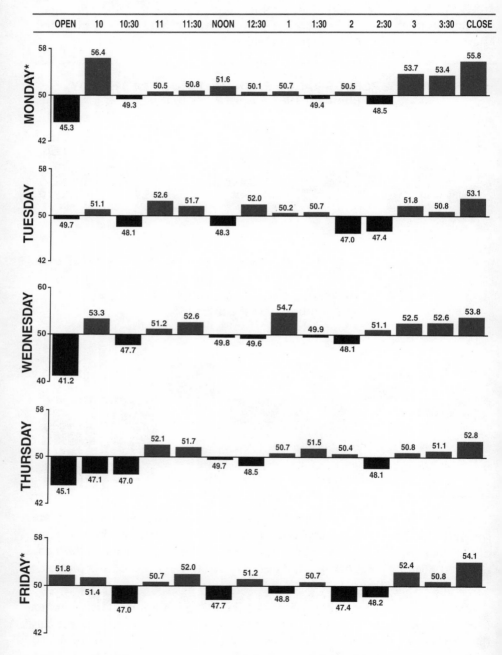

*Monday denotes first trading day of the week, Friday denotes last trading day of the week.

WEDNESDAY NOW MOST PROFITABLE DAY OF WEEK

Between 1952 and 1989 Monday was the worst trading day of the week. The first trading day of the week (including Tuesday, when Monday is a holiday) rose only 44.3% of the time, while the other trading days closed higher 54.8% of the time. (NYSE Saturday trading discontinued June 1952.)

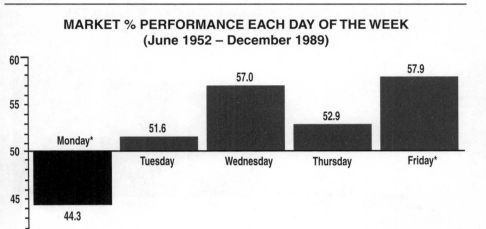

MARKET % PERFORMANCE EACH DAY OF THE WEEK
(June 1952 – December 1989)

A dramatic reversal occurred in 1990—Monday became the most powerful day of the week. However, during the last six and a third years Monday and Friday have battled it out for worst-day-of-the-week status and Wednesday has produced the most gains. Since the top in 2000, traders have not been inclined to stay long over the weekend nor buy up equities at the outset of the week. This is not uncommon during uncertain market times. See pages 68 and 143.

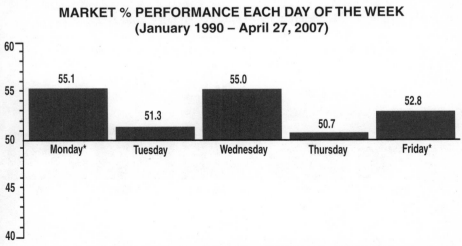

MARKET % PERFORMANCE EACH DAY OF THE WEEK
(January 1990 – April 27, 2007)

Charts based on the number of times S&P 500 index closed higher than previous day.
*Monday denotes first trading day of the week, Friday denotes last trading day of the week.

NASDAQ STRONGEST LAST 3 DAYS OF WEEK

Despite 20 years less data, daily trading patterns on NASDAQ through 1989 appear to be fairly similar to the S&P on page 141 except for more bullishness on Thursdays. During the mostly flat markets of the 1970s and early 1980s, it would appear that apprehensive investors decided to throw in the towel over weekends and sell on Mondays and Tuesdays.

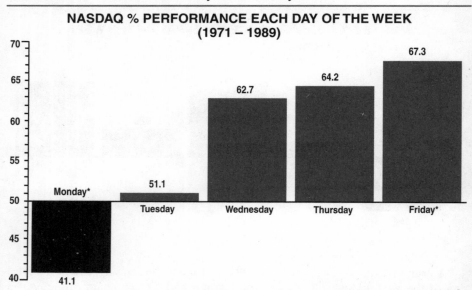

NASDAQ % PERFORMANCE EACH DAY OF THE WEEK
(1971 – 1989)

Notice the vast difference in the daily trading pattern between NASDAQ and S&P from January 1, 1990, to recent times. The reason for so much more bullishness is that NASDAQ moved up 1010%, over three times as much during the 1990-2000 period. The gain for the S&P was 332% and for the Dow Jones industrials, 326%. NASDAQ's weekly patterns are beginning to move in step with the rest of the market. Notice the similarities to the S&P since 2001 on pages 142 and 144, Monday and Friday weakness, mid-week strength.

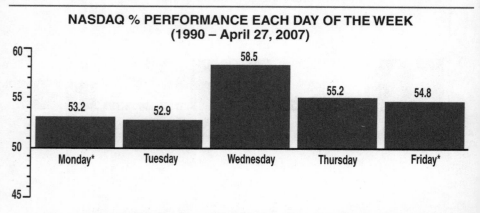

NASDAQ % PERFORMANCE EACH DAY OF THE WEEK
(1990 – April 27, 2007)

Based on NASDAQ composite, prior to February 5, 1971, based on National Quotation Bureau indices.
*Monday denotes first trading day of the week, Friday denotes last trading day of the week.

S&P DAILY PERFORMANCE EACH YEAR SINCE 1952

To determine if market trend alters performance of different days of the week, we separated twenty bear years of 1953, '56, '57, '60, '62, '66, '69, '70, '73, '74, '77, '78, '81, '84, '87, '90, '94, 2000, 2001 and 2002 from 35 bull market years. While Tuesday and Thursday did not vary much between bull and bear years, Mondays and Fridays were sharply affected. There was a swing of 10.6 percentage points in Monday's and 10.7 in Friday's performance. Wednesday is developing a reputation as the best day of the week.

PERCENTAGE OF TIMES MARKET CLOSED HIGHER THAN PREVIOUS DAY
(June 1952 – April 27, 2007)

	Monday*	Tuesday	Wednesday	Thursday	Friday*
1952	48.4%	55.6%	58.1%	51.9%	66.7%
1953	32.7	50.0	54.9	57.5	56.6
1954	50.0	57.5	63.5	59.2	73.1
1955	50.0	45.7	63.5	60.0	78.9
1956	36.5	39.6	46.9	50.0	59.6
1957	25.0	54.0	66.7	48.9	44.2
1958	59.6	52.0	59.6	68.1	72.6
1959	42.3	53.1	55.8	48.9	69.8
1960	34.6	50.0	44.2	54.0	59.6
1961	52.9	54.4	64.7	56.0	67.3
1962	28.3	52.1	54.0	51.0	50.0
1963	46.2	63.3	51.0	57.5	69.2
1964	40.4	48.0	61.5	58.7	77.4
1965	44.2	57.5	55.8	51.0	71.2
1966	36.5	47.8	53.9	42.0	57.7
1967	38.5	50.0	60.8	64.0	69.2
1968†	49.1	57.5	64.3	42.6	54.9
1969	30.8	45.8	50.0	67.4	50.0
1970	38.5	46.0	63.5	48.9	52.8
1971	44.2	64.6	57.7	55.1	51.9
1972	38.5	60.9	57.7	51.0	67.3
1973	32.1	51.1	52.9	44.9	44.2
1974	32.7	57.1	51.0	36.7	30.8
1975	53.9	38.8	61.5	56.3	55.8
1976	55.8	55.3	55.8	40.8	58.5
1977	40.4	40.4	46.2	53.1	53.9
1978	51.9	43.5	59.6	54.0	48.1
1979	54.7	53.2	58.8	66.0	44.2
1980	55.8	54.2	71.7	35.4	59.6
1981	44.2	38.8	55.8	53.2	47.2
1982	46.2	39.6	44.2	44.9	50.0
1983	55.8	46.8	61.5	52.0	55.8
1984	39.6	63.8	31.4	46.0	44.2
1985	44.2	61.2	54.9	56.3	53.9
1986	51.9	44.9	67.3	58.3	55.8
1987	51.9	57.1	63.5	61.7	49.1
1988	51.9	61.7	51.9	48.0	59.6
1989	51.9	47.8	69.2	58.0	69.2
1990	67.9	53.2	52.9	40.0	51.9
1991	44.2	46.9	52.9	49.0	51.9
1992	51.9	49.0	53.9	56.3	45.3
1993	65.4	41.7	55.8	44.9	48.1
1994	55.8	46.8	52.9	48.0	59.6
1995	63.5	56.5	63.5	62.0	63.5
1996	54.7	44.9	51.0	57.1	63.5
1997	67.3	67.4	42.3	41.7	57.7
1998	57.7	62.5	57.7	38.3	60.4
1999	46.2	29.8	67.3	53.1	57.7
2000	51.9	43.5	40.4	56.0	46.2
2001	45.3	51.1	44.0	59.2	43.1
2002	40.4	37.5	56.9	38.8	48.1
2003	59.6	62.5	42.3	58.3	50.0
2004	51.9	61.7	59.6	52.1	52.8
2005	59.6	47.8	59.6	56.0	55.8
2006	55.8	55.6	67.3	52.0	48.1
2007 ‡	52.9	64.3	68.8	50.0	47.1
Average	**47.7%**	**51.3%**	**56.1%**	**52.2%**	**56.4%**
35 Bull Years	**51.5%**	**52.9%**	**58.4%**	**53.2%**	**60.2%**
20 Bear Years	**40.9%**	**48.5%**	**52.1%**	**50.6%**	**49.8%**

Based on S&P 500

† Most Wednesdays closed last 7 months of 1968.   ‡ Four months only, not included in averages.
*Monday denotes first trading day of the week, Friday denotes last trading day of the week.

NASDAQ DAILY PERFORMANCE EACH YEAR SINCE 1971

After dropping a hefty 77.9% from its 2000 high (versus -37.8% on the Dow and -49.1% on the S&P 500), NASDAQ tech stocks still outpace the blue chips and big caps — but not by nearly as much as they did. From January 1, 1971, through April 27, 2007, NASDAQ moved up an impressive 2754%. The Dow (up 1464%) and the S&P (up 1521%) gained just over half as much.

Monday's performance on NASDAQ was lackluster during the three-year bear market of 2000-2002. As NASDAQ rebounded (up 50% in 2003) strength returned to Monday as well as on Tuesday, Wednesday and Thursday during 2003-2006; weakness prevailed Friday. So far in 2007, Wednesday is the strongest.

PERCENTAGE OF TIMES NASDAQ CLOSED HIGHER THAN PREVIOUS DAY
(1971 – April 27, 2007)

	Monday*	Tuesday	Wednesday	Thursday	Friday*
1971	51.9%	52.1%	59.6%	65.3%	71.2%
1972	30.8	60.9	63.5	57.1	78.9
1973	34.0	48.9	52.9	53.1	48.1
1974	30.8	44.9	52.9	51.0	42.3
1975	44.2	42.9	63.5	64.6	63.5
1976	50.0	63.8	67.3	59.2	58.5
1977	51.9	40.4	53.9	63.3	73.1
1978	48.1	47.8	73.1	72.0	84.6
1979	45.3	53.2	64.7	86.0	82.7
1980	46.2	64.6	84.9	52.1	73.1
1981	42.3	32.7	67.3	76.6	69.8
1982	34.6	47.9	59.6	51.0	63.5
1983	42.3	44.7	67.3	68.0	73.1
1984	22.6	53.2	35.3	52.0	51.9
1985	36.5	59.2	62.8	68.8	66.0
1986	38.5	55.1	65.4	72.9	75.0
1987	42.3	49.0	65.4	68.1	66.0
1988	50.0	55.3	61.5	66.0	63.5
1989	38.5	54.4	71.2	72.0	75.0
1990	54.7	42.6	60.8	46.0	55.8
1991	51.9	59.2	66.7	65.3	51.9
1992	44.2	53.1	59.6	60.4	45.3
1993	55.8	56.3	69.2	57.1	67.3
1994	51.9	46.8	54.9	52.0	55.8
1995	50.0	52.2	63.5	64.0	63.5
1996	50.9	57.1	64.7	61.2	63.5
1997	65.4	59.2	53.9	52.1	55.8
1998	59.6	58.3	65.4	44.7	58.5
1999	61.5	40.4	63.5	57.1	65.4
2000	40.4	41.3	42.3	60.0	57.7
2001	41.5	57.8	52.0	55.1	47.1
2002	44.2	37.5	56.9	46.9	46.2
2003	57.7	60.4	40.4	60.4	46.2
2004	57.7	59.6	53.9	50.0	50.9
2005	61.5	47.8	51.9	48.0	59.6
2006	55.8	51.1	65.4	50.0	44.2
2007†	52.9	71.4	68.8	62.5	52.9
Average	**46.8%**	**51.4%**	**60.5%**	**59.7%**	**61.5%**
25 Bull Years	**49.3%**	**53.7%**	**62.9%**	**61.1%**	**64.4%**
10 Bear Years	**40.5%**	**45.5%**	**54.1%**	**56.1%**	**54.1%**

Based on NASDAQ composite; prior to February 5, 1971 based on National Quotation Bureau indices.
† Four months only, not included in averages.
*Monday denotes first trading day of the week, Friday denotes last trading day of the week.

MONTHLY CASH INFLOWS INTO S&P STOCKS

For many years, the last trading day of the month, plus the first four of the following month, were the best market days of the month. This pattern is quite clear in the first chart showing these five consecutive trading days towering above the other 16 trading days of the average month in the 1953-1981 period. The rationale was that individuals and institutions tended to operate similarly, causing a massive flow of cash into stocks near beginnings of months.

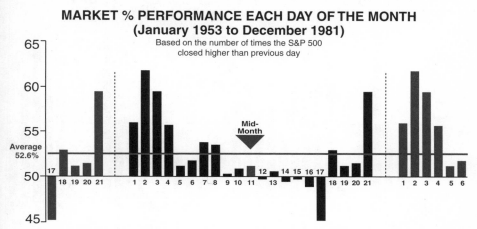

MARKET % PERFORMANCE EACH DAY OF THE MONTH
(January 1953 to December 1981)
Based on the number of times the S&P 500 closed higher than previous day

Clearly "front-running" traders took advantage of this phenomenon, drastically altering the previous pattern. The second chart from 1982 onward shows the trading shift caused by these "anticipators" to the last three trading days of the month plus the first two. Another astonishing development shows the ninth, tenth, and eleventh trading days rising strongly as well. Perhaps the enormous growth of 401(k) retirement plans (participants' salaries are usually paid twice monthly) is responsible for this new mid-month bulge. First trading days of the month have produced the greatest gains in recent years (see page 62).

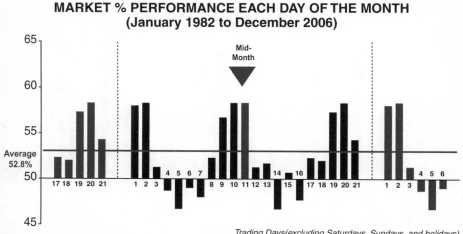

MARKET % PERFORMANCE EACH DAY OF THE MONTH
(January 1982 to December 2006)

Trading Days(excluding Saturdays, Sundays, and holidays).

MONTHLY CASH INFLOWS INTO NASDAQ STOCKS

NASDAQ stocks moved up 58.1% of the time through 1981 compared to 52.6% for the S&P on page 145. Ends and beginnings of the month are fairly similar, specifically the last plus the first four trading days. But notice how investors piled into NASDAQ stocks until mid-month. NASDAQ rose 118.6% from January 1, 1971, to December 31, 1981, compared to 33.0% for the S&P.

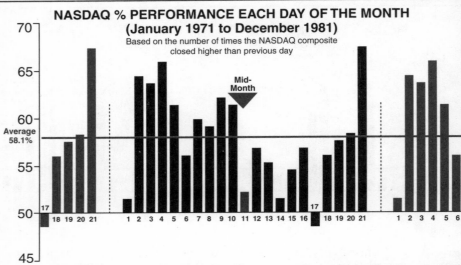

NASDAQ % PERFORMANCE EACH DAY OF THE MONTH
(January 1971 to December 1981)
Based on the number of times the NASDAQ composite closed higher than previous day

After the air was let out of the market 2000-2002, S&P's 1057% gain over the last 25 years is more evenly matched with NASDAQ's 1133% gain. Last three, first four and middle ninth and tenth days rose the most. Where the S&P has six days of the month that go down more often than up, NASDAQ has none. NASDAQ exhibits the most strength on the last trading day of the month.

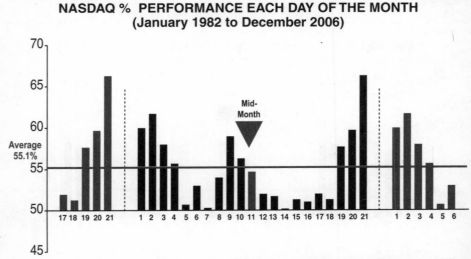

NASDAQ % PERFORMANCE EACH DAY OF THE MONTH
(January 1982 to December 2006)

Trading Days (excluding Saturdays, Sundays, and holidays).
Based on NASDAQ composite, prior to February 5, 1971, based on National Quotation Bureau indices.

NOVEMBER, DECEMBER, AND JANUARY
YEAR'S BEST THREE-MONTH SPAN

The most important observation to be made from a chart showing the average monthly percent change in market prices since 1950 is that institutions (mutual funds, pension funds, banks, etc.) determine the trading patterns in today's market.

The "investment calendar" reflects the annual, semi-annual and quarterly operations of institutions during January, April and July. October, besides being the last campaign month before elections, is also the time when most bear markets seem to end, as in 1946, 1957, 1960, 1966, 1974, 1987, 1990, 1998 and 2002. (August and September tend to combine to make the worst consecutive two-month period.)

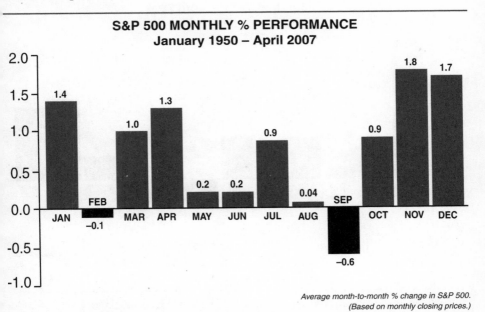

S&P 500 MONTHLY % PERFORMANCE
January 1950 – April 2007

Average month-to-month % change in S&P 500.
(Based on monthly closing prices.)

Unusual year-end strength comes from corporate and private pension funds, producing a 4.9% gain on average between November 1 and January 31. September's dismal performance makes it the worst month of the year. In the last 23 years it has only been up nine times — four in a row 1995-1998. October is the top month since 1991.

In presidential election years since 1950, the best three months are November +2.0% (8-6), June +1.9% (12-2), and December +1.2% (11-3). January drops to sixth with a 0.7% average gain. There are no net monthly losses for the S&P 500.

See page 44 for monthly performance tables for the S&P 500 and the Dow Jones industrials. See pages 48 and 50 for unique six-month switching strategies.

On page 74 you can see how the first month of the first three quarters far outperforms the second and the third months since 1950 and note the improvement in May's and October's performance since 1991.

NOVEMBER THROUGH JUNE
NASDAQ'S EIGHT-MONTH RUN

The two-and-a-half-year plunge of 77.9% in NASDAQ stocks between March 10, 2000, and October 9, 2002, brought several horrendous monthly losses (the two greatest were November 2000, –22.9%, and February 2001, –22.4) which trimmed average monthly performance over the 36¹/₃-year period. Ample Octobers in seven of the last nine years, including two huge turnarounds in 2001 (+12.8%) and 2002 (+13.5%), has put bear-killing October in the number one spot since 1998. January's 3.7% average gain is still awesome, and twice S&P's 1.8% January average since 1971.

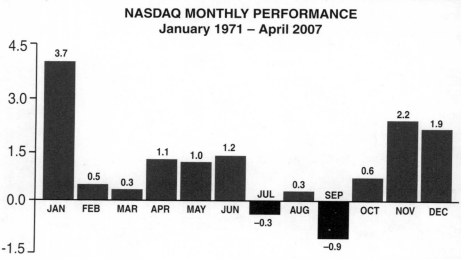

NASDAQ MONTHLY PERFORMANCE
January 1971 – April 2007

Average month-to-month % change in NASDAQ composite, prior to February 5, 1971, based on National Quotation Bureau indices.
(Based on monthly closing prices.)

Bear in mind when comparing NASDAQ to the S&P on page 147 that there are 21 fewer years of data here. During this 36¹/₃-year (1971-April 2007) period, NASDAQ gained 2754%, while the S&P and the Dow rose only 1464% and 1521%, respectively. On page 56 you can see a statistical monthly comparison between NASDAQ and the Dow.

Year-end strength is even more pronounced in NASDAQ, producing a 7.8% gain on average between November 1 and January 31 — 1.6 times greater than that of the S&P 500 on page 147. September is the worst month of the year for the over-the-counter index as well, posting a deeper average loss of –0.9%. These extremes underscore NASDAQ's higher volatility — and potential for moves of greater magnitude.

In presidential election years since 1971, the best three months are February +3.4% (6-3), January +3.4% (7-2), and June +2.9% (6-3). NASDAQ Novembers drop to seventh place with a 0.4% average gain. See page 58 for NASDAQ's impressive eight-month switching strategy using MACD timing.

DOW JONES INDUSTRIALS ANNUAL HIGHS, LOWS & CLOSES SINCE 1901

YEAR	HIGH DATE	HIGH CLOSE	LOW DATE	LOW CLOSE	YEAR CLOSE	YEAR	HIGH DATE	HIGH CLOSE	LOW DATE	LOW CLOSE	YEAR CLOSE
1901	6/17	57.33	12/24	45.07	47.29	1955	12/30	488.40	1/17	388.20	488.40
1902	4/24	50.14	12/15	43.64	47.10	1956	4/6	521.05	1/23	462.35	499.47
1903	2/16	49.59	11/9	30.88	35.98	1957	7/12	520.77	10/22	419.79	435.69
1904	12/5	53.65	3/12	34.00	50.99	1958	12/31	583.65	2/25	436.89	583.65
1905	12/29	70.74	1/25	50.37	70.47	1959	12/31	679.36	2/9	574.46	679.36
1906	1/19	75.45	7/13	62.40	69.12	1960	1/5	685.47	10/25	566.05	615.89
1907	1/7	70.60	11/15	38.83	43.04	1961	12/13	734.91	1/3	610.25	731.14
1908	11/13	64.74	2/13	42.94	63.11	1962	1/3	726.01	6/26	535.76	652.10
1909	11/19	73.64	2/23	58.54	72.56	1963	12/18	767.21	1/2	646.79	762.95
1910	1/3	72.04	7/26	53.93	59.60	1964	11/18	891.71	1/2	766.08	874.13
1911	6/19	63.78	9/25	53.43	59.84	1965	12/31	969.26	6/28	840.59	969.26
1912	9/30	68.97	2/10	58.72	64.37	1966	2/9	995.15	10/7	744.32	785.69
1913	1/9	64.88	6/11	52.83	57.71	1967	9/25	943.08	1/3	786.41	905.11
1914	3/20	61.12	7/30	52.32	54.58	1968	12/3	985.21	3/21	825.13	943.75
1915	12/27	99.21	2/24	54.22	99.15	1969	5/14	968.85	12/17	769.93	800.36
1916	11/21	110.15	4/22	84.96	95.00	1970	12/29	842.00	5/26	631.16	838.92
1917	1/3	99.18	12/19	65.95	74.38	1971	4/28	950.82	11/23	797.97	890.20
1918	10/18	89.07	1/15	73.38	82.20	1972	12/11	1036.27	1/26	889.15	1020.02
1919	11/3	119.62	2/8	79.15	107.23	1973	1/11	1051.70	12/5	788.31	850.86
1920	1/3	109.88	12/21	66.75	71.95	1974	3/13	891.66	12/6	577.60	616.24
1921	12/15	81.50	8/24	63.90	81.10	1975	7/15	881.81	1/2	632.04	852.41
1922	10/14	103.43	1/10	78.59	98.73	1976	9/21	1014.79	1/2	858.71	1004.65
1923	3/20	105.38	10/27	85.76	95.52	1977	1/3	999.75	11/2	800.85	831.17
1924	12/31	120.51	5/20	88.33	120.51	1978	9/8	907.74	2/28	742.12	805.01
1925	11/6	159.39	3/30	115.00	156.66	1979	10/5	897.61	11/7	796.67	838.74
1926	8/14	166.64	3/30	135.20	157.20	1980	11/20	1000.17	4/21	759.13	963.99
1927	12/31	202.40	1/25	152.73	202.40	1981	4/27	1024.05	9/25	824.01	875.00
1928	12/31	300.00	2/20	191.33	300.00	1982	12/27	1070.55	8/12	776.92	1046.54
1929	9/3	381.17	11/13	198.69	248.48	1983	11/29	1287.20	1/3	1027.04	1258.64
1930	4/17	294.07	12/16	157.51	164.58	1984	1/6	1286.64	7/24	1086.57	1211.57
1931	2/24	194.36	12/17	73.79	77.90	1985	12/16	1553.10	1/4	1184.96	1546.67
1932	3/8	88.78	7/8	41.22	59.93	1986	12/2	1955.57	1/22	1502.29	1895.95
1933	7/18	108.67	2/27	50.16	99.90	1987	8/25	2722.42	10/19	1738.74	1938.83
1934	2/5	110.74	7/26	85.51	104.04	1988	10/21	2183.50	1/20	1879.14	2168.57
1935	11/19	148.44	3/14	96.71	144.13	1989	10/9	2791.41	1/3	2144.64	2753.20
1936	11/17	184.90	1/6	143.11	179.90	1990	7/17	2999.75	10/11	2365.10	2633.66
1937	3/10	194.40	11/24	113.64	120.85	1991	12/31	3168.83	1/9	2470.30	3168.83
1938	11/12	158.41	3/31	98.95	154.76	1992	6/1	3413.21	10/9	3136.58	3301.11
1939	9/12	155.92	4/8	121.44	150.24	1993	12/29	3794.33	1/20	3241.95	3754.09
1940	1/3	152.80	6/10	111.84	131.13	1994	1/31	3978.36	4/4	3593.35	3834.44
1941	1/10	133.59	12/23	106.34	110.96	1995	12/13	5216.47	1/30	3832.08	5117.12
1942	12/26	119.71	4/28	92.92	119.40	1996	12/27	6560.91	1/10	5032.94	6448.27
1943	7/14	145.82	1/8	119.26	135.89	1997	8/6	8259.31	4/11	6391.69	7908.25
1944	12/16	152.53	2/7	134.22	152.32	1998	11/23	9374.27	8/31	7539.07	9181.43
1945	12/11	195.82	1/24	151.35	192.91	1999	12/31	11497.12	1/22	9120.67	11497.12
1946	5/29	212.50	10/9	163.12	177.20	2000	1/14	11722.98	3/7	9796.03	10786.85
1947	7/24	186.85	5/17	163.21	181.16	2001	5/21	11337.92	9/21	8235.81	10021.50
1948	6/15	193.16	3/16	165.39	177.30	2002	3/19	10635.25	10/9	7286.27	8341.63
1949	12/30	200.52	6/13	161.60	200.13	2003	12/31	10453.92	3/11	7524.06	10453.92
1950	11/24	235.47	1/13	196.81	235.41	2004	12/28	10854.54	10/25	9749.99	10783.01
1951	9/13	276.37	1/3	238.99	269.23	2005	3/4	10940.55	4/20	10012.36	10717.50
1952	12/30	292.00	5/1	256.35	291.90	2006	12/27	12510.57	1/20	10667.39	12463.15
1953	1/5	293.79	9/14	255.49	280.90	2007*	5/4	13264.62	3/5	12050.41	AT PRESS-TIME
1954	12/31	404.39	1/11	279.87	404.39						

*Through May 4, 2007

149

S&P 500 ANNUALS HIGHS, LOWS & CLOSES SINCE 1930

YEAR	HIGH DATE	HIGH CLOSE	LOW DATE	LOW CLOSE	YEAR CLOSE	YEAR	HIGH DATE	HIGH CLOSE	LOW DATE	LOW CLOSE	YEAR CLOSE
1930	4/10	25.92	12/16	14.44	15.34	1969	5/14	106.16	12/17	89.20	92.06
1931	2/24	18.17	12/17	7.72	8.12	1970	1/5	93.46	5/26	69.29	92.15
1932	9/7	9.31	6/1	4.40	6.89	1971	4/28	104.77	11/23	90.16	102.09
1933	7/18	12.20	2/27	5.53	10.10	1972	12/11	119.12	1/3	101.67	118.05
1934	2/6	11.82	7/26	8.36	9.50	1973	1/11	120.24	12/5	92.16	97.55
1935	11/19	13.46	3/14	8.06	13.43	1974	1/3	99.80	10/3	62.28	68.56
1936	11/9	17.69	1/2	13.40	17.18	1975	7/15	95.61	1/8	70.04	90.19
1937	3/6	18.68	11/24	10.17	10.55	1976	9/21	107.83	1/2	90.90	107.46
1938	11/9	13.79	3/31	8.50	13.21	1977	1/3	107.00	11/2	90.71	95.10
1939	1/4	13.23	4/8	10.18	12.49	1978	9/12	106.99	3/6	86.90	96.11
1940	1/3	12.77	6/10	8.99	10.58	1979	10/5	111.27	2/27	96.13	107.94
1941	1/10	10.86	12/29	8.37	8.69	1980	11/28	140.52	3/27	98.22	135.76
1942	12/31	9.77	4/28	7.47	9.77	1981	1/6	138.12	9/25	112.77	122.55
1943	7/14	12.64	1/2	9.84	11.67	1982	11/9	143.02	8/12	102.42	140.64
1944	12/16	13.29	2/7	11.56	13.28	1983	10/10	172.65	1/3	138.34	164.93
1945	12/10	17.68	1/23	13.21	17.36	1984	11/6	170.41	7/24	147.82	167.24
1946	5/29	19.25	10/9	14.12	15.30	1985	12/16	212.02	1/4	163.68	211.28
1947	2/8	16.20	5/17	13.71	15.30	1986	12/2	254.00	1/22	203.49	242.17
1948	6/15	17.06	2/14	13.84	15.20	1987	8/25	336.77	12/4	223.92	247.08
1949	12/30	16.79	6/13	13.55	16.76	1988	10/21	283.66	1/20	242.63	277.72
1950	12/29	20.43	1/14	16.65	20.41	1989	10/9	359.80	1/3	275.31	353.40
1951	10/15	23.85	1/3	20.69	23.77	1990	7/16	368.95	10/11	295.46	330.22
1952	12/30	26.59	2/20	23.09	26.57	1991	12/31	417.09	1/9	311.49	417.09
1953	1/5	26.66	9/14	22.71	24.81	1992	12/18	441.28	4/8	394.50	435.71
1954	12/31	35.98	1/11	24.80	35.98	1993	12/28	470.94	1/8	429.05	466.45
1955	11/14	46.41	1/17	34.58	45.48	1994	2/2	482.00	4/4	438.92	459.27
1956	8/2	49.74	1/23	43.11	46.67	1995	12/13	621.69	1/3	459.11	615.93
1957	7/15	49.13	10/22	38.98	39.99	1996	11/25	757.03	1/10	598.48	740.74
1958	12/31	55.21	1/2	40.33	55.21	1997	12/5	983.79	1/2	737.01	970.43
1959	8/3	60.71	2/9	53.58	59.89	1998	12/29	1241.81	1/9	927.69	1229.23
1960	1/5	60.39	10/25	52.30	58.11	1999	12/31	1469.25	1/14	1212.19	1469.25
1961	12/12	72.64	1/3	57.57	71.55	2000	3/24	1527.46	12/20	1264.74	1320.28
1962	1/3	71.13	6/26	52.32	63.10	2001	2/1	1373.47	9/21	965.80	1148.08
1963	12/31	75.02	1/2	62.69	75.02	2002	1/4	1172.51	10/9	776.76	879.82
1964	11/20	86.28	1/2	75.43	84.75	2003	12/31	1111.92	3/11	800.73	1111.92
1965	11/15	92.63	6/28	81.60	92.43	2004	12/30	1213.55	8/12	1063.23	1211.92
1966	2/9	94.06	10/7	73.20	80.33	2005	12/14	1272.74	4/20	1137.50	1248.29
1967	9/25	97.59	1/3	80.38	96.47	2006	12/15	1427.09	6/13	1223.69	1418.30
1968	11/29	108.37	3/5	87.72	103.86	2007*	5/4	1505.62	3/5	1374.12	AT PRESS-TIME

*Through May 4, 2007

150

NASDAQ ANNUAL HIGHS, LOWS & CLOSES SINCE 1971

	HIGH		LOW		YEAR		HIGH		LOW		YEAR
YEAR	DATE	CLOSE	DATE	CLOSE	CLOSE	YEAR	DATE	CLOSE	DATE	CLOSE	CLOSE
1971	12/31	114.12	1/5	89.06	114.12	1990	7/16	469.60	10/16	325.44	373.84
1972	12/8	135.15	1/3	113.65	133.73	1991	12/31	586.34	1/14	355.75	586.34
1973	1/11	136.84	12/24	88.67	92.19	1992	12/31	676.95	6/26	547.84	676.95
1974	3/15	96.53	10/3	54.87	59.82	1993	10/15	787.42	4/26	645.87	776.80
1975	7/15	88.00	1/2	60.70	77.62	1994	3/18	803.93	6/24	693.79	751.96
1976	12/31	97.88	1/2	78.06	97.88	1995	12/4	1069.79	1/3	743.58	1052.13
1977	12/30	105.05	4/5	93.66	105.05	1996	12/9	1316.27	1/15	988.57	1291.03
1978	9/13	139.25	1/11	99.09	117.98	1997	10/9	1745.85	4/2	1201.00	1570.35
1979	10/5	152.29	1/2	117.84	151.14	1998	12/31	2192.69	10/8	1419.12	2192.69
1980	11/28	208.15	3/27	124.09	202.34	1999	12/31	4069.31	1/4	2208.05	4069.31
1981	5/29	223.47	9/28	175.03	195.84	2000	3/10	5048.62	12/20	2332.78	2470.52
1982	12/8	240.70	8/13	159.14	232.41	2001	1/24	2859.15	9/21	1423.19	1950.40
1983	6/24	328.91	1/3	230.59	278.60	2002	1/4	2059.38	10/9	1114.11	1335.51
1984	1/6	287.90	7/25	225.30	247.35	2003	12/30	2009.88	3/11	1271.47	2003.37
1985	12/16	325.16	1/2	245.91	324.93	2004	12/30	2178.34	8/12	1752.49	2175.44
1986	7/3	411.16	1/9	323.01	349.33	2005	12/2	2273.37	4/28	1904.18	2205.32
1987	8/26	455.26	10/28	291.88	330.47	2006	11/22	2465.98	7/21	2020.39	2415.29
1988	7/5	396.11	1/12	331.97	381.38	2007*	5/4	2572.15	3/5	2340.68	AT PRESS-TIME
1989	10/9	485.73	1/3	378.56	454.82						

RUSSELL 1000 ANNUAL HIGHS, LOWS & CLOSES SINCE 1979

	HIGH		LOW		YEAR		HIGH		LOW		YEAR
YEAR	DATE	CLOSE	DATE	CLOSE	CLOSE	YEAR	DATE	CLOSE	DATE	CLOSE	CLOSE
1979	10/5	61.18	2/27	51.83	59.87	1994	2/1	258.31	4/4	235.38	244.65
1980	11/28	78.26	3/27	53.68	75.20	1995	12/13	331.18	1/3	244.41	328.89
1981	1/6	76.34	9/25	62.03	67.93	1996	12/2	401.21	1/10	318.24	393.75
1982	11/9	78.47	8/12	55.98	77.24	1997	12/5	519.72	4/11	389.03	513.79
1983	10/10	95.07	1/3	76.04	90.38	1998	12/29	645.36	1/9	490.26	642.87
1984	1/6	92.80	7/24	79.49	90.31	1999	12/31	767.97	2/9	632.53	767.97
1985	12/16	114.97	1/4	88.61	114.39	2000	9/1	813.71	12/20	668.75	700.09
1986	7/2	137.87	1/22	111.14	130.00	2001	1/30	727.35	9/21	507.98	604.94
1987	8/25	176.22	12/4	117.65	130.02	2002	3/19	618.74	10/9	410.52	466.18
1988	10/21	149.94	1/20	128.35	146.99	2003	12/31	594.56	3/11	425.31	594.56
1989	10/9	189.93	1/3	145.78	185.11	2004	12/30	651.76	8/13	566.06	650.99
1990	7/16	191.56	10/11	152.36	171.22	2005	12/14	692.09	4/20	613.37	679.42
1991	12/31	220.61	1/9	161.94	220.61	2006	12/15	775.08	6/13	665.81	770.08
1992	12/18	235.06	4/8	208.87	233.59	2007*	5/4	820.89	3/5	749.85	AT PRESS-TIME
1993	10/15	252.77	1/8	229.91	250.71						

RUSSELL 2000 ANNUAL HIGHS, LOWS & CLOSES SINCE 1979

	HIGH		LOW		YEAR		HIGH		LOW		YEAR
YEAR	DATE	CLOSE	DATE	CLOSE	CLOSE	YEAR	DATE	CLOSE	DATE	CLOSE	CLOSE
1979	12/31	55.91	1/2	40.81	55.91	1994	3/18	271.08	12/9	235.16	250.36
1980	11/28	77.70	3/27	45.36	74.80	1995	9/14	316.12	1/30	246.56	315.97
1981	6/15	85.16	9/25	65.37	73.67	1996	5/22	364.61	1/16	301.75	362.61
1982	12/8	91.01	8/12	60.33	88.90	1997	10/13	465.21	4/25	335.85	437.02
1983	6/24	126.99	1/3	88.29	112.27	1998	4/21	491.41	10/8	310.28	421.96
1984	1/12	116.69	7/25	93.95	101.49	1999	12/31	504.75	3/23	383.37	504.75
1985	12/31	129.87	1/2	101.21	129.87	2000	3/9	606.05	12/20	443.80	483.53
1986	7/3	155.30	1/9	128.23	135.00	2001	5/22	517.23	9/21	378.89	488.50
1987	8/25	174.44	10/28	106.08	120.42	2002	4/16	522.95	10/9	327.04	383.09
1988	7/15	151.42	1/12	121.23	147.37	2003	12/30	565.47	3/12	345.94	556.91
1989	10/9	180.78	1/3	146.79	168.30	2004	12/28	654.57	8/12	517.10	651.57
1990	6/15	170.90	10/30	118.82	132.16	2005	12/2	690.57	4/28	575.02	673.22
1991	12/31	189.94	1/15	125.25	189.94	2006	12/27	797.73	7/21	671.94	787.66
1992	12/31	221.01	7/8	185.81	221.01	2007*	4/26	833.80	3/5	760.06	AT PRESS-TIME
1993	11/2	260.17	2/23	217.55	258.59						

*Through May 4, 2007

DOW JONES INDUSTRIALS MONTHLY PERCENT CHANGE SINCE 1950

	Jan	Feb	Mar	Apr	May	Jun	Jul	Aug	Sep	Oct	Nov	Dec	Year's Change
1950	0.8	0.8	1.3	4.0	4.2	- 6.4	0.1	3.6	4.4	- 0.6	1.2	3.4	17.6
1951	5.7	1.3	- 1.6	4.5	- 3.7	- 2.8	6.3	4.8	0.3	- 3.2	- 0.4	3.0	14.4
1952	0.5	- 3.9	3.6	- 4.4	2.1	4.3	1.9	- 1.6	- 1.6	- 0.5	5.4	2.9	8.4
1953	- 0.7	- 1.9	- 1.5	- 1.8	- 0.9	- 1.5	2.7	- 5.1	1.1	4.5	2.0	- 0.2	- 3.8
1954	4.1	0.7	3.0	5.2	2.6	1.8	4.3	- 3.5	7.3	- 2.3	9.8	4.6	44.0
1955	1.1	0.7	- 0.5	3.9	- 0.2	6.2	3.2	0.5	- 0.3	- 2.5	6.2	1.1	20.8
1956	- 3.6	2.7	5.8	0.8	- 7.4	3.1	5.1	- 3.0	- 5.3	1.0	- 1.5	5.6	2.3
1957	- 4.1	- 3.0	2.2	4.1	2.1	- 0.3	1.0	- 4.8	- 5.8	- 3.3	2.0	- 3.2	-12.8
1958	3.3	- 2.2	1.6	2.0	1.5	3.3	5.2	1.1	4.6	2.1	2.6	4.7	34.0
1959	1.8	1.6	- 0.3	3.7	3.2	- 0.03	4.9	- 1.6	- 4.9	2.4	1.9	3.1	16.4
1960	- 8.4	1.2	- 2.1	- 2.4	4.0	2.4	- 3.7	1.5	- 7.3	0.04	2.9	3.1	- 9.3
1961	5.2	2.1	2.2	0.3	2.7	- 1.8	3.1	2.1	- 2.6	0.4	2.5	1.3	18.7
1962	- 4.3	1.1	- 0.2	- 5.9	- 7.8	- 8.5	6.5	1.9	- 5.0	1.9	10.1	0.4	-10.8
1963	4.7	- 2.9	3.0	5.2	1.3	- 2.8	- 1.6	4.9	0.5	3.1	- 0.6	1.7	17.0
1964	2.9	1.9	1.6	- 0.3	1.2	1.3	1.2	- 0.3	4.4	- 0.3	0.3	- 0.1	14.6
1965	3.3	0.1	- 1.6	3.7	- 0.5	- 5.4	1.6	1.3	4.2	3.2	- 1.5	2.4	10.9
1966	1.5	- 3.2	- 2.8	1.0	- 5.3	- 1.6	- 2.6	- 7.0	- 1.8	4.2	- 1.9	- 0.7	-18.9
1967	8.2	- 1.2	3.2	3.6	- 5.0	0.9	5.1	- 0.3	2.8	- 5.1	- 0.4	3.3	15.2
1968	- 5.5	- 1.7	0.02	8.5	- 1.4	- 0.1	- 1.6	1.5	4.4	1.8	3.4	- 4.2	4.3
1969	0.2	- 4.3	3.3	1.6	- 1.3	- 6.9	- 6.6	2.6	- 2.8	5.3	- 5.1	- 1.5	-15.2
1970	- 7.0	4.5	1.0	- 6.3	- 4.8	- 2.4	7.4	4.1	- 0.5	- 0.7	5.1	5.6	4.8
1971	3.5	1.2	2.9	4.1	- 3.6	- 1.8	- 3.7	4.6	- 1.2	- 5.4	- 0.9	7.1	6.1
1972	1.3	2.9	1.4	1.4	0.7	- 3.3	- 0.5	4.2	- 1.1	0.2	6.6	0.2	14.6
1973	- 2.1	- 4.4	- 0.4	- 3.1	- 2.2	- 1.1	3.9	- 4.2	6.7	1.0	-14.0	3.5	-16.6
1974	0.6	0.6	- 1.6	- 1.2	- 4.1	0.03	- 5.6	-10.4	-10.4	9.5	- 7.0	- 0.4	-27.6
1975	14.2	5.0	3.9	6.9	1.3	5.6	- 5.4	0.5	- 5.0	5.3	2.9	- 1.0	38.3
1976	14.4	- 0.3	2.8	- 0.3	- 2.2	2.8	- 1.8	- 1.1	1.7	- 2.6	- 1.8	6.1	17.9
1977	- 5.0	- 1.9	- 1.8	0.8	- 3.0	2.0	- 2.9	- 3.2	- 1.7	- 3.4	1.4	0.2	-17.3
1978	- 7.4	- 3.6	2.1	10.6	0.4	- 2.6	5.3	1.7	- 1.3	- 8.5	0.8	0.7	- 3.1
1979	4.2	- 3.6	6.6	- 0.8	- 3.8	2.4	0.5	4.9	- 1.0	- 7.2	0.8	2.0	4.2
1980	4.4	- 1.5	- 9.0	4.0	4.1	2.0	7.8	- 0.3	-0.02	- 0.9	7.4	- 3.0	14.9
1981	- 1.7	2.9	3.0	- 0.6	- 0.6	- 1.5	- 2.5	- 7.4	- 3.6	0.3	4.3	- 1.6	- 9.2
1982	- 0.4	- 5.4	- 0.2	3.1	- 3.4	- 0.9	- 0.4	11.5	- 0.6	10.7	4.8	0.7	19.6
1983	2.8	3.4	1.6	8.5	- 2.1	1.8	- 1.9	1.4	1.4	- 0.6	4.1	- 1.4	20.3
1984	- 3.0	- 5.4	0.9	0.5	- 5.6	2.5	- 1.5	9.8	- 1.4	0.1	- 1.5	1.9	- 3.7
1985	6.2	- 0.2	- 1.3	- 0.7	4.6	1.5	0.9	- 1.0	- 0.4	3.4	7.1	5.1	27.7
1986	1.6	8.8	6.4	- 1.9	5.2	0.9	- 6.2	6.9	- 6.9	6.2	1.9	- 1.0	22.6
1987	13.8	3.1	3.6	- 0.8	0.2	5.5	6.3	3.5	- 2.5	-23.2	- 8.0	5.7	2.3
1988	1.0	5.8	- 4.0	2.2	- 0.1	5.4	- 0.6	- 4.6	4.0	1.7	- 1.6	2.6	11.8
1989	8.0	- 3.6	1.6	5.5	2.5	- 1.6	9.0	2.9	- 1.6	- 1.8	2.3	1.7	27.0
1990	- 5.9	1.4	3.0	- 1.9	8.3	0.1	0.9	-10.0	- 6.2	- 0.4	4.8	2.9	- 4.3
1991	3.9	5.3	1.1	- 0.9	4.8	- 4.0	4.1	0.6	- 0.9	1.7	- 5.7	9.5	20.3
1992	1.7	1.4	- 1.0	3.8	1.1	- 2.3	2.3	- 4.0	0.4	- 1.4	2.4	- 0.1	4.2
1993	0.3	1.8	1.9	- 0.2	2.9	- 0.3	0.7	3.2	- 2.6	3.5	0.1	1.9	13.7
1994	6.0	- 3.7	- 5.1	1.3	2.1	- 3.5	3.8	4.0	- 1.8	1.7	- 4.3	2.5	2.1
1995	0.2	4.3	3.7	3.9	3.3	2.0	3.3	- 2.1	3.9	- 0.7	6.7	0.8	33.5
1996	5.4	1.7	1.9	- 0.3	1.3	0.2	- 2.2	1.6	4.7	2.5	8.2	- 1.1	26.0
1997	5.7	0.9	- 4.3	6.5	4.6	4.7	7.2	- 7.3	4.2	- 6.3	5.1	1.1	22.6
1998	- 0.02	8.1	3.0	3.0	- 1.8	0.6	- 0.8	-15.1	4.0	9.6	6.1	0.7	16.1
1999	1.9	- 0.6	5.2	10.2	- 2.1	3.9	- 2.9	1.6	- 4.5	3.8	1.4	5.7	25.2
2000	- 4.8	- 7.4	7.8	- 1.7	- 2.0	- 0.7	0.7	6.6	- 5.0	3.0	- 5.1	3.6	- 6.2
2001	0.9	- 3.6	- 5.9	8.7	1.6	- 3.8	0.2	- 5.4	-11.1	2.6	8.6	1.7	- 7.1
2002	- 1.0	1.9	2.9	- 4.4	- 0.2	- 6.9	- 5.5	- 0.8	-12.4	10.6	5.9	- 6.2	-16.8
2003	- 3.5	- 2.0	1.3	6.1	4.4	1.5	2.8	2.0	- 1.5	5.7	- 0.2	6.9	25.3
2004	0.3	0.9	- 2.1	- 1.3	- 0.4	2.4	- 2.8	0.3	- 0.9	- 0.5	4.0	3.4	3.1
2005	- 2.7	2.6	- 2.4	- 3.0	2.7	- 1.8	3.6	- 1.5	0.8	- 1.2	3.5	- 0.8	- 0.6
2006	1.4	1.2	1.1	2.3	- 1.7	- 0.2	0.3	1.7	2.6	3.4	1.2	2.0	16.3
2007	1.3	- 2.8	0.7	5.7									
TOTALS	77.2	9.6	52.5	107.0	3.8	- 5.7	59.9	- 2.2	- 55.1	33.8	96.3	99.9	
AVG.	1.3	0.2	0.9	1.8	0.1	- 0.1	1.1	- 0.04	- 1.0	0.6	1.7	1.8	
# Up	39	33	37	36	29	28	35	32	21	33	39	41	
# Down	19	25	21	22	28	29	22	25	36	24	18	16	

152

DOW JONES INDUSTRIALS MONTHLY POINT CHANGES SINCE 1950

	Jan	Feb	Mar	Apr	May	Jun	Jul	Aug	Sep	Oct	Nov	Dec	Year's Close
1950	1.66	1.65	2.61	8.28	9.09	−14.31	0.29	7.47	9.49	−1.35	2.59	7.81	235.41
1951	13.42	3.22	−4.11	11.19	−9.48	−7.01	15.22	12.39	0.91	−8.81	−1.08	7.96	269.23
1952	1.46	−10.61	9.38	−11.83	5.31	11.32	5.30	−4.52	−4.43	−1.38	14.43	8.24	291.90
1953	−2.13	−5.50	−4.40	−5.12	−2.47	−4.02	7.12	−14.16	2.82	11.77	5.56	−0.47	280.90
1954	11.49	2.15	8.97	15.82	8.16	6.04	14.39	−12.12	24.66	−8.32	34.63	17.62	404.39
1955	4.44	3.04	−2.17	15.95	−0.79	26.52	14.47	2.33	−1.56	−11.75	28.39	5.14	488.40
1956	−17.66	12.91	28.14	4.33	−38.07	14.73	25.03	−15.77	−26.79	4.60	−7.07	26.69	499.47
1957	−20.31	−14.54	10.19	19.55	10.57	−1.64	5.23	−24.17	−28.05	−15.26	8.83	−14.18	435.69
1958	14.33	−10.10	6.84	9.10	6.84	15.48	24.81	5.64	23.46	11.13	14.24	26.19	583.65
1959	10.31	9.54	−1.79	22.04	20.04	−0.19	31.28	−10.47	−32.73	14.92	12.58	20.18	679.36
1960	−56.74	7.50	−13.53	−14.89	23.80	15.12	−23.89	9.26	−45.85	0.22	16.86	18.67	615.89
1961	32.31	13.88	14.55	2.08	18.01	−12.76	21.41	14.57	−18.73	2.71	17.68	9.54	731.14
1962	−31.14	8.05	−1.10	−41.62	−51.97	−52.08	36.65	11.25	−30.20	10.79	59.53	2.80	652.10
1963	30.75	−19.91	19.58	35.18	9.26	−20.08	−11.45	33.89	3.47	22.44	−4.71	12.43	762.95
1964	22.39	14.80	13.15	−2.52	9.79	10.94	9.60	−2.62	36.89	−2.29	2.35	−1.30	874.13
1965	28.73	0.62	−14.43	33.26	−4.27	−50.01	13.71	11.36	37.48	30.24	−14.11	22.55	969.26
1966	14.25	−31.62	−27.12	8.91	−49.61	−13.97	−22.72	−58.97	−14.19	32.85	−15.48	−5.90	785.69
1967	64.20	−10.52	26.61	31.07	−44.49	7.70	43.98	−2.95	25.37	−46.92	−3.93	29.30	905.11
1968	−49.64	−14.97	0.17	71.55	−13.22	−1.20	−14.80	13.01	39.78	16.60	32.69	−41.33	943.75
1969	2.30	−40.84	30.27	14.70	−12.62	−64.37	−57.72	21.25	−23.63	42.90	−43.69	−11.94	800.36
1970	−56.30	33.53	7.98	−49.50	−35.63	−16.91	50.59	30.46	−3.90	−5.07	38.48	44.83	838.92
1971	29.58	10.33	25.54	37.38	−33.94	−16.67	−32.71	39.64	−10.88	−48.19	−7.66	58.86	890.20
1972	11.97	25.96	12.57	13.47	6.55	−31.69	−4.29	38.99	−10.46	2.25	62.69	1.81	1020.02
1973	−21.00	−43.95	−4.06	−29.58	−20.02	−9.70	34.69	−38.83	59.53	9.48	−134.33	28.61	850.86
1974	4.69	4.98	−13.85	−9.93	−34.58	0.24	−44.98	−78.85	−70.71	57.65	−46.86	−2.42	616.24
1975	87.45	35.36	29.10	53.19	10.95	46.70	−47.48	3.83	−41.46	42.16	24.63	−8.26	852.41
1976	122.87	−2.67	26.84	−2.60	−21.62	27.55	−18.14	−10.90	16.45	−25.26	−17.71	57.43	1004.65
1977	−50.28	−17.95	−17.29	7.77	−28.24	17.64	−26.23	−28.58	−14.38	−28.76	11.35	1.47	831.17
1978	−61.25	−27.80	15.24	79.96	3.29	−21.66	43.32	14.55	−11.00	−73.37	6.58	5.98	805.01
1979	34.21	−30.40	53.36	−7.28	−32.57	19.65	4.44	41.21	−9.05	−62.88	6.65	16.39	838.74
1980	37.11	−12.71	−77.39	31.31	33.79	17.07	67.40	−2.73	−0.17	−7.93	68.85	−29.35	963.99
1981	−16.72	27.31	29.29	−6.12	−6.00	−14.87	−24.54	−70.87	−31.49	2.57	36.43	−13.98	875.00
1982	−3.90	−46.71	−1.62	25.59	−28.82	−7.61	−3.33	92.71	−5.06	95.47	47.56	7.26	1046.54
1983	29.16	36.92	17.41	96.17	−26.22	21.98	−22.74	16.94	16.97	−7.93	50.82	−17.38	1258.64
1984	−38.06	−65.95	10.26	5.86	−65.90	27.55	−17.12	109.10	−17.67	0.67	−18.44	22.63	1211.57
1985	75.20	−2.76	−17.23	−8.72	57.35	20.05	11.99	−13.44	−5.38	45.68	97.82	74.54	1546.67
1986	24.32	138.07	109.55	−34.63	92.73	16.01	−117.41	123.03	−130.76	110.23	36.42	−18.28	1895.95
1987	262.09	65.95	80.70	−18.33	5.21	126.96	153.54	90.88	−66.67	−602.75	−159.98	105.28	1938.83
1988	19.39	113.40	−83.56	44.27	−1.21	110.59	−12.98	−97.08	81.26	35.74	−34.14	54.06	2168.57
1989	173.75	−83.93	35.23	125.18	61.35	−40.09	220.60	76.61	−44.45	−47.74	61.19	46.93	2753.20
1990	−162.66	36.71	79.96	−50.45	219.90	4.03	24.51	−290.84	−161.88	−10.15	117.32	74.01	2633.66
1991	102.73	145.79	31.68	−25.99	139.63	−120.75	118.07	18.78	−26.83	52.33	−174.42	274.15	3168.83
1992	54.56	44.28	−32.20	123.65	37.76	−78.36	75.26	−136.43	14.31	−45.38	78.88	−4.05	3301.11
1993	8.92	60.78	64.30	−7.56	99.88	−11.35	23.39	111.78	−96.13	125.47	3.36	70.14	3754.09
1994	224.27	−146.34	−196.06	45.73	76.68	−133.41	139.54	148.92	−70.23	64.93	−168.89	95.21	3834.44
1995	9.42	167.19	146.64	163.58	143.87	90.96	152.37	−97.91	178.52	−33.60	319.01	42.63	5117.12
1996	278.18	90.32	101.52	−18.06	74.10	11.45	−125.72	87.30	265.96	147.21	492.32	−73.43	6448.27
1997	364.82	64.65	−294.26	425.51	322.05	341.75	549.82	−600.19	322.84	−503.18	381.05	85.12	7908.25
1998	−1.75	639.22	254.09	263.56	−163.42	52.07	−68.73	−1344.22	303.55	749.48	524.45	64.88	9181.43
1999	177.40	−52.25	479.58	1002.88	−229.30	411.06	−315.65	174.13	−492.33	392.91	147.95	619.31	11497.12
2000	−556.59	−812.22	793.61	−188.01	−211.58	−74.44	74.09	693.12	−564.18	320.22	−556.65	372.36	10786.85
2001	100.51	−392.08	−616.50	856.19	176.97	−409.54	20.41	−573.06	−1102.19	227.58	776.42	169.94	10021.50
2002	−101.50	186.13	297.81	−457.72	−20.97	−681.99	−506.67	−73.09	−1071.57	805.10	499.06	−554.46	8341.63
2003	−287.82	−162.73	101.05	487.96	370.17	135.18	248.36	182.02	−140.76	526.06	−18.66	671.46	10453.92
2004	34.15	95.85	−226.22	−132.13	−37.12	247.03	−295.77	34.21	−93.65	−52.80	400.55	354.99	10783.01
2005	−293.07	276.29	−262.47	−311.25	274.97	−92.51	365.94	−159.31	87.10	−128.63	365.80	−88.37	10717.50
2006	147.36	128.55	115.91	257.82	−198.83	−18.09	35.46	195.47	297.92	401.66	141.20	241.22	12463.15
2007	158.54	−353.06	85.72	708.56									
TOTALS	996.17	92.81	1264.04	3724.76	905.11	−267.91	867.21	−1295.98	−2670.66	2636.32	3619.39	2991.52	
# Up	39	33	37	36	29	28	35	32	21	33	39	41	
# Down	19	25	21	22	28	29	22	25	36	24	18	16	

153

DOW JONES INDUSTRIALS MONTHLY CLOSING PRICES SINCE 1950

	Jan	Feb	Mar	Apr	May	Jun	Jul	Aug	Sep	Oct	Nov	Dec
1950	201.79	203.44	206.05	214.33	223.42	209.11	209.40	216.87	226.36	225.01	227.60	235.41
1951	248.83	252.05	247.94	259.13	249.65	242.64	257.86	270.25	271.16	262.35	261.27	269.23
1952	270.69	260.08	269.46	257.63	262.94	274.26	279.56	275.04	270.61	269.23	283.66	291.90
1953	289.77	284.27	279.87	274.75	272.28	268.26	275.38	261.22	264.04	275.81	281.37	280.90
1954	292.39	294.54	303.51	319.33	327.49	333.53	347.92	335.80	360.46	352.14	386.77	404.39
1955	408.83	411.87	409.70	425.65	424.86	451.38	465.85	468.18	466.62	454.87	483.26	488.40
1956	470.74	483.65	511.79	516.12	478.05	492.78	517.81	502.04	475.25	479.85	472.78	499.47
1957	479.16	464.62	474.81	494.36	504.93	503.29	508.52	484.35	456.30	441.04	449.87	435.69
1958	450.02	439.92	446.76	455.86	462.70	478.18	502.99	508.63	532.09	543.22	557.46	583.65
1959	593.96	603.50	601.71	623.75	643.79	643.60	674.88	664.41	631.68	646.60	659.18	679.36
1960	622.62	630.12	616.59	601.70	625.50	640.62	616.73	625.99	580.14	580.36	597.22	615.89
1961	648.20	662.08	676.63	678.71	696.72	683.96	705.37	719.94	701.21	703.92	721.60	731.14
1962	700.00	708.05	706.95	665.33	613.36	561.28	597.93	609.18	578.98	589.77	649.30	652.10
1963	682.85	662.94	682.52	717.70	726.96	706.88	695.43	729.32	732.79	755.23	750.52	762.95
1964	785.34	800.14	813.29	810.77	820.56	831.50	841.10	838.48	875.37	873.08	875.43	874.13
1965	902.86	903.48	889.05	922.31	918.04	868.03	881.74	893.10	930.58	960.82	946.71	969.26
1966	983.51	951.89	924.77	933.68	884.07	870.10	847.38	788.41	774.22	807.07	791.59	785.69
1967	849.89	839.37	865.98	897.05	852.56	860.26	904.24	901.29	926.66	879.74	875.81	905.11
1968	855.47	840.50	840.67	912.22	899.00	897.80	883.00	896.01	935.79	952.39	985.08	943.75
1969	946.05	905.21	935.48	950.18	937.56	873.19	815.47	836.72	813.09	855.99	812.30	800.36
1970	744.06	777.59	785.57	736.07	700.44	683.53	734.12	764.58	760.68	755.61	794.09	838.92
1971	868.50	878.83	904.37	941.75	907.81	891.14	858.43	898.07	887.19	839.00	831.34	890.20
1972	902.17	928.13	940.70	954.17	960.72	929.03	924.74	963.73	953.27	955.52	1018.21	1020.02
1973	999.02	955.07	951.01	921.43	901.41	891.71	926.40	887.57	947.10	956.58	822.25	850.86
1974	855.55	860.53	846.68	836.75	802.17	802.41	757.43	678.58	607.87	665.52	618.66	616.24
1975	703.69	739.05	768.15	821.34	832.29	878.99	831.51	835.34	793.88	836.04	860.67	852.41
1976	975.28	972.61	999.45	996.85	975.23	1002.78	984.64	973.74	990.19	964.93	947.22	1004.65
1977	954.37	936.42	919.13	926.90	898.66	916.30	890.07	861.49	847.11	818.35	829.70	831.17
1978	769.92	742.12	757.36	837.32	840.61	818.95	862.27	876.82	865.82	792.45	799.03	805.01
1979	839.22	808.82	862.18	854.90	822.33	841.98	846.42	887.63	878.58	815.70	822.35	838.74
1980	875.85	863.14	785.75	817.06	850.85	867.92	935.32	932.59	932.42	924.49	993.34	963.99
1981	947.27	974.58	1003.87	997.75	991.75	976.88	952.34	881.47	849.98	852.55	888.98	875.00
1982	871.10	824.39	822.77	848.36	819.54	811.93	808.60	901.31	896.25	991.72	1039.28	1046.54
1983	1075.70	1112.62	1130.03	1226.20	1199.98	1221.96	1199.22	1216.16	1233.13	1225.20	1276.02	1258.64
1984	1220.58	1154.63	1164.89	1170.75	1104.85	1132.40	1115.28	1224.38	1206.71	1207.38	1188.94	1211.57
1985	1286.77	1284.01	1266.78	1258.06	1315.41	1335.46	1347.45	1334.01	1328.63	1374.31	1472.13	1546.67
1986	1570.99	1709.06	1818.61	1783.98	1876.71	1892.72	1775.31	1898.34	1767.58	1877.81	1914.23	1895.95
1987	2158.04	2223.99	2304.69	2286.36	2291.57	2418.53	2572.07	2662.95	2596.28	1993.53	1833.55	1938.83
1988	1958.22	2071.62	1988.06	2032.33	2031.12	2141.71	2128.73	2031.65	2112.91	2148.65	2114.51	2168.57
1989	2342.32	2258.39	2293.62	2418.80	2480.15	2440.06	2660.66	2737.27	2692.82	2645.08	2706.27	2753.20
1990	2590.54	2627.25	2707.21	2656.76	2876.66	2880.69	2905.20	2614.36	2452.48	2442.33	2559.65	2633.66
1991	2736.39	2882.18	2913.86	2887.87	3027.50	2906.75	3024.82	3043.60	3016.77	3069.10	2894.68	3168.83
1992	3223.39	3267.67	3235.47	3359.12	3396.88	3318.52	3393.78	3257.35	3271.66	3226.28	3305.16	3301.11
1993	3310.03	3370.81	3435.11	3427.55	3527.43	3516.08	3539.47	3651.25	3555.12	3680.59	3683.95	3754.09
1994	3978.36	3832.02	3635.96	3681.69	3758.37	3624.96	3764.50	3913.42	3843.19	3908.12	3739.23	3834.44
1995	3843.86	4011.05	4157.69	4321.27	4465.14	4556.10	4708.47	4610.56	4789.08	4755.48	5074.49	5117.12
1996	5395.30	5485.62	5587.14	5569.08	5643.18	5654.63	5528.91	5616.21	5882.17	6029.38	6521.70	6448.27
1997	6813.09	6877.74	6583.48	7008.99	7331.04	7672.79	8222.61	7622.42	7945.26	7442.08	7823.13	7908.25
1998	7906.50	8545.72	8799.81	9063.37	8899.95	8952.02	8883.29	7539.07	7842.62	8592.62	9116.55	9181.43
1999	9358.83	9306.58	9786.16	10789.04	10559.74	10970.80	10655.15	10829.28	10336.95	10729.86	10877.81	11497.12
2000	10940.53	10128.31	10921.92	10733.91	10522.33	10447.89	10521.98	11215.10	10650.92	10971.14	10414.49	10786.85
2001	10887.36	10495.28	9878.78	10734.97	10911.94	10502.40	10522.81	9949.75	8847.56	9075.14	9851.56	10021.50
2002	9920.00	10106.13	10403.94	9946.22	9925.25	9243.26	8736.59	8663.50	7591.93	8397.03	8896.09	8341.63
2003	8053.81	7891.08	7992.13	8480.09	8850.26	8985.44	9233.80	9415.82	9275.06	9801.12	9782.46	10453.92
2004	10488.07	10583.92	10357.70	10225.57	10188.45	10435.48	10139.71	10173.92	10080.27	10027.47	10428.02	10783.01
2005	10489.94	10766.23	10503.76	10192.51	10467.48	10274.97	10640.91	10481.60	10568.70	10440.07	10805.87	10717.50
2006	10864.86	10993.41	11109.32	11367.14	11168.31	11150.22	11185.68	11381.15	11679.07	12080.73	12221.93	12463.15
2007	12621.69	12268.63	12354.35	13062.91								

154

	Jan	Feb	Mar	Apr	May	Jun	Jul	Aug	Sep	Oct	Nov	Dec	Year's Change
1950	1.7	1.0	0.4	4.5	3.9	– 5.8	0.8	3.3	5.6	0.4	– 0.1	4.6	21.8
1951	6.1	0.6	– 1.8	4.8	– 4.1	– 2.6	6.9	3.9	– 0.1	– 1.4	– 0.3	3.9	16.5
1952	1.6	– 3.6	4.8	– 4.3	2.3	4.6	1.8	– 1.5	– 2.0	– 0.1	4.6	3.5	11.8
1953	– 0.7	– 1.8	– 2.4	– 2.6	– 0.3	– 1.6	2.5	– 5.8	0.1	5.1	0.9	0.2	– 6.6
1954	5.1	0.3	3.0	4.9	3.3	0.1	5.7	– 3.4	8.3	– 1.9	8.1	5.1	45.0
1955	1.8	0.4	– 0.5	3.8	– 0.1	8.2	6.1	– 0.8	1.1	– 3.0	7.5	– 0.1	26.4
1956	– 3.6	3.5	6.9	– 0.2	– 6.6	3.9	5.2	– 3.8	– 4.5	0.5	– 1.1	3.5	2.6
1957	– 4.2	– 3.3	2.0	3.7	3.7	– 0.1	1.1	– 5.6	– 6.2	– 3.2	1.6	– 4.1	– 14.3
1958	4.3	– 2.1	3.1	3.2	1.5	2.6	4.3	1.2	4.8	2.5	2.2	5.2	38.1
1959	0.4	– 0.02	0.1	3.9	1.9	– 0.4	3.5	– 1.5	– 4.6	1.1	1.3	2.8	8.5
1960	– 7.1	0.9	– 1.4	– 1.8	2.7	2.0	– 2.5	2.6	– 6.0	– 0.2	4.0	4.6	– 3.0
1961	6.3	2.7	2.6	0.4	1.9	– 2.9	3.3	2.0	– 2.0	2.8	3.9	0.3	23.1
1962	– 3.8	1.6	– 0.6	– 6.2	– 8.6	– 8.2	6.4	1.5	– 4.8	0.4	10.2	1.3	– 11.8
1963	4.9	– 2.9	3.5	4.9	1.4	– 2.0	– 0.3	4.9	– 1.1	3.2	– 1.1	2.4	18.9
1964	2.7	1.0	1.5	0.6	1.1	1.6	1.8	– 1.6	2.9	0.8	– 0.5	0.4	13.0
1965	3.3	– 0.1	– 1.5	3.4	– 0.8	– 4.9	1.3	2.3	3.2	2.7	– 0.9	0.9	9.1
1966	0.5	– 1.8	– 2.2	2.1	– 5.4	– 1.6	– 1.3	– 7.8	– 0.7	4.8	0.3	– 0.1	– 13.1
1967	7.8	0.2	3.9	4.2	– 5.2	1.8	4.5	– 1.2	3.3	– 2.9	0.1	2.6	20.1
1968	– 4.4	– 3.1	0.9	8.2	1.1	0.9	– 1.8	1.1	3.9	0.7	4.8	– 4.2	7.7
1969	– 0.8	– 4.7	3.4	2.1	– 0.2	– 5.6	– 6.0	4.0	– 2.5	4.4	– 3.5	– 1.9	– 11.4
1970	– 7.6	5.3	0.1	– 9.0	– 6.1	– 5.0	7.3	4.4	3.3	– 1.1	4.7	5.7	0.1
1971	4.0	0.9	3.7	3.6	– 4.2	0.1	– 4.1	3.6	– 0.7	– 4.2	– 0.3	8.6	10.8
1972	1.8	2.5	0.6	0.4	1.7	– 2.2	0.2	3.4	– 0.5	0.9	4.6	1.2	15.6
1973	– 1.7	– 3.7	– 0.1	– 4.1	– 1.9	– 0.7	3.8	– 3.7	4.0	– 0.1	– 11.4	1.7	– 17.4
1974	– 1.0	– 0.4	– 2.3	– 3.9	– 3.4	– 1.5	– 7.8	– 9.0	–11.9	16.3	– 5.3	– 2.0	– 29.7
1975	12.3	6.0	2.2	4.7	4.4	4.4	– 6.8	– 2.1	– 3.5	6.2	2.5	– 1.2	31.5
1976	11.8	– 1.1	3.1	– 1.1	– 1.4	4.1	– 0.8	– 0.5	2.3	– 2.2	– 0.8	5.2	19.1
1977	– 5.1	– 2.2	– 1.4	0.02	– 2.4	4.5	– 1.6	– 2.1	– 0.2	– 4.3	2.7	0.3	– 11.5
1978	– 6.2	– 2.5	2.5	8.5	0.4	– 1.8	5.4	2.6	– 0.7	– 9.2	1.7	1.5	1.1
1979	4.0	– 3.7	5.5	0.2	– 2.6	3.9	0.9	5.3	NC	– 6.9	4.3	1.7	12.3
1980	5.8	– 0.4	–10.2	4.1	4.7	2.7	6.5	0.6	2.5	1.6	10.2	– 3.4	25.8
1981	– 4.6	1.3	3.6	– 2.3	– 0.2	– 1.0	– 0.2	– 6.2	– 5.4	4.9	3.7	– 3.0	– 9.7
1982	– 1.8	– 6.1	– 1.0	4.0	– 3.9	– 2.0	– 2.3	11.6	0.8	11.0	3.6	1.5	14.8
1983	3.3	1.9	3.3	7.5	– 1.2	3.5	– 3.3	1.1	1.0	– 1.5	1.7	– 0.9	17.3
1984	– 0.9	– 3.9	1.3	0.5	– 5.9	1.7	– 1.6	10.6	– 0.3	– 0.01	– 1.5	2.2	1.4
1985	7.4	0.9	– 0.3	– 0.5	5.4	1.2	– 0.5	– 1.2	– 3.5	4.3	6.5	4.5	26.3
1986	0.2	7.1	5.3	– 1.4	5.0	1.4	– 5.9	7.1	– 8.5	5.5	2.1	– 2.8	14.6
1987	13.2	3.7	2.6	– 1.1	0.6	4.8	4.8	3.5	– 2.4	–21.8	– 8.5	7.3	2.0
1988	4.0	4.2	– 3.3	0.9	0.3	4.3	– 0.5	– 3.9	4.0	2.6	– 1.9	1.5	12.4
1989	7.1	– 2.9	2.1	5.0	3.5	– 0.8	8.8	1.6	– 0.7	– 2.5	1.7	2.1	27.3
1990	– 6.9	0.9	2.4	– 2.7	9.2	– 0.9	– 0.5	– 9.4	– 5.1	– 0.7	6.0	2.5	– 6.6
1991	4.2	6.7	2.2	0.03	3.9	– 4.8	4.5	2.0	– 1.9	1.2	– 4.4	11.2	26.3
1992	– 2.0	1.0	– 2.2	2.8	0.1	– 1.7	3.9	– 2.4	0.9	0.2	3.0	1.0	4.5
1993	0.7	1.0	1.9	– 2.5	2.3	0.1	– 0.5	3.4	– 1.0	1.9	– 1.3	1.0	7.1
1994	3.3	– 3.0	– 4.6	1.2	1.2	– 2.7	3.1	3.8	– 2.7	2.1	– 4.0	1.2	– 1.5
1995	2.4	3.6	2.7	2.8	3.6	2.1	3.2	– 0.03	4.0	– 0.5	4.1	1.7	34.1
1996	3.3	0.7	0.8	1.3	2.3	0.2	– 4.6	1.9	5.4	2.6	7.3	– 2.2	20.3
1997	6.1	0.6	– 4.3	5.8	5.9	4.3	7.8	– 5.7	5.3	– 3.4	4.5	1.6	31.0
1998	1.0	7.0	5.0	0.9	– 1.9	3.9	– 1.2	–14.6	6.2	8.0	5.9	5.6	26.7
1999	4.1	– 3.2	3.9	3.8	– 2.5	5.4	– 3.2	– 0.6	– 2.9	6.3	1.9	5.8	19.5
2000	– 5.1	– 2.0	9.7	– 3.1	– 2.2	2.4	– 1.6	6.1	– 5.3	– 0.5	– 8.0	0.4	– 10.1
2001	3.5	– 9.2	– 6.4	7.7	0.5	– 2.5	– 1.1	– 6.4	– 8.2	1.8	7.5	0.8	– 13.0
2002	– 1.6	– 2.1	3.7	– 6.1	– 0.9	– 7.2	– 7.9	0.5	–11.0	8.6	5.7	– 6.0	– 23.4
2003	– 2.7	– 1.7	1.0	8.0	5.1	1.1	1.6	1.8	– 1.2	5.5	0.7	5.1	26.4
2004	1.7	1.2	– 1.6	– 1.7	1.2	1.8	– 3.4	0.2	0.9	1.4	3.9	3.2	9.0
2005	– 2.5	1.9	– 1.9	– 2.0	3.0	– 0.01	3.6	– 1.1	0.7	– 1.8	3.5	– 0.1	3.0
2006	2.5	0.1	1.1	1.2	– 3.1	0.01	0.5	2.1	2.5	3.2	1.6	1.3	13.6
2007	1.4	– 2.2	1.0	4.3									
TOTALS	81.3	– 3.1	57.4	77.4	14.0	13.1	49.8	2.1	– 35.1	52.1	100.2	96.7	
AVG.	1.4	– 0.1	1.0	1.3	0.2	0.2	0.9	0.04	– 0.6	0.9	1.8	1.7	
Up	37	31	38	39	32	31	31	31	24	34	39	43	
Down	21	27	20	19	25	26	26	26	32	23	18	14	

STANDARD & POOR'S 500 MONTHLY CLOSING PRICES SINCE 1950

	Jan	Feb	Mar	Apr	May	Jun	Jul	Aug	Sep	Oct	Nov	Dec
1950	17.05	17.22	17.29	18.07	18.78	17.69	17.84	18.42	19.45	19.53	19.51	20.41
1951	21.66	21.80	21.40	22.43	21.52	20.96	22.40	23.28	23.26	22.94	22.88	23.77
1952	24.14	23.26	24.37	23.32	23.86	24.96	25.40	25.03	24.54	24.52	25.66	26.57
1953	26.38	25.90	25.29	24.62	24.54	24.14	24.75	23.32	23.35	24.54	24.76	24.81
1954	26.08	26.15	26.94	28.26	29.19	29.21	30.88	29.83	32.31	31.68	34.24	35.98
1955	36.63	36.76	36.58	37.96	37.91	41.03	43.52	43.18	43.67	42.34	45.51	45.48
1956	43.82	45.34	48.48	48.38	45.20	46.97	49.39	47.51	45.35	45.58	45.08	46.67
1957	44.72	43.26	44.11	45.74	47.43	47.37	47.91	45.22	42.42	41.06	41.72	39.99
1958	41.70	40.84	42.10	43.44	44.09	45.24	47.19	47.75	50.06	51.33	52.48	55.21
1959	55.42	55.41	55.44	57.59	58.68	58.47	60.51	59.60	56.88	57.52	58.28	59.89
1960	55.61	56.12	55.34	54.37	55.83	56.92	55.51	56.96	53.52	53.39	55.54	58.11
1961	61.78	63.44	65.06	65.31	66.56	64.64	66.76	68.07	66.73	68.62	71.32	71.55
1962	68.84	69.96	69.55	65.24	59.63	54.75	58.23	59.12	56.27	56.52	62.26	63.10
1963	66.20	64.29	66.57	69.80	70.80	69.37	69.13	72.50	71.70	74.01	73.23	75.02
1964	77.04	77.80	78.98	79.46	80.37	81.69	83.18	81.83	84.18	84.86	84.42	84.75
1965	87.56	87.43	86.16	89.11	88.42	84.12	85.25	87.17	89.96	92.42	91.61	92.43
1966	92.88	91.22	89.23	91.06	86.13	84.74	83.60	77.10	76.56	80.20	80.45	80.33
1967	86.61	86.78	90.20	94.01	89.08	90.64	94.75	93.64	96.71	93.90	94.00	96.47
1968	92.24	89.36	90.20	97.59	98.68	99.58	97.74	98.86	102.67	103.41	108.37	103.86
1969	103.01	98.13	101.51	103.69	103.46	97.71	91.83	95.51	93.12	97.24	93.81	92.06
1970	85.02	89.50	89.63	81.52	76.55	72.72	78.05	81.52	84.21	83.25	87.20	92.15
1971	95.88	96.75	100.31	103.95	99.63	99.70	95.58	99.03	98.34	94.23	93.99	102.09
1972	103.94	106.57	107.20	107.67	109.53	107.14	107.39	111.09	110.55	111.58	116.67	118.05
1973	116.03	111.68	111.52	106.97	104.95	104.26	108.22	104.25	108.43	108.29	95.96	97.55
1974	96.57	96.22	93.98	90.31	87.28	86.00	79.31	72.15	63.54	73.90	69.97	68.56
1975	76.98	81.59	83.36	87.30	91.15	95.19	88.75	86.88	83.87	89.04	91.24	90.19
1976	100.86	99.71	102.77	101.64	100.18	104.28	103.44	102.91	105.24	102.90	102.10	107.46
1977	102.03	99.82	98.42	98.44	96.12	100.48	98.85	96.77	96.53	92.34	94.83	95.10
1978	89.25	87.04	89.21	96.83	97.24	95.53	100.68	103.29	102.54	93.15	94.70	96.11
1979	99.93	96.28	101.59	101.76	99.08	102.91	103.81	109.32	109.32	101.82	106.16	107.94
1980	114.16	113.66	102.09	106.29	111.24	114.24	121.67	122.38	125.46	127.47	140.52	135.76
1981	129.55	131.27	136.00	132.81	132.59	131.21	130.92	122.79	116.18	121.89	126.35	122.55
1982	120.40	113.11	111.96	116.44	111.88	109.61	107.09	119.51	120.42	133.71	138.54	140.64
1983	145.30	148.06	152.96	164.42	162.39	168.11	162.56	164.40	166.07	163.55	166.40	164.93
1984	163.41	157.06	159.18	160.05	150.55	153.18	150.66	166.68	166.10	166.09	163.58	167.24
1985	179.63	181.18	180.66	179.83	189.55	191.85	190.92	188.63	182.08	189.82	202.17	211.28
1986	211.78	226.92	238.90	235.52	247.35	250.84	236.12	252.93	231.32	243.98	249.22	242.17
1987	274.08	284.20	291.70	288.36	290.10	304.00	318.66	329.80	321.83	251.79	230.30	247.08
1988	257.07	267.82	258.89	261.33	262.16	273.50	272.02	261.52	271.91	278.97	273.70	277.72
1989	297.47	288.86	294.87	309.64	320.52	317.98	346.08	351.45	349.15	340.36	345.99	353.40
1990	329.08	331.89	339.94	330.80	361.23	358.02	356.15	322.56	306.05	304.00	322.22	330.22
1991	343.93	367.07	375.22	375.35	389.83	371.16	387.81	395.43	387.86	392.46	375.22	417.09
1992	408.79	412.70	403.69	414.95	415.35	408.14	424.21	414.03	417.80	418.68	431.35	435.71
1993	438.78	443.38	451.67	440.19	450.19	450.53	448.13	463.56	458.93	467.83	461.79	466.45
1994	481.61	467.14	445.77	450.91	456.50	444.27	458.26	475.49	462.69	472.35	453.69	459.27
1995	470.42	487.39	500.71	514.71	533.40	544.75	562.06	561.88	584.41	581.50	605.37	615.93
1996	636.02	640.43	645.50	654.17	669.12	670.63	639.95	651.99	687.31	705.27	757.02	740.74
1997	786.16	790.82	757.12	801.34	848.28	885.14	954.29	899.47	947.28	914.62	955.40	970.43
1998	980.28	1049.34	1101.75	1111.75	1090.82	1133.84	1120.67	957.28	1017.01	1098.67	1163.63	1229.23
1999	1279.64	1238.33	1286.37	1335.18	1301.84	1372.71	1328.72	1320.41	1282.71	1362.93	1388.91	1469.25
2000	1394.46	1366.42	1498.58	1452.43	1420.60	1454.60	1430.83	1517.68	1436.51	1429.40	1314.95	1320.28
2001	1366.01	1239.94	1160.33	1249.46	1255.82	1224.42	1211.23	1133.58	1040.94	1059.78	1139.45	1148.08
2002	1130.20	1106.73	1147.39	1076.92	1067.14	989.82	911.62	916.07	815.28	885.76	936.31	879.82
2003	855.70	841.15	849.18	916.92	963.59	974.50	990.31	1008.01	995.97	1050.71	1058.20	1111.92
2004	1131.13	1144.94	1126.21	1107.30	1120.68	1140.84	1101.72	1104.24	1114.58	1130.20	1173.82	1211.92
2005	1181.27	1203.60	1180.59	1156.85	1191.50	1191.33	1234.18	1220.33	1228.81	1207.01	1249.48	1248.29
2006	1280.08	1280.66	1294.83	1310.61	1270.09	1270.20	1276.66	1303.82	1335.85	1377.94	1400.63	1418.30
2007	1438.24	1406.82	1420.86	1482.37								

NASDAQ COMPOSITE MONTHLY PERCENT CHANGES SINCE 1971

	Jan	Feb	Mar	Apr	May	Jun	Jul	Aug	Sep	Oct	Nov	Dec	Year's Change
1971	10.2	2.6	4.6	6.0	-3.6	-0.4	-2.3	3.0	0.6	-3.6	-1.1	9.8	27.4
1972	4.2	5.5	2.2	2.5	0.9	-1.8	-1.8	1.7	-0.3	0.5	2.1	0.6	17.2
1973	-4.0	-6.2	-2.4	-8.2	-4.8	-1.6	7.6	-3.5	6.0	-0.9	-15.1	-1.4	-31.1
1974	3.0	-0.6	-2.2	-5.9	-7.7	-5.3	-7.9	-10.9	-10.7	17.2	-3.5	-5.0	-35.1
1975	16.6	4.6	3.6	3.8	5.8	4.7	-4.4	-5.0	-5.9	3.6	2.4	-1.5	29.8
1976	12.1	3.7	0.4	-0.6	-2.3	2.6	1.1	-1.7	1.7	-1.0	0.9	7.4	26.1
1977	-2.4	-1.0	-0.5	1.4	0.1	4.3	0.9	-0.5	0.7	-3.3	5.8	1.8	7.3
1978	-4.0	0.6	4.7	8.5	4.4	0.05	5.0	6.9	-1.6	-16.4	3.2	2.9	12.3
1979	6.6	-2.6	7.5	1.6	-1.8	5.1	2.3	6.4	-0.3	-9.6	6.4	4.8	28.1
1980	7.0	-2.3	-17.1	6.9	7.5	4.9	8.9	5.7	3.4	2.7	8.0	-2.8	33.9
1981	-2.2	0.1	6.1	3.1	3.1	-3.5	-1.9	-7.5	-8.0	8.4	3.1	-2.7	-3.2
1982	-3.8	-4.8	-2.1	5.2	-3.3	-4.1	-2.3	6.2	5.6	13.3	9.3	0.04	18.7
1983	6.9	5.0	3.9	8.2	5.3	3.2	-4.6	-3.8	1.4	-7.4	4.1	-2.5	19.9
1984	-3.7	-5.9	-0.7	-1.3	-5.9	2.9	-4.2	10.9	-1.8	-1.2	-1.8	2.0	-11.2
1985	12.7	2.0	-1.7	0.5	3.6	1.9	1.7	-1.2	-5.8	4.4	7.3	3.5	31.4
1986	3.3	7.1	4.2	2.3	4.4	1.3	-8.4	3.1	-8.4	2.9	-0.3	-2.8	7.5
1987	12.2	8.4	1.2	-2.8	-0.3	2.0	2.4	4.6	-2.3	-27.2	-5.6	8.3	-5.4
1988	4.3	6.5	2.1	1.2	-2.3	6.6	-1.9	-2.8	3.0	-1.4	-2.9	2.7	15.4
1989	5.2	-0.4	1.8	5.1	4.4	-2.4	4.3	3.4	0.8	-3.7	0.1	-0.3	19.3
1990	-8.6	2.4	2.3	-3.6	9.3	0.7	-5.2	-13.0	-9.6	-4.3	8.9	4.1	-17.8
1991	10.8	9.4	6.5	0.5	4.4	-6.0	5.5	4.7	0.2	3.1	-3.5	11.9	56.8
1992	5.8	2.1	-4.7	-4.2	1.1	-3.7	3.1	-3.0	3.6	3.8	7.9	3.7	15.5
1993	2.9	-3.7	2.9	-4.2	5.9	0.5	0.1	5.4	2.7	2.2	-3.2	3.0	14.7
1994	3.0	-1.0	-6.2	-1.3	0.2	-4.0	2.3	6.0	-0.2	1.7	-3.5	0.2	-3.2
1995	0.4	5.1	3.0	3.3	2.4	8.0	7.3	1.9	2.3	-0.7	2.2	-0.7	39.9
1996	0.7	3.8	0.1	8.1	4.4	-4.7	-8.8	5.6	7.5	-0.4	5.8	-0.1	22.7
1997	6.9	-5.1	-6.7	3.2	11.1	3.0	10.5	-0.4	6.2	-5.5	0.4	-1.9	21.6
1998	3.1	9.3	3.7	1.8	-4.8	6.5	-1.2	-19.9	13.0	4.6	10.1	12.5	39.6
1999	14.3	-8.7	7.6	3.3	-2.8	8.7	-1.8	3.8	0.2	8.0	12.5	22.0	85.6
2000	-3.2	19.2	-2.6	-15.6	-11.9	16.6	-5.0	11.7	-12.7	-8.3	-22.9	-4.9	-39.3
2001	12.2	-22.4	-14.5	15.0	-0.3	2.4	-6.2	-10.9	-17.0	12.8	14.2	1.0	-21.1
2002	-0.8	-10.5	6.6	-8.5	-4.3	-9.4	-9.2	-1.0	-10.9	13.5	11.2	-9.7	-31.5
2003	-1.1	1.3	0.3	9.2	9.0	1.7	6.9	4.3	-1.3	8.1	1.5	2.2	50.0
2004	3.1	-1.8	-1.8	-3.7	3.5	3.1	-7.8	-2.6	3.2	4.1	6.2	3.7	8.6
2005	-5.2	-0.5	-2.6	-3.9	7.6	-0.5	6.2	-1.5	-0.02	-1.5	5.3	-1.2	1.4
2006	4.6	-1.1	2.6	-0.7	-6.2	-0.3	-3.7	4.4	3.4	4.8	2.7	-0.7	9.5
2007	2.0	-1.9	0.2	4.3									
TOTALS	135.1	18.2	12.3	40.5	36.1	43.1	-12.5	10.5	-31.3	23.3	78.2	69.9	
AVG.	3.7	0.5	0.3	1.1	1.0	1.2	-0.3	0.3	-0.9	0.6	2.2	1.9	
# Up	26	19	23	23	21	22	17	19	19	19	25	21	
# Down	11	18	14	14	15	14	19	17	17	17	11	15	

Based on NASDAQ composite, prior to February 5, 1971, based on National Quotation Bureau indices

NASDAQ COMPOSITE MONTHLY CLOSING PRICES SINCE 1971

	Jan	Feb	Mar	Apr	May	Jun	Jul	Aug	Sep	Oct	Nov	Dec
1971	98.77	101.34	105.97	112.30	108.25	107.80	105.27	108.42	109.03	105.10	103.97	114.12
1972	118.87	125.38	128.14	131.33	132.53	130.08	127.75	129.95	129.61	130.24	132.96	133.73
1973	128.40	120.41	117.46	107.85	102.64	100.98	108.64	104.87	111.20	110.17	93.51	92.19
1974	94.93	94.35	92.27	86.86	80.20	75.96	69.99	62.37	55.67	65.23	62.95	59.82
1975	69.78	73.00	75.66	78.54	83.10	87.02	83.19	79.01	74.33	76.99	78.80	77.62
1976	87.05	90.26	90.62	90.08	88.04	90.32	91.29	89.70	91.26	90.35	91.12	97.88
1977	95.54	94.57	94.13	95.48	95.59	99.73	100.65	100.10	100.85	97.52	103.15	105.05
1978	100.84	101.47	106.20	115.18	120.24	120.30	126.32	135.01	132.89	111.12	114.69	117.98
1979	125.82	122.56	131.76	133.82	131.42	138.13	141.33	150.44	149.98	135.53	144.26	151.14
1980	161.75	158.03	131.00	139.99	150.45	157.78	171.81	181.52	187.76	192.78	208.15	202.34
1981	197.81	198.01	210.18	216.74	223.47	215.75	211.63	195.75	180.03	195.24	201.37	195.84
1982	188.39	179.43	175.65	184.70	178.54	171.30	167.35	177.71	187.65	212.63	232.31	232.41
1983	248.35	260.67	270.80	293.06	308.73	318.70	303.96	292.42	296.65	274.55	285.67	278.60
1984	268.43	252.57	250.78	247.44	232.82	239.65	229.70	254.64	249.94	247.03	242.53	247.35
1985	278.70	284.17	279.20	280.56	290.80	296.20	301.29	297.71	280.33	292.54	313.95	324.93
1986	335.77	359.53	374.72	383.24	400.16	405.51	371.37	382.86	350.67	360.77	359.57	349.33
1987	392.06	424.97	430.05	417.81	416.54	424.67	434.93	454.97	444.29	323.30	305.16	330.47
1988	344.66	366.95	374.64	379.23	370.34	394.66	387.33	376.55	387.71	382.46	371.45	381.38
1989	401.30	399.71	406.73	427.55	446.17	435.29	453.84	469.33	472.92	455.63	456.09	454.82
1990	415.81	425.83	435.54	420.07	458.97	462.29	438.24	381.21	344.51	329.84	359.06	373.84
1991	414.20	453.05	482.30	484.72	506.11	475.92	502.04	525.68	526.88	542.98	523.90	586.34
1992	620.21	633.47	603.77	578.68	585.31	563.60	580.83	563.12	583.27	605.17	652.73	676.95
1993	696.34	670.77	690.13	661.42	700.53	703.95	704.70	742.84	762.78	779.26	754.39	776.80
1994	800.47	792.50	743.46	733.84	735.19	705.96	722.16	765.62	764.29	777.49	750.32	751.96
1995	755.20	793.73	817.21	843.98	864.58	933.45	1001.21	1020.11	1043.54	1036.06	1059.20	1052.13
1996	1059.79	1100.05	1101.40	1190.52	1243.43	1185.02	1080.59	1141.50	1226.92	1221.51	1292.61	1291.03
1997	1379.85	1309.00	1221.70	1260.76	1400.32	1442.07	1593.81	1587.32	1685.69	1593.61	1600.55	1570.35
1998	1619.36	1770.51	1835.68	1868.41	1778.87	1894.74	1872.39	1499.25	1693.84	1771.39	1949.54	2192.69
1999	2505.89	2288.03	2461.40	2542.85	2470.52	2686.12	2638.49	2739.35	2746.16	2966.43	3336.16	4069.31
2000	3940.35	4696.69	4572.83	3860.66	3400.91	3966.11	3766.99	4206.35	3672.82	3369.63	2597.93	2470.52
2001	2772.73	2151.83	1840.26	2116.24	2110.49	2160.54	2027.13	1805.43	1498.80	1690.20	1930.58	1950.40
2002	1934.03	1731.49	1845.35	1688.23	1615.73	1463.21	1328.26	1314.85	1172.06	1329.75	1478.78	1335.51
2003	1320.91	1337.52	1341.17	1464.31	1595.91	1622.80	1735.02	1810.45	1786.94	1932.21	1960.26	2003.37
2004	2066.15	2029.82	1994.22	1920.15	1986.74	2047.79	1887.36	1838.10	1896.84	1974.99	2096.81	2175.44
2005	2062.41	2051.72	1999.23	1921.65	2068.22	2056.96	2184.83	2152.09	2151.69	2120.30	2232.82	2205.32
2006	2305.82	2281.39	2339.79	2322.57	2178.88	2172.09	2091.47	2183.75	2258.43	2366.71	2431.77	2415.29
2007	2463.93	2416.15	2421.64	2525.09								

Based on NASDAQ composite, prior to February 5, 1971, based on National Quotation Bureau indices.

RUSSELL 1000 INDEX MONTHLY PERCENT CHANGES SINCE 1979

	Jan	Feb	Mar	Apr	May	Jun	Jul	Aug	Sep	Oct	Nov	Dec	Year's Change
1979	4.2	-3.5	6.0	0.3	-2.2	4.3	1.1	5.6	0.02	-7.1	5.1	2.1	16.1
1980	5.9	-0.5	-11.5	4.6	5.0	3.2	6.4	1.1	2.6	1.8	10.1	-3.9	25.6
1981	-4.6	1.0	3.8	-1.9	0.2	-1.2	-0.1	-6.2	-6.4	5.4	4.0	-3.3	-9.7
1982	-2.7	-5.9	-1.3	3.9	-3.6	-2.6	-2.3	11.3	1.2	11.3	4.0	1.3	13.7
1983	3.2	2.1	3.2	7.1	-0.2	3.7	-3.2	0.5	1.3	-2.4	2.0	-1.2	17.0
1984	-1.9	-4.4	1.1	0.3	-5.9	2.1	-1.8	10.8	-0.2	-0.1	-1.4	2.2	-0.1
1985	7.8	1.1	-0.4	-0.3	5.4	1.6	-0.8	-1.0	-3.9	4.5	6.5	4.1	26.7
1986	0.9	7.2	5.1	-1.3	5.0	1.4	-5.9	6.8	-8.5	5.1	1.4	-3.0	13.6
1987	12.7	4.0	1.9	-1.8	0.4	4.5	4.2	3.8	-2.4	-21.9	-8.0	7.2	0.02
1988	4.3	4.4	-2.9	0.7	0.2	4.8	-0.9	-3.3	3.9	2.0	-2.0	1.7	13.1
1989	6.8	-2.5	2.0	4.9	3.8	-0.8	8.2	1.7	-0.5	-2.8	1.5	1.8	25.9
1990	-7.4	1.2	2.2	-2.8	8.9	-0.7	-1.1	-9.6	-5.3	-0.8	6.4	2.7	-7.5
1991	4.5	6.9	2.5	-0.1	3.8	-4.7	4.6	2.2	-1.5	1.4	-4.1	11.2	28.8
1992	-1.4	0.9	-2.4	2.3	0.3	-1.9	4.1	-2.5	1.0	0.7	3.5	1.4	5.9
1993	0.7	0.6	2.2	-2.8	2.4	0.4	-0.4	3.5	-0.5	1.2	-1.7	1.6	7.3
1994	2.9	-2.9	-4.5	1.1	1.0	-2.9	3.1	3.9	-2.6	1.7	-3.9	1.2	-2.4
1995	2.4	3.8	2.3	2.5	3.5	2.4	3.7	0.5	3.9	-0.6	4.2	1.4	34.4
1996	3.1	1.1	0.7	1.4	2.1	-0.1	-4.9	2.5	5.5	2.1	7.1	-1.8	19.7
1997	5.8	0.2	-4.6	5.3	6.2	4.0	8.0	-4.9	5.4	-3.4	4.2	1.9	30.5
1998	0.6	7.0	4.9	0.9	-2.3	3.6	-1.3	-15.1	6.5	7.8	6.1	6.2	25.1
1999	3.5	-3.3	3.7	4.2	-2.3	5.1	-3.2	-1.0	-2.8	6.5	2.5	6.0	19.5
2000	-4.2	-0.4	8.9	-3.3	-2.7	2.5	-1.8	7.4	-4.8	-1.2	-9.3	1.1	-8.8
2001	3.2	-9.5	-6.7	8.0	0.5	-2.4	-1.4	-6.2	-8.6	2.0	7.5	0.9	-13.6
2002	-1.4	-2.1	4.0	-5.8	-1.0	-7.5	-7.5	0.3	-10.9	8.1	5.7	-5.8	-22.9
2003	-2.5	-1.7	0.9	7.9	5.5	1.2	1.8	1.9	-1.2	5.7	1.0	4.6	27.5
2004	1.8	1.2	-1.5	-1.9	1.3	1.7	-3.6	0.3	1.1	1.5	4.1	3.5	9.5
2005	-2.6	2.0	-1.7	-2.0	3.4	0.3	3.8	-1.1	0.8	-1.9	3.5	0.01	4.4
2006	2.7	0.01	1.3	1.1	-3.2	0.003	0.1	2.2	2.3	3.3	1.9	1.1	13.3
2007	1.8	-1.9	0.9	4.1									
TOTALS	50.1	6.1	20.1	36.6	35.5	22.0	8.9	15.4	-24.6	29.9	61.9	46.2	
AVG.	1.7	0.2	0.7	1.3	1.3	0.8	0.3	0.6	-0.9	1.1	2.2	1.7	
Up	20	17	19	18	19	18	12	18	13	18	21	22	
Down	9	12	10	11	9	10	16	10	15	10	7	6	

RUSSELL 1000 INDEX MONTHLY CLOSING PRICES SINCE 1979

	Jan	Feb	Mar	Apr	May	Jun	Jul	Aug	Sep	Oct	Nov	Dec
1979	53.76	51.88	54.97	55.15	53.92	56.25	56.86	60.04	60.05	55.78	58.65	59.87
1980	63.40	63.07	55.79	58.38	61.31	63.27	67.30	68.05	69.84	71.08	78.26	75.20
1981	71.75	72.49	75.21	73.77	73.90	73.01	72.92	68.42	64.06	67.54	70.23	67.93
1982	66.12	62.21	61.43	63.85	61.53	59.92	58.54	65.14	65.89	73.34	76.28	77.24
1983	79.75	81.45	84.06	90.04	89.89	93.18	90.18	90.65	91.85	89.69	91.50	90.38
1984	88.69	84.76	85.73	86.00	80.94	82.61	81.13	89.87	89.67	89.62	88.36	90.31
1985	97.31	98.38	98.03	99.72	103.02	104.65	103.78	102.76	98.75	103.16	109.91	114.39
1986	115.39	123.71	130.07	128.44	134.82	136.75	128.74	137.43	125.70	132.11	133.97	130.00
1987	146.48	152.29	155.20	152.39	152.94	159.84	166.57	172.95	168.83	131.89	121.28	130.02
1988	135.55	141.54	137.45	138.37	138.66	145.31	143.99	139.26	144.68	147.55	144.59	146.99
1989	156.93	152.98	155.99	163.63	169.85	168.49	182.27	185.33	184.40	179.17	181.85	185.11
1990	171.44	173.43	177.28	172.32	187.66	186.29	184.32	166.69	157.83	156.62	166.69	171.22
1991	179.00	191.34	196.15	195.94	203.32	193.78	202.67	207.18	204.02	206.96	198.46	220.61
1992	217.52	219.50	214.29	219.13	219.71	215.60	224.37	218.86	221.15	222.65	230.44	233.59
1993	235.25	236.67	241.80	235.13	240.80	241.78	240.78	249.20	247.95	250.97	246.70	250.71
1994	258.08	250.52	239.19	241.71	244.13	237.11	244.44	254.04	247.49	251.62	241.82	244.65
1995	250.52	260.08	266.11	272.81	282.48	289.29	299.98	301.40	313.28	311.37	324.36	328.89
1996	338.97	342.56	345.01	349.84	357.35	357.10	339.44	347.79	366.77	374.38	401.05	393.75
1997	416.77	417.46	398.19	419.15	445.06	462.95	499.89	475.33	500.78	483.86	504.25	513.79
1998	517.02	553.14	580.31	585.46	572.16	592.57	584.97	496.66	529.11	570.63	605.31	642.87
1999	665.64	643.67	667.49	695.25	679.10	713.61	690.51	683.27	663.83	707.19	724.66	767.97
2000	736.08	733.04	797.99	771.58	750.98	769.68	755.57	811.17	772.60	763.06	692.40	700.09
2001	722.55	654.25	610.36	658.90	662.39	646.64	637.43	597.67	546.46	557.29	599.32	604.94
2002	596.66	583.88	607.35	572.04	566.18	523.72	484.39	486.08	433.22	468.51	495.00	466.18
2003	454.30	446.37	450.35	486.09	512.92	518.94	528.53	538.40	532.15	562.51	568.32	594.56
2004	605.21	612.58	603.42	591.83	599.40	609.31	587.21	589.09	595.66	604.51	629.26	650.99
2005	633.99	646.93	635.78	623.32	644.28	645.92	670.26	663.13	668.53	656.09	679.35	679.42
2006	697.79	697.83	706.74	714.37	691.78	691.80	692.59	707.55	723.48	747.30	761.43	770.08
2007	784.11	768.92	775.97	807.82								

159

RUSSELL 2000 INDEX MONTHLY PERCENT CHANGES SINCE 1979

	Jan	Feb	Mar	Apr	May	Jun	Jul	Aug	Sep	Oct	Nov	Dec	Year's Change
1979	9.0	-3.2	9.7	2.3	-1.8	5.3	2.9	7.8	-0.7	-11.3	8.1	6.6	38.0
1980	8.2	-2.1	-18.5	6.0	8.0	4.0	11.0	6.5	2.9	3.9	7.0	-3.7	33.8
1981	-0.6	0.3	7.7	2.5	3.0	-2.5	-2.6	-8.0	-8.6	8.2	2.8	-2.0	-1.5
1982	-3.7	-5.3	-1.5	5.1	-3.2	-4.0	-1.7	7.5	3.6	14.1	8.8	1.1	20.7
1983	7.5	6.0	2.5	7.2	7.0	4.4	-3.0	-4.0	1.6	-7.0	5.0	-2.1	26.3
1984	-1.8	-5.9	0.4	-0.7	-5.4	2.6	-5.0	11.5	-1.0	-2.0	-2.9	1.4	-9.(
1985	13.1	2.4	-2.2	-1.4	3.4	1.0	2.7	-1.2	-6.2	3.6	6.8	4.2	28.0
1986	1.5	7.0	4.7	1.4	3.3	-0.2	-9.5	3.0	-6.3	3.9	-0.5	-3.1	4.0
1987	11.5	8.2	2.4	-3.0	-0.5	2.3	2.8	2.9	-2.0	-30.8	-5.5	7.8	-10.8
1988	4.0	8.7	4.4	2.0	-2.5	7.0	-0.9	-2.8	2.3	-1.2	-3.6	3.8	22.4
1989	4.4	0.5	2.2	4.3	4.2	-2.4	4.2	2.1	0.01	-6.0	0.4	0.1	14.2
1990	-8.9	2.9	3.7	-3.4	6.8	0.1	-4.5	-13.6	-9.2	-6.2	7.3	3.7	-21.5
1991	9.1	11.0	6.9	-0.2	4.5	-6.0	3.1	3.7	0.6	2.7	-4.7	7.7	43.7
1992	8.0	2.9	-3.5	-3.7	1.2	-5.0	3.2	-3.1	2.2	3.1	7.5	3.4	16.4
1993	3.2	-2.5	3.1	-2.8	4.3	0.5	1.3	4.1	2.7	2.5	-3.4	3.3	17.0
1994	3.1	-0.4	-5.4	0.6	-1.3	-3.6	1.6	5.4	-0.5	-0.4	-4.2	2.5	-3.2
1995	-1.4	3.9	1.6	2.1	1.5	5.0	5.7	1.9	1.7	-4.6	4.2	2.4	26.2
1996	-0.2	3.0	1.8	5.3	3.9	-4.2	-8.8	5.7	3.7	-1.7	4.0	2.4	14.6
1997	1.9	-2.5	-4.9	0.1	11.0	4.1	4.6	2.2	7.2	-4.5	-0.8	1.7	20.5
1998	-1.6	7.4	4.1	0.5	-5.4	0.2	-8.2	-19.5	7.6	4.0	5.2	6.1	-3.4
1999	1.2	-8.2	1.4	8.8	1.4	4.3	-2.8	-3.8	-0.1	0.3	5.9	11.2	19.6
2000	-1.7	16.4	-6.7	-6.1	-5.9	8.6	-3.2	7.4	-3.1	-4.5	-10.4	8.4	-4.2
2001	5.1	-6.7	-5.0	7.7	2.3	3.3	-5.4	-3.3	-13.6	5.8	7.6	6.0	1.0
2002	-1.1	-2.8	7.9	0.8	-4.5	-5.1	-15.2	-0.4	-7.3	3.1	8.8	-5.7	-21.6
2003	-2.9	-3.1	1.1	9.4	10.6	1.7	6.2	4.5	-2.0	8.3	3.5	1.9	45.4
2004	4.3	0.8	0.8	-5.2	1.5	4.1	-6.8	-0.6	4.6	1.9	8.6	2.8	17.(
2005	-4.2	1.6	-3.0	-5.8	6.4	3.7	6.3	-1.9	0.2	-3.2	4.7	-0.6	3.(
2006	8.9	-0.3	4.7	-0.1	-5.7	0.5	-3.3	2.9	0.7	5.7	2.5	0.2	17.0
2007	1.6	-0.9	0.9	1.7									
TOTALS	77.5	39.1	21.3	35.4	48.1	29.7	-25.3	16.9	-19.0	-12.3	72.7	71.5	
AVG.	2.7	1.3	0.7	1.2	1.7	1.1	-0.9	0.6	-0.7	-0.4	2.6	2.6	
# Up	18	16	20	18	18	19	13	16	15	15	19	22	
# Down	11	13	9	11	10	9	15	12	13	13	9	6	

RUSSELL 2000 INDEX MONTHLY CLOSING PRICES SINCE 1979

	Jan	Feb	Mar	Apr	May	Jun	Jul	Aug	Sep	Oct	Nov	Dec
1979	44.18	42.78	46.94	48.00	47.13	49.62	51.08	55.05	54.68	48.51	52.43	55.91
1980	60.50	59.22	48.27	51.18	55.26	57.47	63.81	67.97	69.94	72.64	77.70	74.80
1981	74.33	74.52	80.25	82.25	84.72	82.56	80.41	73.94	67.55	73.06	75.14	73.67
1982	70.96	67.21	66.21	69.59	67.39	64.67	63.59	68.38	70.84	80.86	87.96	88.90
1983	95.53	101.23	103.77	111.20	118.94	124.17	120.43	115.60	117.43	109.17	114.66	112.27
1984	110.21	103.72	104.10	103.34	97.75	100.30	95.25	106.21	105.17	103.07	100.11	101.49
1985	114.77	117.54	114.92	113.35	117.26	118.38	121.56	120.10	112.65	116.73	124.62	129.87
1986	131.78	141.00	147.63	149.66	154.61	154.23	139.65	143.83	134.73	139.95	139.26	135.00
1987	150.48	162.84	166.79	161.82	161.02	164.75	169.42	174.25	170.81	118.26	111.70	120.42
1988	125.24	136.10	142.15	145.01	141.37	151.30	149.89	145.74	149.08	147.25	142.01	147.37
1989	153.84	154.56	157.89	164.68	171.53	167.42	174.50	178.20	178.21	167.47	168.17	168.30
1990	153.27	157.72	163.63	158.09	168.91	169.04	161.51	139.52	126.70	118.83	127.50	132.16
1991	144.17	160.00	171.01	170.61	178.34	167.61	172.76	179.11	180.16	185.00	176.37	189.94
1992	205.16	211.15	203.69	196.25	198.52	188.64	194.74	188.79	192.92	198.90	213.81	221.01
1993	228.10	222.41	229.21	222.68	232.19	233.35	236.46	246.19	252.95	259.18	250.41	258.59
1994	266.52	265.53	251.06	252.55	249.28	240.29	244.06	257.32	256.12	255.02	244.25	250.36
1995	246.85	256.57	260.77	266.17	270.25	283.63	299.72	305.31	310.38	296.25	308.58	315.97
1996	315.38	324.93	330.77	348.28	361.85	346.61	316.00	333.88	346.39	340.57	354.11	362.61
1997	369.45	360.05	342.56	343.00	380.76	396.37	414.48	423.43	453.82	433.26	429.92	437.02
1998	430.05	461.83	480.68	482.89	456.62	457.39	419.75	337.95	363.59	378.16	397.75	421.96
1999	427.22	392.26	397.63	432.81	438.68	457.68	444.77	427.83	427.30	428.64	454.08	504.75
2000	496.23	577.71	539.09	506.25	476.18	517.23	500.64	537.89	521.37	497.68	445.94	483.53
2001	508.34	474.37	450.53	485.32	496.50	512.64	484.78	468.56	404.87	428.17	460.78	488.50
2002	483.10	469.36	506.46	510.67	487.47	462.64	392.42	390.96	362.27	373.50	406.35	383.09
2003	372.17	360.52	364.54	398.68	441.00	448.37	476.02	497.42	487.68	528.22	546.51	556.91
2004	580.76	585.56	590.31	559.80	568.28	591.52	551.29	547.93	572.94	583.79	633.77	651.57
2005	624.02	634.06	615.07	579.38	616.71	639.66	679.75	666.51	667.80	646.61	677.29	673.22
2006	733.20	730.64	765.14	764.54	721.01	724.67	700.56	720.53	725.59	766.84	786.12	787.66
2007	800.34	793.30	800.71	814.57								

10 **BEST** DAYS BY PERCENT & POINT

	BY PERCENT CHANGE				BY POINT CHANGE		
DAY	CLOSE	PNT CHANGE	% CHANGE	DAY	CLOSE	PNT CHANGE	% CHANGE
DJIA 1901 TO 1949							
3/15/33	62.10	8.26	15.3	10/30/29	258.47	28.40	12.3
10/6/31	99.34	12.86	14.9	11/14/29	217.28	18.59	9.4
10/30/29	258.47	28.40	12.3	10/5/29	341.36	16.19	5.0
9/21/32	75.16	7.67	11.4	10/31/29	273.51	15.04	5.8
8/3/32	58.22	5.06	9.5	10/6/31	99.34	12.86	14.9
2/11/32	78.60	6.80	9.5	11/15/29	228.73	11.45	5.3
11/14/29	217.28	18.59	9.4	6/19/30	228.97	10.13	4.6
12/18/31	80.69	6.90	9.4	9/5/39	148.12	10.03	7.3
2/13/32	85.82	7.22	9.2	11/22/28	290.34	9.81	3.5
5/6/32	59.01	4.91	9.1	10/1/30	214.14	9.24	4.5
DJIA 1950 TO APRIL 2007							
10/21/87	2027.85	186.84	10.2	3/16/00	10630.60	499.19	4.9
7/24/02	8191.29	488.95	6.4	7/24/02	8191.29	488.95	6.4
10/20/87	1841.01	102.27	5.9	7/29/02	8711.88	447.49	5.4
7/29/02	8711.88	447.49	5.4	4/5/01	9918.05	402.63	4.2
5/27/70	663.20	32.04	5.1	4/18/01	10615.83	399.10	3.9
9/8/98	8020.78	380.53	5.0	9/8/98	8020.78	380.53	5.0
10/29/87	1938.33	91.51	5.0	10/15/02	8255.68	378.28	4.8
3/16/00	10630.60	499.19	4.9	9/24/01	8603.86	368.05	4.5
8/17/82	831.24	38.81	4.9	10/1/02	7938.79	346.86	4.6
10/15/02	8255.68	378.28	4.8	5/16/01	11215.92	342.95	3.2
S&P 500 1930 TO APRIL 2007							
3/15/33	6.81	0.97	16.6	3/16/00	1458.47	66.32	4.8
10/6/31	9.91	1.09	12.4	1/3/01	1347.56	64.29	5.0
9/21/32	8.52	0.90	11.8	12/5/00	1376.54	51.57	3.9
2/16/35	10.00	0.94	10.4	9/8/98	1023.46	49.57	5.1
8/17/35	11.70	1.08	10.2	4/5/01	1151.44	48.19	4.4
3/16/35	9.05	0.82	10.0	4/25/00	1477.44	47.58	3.3
9/12/38	12.06	1.06	9.6	10/19/00	1388.76	46.63	3.5
9/5/39	12.64	1.11	9.6	4/18/01	1238.16	46.35	3.9
4/17/35	9.01	0.79	9.6	7/29/02	898.96	46.12	5.4
4/20/33	7.82	0.68	9.5	10/28/99	1342.44	45.73	3.5
NASDAQ 1971 TO APRIL 2007							
1/3/01	2616.69	324.83	14.2	1/3/01	2616.69	324.83	14.2
12/5/00	2889.80	274.05	10.5	12/5/00	2889.80	274.05	10.5
4/5/01	1785.00	146.20	8.9	4/18/00	3793.57	254.41	7.2
4/18/01	2079.44	156.22	8.1	5/30/00	3459.48	254.37	7.9
5/30/00	3459.48	254.37	7.9	10/19/00	3418.60	247.04	7.8
10/13/00	3316.77	242.09	7.9	10/13/00	3316.77	242.09	7.9
10/19/00	3418.60	247.04	7.8	6/2/00	3813.38	230.88	6.4
5/8/02	1696.29	122.47	7.8	4/25/00	3711.23	228.75	6.6
12/22/00	2517.02	176.90	7.6	4/17/00	3539.16	217.87	6.6
10/21/87	351.86	24.07	7.3	6/1/00	3582.50	181.59	5.3
RUSSELL 1000 1979 TO APRIL 2007							
10/21/87	135.85	11.15	8.9	3/16/00	777.86	36.60	4.9
7/24/02	448.05	23.87	5.6	1/3/01	712.63	35.74	5.3
7/29/02	477.61	24.69	5.5	12/5/00	728.44	30.36	4.4
1/3/01	712.63	35.74	5.3	4/5/01	604.16	26.31	4.6
9/8/98	529.84	25.40	5.0	4/25/00	780.72	26.16	3.5
3/16/00	777.86	36.60	4.9	10/13/00	732.70	26.01	3.7
10/29/87	127.74	5.91	4.9	9/8/98	529.84	25.40	5.0
10/15/02	465.68	20.78	4.7	5/30/00	752.39	25.30	3.5
10/28/97	486.93	21.49	4.6	10/19/00	740.73	25.14	3.5
4/5/01	604.16	26.31	4.6	4/17/00	740.14	24.94	3.5
RUSSELL 2000 1979 TO APRIL 2007							
10/21/87	130.65	9.26	7.6	4/18/00	486.09	26.83	5.8
10/30/87	118.26	7.46	6.7	6/29/06	714.32	26.28	3.8
4/18/00	486.09	26.83	5.8	6/15/06	701.05	23.96	3.5
7/29/02	400.81	18.55	4.9	1/3/01	484.39	21.90	4.7
3/28/80	47.54	2.18	4.8	12/5/00	471.17	20.78	4.6
1/3/01	484.39	21.90	4.7	7/19/06	702.34	20.70	3.0
12/5/00	471.17	20.78	4.6	6/2/00	513.03	20.56	4.2
4/5/01	444.73	18.99	4.5	4/25/00	489.03	20.49	4.4
10/29/87	110.80	4.72	4.5	4/18/06	769.81	20.34	2.7
4/25/00	489.03	20.49	4.4	2/29/00	577.71	20.03	3.6

10 <u>WORST</u> DAYS BY PERCENT & POINT

	BY PERCENT CHANGE				BY POINT CHANGE		
DAY	CLOSE	PNT CHANGE	% CHANGE	DAY	CLOSE	PNT CHANGE	% CHANGE
DJIA 1901 TO 1949							
10/28/29	260.64	−38.33	−12.8	10/28/29	260.64	−38.33	−12.8
10/29/29	230.07	−30.57	−11.7	10/29/29	230.07	−30.57	−11.7
11/6/29	232.13	−25.55	−9.9	11/6/29	232.13	−25.55	−9.9
8/12/32	63.11	−5.79	−8.4	10/23/29	305.85	−20.66	−6.3
3/14/07	55.84	−5.05	−8.3	11/11/29	220.39	−16.14	−6.8
7/21/33	88.71	−7.55	−7.8	11/4/29	257.68	−15.83	−5.8
10/18/37	125.73	−10.57	−7.8	12/12/29	243.14	−15.30	−5.9
2/1/17	88.52	−6.91	−7.2	10/3/29	329.95	−14.55	−4.2
10/5/32	66.07	−5.09	−7.2	6/16/30	230.05	−14.20	−5.8
9/24/31	107.79	−8.20	−7.1	8/9/29	337.99	−14.11	−4.0
DJIA 1950 TO APRIL 2007							
10/19/87	1738.74	−508.00	−22.6	9/17/01	8920.70	−684.81	−7.1
10/26/87	1793.93	−156.83	−8.0	4/14/00	10305.77	−617.78	−5.7
10/27/97	7161.15	−554.26	−7.2	10/27/97	7161.15	−554.26	−7.2
9/17/01	8920.70	−684.81	−7.1	8/31/98	7539.07	−512.61	−6.4
10/13/89	2569.26	−190.58	−6.9	10/19/87	1738.74	−508.00	−22.6
1/8/88	1911.31	−140.58	−6.9	3/12/01	10208.25	−436.37	−4.1
9/26/55	455.56	−31.89	−6.5	2/27/07	12216.24	−416.02	−3.3
8/31/98	7539.07	−512.61	−6.4	7/19/02	8019.26	−390.23	−4.6
5/28/62	576.93	−34.95	−5.7	9/20/01	8376.21	−382.92	−4.4
4/14/00	10305.77	−617.78	−5.7	10/12/00	10034.58	−379.21	−3.6
S&P 500 1930 TO APRIL 2007							
10/19/87	224.84	−57.86	−20.5	4/14/00	1356.56	−83.95	−5.8
3/18/35	8.14	−0.91	−10.1	8/31/98	957.28	−69.86	−6.8
4/16/35	8.22	−0.91	−10.0	10/27/97	876.99	−64.65	−6.9
9/3/46	15.00	−1.65	−9.9	10/19/87	224.84	−57.86	−20.5
10/18/37	10.76	−1.10	−9.3	1/4/00	1399.42	−55.80	−3.8
7/20/33	10.57	−1.03	−8.9	9/17/01	1038.77	−53.77	−4.9
7/21/33	9.65	−0.92	−8.7	3/12/01	1180.16	−53.26	−4.3
9/10/38	11.00	−1.02	−8.5	2/27/07	1399.04	−50.33	−3.5
10/26/87	227.67	−20.55	−8.3	2/18/00	1346.09	−42.17	−3.0
10/5/32	7.39	−0.66	−8.2	8/27/98	1042.59	−41.60	−3.8
NASDAQ 1971 TO APRIL 2007							
10/19/87	360.21	−46.12	−11.4	4/14/00	3321.29	−355.49	−9.7
4/14/00	3321.29	−355.49	−9.7	4/3/00	4223.68	−349.15	−7.6
10/20/87	327.79	−32.42	−9.0	4/12/00	3769.63	−286.27	−7.1
10/26/87	298.90	−29.55	−9.0	4/10/00	4188.20	−258.25	−5.8
8/31/98	1499.25	−140.43	−8.6	1/4/00	3901.69	−229.46	−5.6
4/3/00	4223.68	−349.15	−7.6	3/14/00	4706.63	−200.61	−4.1
1/2/01	2291.86	−178.66	−7.2	5/10/00	3384.73	−200.28	−5.6
12/20/00	2332.78	−178.93	−7.1	5/23/00	3164.55	−199.66	−5.9
4/12/00	3769.63	−286.27	−7.1	10/25/00	3229.57	−190.22	−5.6
10/27/97	1535.09	−115.83	−7.0	3/29/00	4644.67	−189.22	−3.9
RUSSELL 1000 1979 TO APRIL 2007							
10/19/87	121.04	−28.40	−19.0	4/14/00	715.20	−45.74	−6.0
10/26/87	119.45	−10.74	−8.3	8/31/98	496.66	−35.77	−6.7
8/31/98	496.66	−35.77	−6.7	10/27/97	465.44	−32.96	−6.6
10/27/97	465.44	−32.96	−6.6	1/4/00	731.95	−29.57	−3.9
1/8/88	128.80	−8.33	−6.1	9/17/01	547.04	−28.53	−5.0
4/14/00	715.20	−45.74	−6.0	10/19/87	121.04	−28.40	−19.0
10/13/89	176.82	−10.88	−5.8	3/12/01	621.35	−28.24	−4.4
10/16/87	149.44	−7.81	−5.0	2/27/07	764.79	−27.04	−3.4
9/17/01	547.04	−28.53	−5.0	12/20/00	668.75	−23.60	−3.4
9/11/86	127.34	−6.03	−4.5	1/2/01	676.89	−23.20	−3.3
RUSSELL 2000 1979 TO APRIL 2007							
10/19/87	133.60	−19.14	−12.5	4/14/00	453.72	−35.50	−7.3
10/26/87	110.33	−11.26	−9.3	2/27/07	792.66	−31.03	−3.8
10/20/87	121.39	−12.21	−9.1	10/27/97	420.13	−27.40	−6.1
4/14/00	453.72	−35.50	−7.3	3/20/00	549.20	−25.57	−4.5
3/27/80	45.36	−3.20	−6.6	4/10/00	518.66	−24.33	−4.5
10/27/97	420.13	−27.40	−6.1	6/5/06	713.92	−23.54	−3.2
8/31/98	337.95	−20.59	−5.7	9/17/01	417.67	−23.06	−5.2
9/17/01	417.67	−23.06	−5.2	4/3/00	516.04	−23.05	−4.3
10/9/79	52.53	−2.61	−4.7	1/2/01	462.49	−21.04	−4.4
10/22/87	124.57	−6.08	−4.7	8/31/98	337.95	−20.59	−5.7

10 <u>BEST</u> WEEKS BY PERCENT & POINT

	BY PERCENT CHANGE				BY POINT CHANGE		
WEEK ENDS	CLOSE	PNT CHANGE	% CHANGE	WEEK ENDS	CLOSE	PNT CHANGE	% CHANGE
DJIA 1901 TO 1949							
8/6/32	66.56	12.30	22.7	12/7/29	263.46	24.51	10.3
6/25/38	131.94	18.71	16.5	6/25/38	131.94	18.71	16.5
2/13/32	85.82	11.37	15.3	6/27/31	156.93	17.97	12.9
4/22/33	72.24	9.36	14.9	11/22/29	245.74	17.01	7.4
10/10/31	105.61	12.84	13.8	8/17/29	360.70	15.86	4.6
7/30/32	54.26	6.42	13.4	12/22/28	285.94	15.22	5.6
6/27/31	156.93	17.97	12.9	8/24/29	375.44	14.74	4.1
9/24/32	74.83	8.39	12.6	2/21/29	310.06	14.21	4.8
8/27/32	75.61	8.43	12.6	5/10/30	272.01	13.70	5.3
3/18/33	60.56	6.72	12.5	11/15/30	186.68	13.54	7.8
DJIA 1950 TO APRIL 2007							
10/11/74	658.17	73.61	12.6	3/17/00	10595.23	666.41	6.7
8/20/82	869.29	81.24	10.3	3/21/03	8521.97	662.26	8.4
10/8/82	986.85	79.11	8.7	9/28/01	8847.56	611.75	7.4
3/21/03	8521.97	662.26	8.4	7/2/99	11139.24	586.68	5.6
8/3/84	1202.08	87.46	7.9	4/20/00	10844.05	538.28	5.2
9/28/01	8847.56	611.75	7.4	3/24/00	11112.72	517.49	4.9
9/20/74	670.76	43.57	7.0	10/16/98	8416.76	517.24	6.6
3/17/00	10595.23	666.41	6.7	3/3/00	10367.20	505.08	5.1
10/16/98	8416.76	517.24	6.6	6/2/00	10794.76	495.52	4.8
6/7/74	853.72	51.55	6.4	5/18/01	11301.74	480.43	4.4
S&P 500 1930 TO APRIL 2007							
8/6/32	7.22	1.12	18.4	6/2/00	1477.26	99.24	7.2
6/25/38	11.39	1.72	17.8	4/20/00	1434.54	77.98	5.8
7/30/32	6.10	0.89	17.1	7/2/99	1391.22	75.91	5.8
4/22/33	7.75	1.09	16.4	3/3/00	1409.17	75.81	5.7
10/11/74	71.14	8.80	14.1	9/28/01	1040.94	75.14	7.8
2/13/32	8.80	1.08	14.0	10/16/98	1056.42	72.10	7.3
9/24/32	8.52	1.02	13.6	3/17/00	1464.47	69.40	5.0
10/10/31	10.64	1.27	13.6	2/4/00	1424.37	64.21	4.7
8/27/32	8.57	1.01	13.4	3/24/00	1527.46	62.99	4.3
3/18/33	6.61	0.77	13.2	3/21/03	895.79	62.52	7.5
NASDAQ 1971 TO APRIL 2007							
6/2/00	3813.38	608.27	19.0	6/2/00	3813.38	608.27	19.0
4/12/01	1961.43	241.07	14.0	2/4/00	4244.14	357.07	9.2
4/20/01	2163.41	201.98	10.3	3/3/00	4914.79	324.29	7.1
12/8/00	2917.43	272.14	10.3	4/20/00	3643.88	322.59	9.7
4/20/00	3643.88	322.59	9.7	12/8/00	2917.43	272.14	10.3
10/11/74	60.42	5.26	9.5	4/12/01	1961.43	241.07	14.0
2/4/00	4244.14	357.07	9.2	7/14/00	4246.18	222.98	5.5
1/12/01	2626.50	218.85	9.1	1/12/01	2626.50	218.85	9.1
5/17/02	1741.39	140.54	8.8	4/28/00	3860.66	216.78	6.0
10/16/98	1620.95	128.46	8.6	12/23/99	3969.44	216.38	5.8
RUSSELL 1000 1979 TO APRIL 2007							
8/20/82	61.51	4.83	8.5	6/2/00	785.02	57.93	8.0
6/2/00	785.02	57.93	8.0	4/20/00	757.32	42.12	5.9
9/28/01	546.46	38.48	7.6	3/3/00	756.41	41.55	5.8
10/16/98	546.09	38.45	7.6	7/2/99	723.25	38.80	5.7
8/3/84	87.43	6.13	7.5	9/28/01	546.46	38.48	7.6
3/21/03	474.58	32.69	7.4	10/16/98	546.09	38.45	7.6
10/8/82	71.55	4.90	7.4	12/8/00	729.83	35.67	5.1
5/2/97	426.12	25.75	6.4	10/29/99	707.19	33.83	5.0
11/5/82	78.01	4.67	6.4	2/4/00	752.57	32.90	4.6
10/2/81	65.93	3.90	6.3	3/21/03	474.58	32.69	7.4
RUSSELL 2000 1979 TO APRIL 2007							
6/2/00	513.03	55.66	12.2	6/2/00	513.03	55.66	12.2
10/16/98	342.87	24.47	7.7	3/3/00	597.88	41.14	7.4
12/18/87	116.94	8.31	7.7	6/30/06	724.67	34.53	5.0
3/3/00	597.88	41.14	7.4	8/18/06	711.68	32.64	4.8
10/23/98	367.05	24.18	7.1	3/23/07	809.51	30.74	4.0
8/3/84	102.02	6.71	7.0	8/20/04	547.92	30.53	5.9
1/9/87	146.85	9.60	7.0	4/2/04	603.45	30.53	5.3
9/28/01	404.87	25.98	6.9	4/20/00	481.84	28.12	6.2
2/1/91	145.50	9.01	6.6	7/28/06	700.03	28.09	4.2
11/5/82	86.17	5.31	6.6	11/3/00	507.75	27.90	5.8

10 <u>WORST</u> WEEKS BY PERCENT & POINT

	BY PERCENT CHANGE				BY POINT CHANGE		
WEEK ENDS	CLOSE	PNT CHANGE	% CHANGE	WEEK ENDS	CLOSE	PNT CHANGE	% CHANGE
DJIA 1901 TO 1949							
7/22/33	88.42	−17.68	−16.7	11/8/29	236.53	−36.98	−13.5
5/18/40	122.43	−22.42	−15.5	12/8/28	257.33	−33.47	−11.5
10/8/32	61.17	−10.92	−15.2	6/21/30	215.30	−28.95	−11.9
10/3/31	92.77	−14.59	−13.6	10/19/29	323.87	−28.82	−8.2
11/8/29	236.53	−36.98	−13.5	5/3/30	258.31	−27.15	−9.5
9/17/32	66.44	−10.10	−13.2	10/31/29	273.51	−25.46	−8.5
10/21/33	83.64	−11.95	−12.5	10/26/29	298.97	−24.90	−7.7
12/12/31	78.93	−11.21	−12.4	5/18/40	122.43	−22.42	−15.5
5/8/15	62.77	−8.74	−12.2	2/8/29	301.53	−18.23	−5.7
6/21/30	215.30	−28.95	−11.9	10/11/30	193.05	−18.05	−8.6
DJIA 1950 TO APRIL 2007							
9/21/01	8235.81	−1369.70	−14.3	9/21/01	8235.81	−1369.70	−14.3
10/23/87	1950.76	−295.98	−13.2	3/16/01	9823.41	−821.21	−7.7
10/16/87	2246.74	−235.47	−9.5	4/14/00	10305.77	−805.71	−7.3
10/13/89	2569.26	−216.26	−7.8	7/12/02	8684.53	−694.97	−7.4
3/16/01	9823.41	−821.21	−7.7	7/19/02	8019.26	−665.27	−7.7
7/19/02	8019.26	−665.27	−7.7	10/15/99	10019.71	−630.05	−5.9
12/4/87	1766.74	−143.74	−7.5	2/11/00	10425.21	−538.59	−4.9
9/13/74	627.19	−50.69	−7.5	3/2/07	12114.10	−533.38	−4.2
9/12/86	1758.72	−141.03	−7.4	9/24/99	10279.33	−524.30	−4.9
7/12/02	8684.53	−694.97	−7.4	1/28/00	10738.87	−512.84	−4.6
S&P 500 1930 TO APRIL 2007							
7/22/33	9.71	−2.20	−18.5	4/14/00	1356.56	−159.79	−10.5
5/18/40	9.75	−2.05	−17.4	9/21/01	965.80	−126.74	−11.6
10/8/32	6.77	−1.38	−16.9	10/15/99	1247.41	−88.61	−6.6
9/17/32	7.50	−1.28	−14.6	3/16/01	1150.53	−82.89	−6.7
10/21/33	8.57	−1.31	−13.3	1/28/00	1360.16	−81.20	−5.6
10/3/31	9.37	−1.36	−12.7	7/19/02	847.76	−73.63	−8.0
10/23/87	248.22	−34.48	−12.2	7/12/02	921.39	−67.64	−6.8
12/12/31	8.20	−1.13	−12.1	3/2/07	1387.17	−64.02	−4.4
3/26/38	9.20	−1.21	−11.6	7/23/99	1356.94	−61.84	−4.4
9/21/01	965.80	−126.74	−11.6	11/10/00	1365.98	−60.71	−4.3
NASDAQ 1971 TO APRIL 2007							
4/14/00	3321.29	−1125.16	−25.3	4/14/00	3321.29	−1125.16	−25.3
10/23/87	328.45	−77.88	−19.2	7/28/00	3663.00	−431.45	−10.5
9/21/01	1423.19	−272.19	−16.1	11/10/00	3028.99	−422.59	−12.2
11/10/00	3028.99	−422.59	−12.2	3/31/00	4572.83	−390.20	−7.9
7/28/00	3663.00	−431.45	−10.5	1/28/00	3887.07	−348.33	−8.2
12/15/00	2653.27	−264.16	−9.1	10/6/00	3361.01	−311.81	−8.5
12/1/00	2645.29	−259.09	−8.9	5/12/00	3529.06	−287.76	−7.5
8/28/98	1639.68	−157.93	−8.8	9/21/01	1423.19	−272.19	−16.1
10/20/78	123.82	−11.76	−8.7	12/15/00	2653.27	−264.16	−9.1
10/6/00	3361.01	−311.81	−8.5	12/1/00	2645.29	−259.09	−8.9
RUSSELL 1000 1979 TO APRIL 2007							
10/23/87	130.19	−19.25	−12.9	4/14/00	715.20	−90.39	−11.2
9/21/01	507.98	−67.59	−11.7	9/21/01	507.98	−67.59	−11.7
4/14/00	715.20	−90.39	−11.2	10/15/99	646.79	−43.89	−6.4
10/16/87	149.44	−14.42	−8.8	3/16/01	605.71	−43.88	−6.8
9/12/86	124.95	−10.87	−8.0	1/28/00	719.67	−41.85	−5.5
7/19/02	450.64	−36.13	−7.4	11/10/00	727.48	−37.43	−4.9
12/4/87	117.65	−8.79	−7.0	7/28/00	748.29	−37.21	−4.7
3/16/01	605.71	−43.88	−6.8	7/19/02	450.64	−36.13	−7.4
10/13/89	176.82	−12.63	−6.7	3/2/07	757.82	−35.33	−4.5
7/12/02	486.77	−34.70	−6.7	7/12/02	486.77	−34.70	−6.7
RUSSELL 2000 1979 TO APRIL 2007							
10/23/87	121.59	−31.15	−20.4	4/14/00	453.72	−89.27	−16.4
4/14/00	453.72	−89.27	−16.4	9/21/01	378.89	−61.84	−14.0
9/21/01	378.89	−61.84	−14.0	3/2/07	775.44	−51.20	−6.2
8/28/98	358.54	−37.10	−9.4	5/12/06	742.40	−39.43	−5.0
10/12/79	50.76	−5.09	−9.1	1/7/05	613.21	−38.36	−5.9
10/9/98	318.40	−31.31	−9.0	8/28/98	358.54	−37.10	−9.4
10/16/87	152.74	−13.38	−8.1	6/9/06	701.39	−36.07	−4.9
8/24/90	134.22	−11.41	−7.8	3/31/00	539.09	−34.92	−6.1
3/7/80	54.70	−4.52	−7.6	9/26/03	485.29	−34.91	−6.7
3/28/80	47.54	−3.89	−7.6	7/28/00	490.22	−32.48	−6.2

10 BEST MONTHS BY PERCENT & POINT

MONTH	BY PERCENT CHANGE CLOSE	PNT CHANGE	% CHANGE	MONTH	BY POINT CHANGE CLOSE	PNT CHANGE	% CHANGE
DJIA 1901 TO 1949							
APR-1933	77.66	22.26	40.2	NOV-1928	293.38	41.22	16.3
AUG-1932	73.16	18.90	34.8	JUN-1929	333.79	36.38	12.2
JUL-1932	54.26	11.42	26.7	AUG-1929	380.33	32.63	9.4
JUN-1938	133.88	26.14	24.3	JUN-1938	133.88	26.14	24.3
APR-1915	71.78	10.95	18.0	AUG-1928	240.41	24.41	11.3
JUN-1931	150.18	21.72	16.9	APR-1933	77.66	22.26	40.2
NOV-1928	293.38	41.22	16.3	FEB-1931	189.66	22.11	13.2
NOV-1904	52.76	6.59	14.3	JUN-1931	150.18	21.72	16.9
MAY-1919	105.50	12.62	13.6	AUG-1932	73.16	18.90	34.8
SEP-1939	152.54	18.13	13.5	JAN-1930	267.14	18.66	7.5
DJIA 1950 TO APRIL 2007							
JAN-1976	975.28	122.87	14.4	APR-1999	10789.04	1002.88	10.2
JAN-1975	703.69	87.45	14.2	APR-2001	10734.97	856.19	8.7
JAN-1987	2158.04	262.09	13.8	OCT-2002	8397.03	805.10	10.6
AUG-1982	901.31	92.71	11.5	MAR-2000	10921.92	793.61	7.8
OCT-1982	991.72	95.47	10.7	NOV-2001	9851.56	776.42	8.6
OCT-2002	8397.03	805.10	10.6	OCT-1998	8592.10	749.48	9.6
APR-1978	837.32	79.96	10.6	APR-2007	13062.91	708.56	5.7
APR-1999	10789.04	1002.88	10.2	AUG-2000	11215.10	693.12	6.6
NOV-1962	649.30	59.53	10.1	DEC-2003	10453.92	671.46	6.9
NOV-1954	386.77	34.63	9.8	FEB-1998	8545.72	639.22	8.1
S&P 500 1930 TO APRIL 2007							
APR-1933	8.32	2.47	42.2	MAR-2000	1498.58	132.16	9.7
JUL-1932	6.10	1.67	37.7	APR-2001	1249.46	89.13	7.7
AUG-1932	8.39	2.29	37.5	AUG-2000	1517.68	86.85	6.1
JUN-1938	11.56	2.29	24.7	OCT-1998	1098.67	81.66	8.0
SEP-1939	13.02	1.84	16.5	DEC-1999	1469.25	80.34	5.8
OCT-1974	73.90	10.36	16.3	OCT-1999	1362.93	80.22	6.3
MAY-1933	9.64	1.32	15.9	NOV-2001	1139.45	79.67	7.5
APR-1938	9.70	1.20	14.1	JUN-1999	1372.71	70.87	5.4
JUN-1931	14.83	1.81	13.9	OCT-2002	885.76	70.48	8.6
JAN-1987	274.08	31.91	13.2	JUL-1997	954.29	69.15	7.8
NASDAQ 1971 TO APRIL 2007							
DEC-1999	4069.31	733.15	22.0	FEB-2000	4696.69	756.34	19.2
FEB-2000	4696.69	756.34	19.2	DEC-1999	4069.31	733.15	22.0
OCT-1974	65.23	9.56	17.2	JUN-2000	3966.11	565.20	16.6
JAN-1975	69.78	9.96	16.6	AUG-2000	4206.35	439.36	11.7
JUN-2000	3966.11	565.20	16.6	NOV-1999	3336.16	369.73	12.5
APR-2001	2116.24	275.98	15.0	JAN-1999	2505.89	313.20	14.3
JAN-1999	2505.89	313.20	14.3	JAN-2001	2772.73	302.21	12.2
NOV-2001	1930.58	240.38	14.2	APR-2001	2116.24	275.98	15.0
OCT-2002	1329.75	157.69	13.5	DEC-1998	2192.69	243.15	12.5
OCT-1982	212.63	24.98	13.3	NOV-2001	1930.58	240.38	14.2
RUSSELL 1000 1979 TO APRIL 2007							
JAN-1987	146.48	16.48	12.7	MAR-2000	797.99	64.95	8.9
OCT-1982	73.34	7.45	11.3	AUG-2000	811.17	55.60	7.4
AUG-1982	65.14	6.60	11.3	APR-2001	658.90	48.54	8.0
DEC-1991	220.61	22.15	11.2	OCT-1999	707.19	43.36	6.5
AUG-1984	89.87	8.74	10.8	DEC-1999	767.97	43.31	6.0
NOV-1980	78.26	7.18	10.1	NOV-2001	599.32	42.03	7.5
MAY-1990	187.66	15.34	8.9	OCT-1998	570.63	41.52	7.8
MAR-2000	797.99	64.95	8.9	DEC-1998	642.87	37.56	6.2
JUL-1989	182.27	13.78	8.2	JUL-1997	499.89	36.94	8.0
OCT-2002	468.51	35.29	8.1	FEB-1998	553.14	36.12	7.0
RUSSELL 2000 1979 TO APRIL 2007							
FEB-2000	577.71	81.48	16.4	FEB-2000	577.71	81.48	16.4
OCT-1982	80.86	10.02	14.1	JAN-2006	733.20	59.98	8.9
JAN-1985	114.77	13.28	13.1	DEC-1999	504.75	50.67	11.2
AUG-1984	106.21	10.96	11.5	NOV-2004	633.77	49.98	8.6
JAN-1987	150.48	15.48	11.5	MAY-2003	441.00	42.32	10.6
DEC-1999	504.75	50.67	11.2	OCT-2006	766.84	41.25	5.7
JUL-1980	63.81	6.34	11.0	JUN-2000	517.23	41.05	8.6
MAY-1997	380.76	37.76	11.0	OCT-2003	528.22	40.54	8.3
FEB-1991	160.00	15.83	11.0	JUL-2005	679.75	40.09	6.3
MAY-2003	441.00	42.32	10.6	MAY-1997	380.76	37.76	11.0

10 <u>WORST</u> MONTHS BY PERCENT & POINT

	BY PERCENT CHANGE				BY POINT CHANGE		
MONTH	CLOSE	PNT CHANGE	% CHANGE	MONTH	CLOSE	PNT CHANGE	% CHANGE
DJIA 1901 TO 1949							
SEP-1931	96.61	−42.80	−30.7	OCT-1929	273.51	−69.94	−20.4
MAR-1938	98.95	−30.69	−23.7	JUN-1930	226.34	−48.73	−17.7
APR-1932	56.11	−17.17	−23.4	SEP-1931	96.61	−42.80	−30.7
MAY-1940	116.22	−32.21	−21.7	SEP-1929	343.45	−36.88	−9.7
OCT-1929	273.51	−69.94	−20.4	SEP-1930	204.90	−35.52	−14.8
MAY-1932	44.74	−11.37	−20.3	NOV-1929	238.95	−34.56	−12.6
JUN-1930	226.34	−48.73	−17.7	MAY-1940	116.22	−32.21	−21.7
DEC-1931	77.90	−15.97	−17.0	MAR-1938	98.95	−30.69	−23.7
FEB-1933	51.39	−9.51	−15.6	SEP-1937	154.57	−22.84	−12.9
MAY-1931	128.46	−22.73	−15.0	MAY-1931	128.46	−22.73	−15.0
DJIA 1950 TO APRIL 2007							
OCT-1987	1993.53	−602.75	−23.2	AUG-1998	7539.07	−1344.22	−15.1
AUG-1998	7539.07	−1344.22	−15.1	SEP-2001	8847.56	−1102.19	−11.1
NOV-1973	822.25	−134.33	−14.0	SEP-2002	7591.93	−1071.57	−12.4
SEP-2002	7591.93	−1071.57	−12.4	FEB-2000	10128.31	−812.22	−7.4
SEP-2001	8847.56	−1102.19	−11.1	JUN-2002	9243.26	−681.99	−6.9
SEP-1974	607.87	−70.71	−10.4	MAR-2001	9878.78	−616.50	−5.9
AUG-1974	678.58	−78.85	−10.4	OCT-1987	1993.53	−602.75	−23.2
AUG-1990	2614.36	−290.84	−10.0	AUG-1997	7622.42	−600.19	−7.3
MAR-1980	785.75	−77.39	−9.0	AUG-2001	9949.75	−573.06	−5.4
JUN-1962	561.28	−52.08	−8.5	SEP-2000	10650.92	−564.18	−5.0
S&P 500 1930 TO APRIL 2007							
SEP-1931	9.71	−4.15	−29.9	AUG-1998	957.28	−163.39	−14.6
MAR-1938	8.50	−2.84	−25.0	FEB-2001	1239.94	−126.07	−9.2
MAY-1940	9.27	−2.92	−24.0	NOV-2000	1314.95	−114.45	−8.0
MAY-1932	4.47	−1.36	−23.3	SEP-2002	815.28	−100.79	−11.0
OCT-1987	251.79	−70.04	−21.8	SEP-2001	1040.94	−92.64	−8.2
APR-1932	5.83	−1.48	−20.2	SEP-2000	1436.51	−81.17	−5.3
FEB-1933	5.66	−1.28	−18.4	MAR-2001	1160.33	−79.61	−6.4
JUN-1930	20.46	−4.03	−16.5	JUL-2002	911.62	−78.20	−7.9
AUG-1998	957.28	−163.39	−14.6	AUG-2001	1133.58	−77.65	−6.4
DEC-1931	8.12	−1.38	−14.5	JUN-2002	989.82	−77.32	−7.2
NASDAQ 1971 TO APRIL 2007							
OCT-1987	323.30	−120.99	−27.2	NOV-2000	2597.93	−771.70	−22.9
NOV-2000	2597.93	−771.70	−22.9	APR-2000	3860.66	−712.17	−15.6
FEB-2001	2151.83	−620.90	−22.4	FEB-2001	2151.83	−620.90	−22.4
AUG-1998	1499.25	−373.14	−19.9	SEP-2000	3672.82	−533.53	−12.7
MAR-1980	131.00	−27.03	−17.1	MAY-2000	3400.91	−459.75	−11.9
SEP-2001	1498.80	−306.63	−17.0	AUG-1998	1499.25	−373.14	−19.9
OCT-1978	111.12	−21.77	−16.4	MAR-2001	1840.26	−311.57	−14.5
APR-2000	3860.66	−712.17	−15.6	SEP-2001	1498.80	−306.63	−17.0
NOV-1973	93.51	−16.66	−15.1	OCT-2001	3369.63	−303.19	−8.3
MAR-2001	1840.26	−311.57	−14.5	AUG-2001	1805.43	−221.70	−10.9
RUSSELL 1000 1979 TO APRIL 2007							
OCT-1987	131.89	−36.94	−21.9	AUG-1998	496.66	−88.31	−15.1
AUG-1998	496.66	−88.31	−15.1	NOV-2000	692.40	−70.66	−9.3
MAR-1980	55.79	−7.28	−11.5	FEB-2001	654.25	−68.30	−9.5
SEP-2002	433.22	−52.86	−10.9	SEP-2002	433.22	−52.86	−10.9
AUG-1990	166.69	−17.63	−9.6	SEP-2001	546.46	−51.21	−8.6
FEB-2001	654.25	−68.30	−9.5	MAR-2001	610.36	−43.89	−6.7
NOV-2000	692.40	−70.66	−9.3	JUN-2002	523.72	−42.46	−7.5
SEP-2001	546.46	−51.21	−8.6	AUG-2001	597.67	−39.76	−6.2
SEP-1986	125.70	−11.73	−8.5	JUL-2002	484.39	−39.33	−7.5
NOV-1987	121.28	−10.61	−8.0	SEP-2000	772.60	−38.57	−4.8
RUSSELL 2000 1979 TO APRIL 2007							
OCT-1987	118.26	−52.55	−30.8	AUG-1998	337.95	−81.80	−19.5
AUG-1998	337.95	−81.80	−19.5	JUL-2002	392.42	−70.22	−15.2
MAR-1980	48.27	−10.95	−18.5	SEP-2001	404.87	−63.69	−13.6
JUL-2002	392.42	−70.22	−15.2	OCT-1987	118.26	−52.55	−30.8
AUG-1990	139.52	−21.99	−13.6	NOV-2000	445.94	−51.74	−10.4
SEP-2001	404.87	−63.69	−13.6	MAY-2006	721.01	−43.53	−5.7
OCT-1979	48.51	−6.17	−11.3	JUL-2004	551.29	−40.23	−6.8
NOV-2000	445.94	−51.74	−10.4	MAR-2000	539.09	−38.62	−6.7
JUL-1986	139.65	−14.58	−9.5	JUL-1998	419.75	−37.64	−8.2
SEP-1990	126.70	−12.82	−9.2	APR-2005	579.38	−35.69	−5.8

10 <u>BEST</u> QUARTERS BY PERCENT & POINT

	BY PERCENT CHANGE				BY POINT CHANGE		
QUARTER	CLOSE	PNT CHANGE	% CHANGE	QUARTER	CLOSE	PNT CHANGE	% CHANGE
DJIA 1901 TO 1949							
JUN-1933	98.14	42.74	77.1	DEC-1928	300.00	60.57	25.3
SEP-1932	71.56	28.72	67.0	JUN-1933	98.14	42.74	77.1
JUN-1938	133.88	34.93	35.3	MAR-1930	286.10	37.62	15.1
SEP-1915	90.58	20.52	29.3	JUN-1938	133.88	34.93	35.3
DEC-1928	300.00	60.57	25.3	SEP-1927	197.59	31.36	18.9
DEC-1904	50.99	8.80	20.9	SEP-1928	239.43	28.88	13.7
JUN-1919	106.98	18.13	20.4	SEP-1932	71.56	28.72	67.0
SEP-1927	197.59	31.36	18.9	JUN-1929	333.79	24.94	8.1
DEC-1905	70.47	10.47	17.4	SEP-1939	152.54	21.91	16.8
JUN-1935	118.21	17.40	17.3	SEP-1915	90.58	20.52	29.3
DJIA 1950 TO APRIL 2007							
MAR-1975	768.15	151.91	24.7	DEC-1998	9181.43	1338.81	17.1
MAR-1987	2304.69	408.74	21.6	JUN-1999	10970.80	1184.64	12.1
MAR-1986	1818.61	271.94	17.6	DEC-2003	10453.92	1178.86	12.7
MAR-1976	999.45	147.04	17.2	DEC-2001	10021.50	1173.94	13.3
DEC-1998	9181.43	1338.81	17.1	DEC-1999	11497.12	1160.17	11.2
DEC-1982	1046.54	150.29	16.8	JUN-1997	7672.79	1089.31	16.5
JUN-1997	7672.79	1089.31	16.5	JUN-2003	8985.44	993.31	12.4
DEC-1985	1546.67	218.04	16.4	MAR-1998	8799.81	891.56	11.3
JUN-1975	878.99	110.84	14.4	DEC-2006	12463.15	784.08	6.7
DEC-2001	10021.50	1173.94	13.3	DEC-2002	8341.63	749.70	9.9
S&P 500 1930 TO APRIL 2007							
JUN-1933	10.91	5.06	86.5	DEC-1998	1229.23	212.22	20.9
SEP-1932	8.08	3.65	82.4	DEC-1999	1469.25	186.54	14.5
JUN-1938	11.56	3.06	36.0	MAR-1998	1101.75	131.32	13.5
MAR-1975	83.36	14.80	21.6	JUN-1997	885.14	128.02	16.9
DEC-1998	1229.23	212.22	20.9	JUN-2003	974.50	125.32	14.8
JUN-1935	10.23	1.76	20.8	DEC-2003	1111.92	115.95	11.6
MAR-1987	291.70	49.53	20.5	DEC-2001	1148.08	107.14	10.3
SEP-1939	13.02	2.16	19.9	DEC-2004	1211.92	97.34	8.7
MAR-1943	11.58	1.81	18.5	JUN-1999	1372.71	86.34	6.7
MAR-1930	25.14	3.69	17.2	DEC-2006	1418.30	82.45	6.2
NASDAQ 1971 TO APRIL 2007							
DEC-1999	4069.31	1323.15	48.2	DEC-1999	4069.31	1323.15	48.2
DEC-2001	1950.40	451.60	30.1	MAR-2000	4572.83	503.52	12.4
DEC-1998	2192.69	498.85	29.5	DEC-1998	2192.69	498.85	29.5
MAR-1991	482.30	108.46	29.0	DEC-2001	1950.40	451.60	30.1
MAR-1975	75.66	15.84	26.5	JUN-2001	2160.54	320.28	17.4
DEC-1982	232.41	44.76	23.9	JUN-2003	1622.80	281.63	21.0
MAR-1987	430.05	80.72	23.1	DEC-2004	2175.44	278.60	14.7
JUN-2003	1622.80	281.63	21.0	MAR-1999	2461.40	268.71	12.3
JUN-1980	157.78	26.78	20.4	MAR-1998	1835.68	265.33	16.9
SEP-1980	187.76	29.98	19.0	SEP-1997	1685.69	243.62	16.9
RUSSELL 1000 1979 TO APRIL 2007							
DEC-1998	642.87	113.76	21.5	DEC-1998	642.87	113.76	21.5
MAR-1987	155.20	25.20	19.4	DEC-1999	767.97	104.14	15.7
DEC-1982	77.24	11.35	17.2	JUN-2003	518.94	68.59	15.2
JUN-1997	462.95	64.76	16.3	MAR-1998	580.31	66.52	12.9
DEC-1985	114.39	15.64	15.8	JUN-1997	462.95	64.76	16.3
DEC-1999	767.97	104.14	15.7	DEC-2003	594.56	62.41	11.7
JUN-2003	518.94	68.59	15.2	DEC-2001	604.94	58.48	10.7
MAR-1991	196.15	24.93	14.6	DEC-2004	650.99	55.33	9.3
MAR-1986	130.07	15.68	13.7	DEC-2006	770.08	46.60	6.4
JUN-1980	63.27	7.48	13.4	JUN-1999	713.61	46.12	6.9
RUSSELL 2000 1979 TO APRIL 2007							
MAR-1991	171.01	38.85	29.4	MAR-2006	765.14	91.92	13.7
DEC-1982	88.90	18.06	25.5	JUN-2003	448.37	83.83	23.0
MAR-1987	166.79	31.79	23.5	DEC-2001	488.50	83.63	20.7
JUN-2003	448.37	83.83	23.0	DEC-2004	651.57	78.63	13.7
SEP-1980	69.94	12.47	21.7	DEC-1999	504.75	77.45	18.1
DEC-2001	488.50	83.63	20.7	DEC-2003	556.91	69.23	14.2
JUN-1983	124.17	20.40	19.7	JUN-2001	512.64	62.11	13.8
JUN-1980	57.47	9.20	19.1	DEC-2006	787.66	62.07	8.6
DEC-1999	504.75	77.45	18.1	JUN-1999	457.68	60.05	15.1
MAR-1988	142.15	21.73	18.0	DEC-1998	421.96	58.37	16.1

10 <u>WORST</u> QUARTERS BY PERCENT & POINT

	BY PERCENT CHANGE				BY POINT CHANGE		
QUARTER	CLOSE	PNT CHANGE	% CHANGE	QUARTER	CLOSE	PNT CHANGE	% CHANGE
DJIA 1901 TO 1949							
JUN-1932	42.84	−30.44	−41.5	DEC-1929	248.48	−94.97	−27.7
SEP-1931	96.61	−53.57	−35.7	JUN-1930	226.34	−59.76	−20.9
DEC-1929	248.48	−94.97	−27.7	SEP-1931	96.61	−53.57	−35.7
SEP-1903	33.55	−9.73	−22.5	DEC-1930	164.58	−40.32	−19.7
DEC-1937	120.85	−33.72	−21.8	DEC-1937	120.85	−33.72	−21.8
JUN-1930	226.34	−59.76	−20.9	SEP-1946	172.42	−33.20	−16.1
DEC-1930	164.58	−40.32	−19.7	JUN-1932	42.84	−30.44	−41.5
DEC-1931	77.90	−18.71	−19.4	JUN-1940	121.87	−26.08	−17.6
MAR-1938	98.95	−21.90	−18.1	MAR-1939	131.84	−22.92	−14.8
JUN-1940	121.87	−26.08	−17.6	JUN-1931	150.18	−22.18	−12.9
DJIA 1950 TO APRIL 2007							
DEC-1987	1938.83	−657.45	−25.3	SEP-2001	8847.56	−1654.84	−15.8
SEP-1974	607.87	−194.54	−24.2	SEP-2002	7591.93	−1651.33	−17.9
JUN-1962	561.28	−145.67	−20.6	JUN-2002	9243.26	−1160.68	−11.2
SEP-2002	7591.93	−1651.33	−17.9	SEP-1998	7842.62	−1109.40	−12.4
SEP-2001	8847.56	−1654.84	−15.8	MAR-2001	9878.78	−908.07	−8.4
SEP-1990	2452.48	−428.21	−14.9	DEC-1987	1938.83	−657.45	−25.3
SEP-1981	849.98	−126.90	−13.0	SEP-1999	10336.95	−633.85	−5.8
JUN-1970	683.53	−102.04	−13.0	MAR-2000	10921.92	−575.20	−5.0
SEP-1998	7842.62	−1109.40	−12.4	JUN-2000	10447.89	−474.03	−4.3
JUN-2002	9243.26	−1160.68	−11.2	SEP-1990	2452.48	−428.21	−14.9
S&P 500 1930 TO APRIL 2007							
JUN-1932	4.43	−2.88	−39.4	SEP-2001	1040.94	−183.48	−15.0
SEP-1931	9.71	−5.12	−34.5	SEP-2002	815.28	−174.54	−17.6
SEP-1974	63.54	−22.46	−26.1	MAR-2001	1160.33	−159.95	−12.1
DEC-1937	10.55	−3.21	−23.3	JUN-2002	989.82	−157.57	−13.7
DEC-1987	247.08	−74.75	−23.2	SEP-1998	1017.01	−116.83	−10.3
JUN-1962	54.75	−14.80	−21.3	DEC-2000	1320.28	−116.23	−8.1
MAR-1938	8.50	−2.05	−19.4	SEP-1999	1282.71	−90.00	−6.6
JUN-1970	72.72	−16.91	−18.9	DEC-1987	247.08	−74.75	−23.2
SEP-1946	14.96	−3.47	−18.8	SEP-1990	306.05	−51.97	−14.5
JUN-1930	20.46	−4.68	−18.6	JUN-2000	1454.60	−43.98	−2.9
NASDAQ 1971 TO APRIL 2007							
DEC-2000	2470.52	−1202.30	−32.7	DEC-2000	2470.52	−1202.30	−32.7
SEP-2001	1498.80	−661.74	−30.6	SEP-2001	1498.80	−661.74	−30.6
SEP-1974	55.67	−20.29	−26.7	MAR-2001	1840.26	−630.26	−25.5
DEC-1987	330.47	−113.82	−25.6	JUN-2000	3966.11	−606.72	−13.3
MAR-2001	1840.26	−630.26	−25.5	JUN-2002	1463.21	−382.14	−20.7
SEP-1990	344.51	−117.78	−25.5	SEP-2000	3672.82	−293.29	−7.4
JUN-2002	1463.21	−382.14	−20.7	SEP-2002	1172.06	−291.15	−19.9
SEP-2002	1172.06	−291.15	−19.9	SEP-1998	1693.84	−200.90	−10.6
JUN-1974	75.96	−16.31	−17.7	MAR-2005	1999.23	−176.21	−8.1
DEC-1973	92.19	−19.01	−17.1	JUN-2006	2172.09	−167.70	−7.0
RUSSELL 1000 1979 TO APRIL 2007							
DEC-1987	130.02	−38.81	−23.0	SEP-2001	546.46	−100.18	−15.5
SEP-2002	433.22	−90.50	−17.3	SEP-2002	433.22	−90.50	−17.3
SEP-2001	546.46	−100.18	−15.5	MAR-2001	610.36	−89.73	−12.8
SEP-1990	157.83	−28.46	−15.3	JUN-2002	523.72	−83.63	−13.8
JUN-2002	523.72	−83.63	−13.8	DEC-2000	700.09	−72.51	−9.4
MAR-2001	610.36	−89.73	−12.8	SEP-1998	529.11	−63.46	−10.7
SEP-1981	64.06	−8.95	−12.3	SEP-1999	663.83	−49.78	−7.0
SEP-1998	529.11	−63.46	−10.7	DEC-1987	130.02	−38.81	−23.0
MAR-1982	61.43	−6.50	−9.6	SEP-1990	157.83	−28.46	−15.3
DEC-2000	700.09	−72.51	−9.4	JUN-2000	769.68	−28.31	−3.5
RUSSELL 2000 1979 TO APRIL 2007							
DEC-1987	120.42	−50.39	−29.5	SEP-2001	404.87	−107.77	−21.0
SEP-1990	126.70	−42.34	−25.0	SEP-2002	362.27	−100.37	−21.7
SEP-2002	362.27	−100.37	−21.7	SEP-1998	363.59	−93.80	−20.5
SEP-2001	404.87	−107.77	−21.0	DEC-1987	120.42	−50.39	−29.5
SEP-1998	363.59	−93.80	−20.5	JUN-2002	462.64	−43.82	−8.7
SEP-1981	67.55	−15.01	−18.2	SEP-1990	126.70	−42.34	−25.0
MAR-1980	48.27	−7.64	−13.7	JUN-2006	724.67	−40.47	−5.3
SEP-1986	134.73	−19.50	−12.6	DEC-2000	483.53	−37.84	−7.3
MAR-1982	66.21	−7.46	−10.1	MAR-2005	615.07	−36.50	−5.6
JUN-2002	462.64	−43.82	−8.7	MAR-2001	450.53	−33.00	−6.8

10 <u>BEST</u> YEARS BY PERCENT & POINT

	BY PERCENT CHANGE				BY POINT CHANGE		
YEAR	CLOSE	PNT CHANGE	% CHANGE	YEAR	CLOSE	PNT CHANGE	% CHANGE
			DJIA 1901 TO 1949				
1915	99.15	44.57	81.7	1928	300.00	97.60	48.2
1933	99.90	39.97	66.7	1927	202.40	45.20	28.8
1928	300.00	97.60	48.2	1915	99.15	44.57	81.7
1908	63.11	20.07	46.6	1945	192.91	40.59	26.6
1904	50.99	15.01	41.7	1935	144.13	40.09	38.5
1935	144.13	40.09	38.5	1933	99.90	39.97	66.7
1905	70.47	19.48	38.2	1925	156.66	36.15	30.0
1919	107.23	25.03	30.5	1936	179.90	35.77	24.8
1925	156.66	36.15	30.0	1938	154.76	33.91	28.1
1927	202.40	45.20	28.8	1919	107.23	25.03	30.5
			DJIA 1950 TO APRIL 2007				
1954	404.39	123.49	44.0	1999	11497.12	2315.69	25.2
1975	852.41	236.17	38.3	2003	10453.92	2112.29	25.3
1958	583.65	147.96	34.0	2006	12463.15	1745.65	16.3
1995	5117.12	1282.68	33.5	1997	7908.25	1459.98	22.6
1985	1546.67	335.10	27.7	1996	6448.27	1331.15	26.0
1989	2753.20	584.63	27.0	1995	5117.12	1282.68	33.5
1996	6448.27	1331.15	26.0	1998	9181.43	1273.18	16.1
2003	10453.92	2112.29	25.3	1989	2753.20	584.63	27.0
1999	11497.12	2315.69	25.2	1991	3168.83	535.17	20.3
1997	7908.25	1459.98	22.6	1993	3754.09	452.98	13.7
			S&P 500 1930 TO APRIL 2007				
1933	10.10	3.21	46.6	1998	1229.23	258.80	26.7
1954	35.98	11.17	45.0	1999	1469.25	240.02	19.5
1935	13.43	3.93	41.4	2003	1111.92	232.10	26.4
1958	55.21	15.22	38.1	1997	970.43	229.69	31.0
1995	615.93	156.66	34.1	2006	1418.30	170.01	13.6
1975	90.19	21.63	31.5	1995	615.93	156.66	34.1
1997	970.43	229.69	31.0	1996	740.74	124.81	20.3
1945	17.36	4.08	30.7	2004	1211.92	100.00	9.0
1936	17.18	3.75	27.9	1991	417.09	86.87	26.3
1989	353.40	75.68	27.3	1989	353.40	75.68	27.3
			NASDAQ 1971 TO APRIL 2007				
1999	4069.31	1876.62	85.6	1999	4069.31	1876.62	85.6
1991	586.34	212.50	56.8	2003	2003.37	667.86	50.0
2003	2003.37	667.86	50.0	1998	2192.69	622.34	39.6
1995	1052.13	300.17	39.9	1995	1052.13	300.17	39.9
1998	2192.69	622.34	39.6	1997	1570.35	279.32	21.6
1980	202.34	51.20	33.9	1996	1291.03	238.90	22.7
1985	324.93	77.58	31.4	1991	586.34	212.50	56.8
1975	77.62	17.80	29.8	2006	2415.29	209.97	9.5
1979	151.14	33.16	28.1	2004	2175.44	172.07	8.6
1971	114.12	24.51	27.4	1993	776.80	99.85	14.7
			RUSSELL 1000 1979 TO APRIL 2007				
1995	328.89	84.24	34.4	1998	642.87	129.08	25.1
1997	513.79	120.04	30.5	2003	594.56	128.38	27.5
1991	220.61	49.39	28.8	1999	767.97	125.10	19.5
2003	594.56	128.38	27.5	1997	513.79	120.04	30.5
1985	114.39	24.08	26.7	2006	770.08	90.66	13.3
1989	185.11	38.12	25.9	1995	328.89	84.24	34.4
1980	75.20	15.33	25.6	1996	393.75	64.86	19.7
1998	642.87	129.08	25.1	2004	650.99	56.43	9.5
1996	393.75	64.86	19.7	1991	220.61	49.39	28.8
1999	767.97	125.10	19.5	1989	185.11	38.12	25.9
			RUSSELL 2000 1979 TO APRIL 2007				
2003	556.91	173.82	45.4	2003	556.91	173.82	45.4
1991	189.94	57.78	43.7	2006	787.66	114.44	17.0
1979	55.91	15.39	38.0	2004	651.57	94.66	17.0
1980	74.80	18.89	33.8	1999	504.75	82.79	19.6
1985	129.87	28.38	28.0	1997	437.02	74.41	20.5
1983	112.27	23.37	26.3	1995	315.97	65.61	26.2
1995	315.97	65.61	26.2	1991	189.94	57.78	43.7
1988	147.37	26.95	22.4	1996	362.61	46.64	14.8
1982	88.90	15.23	20.7	1993	258.59	37.58	17.0
1997	437.02	74.41	20.5	1992	221.01	31.07	16.4

10 <u>WORST</u> YEARS BY PERCENT & POINT

BY PERCENT CHANGE				BY POINT CHANGE			
YEAR	CLOSE	PNT CHANGE	% CHANGE	YEAR	CLOSE	PNT CHANGE	% CHANGE
DJIA 1901 TO 1949							
1931	77.90	−86.68	−52.7	1931	77.90	−86.68	−52.7
1907	43.04	−26.08	−37.7	1930	164.58	−83.90	−33.8
1930	164.58	−83.90	−33.8	1937	120.85	−59.05	−32.8
1920	71.95	−35.28	−32.9	1929	248.48	−51.52	−17.2
1937	120.85	−59.05	−32.8	1920	71.95	−35.28	−32.9
1903	35.98	−11.12	−23.6	1907	43.04	−26.08	−37.7
1932	59.93	−17.97	−23.1	1917	74.38	−20.62	−21.7
1917	74.38	−20.62	−21.7	1941	110.96	−20.17	−15.4
1910	59.60	−12.96	−17.9	1940	131.13	−19.11	−12.7
1929	248.48	−51.52	−17.2	1932	59.93	−17.97	−23.1
DJIA 1950 TO APRIL 2007							
1974	616.24	−234.62	−27.6	2002	8341.63	−1679.87	−16.8
1966	785.69	−183.57	−18.9	2001	10021.50	−765.35	−7.1
1977	831.17	−173.48	−17.3	2000	10786.85	−710.27	−6.2
2002	8341.63	−1679.87	−16.8	1974	616.24	−234.62	−27.6
1973	850.86	−169.16	−16.6	1966	785.69	−183.57	−18.9
1969	800.36	−143.39	−15.2	1977	831.17	−173.48	−17.3
1957	435.69	−63.78	−12.8	1973	850.86	−169.16	−16.6
1962	652.10	−79.04	−10.8	1969	800.36	−143.39	−15.2
1960	615.89	−63.47	−9.3	1990	2633.66	−119.54	−4.3
1981	875.00	−88.99	−9.2	1981	875.00	−88.99	−9.2
S&P 500 1930 TO APRIL 2007							
1931	8.12	−7.22	−47.1	2002	879.82	−268.26	−23.4
1937	10.55	−6.63	−38.6	2001	1148.08	−172.20	−13.0
1974	68.56	−28.99	−29.7	2000	1320.28	−148.97	−10.1
1930	15.34	−6.11	−28.5	1974	68.56	−28.99	−29.7
2002	879.82	−268.26	−23.4	1990	330.22	−23.18	−6.6
1941	8.69	−1.89	−17.9	1973	97.55	−20.50	−17.4
1973	97.55	−20.50	−17.4	1981	122.55	−13.21	−9.7
1940	10.58	−1.91	−15.3	1977	95.10	−12.36	−11.5
1932	6.89	−1.23	−15.1	1966	80.33	−12.10	−13.1
1957	39.99	−6.68	−14.3	1969	92.06	−11.80	−11.4
NASDAQ 1971 TO APRIL 2007							
2000	2470.52	−1598.79	−39.3	2000	2470.52	−1598.79	−39.3
1974	59.82	−32.37	−35.1	2002	1335.51	−614.89	−31.5
2002	1335.51	−614.89	−31.5	2001	1950.40	−520.12	−21.1
1973	92.19	−41.54	−31.1	1990	373.84	−80.98	−17.8
2001	1950.40	−520.12	−21.1	1973	92.19	−41.54	−31.1
1990	373.84	−80.98	−17.8	1974	59.82	−32.37	−35.1
1984	247.35	−31.25	−11.2	1984	247.35	−31.25	−11.2
1987	330.47	−18.86	−5.4	1994	751.96	−24.84	−3.2
1981	195.84	−6.50	−3.2	1987	330.47	−18.86	−5.4
1994	751.96	−24.84	−3.2	1981	195.84	−6.50	−3.2
RUSSELL 1000 1979 TO APRIL 2007							
2002	466.18	−138.76	−22.9	2002	466.18	−138.76	−22.9
2001	604.94	−95.15	−13.6	2001	604.94	−95.15	−13.6
1981	67.93	−7.27	−9.7	2000	700.09	−67.88	−8.8
2000	700.09	−67.88	−8.8	1990	171.22	−13.89	−7.5
1990	171.22	−13.89	−7.5	1981	67.93	−7.27	−9.7
1994	244.65	−6.06	−2.4	1994	244.65	−6.06	−2.4
1984	90.31	−0.07	−0.1	1984	90.31	−0.07	−0.1
1987	130.02	0.02	0.02	1987	130.02	0.02	0.02
2005	679.42	28.43	4.4	1979	59.87	8.29	16.1
1992	233.59	12.98	5.9	1982	77.24	9.31	13.7
RUSSELL 2000 1979 TO APRIL 2007							
2002	383.09	−105.41	−21.6	2002	383.09	−105.41	−21.6
1990	132.16	−36.14	−21.5	1990	132.16	−36.14	−21.5
1987	120.42	−14.58	−10.8	2000	483.53	−21.22	−4.2
1984	101.49	−10.78	−9.6	1998	421.96	−15.06	−3.4
2000	483.53	−21.22	−4.2	1987	120.42	−14.58	−10.8
1998	421.96	−15.06	−3.4	1984	101.49	−10.78	−9.6
1994	250.36	−8.23	−3.2	1994	250.36	−8.23	−3.2
1981	73.67	−1.13	−1.5	1981	73.67	−1.13	−1.5
2001	488.50	4.97	1.0	2001	488.50	4.97	1.0
2005	673.22	21.65	3.3	1986	135.00	5.13	4.0

STRATEGY PLANNING AND RECORD SECTION

CONTENTS

PORTFOLIO AT START OF 2008

DATE ACQUIRED	NO. OF SHARES	SECURITY	PRICE	TOTAL COST	PAPER PROFITS	PAPER LOSSES

ADDITIONAL PURCHASES

DATE ACQUIRED	NO. OF SHARES	SECURITY	PRICE	TOTAL COST	REASON FOR PURCHASE PRIME OBJECTIVE, ETC.

ADDITIONAL PURCHASES

DATE ACQUIRED	NO. OF SHARES	SECURITY	PRICE	TOTAL COST	REASON FOR PURCHASE PRIME OBJECTIVE, ETC.

SHORT-TERM TRANSACTIONS

Pages 175-178 can accompany next year's income tax return (Schedule D). Enter transactions as completed to avoid last-minute pressures.

NO. OF SHARES	SECURITY	DATE ACQUIRED	DATE SOLD	SALE PRICE	COST	LOSS	GAIN

TOTALS: Carry over to next page

175

SHORT-TERM TRANSACTIONS (continued)

NO. OF SHARES	SECURITY	DATE ACQUIRED	DATE SOLD	SALE PRICE	COST	LOSS	GAIN

TOTALS:

LONG-TERM TRANSACTIONS

Pages 175-178 can accompany next year's income tax return (Schedule D). Enter transactions as completed to avoid last-minute pressures.

NO. OF SHARES	SECURITY	DATE ACQUIRED	DATE SOLD	SALE PRICE	COST	LOSS	GAIN

TOTALS:

Carry over to next page

177

LONG–TERM TRANSACTIONS *(continued)*

NO. OF SHARES	SECURITY	DATE ACQUIRED	DATE SOLD	SALE PRICE	COST	LOSS	GAIN

TOTALS:

INTEREST/DIVIDENDS RECEIVED DURING 2008

SHARES	STOCK/BOND	FIRST QUARTER		SECOND QUARTER		THIRD QUARTER		FOURTH QUARTER	
		$		$		$		$	

BROKERAGE ACCOUNT DATA 2008

	MARGIN INTEREST	TRANSFER TAXES	CAPITAL ADDED	CAPITAL WITHDRAWN
JAN				
FEB				
MAR				
APR				
MAY				
JUN				
JUL				
AUG				
SEP				
OCT				
NOV				
DEC				

PORTFOLIO PRICE RECORD 2008 (FIRST HALF)

Place purchase price above stock name and weekly closes below

	STOCKS / Week Ending	1	2	3	4	5	6	7	8	9	10
JANUARY	4										
	11										
	18										
	25										
FEBRUARY	1										
	8										
	15										
	22										
	29										
MARCH	7										
	14										
	21										
	28										
APRIL	4										
	11										
	18										
	25										
MAY	2										
	9										
	16										
	23										
	30										
JUNE	6										
	13										
	20										
	27										

PORTFOLIO PRICE RECORD 2008 (SECOND HALF)

Place purchase price above stock name and weekly closes below

STOCKS Week Ending	1	2	3	4	5	6	7	8	9	10
4										
11										
18										
25										
1										
8										
15										
22										
29										
5										
12										
19										
26										
3										
10										
17										
24										
31										
7										
14										
21										
28										
5										
12										
19										
26										

WEEKLY INDICATOR DATA 2008 (FIRST HALF)

	Week Ending	Dow Jones Industrial Average	Net Change for Week	Net Change on Friday	Net Change Next Monday	S&P or NASDAQ	NYSE Advances	NYSE Declines	New Highs	New Lows	CBOE Put/Call Ratio	90-Day Treas. Rate	Moody's AAA Rate
JANUARY	4												
	11												
	18												
	25												
FEBRUARY	1												
	8												
	15												
	22												
	29												
MARCH	7												
	14												
	21												
	28												
APRIL	4												
	11												
	18												
	25												
MAY	2												
	9												
	16												
	23												
	30												
JUNE	6												
	13												
	20												
	27												

WEEKLY INDICATOR DATA 2008 (SECOND HALF)

Week Ending	Dow Jones Industrial Average	Net Change for Week	Net Change on Friday	Net Change Next Monday	S&P or NASDAQ	NYSE Ad-vances	NYSE De-clines	New Highs	New Lows	CBOE Put/Call Ratio	90-Day Treas. Rate	Moody's AAA Rate
4												
11												
18												
25												
1												
8												
15												
22												
29												
5												
12												
19												
26												
3												
10												
17												
24												
31												
7												
14												
21												
28												
5												
12												
19												
26												

MONTHLY INDICATOR DATA 2008

	DJIA% Last 3 + 1st 2 Days	DJIA% 9th - 11th Trading Days	DJIA% Change Rest Of Month	DJIA% Change Whole Month	% Change Your Stocks	Gross Domestic Product	Prime Rate	Trade Deficit $ Billion	CPI % Change	% Unem- ployment Rate
JAN										
FEB										
MAR										
APR										
MAY										
JUN										
JUL										
AUG										
SEP										
OCT										
NOV										
DEC										

INSTRUCTIONS:

Weekly Indicator Data (pages 182-183). Keeping data on several indicators may give you a better feel of the market. In addition to the closing DJIA and its net change for the week, post the net change for Friday's Dow and also the following Monday's. A series of "down Fridays" followed by "down Mondays" often precedes a downswing. Tracking either the S&P or NASDAQ composite, and advances and declines, will help prevent the Dow from misleading you. New highs and lows and put/call ratios (www.cboe.com) are also useful indicators. All these weekly figures appear in weekend papers or *Barron's*. Data for 90-day Treasury Rate and Moody's AAA Bond Rate are quite important to track short- and long-term interest rates. These figures are available from:

Weekly U.S. Financial Data
Federal Reserve Bank of St. Louis
P.O. Box 442
St. Louis MO 63166
http://research.stlouisfed.org

Monthly Indicator Data. The purpose of the first three columns is to enable you to track the market's bullish bias near the end, beginning and middle of the month, which has been shifting lately (see pages 88, 136 & 137). Market direction, performance of your stocks, Gross Domestic Product, Prime Rate, Trade Deficit, Consumer Price Index, and Unemployment Rate are worthwhile indicators to follow. Or, readers may wish to gauge other data.

PORTFOLIO AT END OF 2008

DATE ACQUIRED	NO. OF SHARES	SECURITY	PRICE	TOTAL COST	PAPER PROFITS	PAPER LOSSES

IF YOU DON'T PROFIT FROM YOUR INVESTMENT MISTAKES, SOMEONE ELSE WILL

No matter how much we may deny it, almost every successful person in Wall Street pays a great deal of attention to trading suggestions — especially when they come from "the right sources."

One of the hardest things to learn is to distinguish between good tips and bad ones. Usually the best tips have a logical reason in back of them, which accompanies the tip. Poor tips usually have no reason to support them.

The important thing to remember is that the market discounts. It does not review, it does not reflect. The Street's real interest in "tips," inside information, buying and selling suggestions, and everything else of this kind emanates from a desire to find out just what the market has on hand to discount. The process of finding out involves separating the wheat from the chaff — and there is plenty of chaff.

HOW TO MAKE USE OF STOCK "TIPS"

- The source should be **reliable**. (By listing all "tips" and suggestions on a Performance Record of Recommendations, such as below, and then periodically evaluating the outcomes, you will soon know the "batting average" of your sources.)

- The story should make sense. Would the merger violate anti-trust laws? Are there too many computers on the market already? How many years will it take to become profitable?

- The stock should not have had a recent sharp run-up. Otherwise, the story may already be discounted and confirmation or denial in the press would most likely be accompanied by a sell-off in the stock.

PERFORMANCE RECORD OF RECOMMENDATIONS

STOCK RECOMMENDED	BY WHOM	DATE	PRICE	REASON FOR RECOMMENDATION	SUBSEQUENT ACTION OF STOCK

INDIVIDUAL RETIREMENT ACCOUNTS: MOST AWESOME INVESTMENT INCENTIVE EVER DEVISED

MAX IRA INVESTMENTS OF $5,000 A YEAR COMPOUNDED AT VARIOUS RATES OF RETURN FOR DIFFERENT PERIODS

Annual Rate	5 Yrs	10 Yrs	15 Yrs	20 Yrs	25 Yrs	30 Yrs	35 Yrs	40 Yrs	45 Yrs	50 Yrs
1%	$25,760	$52,834	$81,289	$111,196	$142,628	$175,664	$210,384	$246,876	$285,229	$325,539
2%	26,541	55,844	88,196	123,917	163,355	206,897	254,972	308,050	366,653	431,355
3%	27,342	59,039	95,784	138,382	187,765	245,013	311,380	388,316	477,507	580,904
4%	28,165	62,432	104,123	154,846	216,559	291,642	382,992	494,133	629,353	793,869
5%	29,010	66,034	113,287	173,596	250,567	348,804	474,182	634,199	838,426	1,099,077
6%	29,877	69,858	123,363	194,964	290,782	419,008	590,604	820,238	1,127,541	1,538,780
7%	30,766	73,918	134,440	219,326	338,382	505,365	739,567	1,068,048	1,528,759	2,174,930
8%	31,680	78,227	146,621	247,115	394,772	611,729	930,511	1,398,905	2,087,130	3,098,359
9%	32,617	82,801	160,017	278,823	461,620	742,876	1,175,624	1,841,459	2,865,930	4,442,205
10%	33,578	87,656	174,749	315,012	540,909	904,717	1,490,634	2,434,259	3,953,977	6,401,497
11%	34,564	92,807	190,950	356,326	634,994	1,104,566	1,895,822	3,229,135	5,475,844	9,261,680
12%	35,576	98,273	208,766	403,494	746,670	1,351,463	2,417,316	4,295,712	7,606,088	13,440,102
13%	36,614	104,072	228,359	457,350	879,250	1,656,576	3,088,747	5,727,429	10,589,030	19,546,215
14%	37,678	110,223	249,902	518,842	1,036,664	2,033,685	3,953,364	7,649,543	14,766,219	28,468,772
15%	38,769	116,746	273,587	589,051	1,223,560	2,499,785	5,066,728	10,229,769	20,614,489	41,501,869
16%	39,887	123,665	299,625	669,203	1,445,441	3,075,808	6,500,135	13,692,392	28,798,589	60,526,763
17%	41,034	131,000	328,244	760,693	1,708,813	3,787,519	8,344,972	18,336,953	40,243,850	88,273,585
18%	42,210	138,776	359,695	865,105	2,021,361	4,666,593	10,718,245	24,562,957	56,236,305	128,697,253
19%	43,415	147,018	394,251	984,237	2,392,153	5,751,937	13,769,572	32,902,482	78,560,374	187,516,251
20%	44,650	155,752	432,211	1,120,128	2,831,886	7,091,289	17,690,047	44,063,147	109,687,860	272,983,145

TOP 300 EXCHANGE TRADED FUNDS (As of 4/30/2007)

By Market Cap & Volume. See pages 114 & 116, Almanac Investor & stocktradersalmanac.com for more.

Ticker	Name	Ticker	Name
SPY	S&P 500 Spyder	VGK	European VIPERS
QQQQ	PowerShares QQQ	IJJ	iShares S&P Md Cp 400/BARRA Va
IWM	iShares Russell 2000	IYT	iShares DJ Transports
EFA	iShares EAFE	BBH	Biotech HOLDRs
EWJ	iShares Japan	PBW	PowerShares Wilder Hill Energy
EEM	iShares Emerging Market Income	GDX	Market Vectors Gold Miners
XLE	SPDR Energy	QLD	ProShares Ultra QQQ
DIA	Diamonds DJIA 30	DBC	PowerShares DB Commodity
GLD	streetTRACKS Gold	IJS	iShares S&P Sm Cp 600/BARRA Va
XLF	SPDR Financial	VTV	Vanguard Value VIPERS
MDY	S&P Mid Cap 400 SPDR	VNQ	REIT VIPERS
OIH	Oil Service HOLDRs	VUG	Vanguard Growth VIPERS
SMH	Semiconductor HOLDRs	IJK	iShares S&P Md Cp 400/BARRA Gr
EWZ	iShares Brazil	IGE	iShares Natural Resources
IVV	iShares S&P 500	IYH	iShares DJ US Healthcare
XLU	SPDR Utilities	PRF	Powershares FTSE RAFI US 1000
EWT	iShares Taiwan	EWP	iShares Spain
IWF	iShares Russell 1000 Growth	IAU	iShares Comex Gold
IWD	iShares Russell 1000 Value	VO	Mid Cap VIPERS
FXI	iShares FTSE/Xinhua China 25	HHH	Internet HOLDRs
IWN	iShares Russell 2000 Value	PGJ	PowerShares Golden Dragon
IJR	iShares S&P Small Cap 600	VB	Small Cap VIPERS
IWO	iShares Russell 2000 Growth	EFV	iShares MSCI EAFE Value
OEF	iShares S&P 100	EWD	iShares Sweden
IYR	iShares DJ US Real Estate	VPL	Pacific VIPERS
EWS	iShares Singapore	IYE	iShares DJ US Energy
QID	ProShares UltraShort QQQ	FXE	CurrencyShares Euro
XLV	SPDR Healthcare	RWR	StreetTRACKS Wilshire REIT
XLI	SPDR Industrial	IJT	iShares S&P Sm Cp 600 BARRA Gr
USO	United States Oil Fund	IYM	iShares DJ US Basic Materials
XLB	SPDR Materials	IXJ	iShares S&P Global Healthcare
EWW	iShares Mexico	KRE	streetTRACKS KBW Regional Bank
XLK	SPDR Tech	PID	PowerShares Int' Dvdnd
SHY	iShares Lehman 1-3 Yr Bonds	RWX	SPDR DJ Wilshire Int Rl Estate
EWH	iShares Hong Kong	DXD	ProShares UltraShort Dow 30
DVY	iShares DJ Select Dvdnd Index	UTH	Utilities HOLDRs
IBB	iShares NASDAQ Biotech	ADRE	BLDRS Emerging Market 50
XLP	SPDR Consumer Staples	PWC	PowerShares Dynamic Market
EWM	iShares Malaysia	EZA	iShares S Africa Index
PPH	Pharmaceutical HOLDRs	PIV	PowerShares VL Time Select
IVW	iShares S&P 500 BARRA Growth	IXC	iShares S&P Global Energy
EWY	iShares South Korea	FEZ	streetTRACKS DJ Euro STOXX 50
VTI	Vanguard Total Market VIPERS	PEY	PowerShares High Yield
RTH	Retail HOLDRs	PWV	PowerShares Dynamic Lg Cap Val
AGG	iShares Lehman Aggregate Bond	PXJ	PowerShares Oil Services
IJH	iShares S&P Mid Cap 400	VV	Vanguard Large Cap VIPERS
EWA	iShares Australia	EWN	iShares Netherlands
TLT	iShares Lehman 20+yr Bond	IWW	iShares Russell 3000 Value
IVE	iShares S&P 500/BARRA Value	IDU	iShares DJ US Utilities
EWG	iShares Germany	IYW	iShares DJ US Tech
XLY	SPDR Consumer Discretionary	KBE	streetTRACKS KBW Bank
ICF	iShares Cohen & Steers Realty	EWL	iShares Switzerland
IEV	iShares S&P Europe 350	EWQ	iShares France
IWV	iShares Russell 3000	DBA	PowerShares DB Agriculture
IWR	iShares Russell Mid Cap	EWK	iShares Belgium
XHB	SPDR Homebuilders	IGW	iShares Semiconductor
EPP	iShares Pacific Ex-Japan	DLS	WisdomTree Int SmallCap
IWB	iShares Russell 1000	EFG	iShares MSCI EAFE Growth
TIP	iShares Lehman TIPS Bond	IOO	iShares S&P Global 100
SLV	iShares Silver Trust	IGM	iShares Technology
RSP	Rydex S&P Equal Weight	VEU	Vanguard FTSE All-World ex-US
VWO	Emerging Markets VIPERS	TTH	Telecom HOLDRs
IWS	iShares Russell Mid Cap Val	IAI	iShares DJ US Broker-Dealers
EWU	iShares United Kingdom	GSG	iShares GSCI Commodity-Indexed
PHO	PowerShares Water Resource	PBE	PowerShares Dyn Bio & Genom
IEF	iShares Lehman 7-10 Year	BDH	Broadband HOLDRs
RKH	Regional Bank HOLDRs	SSO	ProShares Ultra S&P 500
EZU	iShares EMU	IYF	iShares DJ US Financial
ILF	iShares S&P Latin America 40	IGN	iShares Multimedia Networking
EWC	iShares Canada	EWI	iShares Italy
IWP	iShares Russell Mid Cap Gr	KCE	streetTRACKS KBW Capital Mkts
LQD	iShares GS Corporate Bond	IWC	iShares Russell Microcap
IYZ	iShares DJ US Telecom	NY	iShares NYSE 100
EWO	iShares Austria	XLG	Rydex Russell Top 50
SDS	ProShares UltraShort S&P 500	VBR	Vanguard Small Cap Val VIPERS

TOP 300 EXCHANGE TRADED FUNDS (As of 4/30/2007)

By Market Cap & Volume. See pages 114 & 116, Almanac Investor & stocktradersalmanac.com for more.

VBK	Small Cap Growth VIPERS		PWO	PowerShares OTC
FVD	First Trust Value Line Dvdnd		PSJ	PowerShares Dynamic Software
IYY	iShares DJ US Total Market		IEO	iShares DJ US Oil&Gas Exp&Prod
ITB	iShares DJ US Home Const		ADRA	BLDRS Asia 50 ADR
IYK	iShares DJ US Consumer Goods		DOL	WisdomTree Int LargeCap Dvdnd
SWH	Software HOLDRs		ADRD	BLDRS Developed Market 100
XRT	SPDR Retail		VOX	Telecom VIPERS
PSI	PowerShares Dynamic Semis		SHV	iShares Lehman Shrt-Term Trsry
MZZ	ProShares UltraShrt Md Cp 400		ONEQ	Fidelity NASDAQ Composite
PWB	PowerShares Large Cap Growth		SRS	ProShares UltraShort Rl Estate
VDE	Energy VIPERS		VIS	Industrial VIPERS
IGV	iShares Software		DND	WisdomTree Pac ex-Jp Tot Div
DLN	WisdomTree LargeCap Dvdnd		DES	WisdomTree SmallCap Dividend
IHF	iShares DJ US Health Care Prov		PGF	PowerShares Fin Preferred
DWM	WisdomTree DIEFA		UWM	ProShares Ultra Russell 2000
PPA	PowerShares Aero & Defense		MTK	streetTRACKS MS Technology
VHT	Vanguard Health Care VIPERS		PSP	PowerShares Listed Private Eq
DOO	WisdomTree Int Dvdnd Top 100		DBE	PowerShares DB Energy
IYC	iShares DJ US Consumer Serv		VCR	Consumer Discretionary VIPERS
VPU	Utilities VIPERS		DTD	WisdomTree Total Dividend
JKF	iShares Morningstar Lg Cap Val		PTH	PowerShares Dyn Heathcare
VFH	Financial VIPERS		XRO	Claymore/Zacks Sector Rotation
PWJ	PowerShares Dynamic Mid Cap Gr		PIQ	PowerShares Dyn MagniQuant
KIE	streetTRACKS KBW Insurance		JPP	streetTRACKS Russ/Nom PRIME Jp
VXF	Extended Market VIPERS		DFJ	WisdomTree Japan SmallCap
DIM	WisdomTree Int MidCap Dvdnd		XBI	SPDR Biotech
PXN	PowerShares Lux Nanotech		JKD	iShares Morningstar Large Cap
XSD	SPDR Semiconductors		PWT	PowerShares Dynamic Sm Cap Gr
IXG	iShares S&P Global Financial		DGT	streetTRACKS DJ Glob Titans 50
PZI	PowerShares Zacks Micro Cap		PZJ	PowerShares Zacks Small Cap
XME	SPDR Metals & Mining		XES	SPDR Oil & Gas Equip & Service
SH	ProShares Short S&P 500		DON	WisdomTree MidCap Dvdnd
IYG	iShares DJ US Financial Serv		JKJ	iShares Morningstar Small Cap
DTH	WisdomTree DIEFA High-Yielding		VOE	Vanguard Mid-Cap Value
IXP	iShares S&P Global Telecom		FDL	Morningstar Dividend Leaders
ELG	streetTRACKS DJ US LC Growth		FEU	streetTRACKS DJ STOXX 50
PXE	PowerShares Energy Exp & Prod		CWI	SPDR MSCI ACWI ex-US
IEZ	iShares DJ US Oil Equip & Serv		DGL	PowerShares DB Gold
IWZ	iShares Russell 3000 Growth		FBT	First Trust Amex Biotech
EEB	Claymore/BNY BRIC		IHE	iShares DJ US Pharmaceutical
IXN	iShares S&P Global IT		CVY	Claymore/Zacks Yield Hog
IYJ	iShares DJ US Industrial		JKG	iShares Morningstar Mid Cap
DBV	PowerShares DB G10 Currency		PFM	PowerShares Dividend Achievers
FXY	CurrencyShares Japanese Yen		DBB	PowerShares DB Base Metals
ITA	iShares DJ US Aero & Def		VIG	Vanguard Dividend Appreciation
VGT	IT VIPERS		PEJ	PowerShares Dyn Leis & Ent
VDC	Consumer Staples VIPERS		BHH	B2B Internet HOLDRs
ITF	iShares S&P/TOPIX 150		PKW	PowerShares Buyback Achievers
PSQ	ProShares Short QQQ		DBO	PowerShares DB Oil
PUI	PowerShares Utilities		PIC	PowerShares Insurance
TWM	ProShares UltraShort R2K		UUP	PowerShares DB US Dollar-Bull
DNH	WisdomTree Pac ex-Jp High-Yld		JKK	iShares Morningstar Sm Cap Gr
IHI	iShares DJ US Medical Devices		KXI	iShares S&P Global Cnsmr Stapl
PDP	PowerShares DWA Technical Ldrs		DEW	WisdomTree Europe High-Yield
DHS	WisdomTree High-Yielding		ELV	streetTRACKS DJ US LC Value
IIH	Internet Infrastructure HOLDRs		FXF	CurrencyShares Swiss Franc
IAH	Internet Architecture HOLDRs		TLH	iShares Lehman 10-20 Yr Trsry
DFE	WisdomTree Europe SmallCap		PBJ	PowerShares Dyn Food & Bev
DDM	ProShares Ultra Dow 30		TMW	streetTRACKS Fortune 500
MXI	iShares S&P Global Materials		DBS	PowerShares DB Silver
SDY	SPDR Dividend		EXT	WisdomTree Total Earnings
VAW	Materials VIPERS		EZY	WisdomTree Low P/E
DTN	WisdomTree Dividend Top 100		VOT	Vanguard Mid-Cap Growth
MYY	ProShares Short Mid Cap 400		DDI	WisdomTree Int Industrial
SLX	Market Vectors Steel		DSV	streetTRACKS DJ Small Cap Val
PWY	PowerShares Dyn Mid Cap Val		PTE	PowerShares Dyn Tel & Wireless
JKE	iShares Morningstar Lg Cap Gr		DBN	WisdomTree Int Basic Materials
PWP	PowerShares Dynamic Mid Cp Val		RPV	Rydex S&P 500 Va
ISI	iShares S&P 1500		SKF	ProShares UltraShort Financial
DOG	ProShares Short Dow 30		NYC	iShares NYSE Composite
JKH	iShares Morningstar Mid Cap Gr		EEZ	WisdomTree Earnings Top 100
MVV	ProShares Ultra Mid Cap 400		PXQ	PowerShares Dyn Networking
JKI	iShares Morningstar Mid Cp Val		UDN	PowerShares DB US Dollar-Bear
XOP	SPDR Oil & Gas Explore & Prod		FDN	First Trust DJ Internet
PJP	PowerShares Dyn Pharma		ADRU	BLDRS Europe 100 ADR

OPTION TRADING CODES

The Basics:

Options symbols contain a security's ticker symbol, an expiration month code, and a strike (exercise) price code.

For NASDAQ stocks with more than three letters in the stock code, the option ticker symbol is shortened to three letters, usually ending in Q. For example, Microsoft's stock symbol is MSFT, so its option ticker symbol is MSQ.

Each expiration month has a separate code for both Calls and Puts. Also, each strike price has a separate code, which is identical for Calls and Puts. In an option listing, the ticker symbol is first, followed by the expiration month code, and then the strike price code. For example, the Microsoft January 25 Call would have the code MSQAE, and the Microsoft January 25 Put would have the code MSQME.

					EXPIRATION MONTH CODES							
	JAN	FEB	MAR	APR	MAY	JUN	JUL	AUG	SEP	OCT	NOV	DEC
CALLS	A	B	C	D	E	F	G	H	I	J	K	L
PUTS	M	N	O	P	Q	R	S	T	U	V	W	X

					STRIKE PRICE CODES							
A	B	C	D	E	F	G	H	I	J	K	L	M
5	10	15	20	25	30	35	40	45	50	55	60	65
105	110	115	120	125	130	135	140	145	150	155	160	165
205	210	215	220	225	230	235	240	245	250	255	260	265
305	310	315	320	325	330	335	340	345	350	355	360	365
405	410	415	420	425	430	435	440	445	450	455	460	465
505	510	515	520	525	530	535	540	545	550	555	560	565
605	610	615	620	625	630	635	640	645	650	655	660	665
705	710	715	720	725	730	735	740	745	750	755	760	765

N	O	P	Q	R	S	T	U	V	W	X	Y	Z
70	75	80	85	90	95	100	7 1/2	12 1/2	17 1/2	22 1/2	27 1/2	32 1/2
170	175	180	185	190	195	200	37 1/2	42 1/2	47 1/2	52 1/2	57 1/2	62 1/2
270	275	280	285	290	295	300	67 1/2	72 1/2	77 1/2	82 1/2	87 1/2	92 1/2
370	375	380	385	390	395	400	97 1/2	102 1/2	107 1/2	112 1/2	117 1/2	122 1/2
470	475	480	485	490	495	500	127 1/2	132 1/2	137 1/2	142 1/2	147 1/2	152 1/2
570	575	580	585	590	595	600	157 1/2	162 1/2	167 1/2	172 1/2	177 1/2	182 1/2
670	675	680	685	690	695	700	187 1/2	192 1/2	197 1/2	202 1/2	207 1/2	212 1/2
770	775	780	785	790	795	800	217 1/2	222 1/2	227 1/2	232 1/2	237 1/2	242 1/2

Single Letter Strike Prices & *Wraps*:

Expanding equity and ETF markets in recent years have mushroomed, creating problems for single letter strike price codes. So we consulted with options guru, Larry McMillan at *www.optionstrategist.com*. Stocks and ETFs that have option strike prices spaced less than five points apart and LEAPS (long-term options) often use up all the codes. In this case, the Options Clearing Corporation (OCC) rather arbitrarily assigns the letters that correspond to the striking prices. It might be H = 60, I = 61, J = 62, K = 63, L = 64, and so forth. Each stock or ETF is frequently different.

Once all 26 available letters have been assigned, a new base symbol is created by the OCC, called a *wrap symbol*. These newly created wrap symbols often have little in common with the stock or ETF itself. The OCC can use any three-character designation that is not already in use. For example, the current symbol for the Microsoft January 2009 25 Call is VMFAE.

Now, more than ever, any potential option trade requires a comprehensive review to ensure that the symbol actually represents the trade to be executed. Additional information can be found online at www.cboe.com and www.amex.com provides excellent data on ETFs and ETF options.

Sources: Larry McMillan, cboe.com and amex.com

G.M. LOEB'S "BATTLE PLAN" FOR INVESTMENT SURVIVAL

LIFE IS CHANGE: Nothing can ever be the same a minute from now as it was a minute ago. Everything you own is changing in price and value. You can find that last price of an active security on the stock ticker, but you cannot find the next price anywhere. The value of your money is changing. Even the value of your home is changing, though no one walks in front of it with a sandwich board consistently posting the changes.

RECOGNIZE CHANGE: Your basic objective should be to profit from change. The art of investing is being able to recognize change and to adjust investment goals accordingly.

WRITE THINGS DOWN: You will score more investment success and avoid more investment failures if you write things down. Very few investors have the drive and inclination to do this.

KEEP A CHECKLIST: If you aim to improve your investment results, get into the habit of keeping a checklist on every issue you consider buying. Before making a commitment, it will pay you to write down the answers to at least some of the basic questions — How much am I investing in this company? How much do I think I can make? How much do I have to risk? How long do I expect to take to reach my goal?

HAVE A SINGLE RULING REASON: Above all, writing things down is the best way to find "the ruling reason." When all is said and done, there is invariably a single reason that stands out above all others why a particular security transaction can be expected to show a profit. All too often many relatively unimportant statistics are allowed to obscure this single important point.

Any one of a dozen factors may be the point of a particular purchase or sale. It could be a technical reason — an increase in earnings or dividend not yet discounted in the market price — a change of management — a promising new product — an expected improvement in the market's valuation of earnings — or many others. But, in any given case, one of these factors will almost certainly be more important than all the rest put together.

CLOSING OUT A COMMITMENT: If you have a loss, the solution is automatic, provided you decide what to do at the time you buy. Otherwise, the question divides itself into two parts. Are we in a bull or bear market? Few of us really know until it is too late. For the sake of the record, if you think it is a bear market, just put that consideration first and sell as much as your conviction suggests and your nature allows.

If you think it is a bull market, or at least a market where some stocks move up, some mark time and only a few decline, do not sell unless:

✓ You see a bear market ahead.

✓ You see trouble for a particular company in which you own shares.

✓ Time and circumstances have turned up a new and seemingly far better buy than the issue you like least in your list.

✓ Your shares stop going up and start going down.

A subsidiary question is, which stock to sell first? Two further observations may help:

✓ Do not sell solely because you think a stock is "overvalued."

✓ If you want to sell some of your stocks and not all, in most cases it is better to go against your emotional inclinations and sell first the issues with losses, small profits or none at all, the weakest, the most disappointing, etc.

Mr. Loeb is the author of *The Battle for Investment Survival*, John Wiley & Sons.

G.M. LOEB'S INVESTMENT SURVIVAL CHECKLIST

OBJECTIVES AND RISKS

Security		Price	Shares	Date

"Ruling reason" for commitment	Amount of commitment
	$ _____
	% of my investment capital
	_____%

Price objective	Est. time to achieve it	I will risk _____ points	Which would be $ _____

TECHNICAL POSITION

Price action of stock:

☐ hitting new highs   ☐ in a trading range

☐ pausing in an uptrend   ☐ moving up from low ground

☐ acting stronger than market   ☐ _____

Dow Jones Industrial Average

Trend of Market

SELECTED YARDSTICKS

	Price Range		Earnings Per Share Actual or Projected	Price/Earnings Ratio Actual or Projected
	High	Low		
Current Year				
Previous Year				
Merger Possibilities				Years for earnings to double in past
Comment on Future				Years for market price to double in past

PERIODIC RE-CHECKS

Date	Stock Price	DJIA	Comment	Action taken, if any

COMPLETED TRANSACTIONS

Date Closed	Period of time held	Profit or loss

Reason for profit or loss